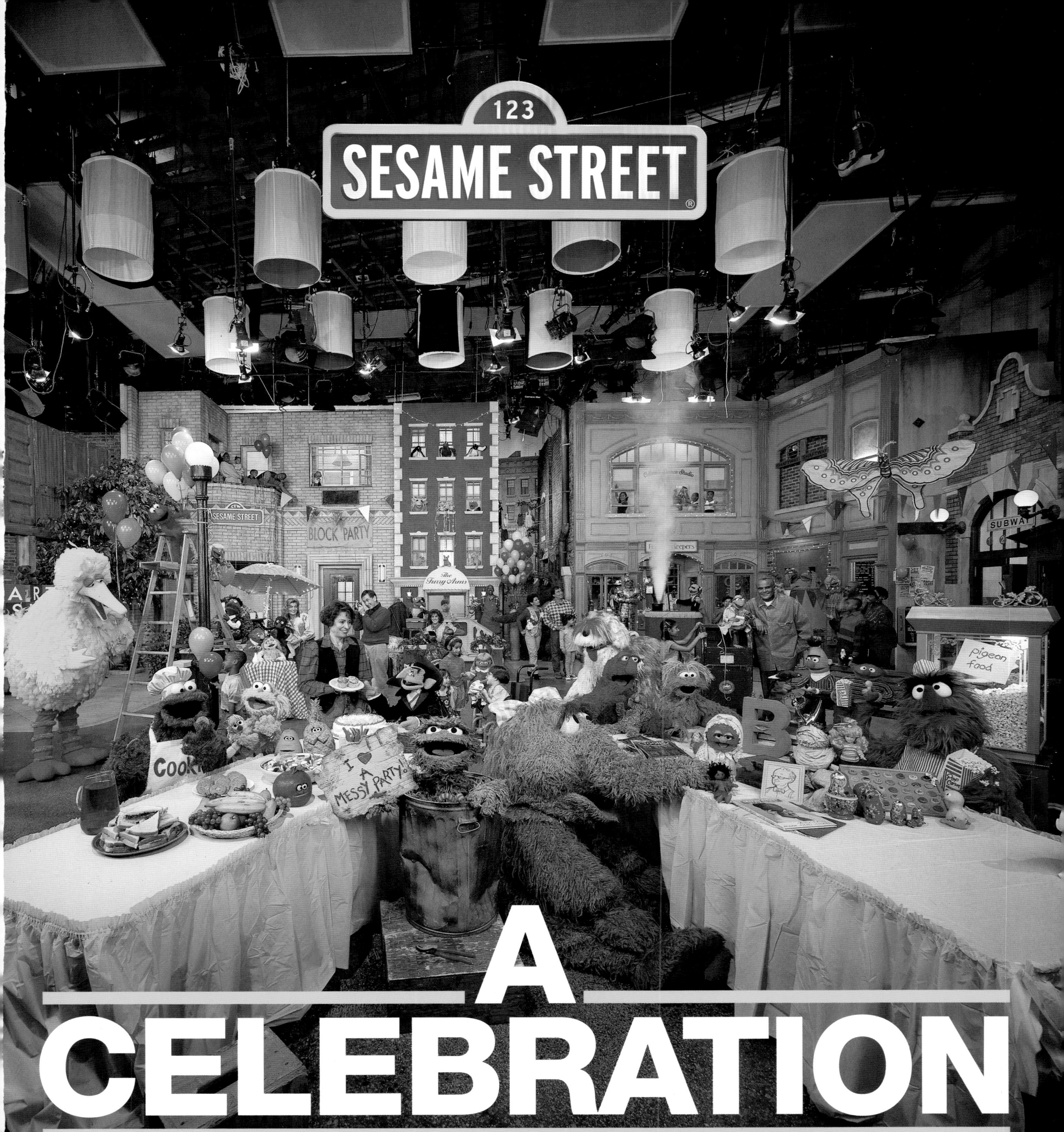

123
SESAME STREET ®

SESAME STREET

BLOCK PARTY

The Furry Arms

pigeon food

Cook

I ♥ A MESSY PARTY

SUBWAY

B

A
CELEBRATION

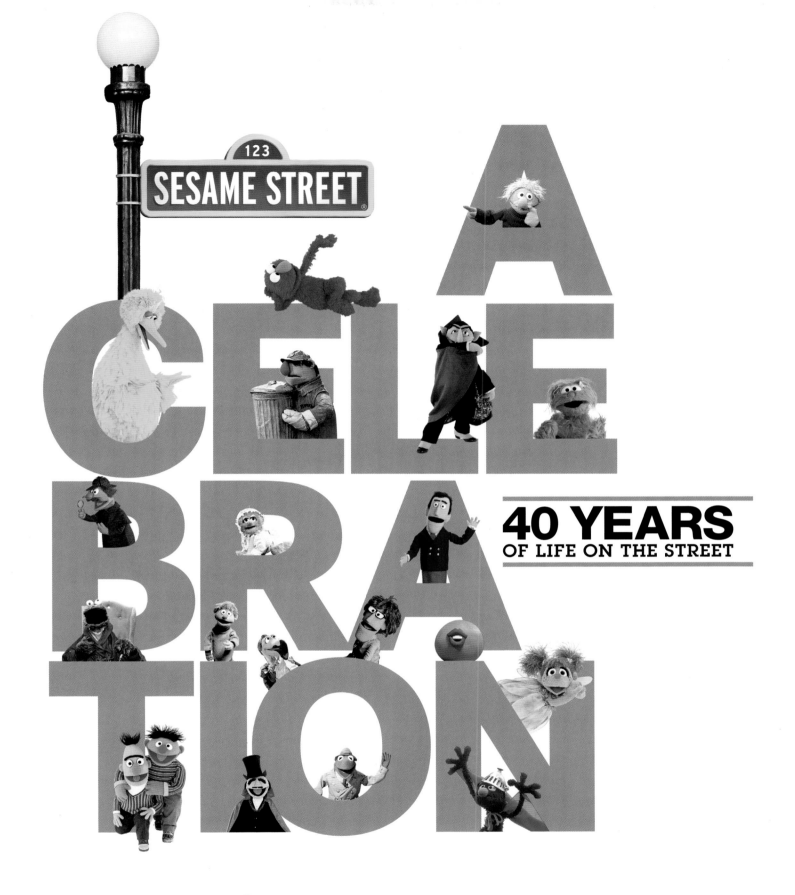

SESAME STREET

A CELEBRATION

40 YEARS
OF LIFE ON THE STREET

Louise A. Gikow

CONTRIBUTING EDITOR, BETSY LOREDO

BLACK DOG
& LEVENTHAL
PUBLISHERS

Published by
Black Dog & Leventhal Publishers, Inc.
151 West 19th Street
New York, NY 10011

Distributed by
Workman Publishing Company
225 Varick Street
New York, NY 10014

Manufactured in China

Cover and interior design by ohioboy art & design

Art Direction by Colleen Pidel

Front and Back Cover photographs by John E. Barrett; Charlotte Brooks, LOOK Magazine Collection, Library of Congress, Prints & Photographs Division, Reproduction no. LC-L9-69-5159; Robert Fuhring; Eric Jacobson; Judy Ross; Richard Termine; Geert Teuwen; and Sesame Workshop

ISBN-13: 978-1-57912-638-4

h g f e d c b a

Library of Congress Cataloging-in-Publication Data is available on file.

www.blackdogandleventhal.com
www.sesameworkshop.org
www.sesamestreet.org

ACKNOWLEDGMENTS

"To truly acknowledge everyone who was involved in the making of this book would mean listing the names of every individual who ever worked on or for *Sesame Street*. Each one of them left an indelible imprint . . . some small, some very large indeed . . . on the show, its products, its outreach and international efforts, on all the children who have watched the show over the last forty years. Without all of them, this book would and could not have been written. I can't name everyone... but know that you are in the fabric of this book and in my heart.

Thank you to J.P. Leventhal, brilliant publisher of Black Dog & Leventhal, who hired me to write this book (and to Jane Leventhal, who mentioned my name to him in the first place). Thanks to Black Dog's True Sims, Production Director; Nathaniel Marunas, Associate Publisher; Liz Hartman, Publicity and Marketing Manager; and to Allison Frascatore, Editorial Assistant, who worked above and beyond the call of duty. Thank you to copy editor extraordinaire Kelly Waggoner and to photo researcher Susie Tofte. Susie, I know you had no idea what you were signing on for . . . but thanks for your amazing job on photo research, art logging, and organizing all the visual materials in the book. And thanks to Judy Pray, my original editor at BD&L . . . and most of all to Liz Van Doren, my current editor, without whose mammoth efforts this book would never have come to be.

Then there's everyone at Sesame Workshop. First and foremost is Executive Editor Betsy Loredo. We all shared a vision for this book from the beginning, and without Betsy, who was indispensable throughout the process, it simply would not have happened. Thanks, too, to Jennifer A. Perry, Assistant Vice President & Editorial Director, who coordinated the project's myriad details and, with steadfast equanimity and consummate skill, helped us realize that vision; and to Scott Chambers, Vice President and General Manager, Worldwide Media Distribution, for his unwavering support.

I'd also like to thank the many, many *Sesame Street* cast, crew, and staff members we managed to interview; you were all incredibly patient and generous. I would like to mention a few individuals who not only helped on the book but have been an important part of my Sesame and Muppet life: Chris Cerf; Norman Stiles; Sharon Lerner; Lisa Simon; Lewis Bernstein; Cheryl, Brian, Lisa, John, Heather, and Jane Henson; Sarah Durkee; Paul Jacobs; Cooper Wright; and Mark Saltzman (who got me my first Sesame job). Thanks, too, to all the Workshop personnel, especially Gary Knell, CEO, and Mel Ming, COO, who steer the Sesame Workshop ship with integrity and creativity.

I'd like to acknowledge The Academy of Television Arts & Sciences Foundation for their series of interviews of some of the principal Sesame players, including Joan Ganz Cooney and Lloyd Morrisett. I'd like to thank Victor DiNapoli, who in addition to being a good friend and endless source of information, provided me with his interviews of some principal players, especially Jon Stone, that proved invaluable. And I want also to thank Danny Horn for both contributing some reminiscences and for his and others' work on the Muppet and Sesame sections of Wikipedia, which itself deserves thanks as an invaluable resource. I hope the book lives up to all of that community's extraordinary standards.

I'd particularly like to remember those *Sesame Street* veterans whom we've lost. Some, like the wonderful Arlene Sherman and the brilliant, quirky Kermit Love, have only recently left us. Others, like Jim Henson, Richard Hunt, Jon Stone, Joe Raposo, Jeff Moss, Will Lee, Northern Calloway, and Nina Elias, have been gone for far too long. I had the pleasure of knowing most of them and working with many of them, and I can vouch for the fact that they were far more special than I could possibly convey.

Most personally, thanks to all my friends, who lived with this book far more than they probably should have. And a special thanks to Erik and Rachel. I love you both very much.

Last but not least, I'd like to pay homage to Joan Ganz Cooney and Lloyd Morrisett for coming up with the idea of *Sesame Street* and for making it happen. Without both of you, the world would be a different and far less friendly place.

Thank you all, for showing me how to get to *Sesame Street*."

In addition to everyone already mentioned, as well as the scores of contributors to this project, Sesame Workshop would like to thank all those people whose names don't appear in this book but whose passionate support and help, though invisible, was invaluable.

Catherine Alexander, Annette Augeri, Ann Marie Aversano, Barbara Bevel, Ariel Birdoff, Kathy Blomquist, Alex Brown, Ben Campisi, Taska Carrigan, Tim Carter, Phillip Chapman, Jovanka Ciares, Robert Davidson, James Day, Dan Donohue, Alicia Durand, Karen Falk, Julie Fefferman, Len Forgione, John Gallacher, Nicole Goldman, Will Greene, Pam Hacker, Karen Halpenny, Anna Jane Hayes, William Hernandez, Lynda Holder-Settles, The Jim Henson Company, Inc., The Jim Henson Legacy, George James, Mike Khouri, Leslie Kimmelman, Jane Lee, Jodi Lefkowitz, Jocelyn Leong, Ellen Lewis, Sharon Lyew, Kelly Mac Lellan, Mark Magner, Tracy Martin, Renee Mascara, Carrie Miller, Tomoko Nagano, Dionne Nosek, Deborah November, Jodi Nussbaum, Margaret Pepe, Jill Peterson, Susanna Phillips, June Reich, Paul Roberts, Jennifer Rupnik, Carol-Anne Ryce-Paul, Anthony Saggese, Jr., Syndi Shumer, Dwayne Smith, the team at Spectragraphic, Inc., Kurt Swenson, Pamela Thomas, Peter van Roden, Jason Weber, Sherrie Westin, Beth Wexelman, Janet Wolf, Greg Wong, Jowill Woodman, and Mayumi Yokomizo

Finally, the editors extend special appreciation to the individuals who shared an array of images from their personal collections: Charles Baum, Bonnie Erickson, Danny Epstein, Bob McGrath, Sonia Manzano, Paul McGinniss, Michael Melford Studio and Gae McGregor, Bill Pierce, Walt Rauffer, Caroll and Debra Spinney, Nancy Stevenson, and Richard Termine

And our deep gratitude to the families and estates of Joe Raposo and Jeff Moss

CONTENTS

Dear Friends:

    Hullo there.

    I'm so glad you've come to visit. Welcome to Sesame Street—*my* street.

    I've lived on Sesame Street a real long time now, ever since I was an egg. I remember leaving my nest for the very first time and walking down the street, looking up at all the buildings and wondering who lived behind all those windows. Now I know. And I bet you do, too!

    I'll bet you know *exactly* where you can find Bert and Ernie's window. That's right, just next door, in the basement of 123. You probably even know that Susan and Gordon live there, too. Or that Elmo moved into the building behind Hooper's Store—it seems like forever ago, even though he's only three and a half.

    Go on, look around. A few of the neighbors may be a little grouchy, but mostly they'll be glad to see you. Just don't be surprised if things look a little different from the first time you stopped by. 'Cause since I first walked down the block, there sure have been a *lot* of changes around here.

    But some things don't ever change. I still walk through a big wall of doors to get to my nest (even though they were once blown down by a hurricane). Ernie and Bert are still wearing the same clothes. And the birdseed milk shakes at Hooper's Store are still the same, even though my friend Mr. Dooper isn't there anymore.

    And Sesame Street is still my favorite place in the whole world. Golly, on Sesame Street, you learn something new every day. For instance, did you know that *abcdefghijklmnopqrstuvwxyz* is not just a big word?* It's the *alphabet*, a list of all the letters that *make* words. Isn't that amazing?

    So take a walk around the block. Or roller-skate—that's my favorite way to travel. Stay as long as you like. Then maybe we can go for some birdseed milk shakes. You'll like 'em! I know I do.

Yours sincerely,

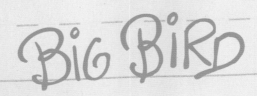

*I used to think it was the word for a rare
kind of turkey, and I said it like this:
ab-ca-def-ghee-jekyl-men-op-qurst-stu-wyx-zez.
It's a common mistake among birds.

To Whom It May Concern (which is probably none of you):

Arghhh! I can't believe they asked me to write this introduction! Just thinking about saying something un-yucky about *Sesame Street* makes my fur crawl. All those nice people making such a nice show ... it's enough to make a Grouch miserable.

In fact, how did a perfectly normal orange Grouch like me, you might ask, ever end up on a happy place like *Sesame Street*? Well, I'm not gonna tell you!

Okay, okay, I'll tell you. It all started with two people— a disgustingly tidy lady named Joan Ganz Cooney and some hairy guy named Jon Stone. Back in the 1960s, she decided to make a television show that would help inner-city kids learn stuff. And as if that wasn't bad enough, *he* agreed to help and hired some hippie named Jim Henson. Jim Henson was the guy who roped me in.

Not that I made it easy for him. When he first came calling, all I did was yell, "Go away!" But he stuck around and you know what he said to me? "Come to New York and we can talk about the Muppets."

Muppets? What kind of word is that?

That Henson guy wouldn't leave me alone. Finally, I figured the best way to stop him from pestering me was to go to New York to be in his nutty television show. "Just the first episode," I told him. "After that, I'm outta here."

The next thing I know, here I am, on this crazy street, with an eight-foot, two-inch weirdo named Big Bird and some odd couple next door, plus a crowd of people around, called Susan and Gordon and Bob and Mr. Hooper, who are just plain . . . *nice*. Quadruple yuck! During the first show, they tried to get me to come out and say hello. I remember exactly what I said: "Don't bang on my can!"

Not that anybody listened.

Boy, was I happy to leave the set after that first episode wrapped. I headed straight to Swamp Mushy Muddy to recover. But the next day, I found out that my agent, Bernie—despite specific instructions!—had negotiated some goofy contract that meant I had to do the ENTIRE RUN OF THE SHOW!!! I was so mad that I turned green!!!! And I've been bile-colored ever since. Still, I was sure the nutty thing wouldn't run more than six months.

Boy, was I wrong.

The show's been goin' on the air for *decades*. Years of slamming my trash can lid. Years of yelling at people to get lost! It's the most miserable job I can imagine.

Which is not bad for a Grouch, now that I think of it.

Anyway, you won't catch me celebrating any 40th birthday. I hope that reading this book makes you as grouchy as I've been. Heh heh heh. Now, SCRAM!

OSCAR THE GROUCH!

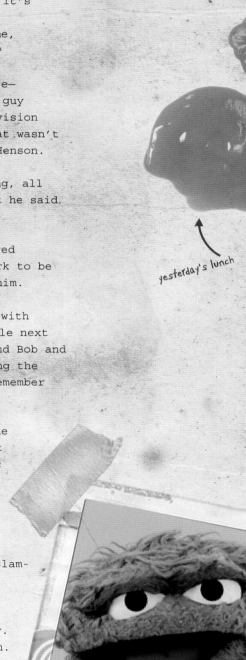

yesterday's lunch

grape juice

unidentifiable

November 2009

I first walked on to the set of *Sesame Street* in July of 1969, and for me it was like entering a dream except that it was a dream come true. I had done the study for Carnegie Corporation in 1966, which led to the creation of the Workshop. With foundation executive Lloyd Morrisett, who started it all with a group of us, I had been working toward the goal of getting a preschool educational show on the air for the past eighteen months. And now it was real. Suddenly, I was entering the Street itself.

Jon Stone, one of our brilliant producers, had come up with the idea of an urban street as a setting for the show, and he recalled in his memoirs that I turned pale at the suggestion. Children's programs were always set in some fantasy place or a playroom or a suburban neighborhood. Now here I was looking at the re-creation of an actual street in New York . . . with a brownstone, a stoop, a fix-it shop, a garbage can (with Oscar inside), a small playground—a very far cry from what children were used to seeing on a children's television show. We had no idea how this dramatic departure from the usual would be received by critics and parents who lived outside of urban areas.

Nonetheless, I was thrilled upon seeing it and more than thrilled with the research and creative work that had gone into the creation of the show. Our three very talented and experienced producers, Dave Connell, Jon Stone, and Sam Gibbon, together with two of the most gifted artists in their fields, Jim Henson and Joe Raposo, had created a show unlike any children's program in history. They were aided and abetted by the research of Ed Palmer and the advice of Harvard professor Gerry Lesser, both of whom rolled up their sleeves and worked side by side in perfect harmony with the creative people.

On that first visit to the set, I could not have imagined what would transpire over the next forty years. The show was unbelievably well received and soon, foreign countries were asking us to help them create their own versions of *Sesame Street* until it became the longest street in the world. During that time, I have collected pictures of visits to the set by nearly all of the first ladies who have been in office since the 1970s. My grandchildren have visited many times, as have the children of friends. I never tire of accompanying a child to meet the Muppets and all the wonderful people who do their magic in the studio.

Recently, I went to a taping when Michelle Obama came to *Sesame Street* to do a public service announcement about healthy eating. I saw the street anew through her eyes and understood perfectly why she seemed so happy to be there—in a familiar place with a new generation of children and old friends Elmo and Big Bird.

I cherish the colorful and happy memories of those early days. But what I never could have predicted is that forty years later, I'd still be gathering new memories on my joyful visits to *Sesame Street*.

First day on set, 1969

Joan Ganz Cooney

Cofounder and Creator of *Sesame Street*

123
SESAME STREET

sesameworkshop.
The nonprofit educational organization
behind Sesame Street and so much more

Mideast trip, 2007

November 2009

Early on in the production of *Sesame Street*, Joan Ganz Cooney was asked about the most far-reaching goal the program could possibly achieve. She responded by telling of a dream she harbored that Israelis and Palestinians would be at the negotiating table, and Bert and Ernie would somehow find a way to "break the ice," resulting in the breakthrough to create a lasting peace.

Seemed a bit dreamy, huh?

Well, with that as an inspirational framework, my colleagues and I set out on a journey that has now taken *Sesame Street* to 140 countries around the world and is viewed today as one of the most successful examples of public diplomacy to have ever been launched.

For more than forty years, the power of Muppets and the power of creative talent committed to offering each generation a better world has enabled *Sesame Street* to impart important life lessons to children. And no matter on which *Sesame Street* broadcast the messages originate, they resound worldwide: that in South Africa, you can be friends with a schoolmate who is HIV positive; that the Arab child in the village near your home in Haifa has aspirations to be a doctor, just like you; that girls in Cairo aspire to visit the moon; that in Tanzania, you need not become sick from a mosquito bite if you use a bed net properly; that in Mexico, Germany, Australia, and the United States, you can be healthy if you eat your colors.

Of all of the many, many wonderful experiences this position has given me, seeing children laughing, singing, and learning with the show—in their language, on their terms—never gets old. It is a new, wonderful experience of hope, revisited with child after child. It is my goal that each child's unique discoveries of the world, propelled by a profound curiosity about why things work the way they do, will be bolstered by *Sesame Street*.

In my job, I am called upon to negotiate, protect, and promote a global cultural icon, which has now found success across centuries. It is a tool that exports creativity and education. It is about optimism . . . because even those who have fought and struggled still want to find that special place of hope for their children and grandchildren.

It's about hope in Northern Ireland, where Gerry Adams of Sinn Fein wears a Cookie Monster watch. It's about President Obama growing up watching the show with his little sister. It's about the German Consulate making Bert and Ernie "dual citizens" of the U.S. and Germany. It's about hundreds of children gathering around a rickshaw outside Dacca, Bangladesh, to catch their first glimpses of the Bengali Muppets.

It's about changing the world.

Gary E. Knell

President and Chief Executive Officer

123
SESAME STREET

sesameworkshop.
**The nonprofit educational organization
behind Sesame Street and so much more**

1

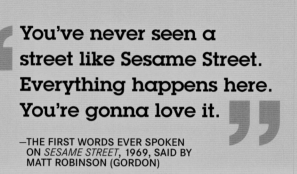

"You've never seen a
street like Sesame Street.
Everything happens here.
You're gonna love it."

—THE FIRST WORDS EVER SPOKEN
ON *SESAME STREET*, 1969, SAID BY
MATT ROBINSON (GORDON)

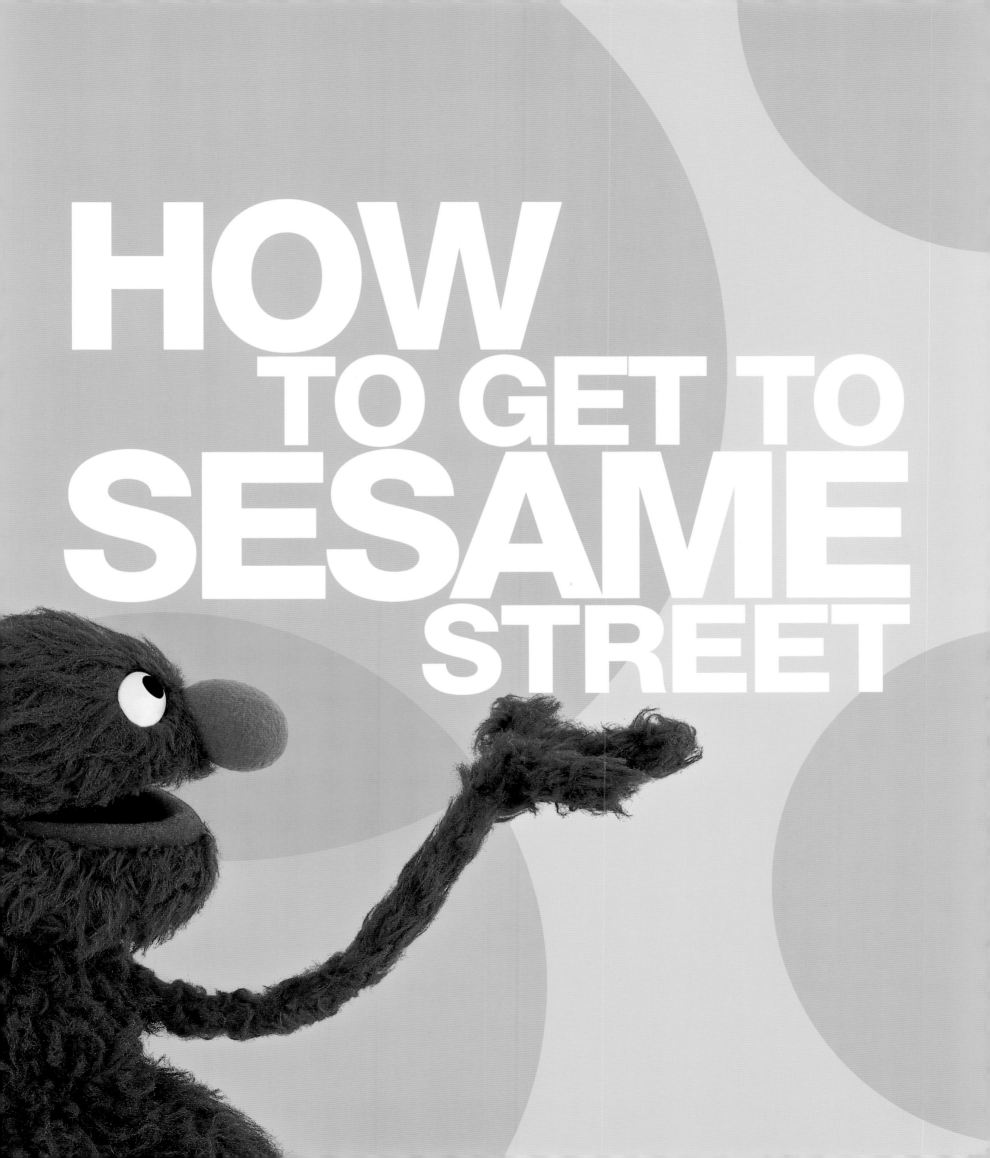

HOW
TO GET TO
SESAME
STREET

> **One of our biggest problems was naming this street.**
>
> —JOAN GANZ COONEY,
> *SESAME STREET* COFOUNDER

on the set
on the set
on the set

EPISODE
4141

On an icy December morning, the sun hasn't yet risen over the small, tidy houses and empty streets of Astoria, Queens. Here, on a sound stage buried deep in New York City's largest borough, Sesame Street is dark, too. A "closed" sign hangs in the door of Hooper's Store. Big Bird's nest is empty, and if Oscar is asleep in his trash can, he's not snoring.

The street where millions of children learn their ABCs and numbers is shadowy and still.

Frankie Biondo—a cameraman with a gravelly voice, quick sense of humor, and love of ballroom dancing—is the first member of the crew to arrive. At 6 A.M. he pulls his car into a parking lot across the street from Kaufman Astoria Studios, a beige concrete slab of a building that sprawls over an entire block in this mostly residential New York neighborhood. He likes to drive early, when there's no traffic.

Once inside, Frankie doesn't even glance at the famous street and familiar brownstone just down the hall. In the third-floor green room, a kind of holding pen for cast members between shots, he shrugs off his coat, stretches out on one of the three couches, and closes his eyes. He'll finish his night's sleep right here.

"In the old studio, I'd fall asleep on the stoop," he recalls. He's talking about the original set in the very first studio—Frankie's been with *Sesame Street* since it began airing in 1969. In forty years, his sleeping habits have become the stuff of legend. "The whole crew would make fun of me. I was out like a light."

This morning is no different. Frankie's out cold until 7:30 A.M., when the Street finally starts to come awake.

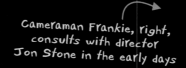

Cameraman Frankie, right, consults with director Jon Stone in the early days

Frankie Biondo shares a moment with his Muppet doppelgänger, who debuted in episode #4125 and makes a guest appearance in season 40. Puppet impersonations are common in the show's parodies of celebs but are a rare honor for those not in the spotlight. Senior cameraman Frankie earned his by sticking with *Sesame Street* since its very first show.

Executive Producer Carol-Lynn Parente consults with writer Lou Berger and director Emily Squires. Given the unique challenges of taping humans and Muppets together, there are often last-minute rewrites needed to work around unexpected problems.

The action really starts with the early-morning arrival of Executive Producer Carol-Lynn Parente, along with a number of producers and stage managers. Members of wardrobe and hair and makeup haul out clothes racks, lipsticks and hair dryers, ready for the moment human performers arrive. Frankie, awake and busy now, rolls his camera into place. In the growing bustle, only the Muppets rest quietly, patiently waiting on their stands in a staging area just off the set, a workspace commonly known as the "Muppet box."

The talent—the puppeteers and human stars on the show—join the crowd sometime around 8:00 A.M. The atmosphere is relaxed and a bit sleepy. Human cast members check in with hair and makeup. Puppeteers head for the green room to study scripts, grabbing some of the admittedly terrible coffee on the way.

Tape operator Ernie Albritton—another *Sesame Street* veteran from 1969—is heard but not seen among all the bustle. Often, no one will know Ernie has shown up until they hear his deep, reassuring voice over the studio's sound system when tape is rolling. That's because he's camped out in a trailer parked outside.

Tech people, camera operators, and the sound department slowly fill the soundstage and are greeted by the director, who swiftly walks the talent through the upcoming scene. It's nearly time to shoot another episode of the longest-running and most successful children's television show in the world.

At exactly 9:00 A.M., lighting board operator Karen Sunderlin, sitting in a room behind the set at the lighting board, hits a switch.

The lights go up. It's another sunny day on *Sesame Street*.

Alan Muraoka gets readied for his close-up by a makeup artist while puppets wait beside the Muppet box for their turn to be primped

Director Lisa Simon hobnobs with puppeteer Jerry Nelson, better known to fans as Count von Count.
Above and below are sneak peeks behind the scenes of season 40 with the ensemble cast, Big Bird, Grover, and Buster the horse. Plus, multiple Elmos.

"You know you're part of something that is significant, and it's a thrill to be around."

—LISA SIMON, DIRECTOR

The human cast watches playback of an episode where Big Bird prepares to migrate away from Sesame Street— then realizes that's his habitat

Former FCC Chairman Newton N. Minow congratulates Joan on her senate subcommittee testimony—in 1971 Joan calls for continued government funding of PBS: "Only then will future Sesame Streets be possible."

How It All Began

One chilly February morning in the late 1960s, a young television publicist named Joan Ganz Cooney picked up a newspaper. An article about public television caught her eye, and she settled back in her chair and began to read. It was a moment that would lead to a change in millions of children's lives around the globe.

After giving up an early dream of becoming an actress, the young education major from the University of Arizona had begun her working life as a typist for the State Department in Washington, D.C. This was followed by a stint on the Phoenix newspaper *The Arizona Republic*. But Joan wanted to live in New York, and after she saved enough money to move, she ended up in the Big Apple.

Joan had been introduced to television in 1952 when, on a neighbor's small black-and-white set, she watched Adlai Stevenson's nomination at the Democratic National Convention. A year later in New York, her journalist background landed her a job as a TV publicist. Over the next decade or so, she filled that role first at RCA, then NBC, and finally at the U.S. Steel Corporation, promoting their live dramatic series, *The United States Steel Hour*, on CBS.

The show was biweekly, which left her with time on her hands. So she volunteered her writing and organizational talents to local political clubs and to the literary journal *Partisan Review*. The experience of being a fly on the wall among these New York intellectuals was "incredibly heady stuff," she recalls. But although her work in television was considered frivolous by the denizens of this rarified atmosphere, Joan remained committed to the fledgling media.

When she heard that a colleague was leaving to work for a station called WGBH, in Boston, it was a life-changing moment.

"I said '*What?!?* There is *educational* television?!?'" Joan's face lights up when talking about it, even decades later.

Joan began avidly tracking the progress of an organization that would later become known as the Educational Broadcasting Corporation, which provided programming to stations reserved by the Federal Communications Commission for public use. The article she noticed on that February morning described the EBC's acquisition of a nearby television station, Channel Thirteen. Within days, she was asking for a job there, only to discover that the few job openings were for television producers.

"Oh, I can do that," she said.

She had never produced before.

Her literary contacts, political savvy, and vast interest in the "world of ideas"—in addition to disarming self-confidence—got her hired. Her masterful organization skills and intuitive grasp of the zeitgeist of the times won her success. Joan produced portions of the station's live talking-head programming and, later, a series of respected documentaries. Among Joan's EBC productions were a debate between school-separationist Malcolm X and integrationist Reverend Calvin Butts, and another that anticipated by days the Cuban missile crisis.

"I felt like I'd died and gone to heaven," she would say of those days, "dealing with foreign policy and domestic policy and civil rights, which became the great passion in those years for me."

F.C.C. Head Bids TV Men Reform 'Vast Wasteland'

Minow Charges Failure in Public Duty—Threatens to Use License Power

Excerpts from Minow's speech to broadcasters, Page 91.

By VAL ADAMS
Special to The New York Times.

WASHINGTON, May 9 — Newton N. Minow, the new chairman of the Federal Communications Commission, presented a scorching indictment of contemporary television at the National Association of Broadcasters convention today.

Addressing more than 2,000 broadcasters, Mr. Minow described TV's program output as a "vast wasteland." He excoriated the amount of violence and mediocrity in shows and said the F. C. C. would no longer automatically renew station licenses.

He called upon viewers to speak up at public hearings that he plans to hold at the community level when a station's license is up for renewal.

Calling for diversification in programing, Mr. Minow invited

Newton N. Minow
Associated Press

each station operator to view his station's programs for one day, from sign-on to sign-off.

"You will see," he said, "a procession of game shows, violence, audience participation shows, formula comedies about totally unbelievable families, blood and thunder, mayhem, violence, sadism, murder, West-

Continued on Page 91, Column 1

FCC Chairman Newton N. Minow's infamous "vast wasteland" speech in 1961 set in motion a wave of pressure for quality television. Years later, in support of PBS, Joan testified at Senate hearings over funding for the stations, which brought her face-to-face with Minow (seen chatting with her between sessions on the facing page). Joan's own involvement in educational television was initially sparked by Jack Gould's article in *The New York Times*, below. Joan and Jack were also subsequently brought together by *Sesame Street*, when the television critic chronicled the show's launch in 1969.

BIG OPPORTUNITY

Sale of Channel 13 to Educational TV Interests Could Enrich Audiences

By JACK GOULD

THE idea of a noncommercial educational television station for the metropolitan New York area, drawing on the city's cultural resources for programing that not only could benefit the immediate viewing audience but also have substantial national influence, has come to the fore again. It could represent an opportunity that might not recur for a long time.

A small group of prominent New Yorkers, working with the National Educational Television Center, has made an

that might come into economic conflict.

But if there is even an outside chance to gain an educational outlet for metropolitan New York, by all means it should be pursued with the utmost diligence. Coldly and realistically, six stations operating under commercial philosophy is ample representation of one form of TV; the medium's base desperately needs broadening in terms of a fundamentally different operating credo.

Speaking in national terms, a New York educational outlet in all probability would become

> I knew that I was born to be in educational television.
>
> —JOAN GANZ COONEY

Joan's political, social, and educational interests merged in a series of EBC documentaries she produced about urban literacy initiatives, shows directed by Bob Myhrum, who would eventually join her on *Sesame Street*. The powerful programs won Joan a local Emmy Award and were later adopted by the federally funded Head Start program to train teachers in its urban education classrooms.

It was at a dinner party celebrating that award win in 1966 that Joan played host to Lewis Freedman, her boss at WNET. Also at the table was Lloyd Morrisett, at the time vice president of the Carnegie Corporation, a philanthropic foundation with a special interest in education. On the menu? Beef Wellington and a conversation about the educational potential of television.

From its genesis as a feasibility study though the segments shot for the most recent season, research has been an integral element of *Sesame Street*. In 1969, Joan conducts early interviews with kids, with the assistance of field researchers like Sharon Lerner, top left. At right, Lloyd Morrisett and Dr. Ed Palmer, head of the show's research team, review early test results with a team of advisors.

PROPOSAL

TO: Carnegie Corporation
FROM: Educational Broadcasting Corporation, Channel 13
      Lewis Freedman, ~~Executive~~ Director of Programming
SUBJECT: ~~Fourteen-week~~ Research project to investigate & evaluate
         possible ways and means of producing and broadcasting
         educational programs for pre-school children.

APPROXIMATE STARTING DATE: June 13, 1966
PROPOSED DURATION OF PROJECT: 14 weeks (with a four-week contingency)
AMOUNT ~~asked~~ REQUESTED: $11,000 for 14 weeks ($14,000 for 18 weeks)

Funds are requested to set up a 14-week research project
which would investigate and evaluate possible ways and
means of producing and ~~broadcasting~~ quality television
programming, with a high degree of educational content,
for pre-school children, ranging in ages from 3 to 5
years of age.

Channel 13 proposes the hiring of a project director who
would confer with pre-school education authorities ~~who~~
throughout the country, and examine theories and techniques
being applied in the education of pre-school children; and
who would ~~research~~ (Review) and past/present television programming
for young children, and confer with noted children's
program producers, in order to:

1) ascertain if high quality, educational programming,
   broadcast on a regular basis, for pre-school children
   would meet a real need in the view of educators; and if
   it is feasible in broadcasting ~~back~~ terms;
2) make recommendations for the production and format/of
   such programming, if the above conditions are met.

"It became clear that
we didn't know enough
to have an answer to the
question, Can television
be used to teach
young children . . . ?"

—LLOYD MORRISETT

*It all begins here—the
original draft of Joan's
request in 1966 for grant
money from
the Carnegie Foundation
to research an answer to
Lloyd's question, above*

Over the meal, Lloyd shared his family's experience of a medium that was still relatively new—color televison. It had been around for only a little more than a decade.

"I would come out on a Sunday morning," he recalled sometime later. "My daughter Sarah [a preschooler] would be in front of the television set in the living room watching the station identification signal." Sarah, who routinely amused her family by singing product jingles, was waiting for the first cartoon to come on. But she seemed just as fascinated by the static image that aired before the day's broadcasting even began—something that clearly wasn't intended for anyone to watch. "And it struck me," Lloyd would tell the dinner guests that night, "there was something fascinating for Sarah about television."

Carnegie was already financing research into education for young children. Why not, Lloyd suggested, include television in that study? Could an experimental program for young children help them learn numbers and letters? To read and do math?

The conversation continued well after the dinner ended.

"We talked around the idea of having a feasibility study done." Lloyd remembers that Joan's boss didn't think she'd be interested. "And Joan spoke up and said, 'Oh, yes, I would!'"

Joan hastily developed a proposal (see her early draft, above) and, within weeks, Carnegie agreed to fund the study.

On hiatus from Channel Thirteen, Joan began a cross-country odyssey, talking with preschool educators, social scientists, psychologists, television experts, and, of course, children. The report of Joan's findings, "The Potential Uses of Television in Preschool Education," reads like a schematic for the show *Sesame Street* would become.

Against all odds, given the undertaking's experimental nature, Lloyd managed to raise $8 million from Carnegie, the U.S. Office of Education, the Ford Foundation, and the Corporation for Public Broadcasting during the following year. These funds would enable Joan to realize the television show envisioned in her report. At a time when commercials cost $60,000 a minute, she argued, a similar expenditure would be needed to create an appealing kids show, to ensure that the quality of this educational offering was as high as the commercial programming competing for audience attention.

In March of 1968, Joan and Lloyd announced the formation of their vision: Children's Television Workshop. At a time when few women producers controlled such huge sums, none of the people who could help build such an ambitious show had ever heard of Joan Ganz Cooney.

That was about to change.

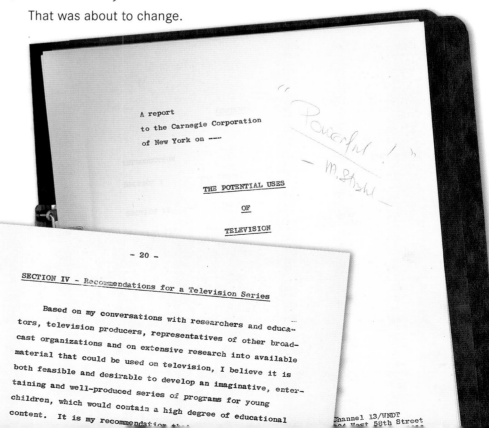

A report
to the Carnegie Corporation
of New York on ----

"Powerful !"
— M. Shaw

THE POTENTIAL USES
OF
TELEVISION

- 20 -

SECTION IV - Recommendations for a Television Series

Based on my conversations with researchers and educators, television producers, representatives of other broadcast organizations and on extensive research into available
material that could be used on television, I believe it is
both feasible and desirable to develop an imaginative, entertaining and well-produced series of programs for young
children, which would contain a high degree of educational
content. It is my recommendation that

Channel 13/WNDT
304 West 58th Street

Joan and Dave

Sam Gibbon Dave Connell Jon Stone

The Dream Team

When the funding for *Sesame Street* came through, the first role Joan had to fill was that of executive producer (EP). One hundred fifty-two hour-long shows would have to be shot in a matter of months, and she needed someone with hands-on experience making television efficiently and well.

An executive producer manages personnel—hiring the director, writers, and actors—and oversees the budget, which involves issues like where, when, and how the series is shot. The EP is also the liaison between the crew and the studio (in this case, Children's Television Workshop). But on *Sesame Street*, the EP would also act as a go-between for the creative talent and the educational advisors . . . all of this under a crushing schedule.

Highly respected CBS producer Mike Dann told Joan, "You've got to have someone who, as Dave Connell says, knows how to run a sausage factory, because that's what you're really doing."

It was the first time Joan had heard Dave's name.

Dave Connell had recently retired as EP of television's *Captain Kangaroo*—one of the few children's programs (such as *Mister Rogers' Neighborhood*) that Joan respected. She soon became convinced Dave was the ideal candidate for her show.

Dave was reluctant to come back from retirement for another round of children's programming, especially one that would be governed by educational mandates. "There's $8 million down the drain," is how he would later describe his reaction to news about the show's ties to an advisory board. Dubious also of Joan's lack of kids'-show experience, he nevertheless listened to her pitch.

"I told him I had some 'nonnegotiable demands'—but not very many!" she has said of their early talks. "I wanted our new children's program to use the short segments and multiple formats that made *Laugh-In* so entertaining and the most popular show on television at the time. Because I knew that children paid attention to TV, I wanted to use 'commercials' to teach letters and numbers. I wanted to see a multiracial cast and both sexes on the show—no one star. But I told Dave that as executive producer, he'd be in charge. I wouldn't be second-guessing creative decisions."

The offer and the challenge proved irresistible. Dave agreed to join the team, taking a salary cut to work for the fledgling nonprofit (a status the Workshop maintains today). He served as the show's EP from 1968 to 1971, then added vice president of production to his title. He was still a valued producer at the Workshop, working on an array of projects, when he passed away in 1995.

Joan also had her eye on two other alumni of *Captain Kangaroo*, both with long careers in children's television.

> ❝ **I know she's got the best possible staff to do the job—she stole them all from me.** ❞
>
> —BOB KEESHAN, TELEVISION'S CAPTAIN KANGAROO,
> AT AN EDUCATIONAL CONFERENCE, GENTLY POKING FUN
> BEFORE EXHORTING THE CROWD TO SUPPORT JOAN'S SHOW

Joan refuses NET's original suggestion to act as executive producer herself, turning that role over to Dave Connell so she can focus on planning and outreach; Dave, seen here on the first set, is able to corral the best talent in children's media

A behind-the-scenes staffer, whose name is unknown to many, was Robert A. Hatch. Bob worked for the Peace Corps before joining the Workshop in 1969 to help promote *Sesame Street* to local PBS stations, schools, and libraries. It's largely due to his efforts that the show was "picked up" across the country.

> ... Every piece of education would be entertaining and every piece of entertainment would be educational.
>
> —JOAN GANZ COONEY

One was producer Samuel Y. Gibbon, Jr. Sam was an expert in putting curriculum and entertainment together, and Joan knew she needed him. "Sam was the one who really understood how to get curriculum into the show," she later said.

Joan begged Sam to come on board. But he kept saying no . . . until April 4, 1968. That was the day Martin Luther King, Jr., was shot. Sam responded deeply to the tragedy. "It felt to most of us as though the country was in real danger of crumbling," he remembered, describing that terrible event.

In an interview with assistant director Bob Davidson, Sam recalled going to a memorial service in New York's Central Park with his wife and being tremendously moved by the tear-stained faces of all races in the crowd. "The notion that maybe it was time to do something useful was pretty overpowering."

The next morning, he called Joan. "If you want me, I'm yours," Sam informed her.

The second member Joan earmarked for the team was a man who puppeteer Frank Oz would later describe as "the main guy, kind of the father of *Sesame Street*." Joan originally tried to hire him for the EP job, but he was busy building a house in Vermont and showed no interest. Besides, he didn't want to take an administrative job. His strength, he felt, was in the creative arena.

His name was Jon Stone.

Producer Sam Gibbon, in the top two photos with Joan, was credited by colleagues as being able to crank out shows tirelessly—to meet deadlines that first season, the team was taping one hour-long show a day. Lutrelle "Lu" Horne, pictured here screening a "Dot Bridge" animation, was brought in as a coproducer that first season. The team was still taping mid-season shows when the first episode went on the air.

Rolleeolee-oleeyo!*

> " He was an artist . . . in many ways the key creative talent on *Sesame Street*. "
>
> —JOAN GANZ COONEY

J on Stone was a grizzly bear of a guy with a twinkle in his eye and a gift for slapstick. Most people remember him striding around the set with a pencil stuck in his beard, ready to do whatever was needed—rewrite a script, help a puppeteer with a performance, give someone an encouraging hug.

When Jon came on board, the show found a critical champion and visionary. It was Jon who recommended a puppeteer named Jim Henson be hired, Jon who envisioned the set's unique look. It was Jon co-wrote the theme-song lyrics and many of the show's indelible comic moments—Joan would later call him "probably the most brilliant writer of children's television material in America." It was Jon who eventually took over as EP when Dave Connell moved on to other Workshop productions, and it was Jon who became *Sesame Street*'s principal director for the next twenty-odd years. "He was the father of *Sesame Street*," states puppeteer Frank Oz.

Jon could do it *all* brilliantly. As a director, he coaxed nuanced performances from both the Muppets and the show's

child actors. In the early years, he, Jim, and Frank would rally every Friday to create the Muppet insert pieces on a separate stage. That's perhaps where Jon's special genius for spontaneity and wit shone most brightly. It was almost as if he were a third puppeteer—laughing with Jim and Frank, helping to shape their performances, crafting what would become the show's signature style.

As a writer, Jon could take a script and, on the floor and on the fly, edit and rewrite it in minutes so that it was twice as funny. Show writer Chris Cerf fondly remembers Jon's fallback for getting kid viewers and the crew to belly laugh: Muppet-tossing. "He was a little bit of an anarchist. He loved it if there was a sketch in which he could throw puppet sheep up in the air."

*That means: "Roll tape!"

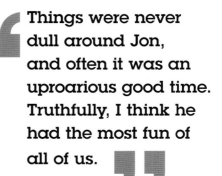

NEWS FLASH

"It's a delightful atmosphere to work in," Jon said of the *Sesame Street* set. Many on the crew during Jon's 29 years at the helm credit him for setting that tone, and his puckish sense of humor is still infamous on the set. Director Emily Squires recalls him huddling with puppeteers, snickering and cooking up bits of silliness, and then shouting "Rolleeoleeoleeyo" to start tape rolling. No one knew what would happen next. "He had a way of making even the smallest moments fun," Emily says. Jon's humor is spotted in other Henson projects, too. His script, "Sex and Violence with the Muppets," would become the pilot for what eventually became Jim Henson's next phenomenon: *The Muppet Show.*

And as an administrator, Jon was generous and supportive, willing to take a chance. Director Lisa Simon provides one example of this.

"The way I first got to direct is, we were shooting on location and we had one more bit to do," she recalls, "and Jon came over to me and said, 'You do it,' and then just walked away." She shakes her head in wonder. "I had never thought about directing. I don't even remember what I was doing that day—I might have been stage-managing—but he just said, 'See you later.' And he walked away."

Jon's instincts were so accurate that things almost invariably paid off. Lisa went on to produce *the show* for years and is one of the show's Emmy Award–winning directors.

"He had like a little light," says Sonia Manzano, who plays the role of Maria. "He had a way of getting people to break their necks for his approval, because he was so inspiring."

"I've always said of our original team that developed and produced *Sesame Street*: Collectively, we were a genius."

—JOAN GANZ COONEY

Charlotte Brooks gets a ladder's—eye view of the cast and crew for photos featured in Look magazine.

Joan poses on the set during taping of the first season with many of the production crew and research staff. Photographer Charlotte Brooks documented the process for a *Look* magazine feature. The show's debut was the focus of an enormous amount of media attention, largely due to the efforts of the community outreach team at the newly formed Children's Television Workshop.

By early 1969, the set was established as a quintessential city block. But *Sesame Street* might have looked very different if not for Jon Stone, who was committed to the idea of an inner-city location throughout impassioned internal debate. "I wanted something really funky and down-to-earth," Jon said in later years. "A real inner-city street." He was inspired by the idea of urban ghettos, where "the street outside is where it's really happening . . . where the action is." By setting the show in the reality of its neediest viewers, Jon contended, kids would be able to envision themselves using the show's lessons and behaviors. However, filmmaker Clark Gesner, who was initially tapped to design the show's look, argued for a very different vision of the show: an abstract locale peopled by nonhuman forms. Jon later described that approach as "clean and high tech, plastic-looking . . . the exact *antithesis* of what I was thinking." Jon's gritty street won the day, but Clark's vision lives on in a series of surreal dot animations, below, that entranced young viewers and occasionally still air on the show.

 **NEWS FLASH** The Street set was built in a single long line, with a dirt patch separating the 123 Sesame Street brownstone apartment house (where Bert and Ernie live) from the next building. This is a set rarely seen by fans, as it was quickly replaced, after the pilots were shot, by a curved street, which allowed more camera angles.

   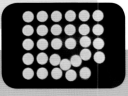

On-location shoots such as this one cemented for viewers the notion that Sesame Street was a real place somewhere in New York City, but debate still rages over whether that locale is in Manhattan or Brooklyn

These screen grabs of the show opener will look familiar to viewers of the first season

Few musical phrases trigger as heady a wave of nostalgia as the iconic three-note lead-in to *Sesame Street*'s opening number. People often refer to this tune as "Sunny Day," but in house, the song dreamed up by the team of Joe Raposo, Bruce Hart, and Jon Stone is known simply as "The Sesame Street Theme." The arrangement has changed only a half dozen times in 40 years, and the words remain exactly the same.

How Sesame Street Got Its Name

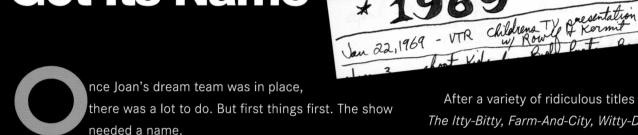

Once Joan's dream team was in place, there was a lot to do. But first things first. The show needed a name.

Settling on one proved a challenge for the show's cofounders. When Muppet founder, builder, performer, and all-around genius Jim Henson was first commissioned to create a promotional film for the show, to be shown to National Educational Television (NET) executives, there still wasn't one in place. Jim and scriptwriter Jon Stone took full advantage of the comic possibilities that this uncertainty provided. The promo film would be funny—in fact, irreverent. It would set the tone for the teasing and joyous human–puppet interaction that would later become a hallmark of the show.

And it would reference the show's naming dilemma.

In the film, Dr. Gerald Lesser, chairman to the advisory board and one of the premier educational experts on the show, outlines its intentions and research process for a dog and a frog. Those earnest segments are sandwiched between scenes of a crowd of ad-men-type Muppets debating potential show names.

After a variety of ridiculous titles are suggested—culminating in *The Itty-Bitty, Farm-And-City, Witty-Ditty, Nitty-Gritty, Dog-And-Kitty, Pretty-Little-Kiddie Show*—Rowlf the Dog fires the conference room of Muppets, and Kermit the Frog himself comes up with the name *Sesame Street*: "You know, like 'Open sesame.' It kind of gives the idea of a street where neat stuff happens," he suggests in his reasonable, yet unmistakably froggy voice.

In real life, arriving at that name had been a bit harder. Suggested monikers included *The Video Classroom* and *1-2-3 Avenue B* (after a New York Lower East Side avenue). "Everything from the mundane *'Fun Street*,'" Joan would later recall ruefully. "Of course, it didn't matter, we could have called it anything if it was a success."

She laughs now over her own reluctance to the show's final name, inspired by Ali Baba's magical phrase, "Open sesame." *Sesame Street* was dreamed up by staff writer Virginia Schone, according to Workshop memories. Like Joan, no one on the team was overly fond of it. Among other things, some felt the word *sesame* would be too difficult for kids to sound out in print, that kids would pronounce it "see same."

Finally, some potential names were tested on neighborhood children one weekend. No prizes for guessing the winner.

The completed promo film (which credits Kermit on-screen with dreaming up the name *Sesame Street*) was shipped to stations all over the country in the early months of 1969, in an effort to convince them to air the show at 9 A.M. *Captain Kangaroo* was on at 8 A.M. on the East Coast, and Joan was adamant about not competing with the Captain's series, which she singled out alongside *Mister Rogers' Neighborhood* as "the only other decent show on the air."

It took personal meetings and much convincing, but more than 180 NET stations agreed to air *Sesame Street* beginning fall 1969.

Now the show would have to be fully cast and produced. It was time for the Muppets and their human neighbors to take center stage.

Dr. Gerald "Gerry" Lesser rehearses with Kermit

> " . . . all the teaching stuff is mixed in with stories and cartoons and us Muppets and real people and like that. "
>
> —ROWLF THE DOG,
> IN THE SHOW'S PITCH REEL

> " How about we call it *The Itty-Bitty, Farm-And-City, Witty-Ditty, Nitty-Gritty, Dog-And-Kitty, Pretty-Little-Kiddie Show*? "
>
> —ANYTHING MUPPET AD MAN,
> IN THE SHOW'S PITCH REEL

Blue AM: How about this for a title? *The Two and Two Are Five Show*.

Pink AM: Are you crazy? Now, this is supposed to be an educational show. Two plus two don't make five!

Blue AM: They don't?

Pink AM: No, you meatball!

Blue AM: Then how about *The Two and Two Ain't Five Show*?

Joan tests portions of the pitch reel with kids before shopping it to the PBS stations. New York City's local affiliate, Channel Thirteen, passed on the show. So Joan cannily negotiated a waiver from unions to air the show on the commercial network WPIX channel 11 until Thirteen opted to pick up the show in season two.

THIS CHAPTER HAS BEEN BROUGHT TO YOU BY THE LETTER J AND THE NUMBER 13.

The letter J is for Joan Ganz Cooney, who made it all happen. It's also for Jon Stone, Jim Henson, and a number of other "J" jewels in the *Sesame Street* crown—Jeff Moss, Joe Raposo, and Jerry Nelson among them. Don't worry, you'll meet them all soon. **The number 13** is for Channel Thirteen, the name of the local public broadcasting station in the New York area, where Joan once worked as a producer. At the time Joan started there, it was called WNET. As the Count would no doubt agree, the number's much catchier.

2

"You don't think of them as Muppets. If you're gonna stand around talking to a rag, you better think of him as Oscar."

—DR. LORETTA LONG (SUSAN ROBINSON)

EPISODE
4151

When Slimey started on *Sesame Street* in season two, he had no words—just squeaky sounds. Recently, he's acquired an English vocabulary. One of the few Muppets not voiced by a puppeteer, Slimey's vocals come from sound engineer Dick Maitland. Dick records his own voice and then digitally manipulates it.

"Puppeteers under!" Stage manager Shawn Havens's baritone resonates easily above the conversations and clatter on the *Sesame Street* set.

"Find your worms!"

Unmoved by the bedlam, five small Muppet worms lounge on the counter in Hooper's Store. They recline in tiny bentwood chairs at a dollhouse-sized picnic table, under a minuscule umbrella.

Nearby, puppeteers cram themselves into an area not more than six feet square, under the worms' faux grass playing field. Two rods per puppet feed through holes in the turf, under which the compressed and contorted performers sort out who's holding what.

"You guys should make yourselves comfortable," Shawn tells them dryly. "You're gonna be in there for hours."

On the schedule for today? "The Worm Games," written by Belinda Ward, directed by former puppeteer Jim Martin, and brought to us by the letter K and the number 19. The episode stars one of *Sesame Street*'s largest characters—Big Bird, clocking in at 8 feet 2 inches tall with a not-so-trim waistline of 92 inches—and one of its smallest, Slimey, a 7-inch worm. It's just another day of bending the laws of physics on *Sesame Street*.

In this episode, Slimey is competing in the international Worm Games, a kind of invertebrate soccer. While the worms rehearse, puppeteer Caroll Spinney runs lines with the director, his gentle face alert and attentive, even a little mischievous. When he reappears on set a few moments later, Caroll is wearing Big Bird's familiar striped orange legs, which cover his own legs and feet, held in place with a pair of reinforced suspenders. He wears a harness that contains a tiny TV receiver and wireless microphone over his T-shirt.

Muppet worms are composed of nine tiny sections. Two metal rods are used to manipulate them, and monofilament thread opens and shuts their mouths. Left, an intern assists Muppet wranglers making on-set adjustments to a worm in its dollhouse-sized chair.

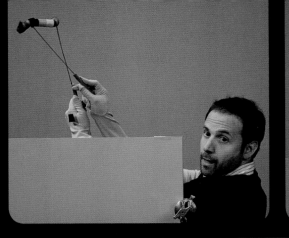
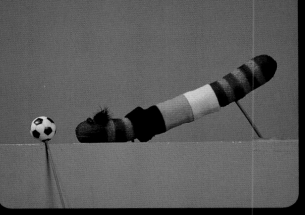

on the set
on the set
on the set
on the set

Joey Mazzarino demonstrates how to make a worm squirm

" **In puppetry, it's the magic that matters.** "

—JERRY NELSON,
PUPPETEER

Puppeteers are sometimes stuck in backbreaking positions for over an hour until somebody desperately needs to stretch. Below, Noel MacNeal, Matt Vogel, Eric Jacobson, and Marty Robinson await cues. At right, Marty rehearses Slimey's gold-medal-winning moves.

The tiny video monitor used inside Big Bird is the original one techie Walt Rauffer rigged up for Caroll back in 1968. The idea came from director Bob Myhrum, Caroll recalls. "He said, 'Can't we get one of those TV things people take to ball games, so they can see the replay from the stands?'" Walt rigged it to a harness. "We call it the electronic bra," says Caroll, pictured here with director Jim Martin.

Soon the upper half of Big Bird, sitting on a hinged stand, is wheeled in by senior Muppet wrangler Michelle Hickey. Wranglers are responsible for the care and repair of the Muppets.

Nothing prepares you for Big Bird. First of all, he really is big—big and fluffy and an almost electric yellow. And he's beautiful; his feathers glisten in the bright, flat studio light.

Looking oddly formal in a pair of white cotton gloves, worn to keep feathers clean, Michelle slips the Bird off his stand in one quick motion. Holding the beak in one hand and a hidden tab of cloth in the other, she maneuvers the puppet over Caroll's shoulders. Caroll's right arm slides up into Bird's neck; his right hand controls the head. He uses his little finger on a lever to control Bird's eyes, and his thumb to open and close the beak. His left arm operates Bird's left wing, counterbalanced by the right wing, operated with a nearly invisible filament. Caroll's own head is wedged at an awkward angle in the Bird's neck. Yet as contorted as he is, Caroll still manages to always give a heartfelt performance.

"The first day on set, I had no TV inside," Caroll remembers ruefully. "I could hardly see what I was doing. They didn't show playbacks, so I didn't see how bad it was. I'm amazed I kept the job."

Even with a video monitor, performing Big Bird is a visual challenge. Caroll sees what the director and camera operators see—a third-person view of the action. But since monitors show images in reverse, when Caroll wants to move camera left, he must instinctively shift to the right.

"Wait'll you see him dribble," someone on the crew whispers to a guest. "Remember: He's almost blind in there!"

Sure enough, in the next scene, Big Bird bounces a basketball as he heads for Hooper's Store to watch his tiny pal compete on TV. It's incredible to imagine the actor inside, gracefully navigating the crowded set in spite of his mind-bending thirdhand viewpoint through the monitor buried in the Bird. And as if that isn't enough, director Jim Martin wants higher energy in the scene. The full-body Bird puppet is lifted off Caroll's shoulders briefly as the actor consults with Jim on a line change. Then he suits up again.

"Roll record," calls Shawn Havens. Two bells ring. Tape is rolling.

"Slimey is an intelligent worm," Marty says. "Except for Buster the horse, he may be the smartest guy on the Street." He's also the tiniest (if you don't count the invisible fleas in the flea circus). Ironically, Marty Robinson plays both the worm and the show's *biggest* character—he puppeteers Snuffleupagus with Bryant Young.

There's always a lot of downtime on set. No one wants to spend all that time in a full-body character like Big Bird. The heat is unbearable, and it's extraordinarily difficult to hold Big Bird's head aloft. Big Bird's body "suit" weighs in at about ten pounds, and his head is an additional four and a half. "The hardest thing is to keep my arm up," says Caroll Spinney. "Try holding your hand up for two minutes and see how it feels. Then put four pounds on it. After ten minutes, I sag."

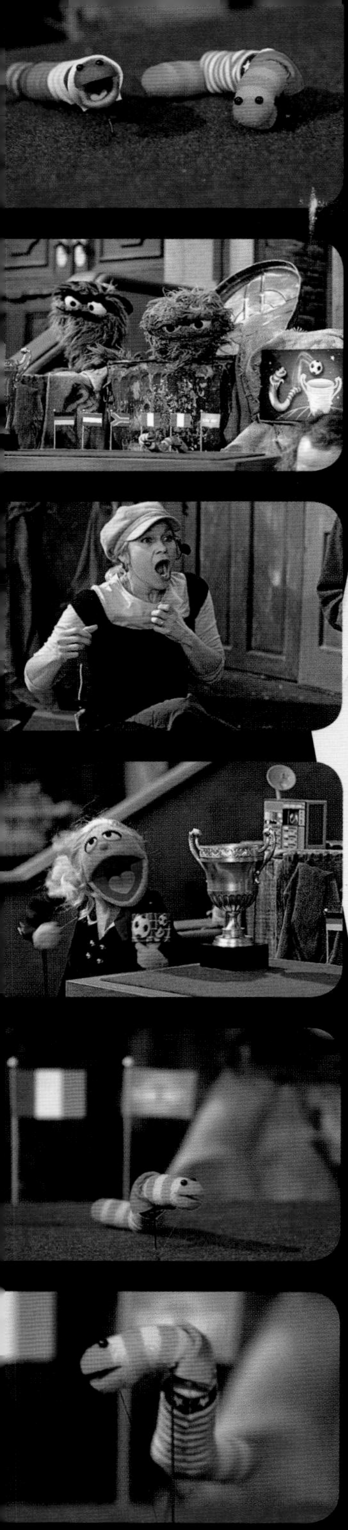

SESAME STREET

PRODUCTION MEETING COPY — WARD
16   SHOW 4151

TECH: THE INSTANT REPLAY OF SQUIRMADENE SAYING "NYAH, NYAH, NYAH, NYAH, NYAH."

SPORTSCASTER: (TO CAM) I believe Squirmadene's exact words were (DISTINCTLY) "Nyah, nyah, nyah, nyah, nyah." As you all know, that's teasing and against the rules of the Worm Cup. The referee is giving Squirmadene a warning.

CLOSE ON THE REFEREE WORM GIVING A GOOD TALKING TO SQUIRMADENE.

OSCAR: (TO THE REFEREE) A warning? Just a warning? You should throw the worm out of the game!

SPORTSCASTER: (TO OSCAR) Never argue with the referee.

OSCAR: Hey, I'm a grouch! I'll argue with anyone! Even you.

THE SPORTSCASTER LOOKS SURPRISED.

OSCAR: (CONT, TO SLIMEY) Don't let Squirmadene get to you, Slimey. Just go out there and give it your personal worm best.

SLIMEY NODS AND CRAWLS ONTO THE FIELD.

SPORTSCASTER: (TO CAM) Here com Slimey!

SFX: SPECTATOR CHEERS.

(CONTINUED)

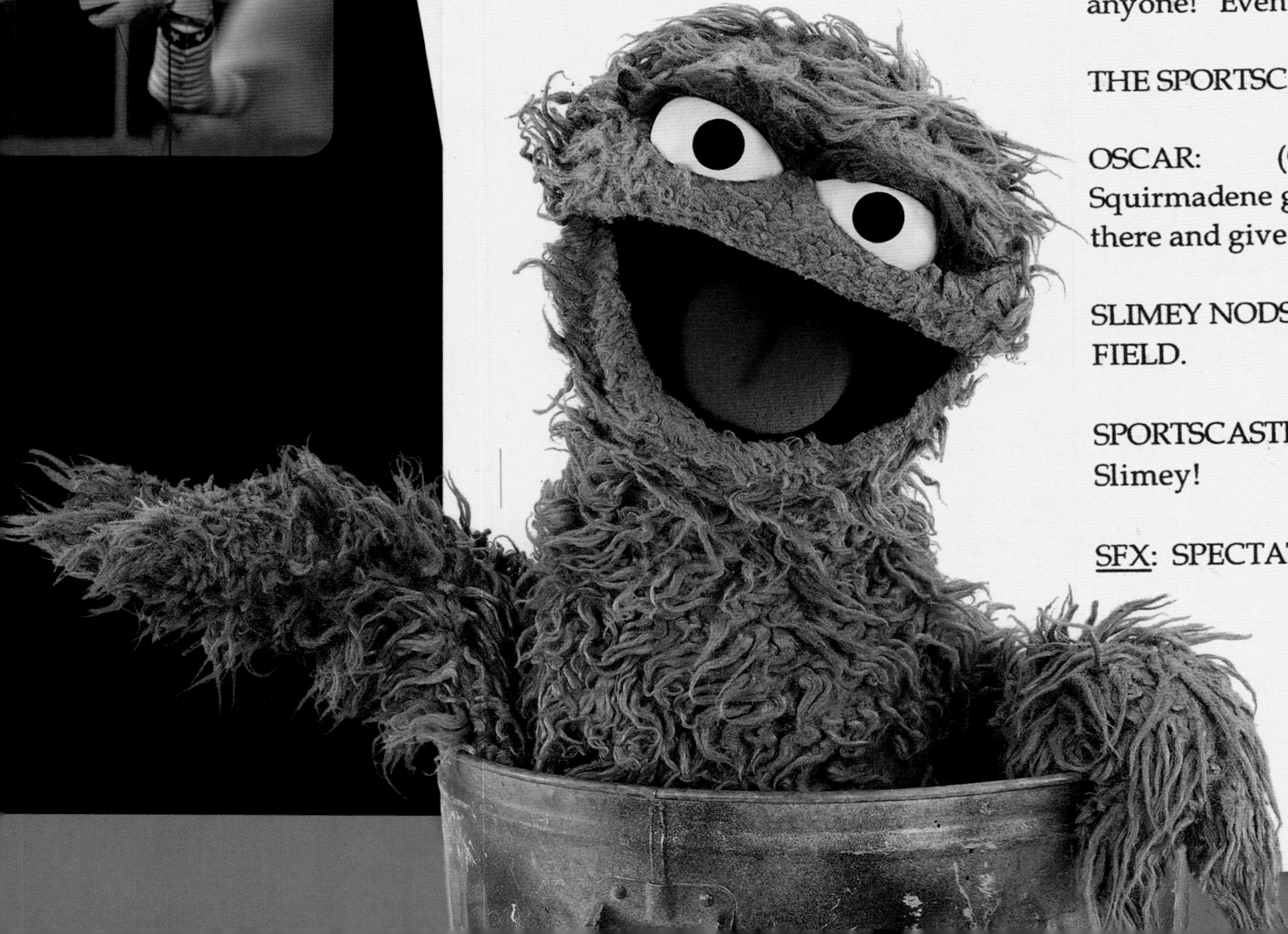

Rehearsing the scene, puppeteer Leslie Carrara-Rudolph eerily re-sembles her sportscaster Muppet

SESAME STREET

PRODUCTION MEETING COPY - WARD
17
SHOW 4151

Each script is reproduced in this book complete with the original typos

SLIMEY BACKS UP AND CRAWLS TOWARDS
THE BALL AS FAST AS HIS CAN.

SPORTSCASTER: (CONT) Slimey is getting a
crawling start! Look at that worm crawl! He's
gaining speed and he kicks the ball!

SLIMEY KICKS THE BALL.

                                                    CUT TO:
TECH: SQUIRMADENE LEAPING UP IN SLOW
MOTION.

THE BALL FLIES OVER HIS HEAD.

                                                    CUT TO:
THE BALL LANDING IN THE CUP.

SPORTSCASTER: (VO)   Squirmadene tries
to stop him, but he can't! Slimey scores!

                                                    CUT TO:
INT. - HOOPER'S STORE - SAME

BIG BIRD/ALAN/KID/AMERICAN WORMS:
(CHEERING) Yay! Slimey!

                                                    CUT BACK TO:
EXT. - WORM GAMES (CAN AREA) - SAME

SPORTSCASTER: (TO CAM) The worms are
tied. The score is now Squirmadene-one and
Slimey-one.   And now it's Squirmadene's turn
again. Looks like he is winding up for his
famous back flip kick!

(CONTINUED)

The color of a script's pages indicates which revision the cast is looking at, according to Script Supervisor Syndi Shumer and Coordinator Lynda Holder-Settles. Here's the color code that lets you know: white (orginal draft); canary yellow (1st revise); salmon (2nd); pink (3rd); green (4th); goldenrod (5th); cherry (6th); gray (7th). Then the cycle repeats. Here, puppeteer Kevin Clash bones up on Elmo's lines, using an original draft of the script.

Heigh-Ho!
Kermit the Frog Here!

You must have heard: the first Kermit was built from Jim's mother's green coat

If not for a wide-mouthed frog made from an old coat, *Sesame Street* might look very different.

For one thing, it probably wouldn't have any puppets. Rumor has it that Executive Producer Dave Connell and Producer/Writer/Director Jon Stone felt that if they couldn't get Jim Henson's Muppets, they wouldn't use any puppets at all.

Controversy still exists about whose idea it was to call Jim Henson and offer him the job. But most agree it was probably Jon. He and Jim met on a special for ABC that aired in 1969, called *Hey Cinderella*. (Music director Joe Raposo—who helped create *Sesame Street*'s signature sound—also worked on that program.)

Joan Cooney remembers falling in the aisle laughing over a reel of commercials by Jim some time before *Sesame Street* began. But she never thought they could get the talented puppeteer. After all, he already had a successful career.

Jim had been performing his Muppet characters ever since he was seventeen, when he built a character named Kermit out of his mother's discarded green felt topper. Later, he created some additional Muppets, including Yorick, Harry the Hipster, and Sam, for *Sam and Friends*, a local Washington, D.C., TV show that launched his career. Muppet appearances followed on national television shows such as *The Today Show*, *The Ed Sullivan Show*, and *The Jimmy Dean Show,* as well as a variety of local and national TV commercials, including some for La Choy Chinese food. For that series of ads, Jim built the long-tailed La Choy Dragon, who had a habit of setting grocery aisles alight with his fiery breath.

One of Joan Ganz Cooney's ideas for her fledgling show had been to create educational segments based on the short, punchy TV commercial model. She had noticed that even the youngest kids sang the jingles for commercials. Clearly, they were learning something from them.

When Jim found out about this idea, he was intrigued.

One hot New York summer day in August 1968, Joan sat in a Waldorf-Astoria Hotel conference room, attending the first of five educational seminars organized by her handpicked team of curriculum advisers. Executive Producer Dave Connell was sitting beside her when the door opened and a long-haired, bearded man in leather pants entered the room and edged into a seat in the back.

A summer filled with threats from the underground organization The Weathermen made Joan look nervously over her shoulder. "How do we know that that man isn't going to throw a bomb up here and kill us?" she whispered to Dave.

Dave glanced behind, then grinned. "No, no," he replied reassuringly. "That's Jim Henson."

> **Anywhere I am is here. Anywhere I am not is there.**
>
> —KERMIT THE FROG

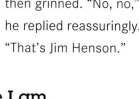

> "Unlike any adult I've ever known, Jim could talk about wanting a world of peace and love without a trace of irony or self-consciousness."
>
> —JOAN GANZ COONEY

Dr. Loretta Long, who plays Susan, recalls Jim's sartorial influence on the other men on the set and even among the research staff; soon formerly clean-cut guys like Caroll Spinney were all wearing their hair long and growing beards

"Cookie originally was a different physical monster than you see now—a different puppet," Frank Oz recalls. "Jim had a two-minute routine we did for *The Ed Sullivan Show* called 'Beautiful Day,' and a monster was part of it." That puppet, called Beautiful Day Monster [shown below in Jim's Oscar-nominated short "Timepiece"], was used interchangeably with another puppet for the first few seasons until Cookie Monster's character and toothless look became firmly established on *Sesame Street*.

Kermit, as a preexisting Muppet character, was solely owned by Jim when he joined the *Sesame Street* cast, leaving him free to perform in *The Muppet Show* and other Henson productions. In an instructional video created in the '70s, *Muppets on Puppets*, Jim and puppet designer Michael Frith discussed the frog.

Jim: Hi there, I'm Jim Henson. This is Kermit the Frog, here.

Kermit: Heigh-ho.

Jim: He's one of the very simplest puppets because inside of his head there's nothing in there but my hand. And so it's just a little cloth pattern. . . . Originally he was done with a couple of Ping-Pong balls—the eyes were—so they are just half spheres. . . . He's virtually a glorified sock puppet.

Michael: . . . Remember that the basic skeleton of the puppet is the human hand and arm . . . It's *very* dramatically illustrated in Kermit when you look at him in profile, because you can really see the shape of the hand in there.

> " **The most sophisticated people I know . . . inside, they are all children.** "
>
> —JIM HENSON

Jim HENSON

ERNIE, KERMIT, YIP-YIP, GUY SMILEY, COUNTLESS ANYTHING MUPPETS

> " No frog of mine ever said
> 'wiggit-wiggit' in my life! "
>
> —KERMIT, IN RESPONSE TO A GIRL
> TRYING TO SPEAK FROG

Although Jim Henson personified some of the funniest and silliest characters on *Sesame Street* and *The Muppet Show*, you'd never know it from meeting him.

Jim was tall, slightly stooped, and always appeared relaxed and calm. Nothing fazed him, and he never seemed to get angry. In meetings, if he didn't like an idea, all he'd do was sit back and say, "Hmmmm," in a quizzical tone. On TV and movie sets, visitors who knew how tense production could be were amazed that he never, ever raised his voice.

In fact, he was a lot like Kermit—except that Kermit occasionally lost his temper.

"I remember one time, they were doing a very complicated Muppet piece with maybe six or seven puppeteers," recalls Bob McGrath (Bob). "It looked like a car crash behind the scenes.

"And right at the very end of this piece, which they had worked on for a couple of hours, this younger girl puppeteer crashed and the piece went to pieces. The girl was probably dying in her boots. And Jim—he sounded a little bit like Kermit, you know, in real life—said, 'I think we can probably do another one, don't you?'

"That was the extent of it. There was no criticism."

Kevin Clash, performer of Elmo, admires this about Jim.

"That's why I loved Henson," he says. "In doing that, he took away the shyness, 'cause a lot of us, even actors and comedians, we're all shy at the beginning. But once you got that acceptance, then you could shine."

Jim was a doodler—often of complex, abstract

designs, though his puppet creations were frequently realized from the sketchiest of drawings. He overflowed with ideas.

"He was always making things or doing art projects with us," says Jim Henson's daughter Cheryl Henson of her father. "He didn't really bring the work home . . . it's more like he brought the spirit of home back to the work."

"Jim was an extraordinarily serious yet silly man," says Fran Brill, the puppeteer who performs Prairie Dawn and Zoe on *Sesame Street*. "He would encourage you to be as crazy as possible, because when you're inhibited as a performer, you can't be creative. Because he would be silly, everybody else would be silly."

He was also tenacious. From the time he fell in love with television, when his dad brought home their first set, he never gave up on his dream of working on TV. He likewise encouraged and promoted other people's dreams.

"He treated everybody with incredible grace and dignity, whether it was the head of the network or the guy picking up the trash," Fran recalls. "And he had a very good instinct about people, too, because he really did not hire too many bad eggs. They were all good people, generous people, kind people, and I think that's amazing."

Jane Henson, Jim's wife and frequent puppeteering partner in the early years, as seen above, remembers the Mississippi home that shaped the man he would later become:

"The Hensons always had porch furniture that rocked this way and that, and they would sit and rock and talk for hours. They definitely had that Southern storytelling tradition. Jim's work always had a poignant, sweet sadness. A lot of his sensitivity and caring and tenderness came from growing up in that family."

Jim's sketches show the development of what truly distinguishes Ernie from Bert—the shapes of their heads, which reflect their essential characters: soft and sharp

"I'm so busy and obsessed puppeteering that I have no recollection afterward of what I've done. It just disappears."
—FRANK OZ

Frank OZ

BERT, COOKIE MONSTER, GROVER, LEFTY THE SALESMAN, ETC.

> **Why me?**
> —BERT

One of the people Jim hired early in his career was Frank Oz. Frank came from a family of puppeteers—his parents, Frances and Isidore Oznowicz, were highly respected performers. Frank was just seventeen years old when he first met Jim at a puppetry festival. Two years later, in 1963, Jim hired him to work part-time for his fledg-

ling company, and Frank headed to New York. It was immediately obvious that he would bring something immeasurable to Jim's work—and, subsequently, to *Sesame Street*. His serious, sometimes slightly dour demeanor hides a wicked sense of humor, ready to pop out at a moment's notice. He takes his performances to extremes—from the insanely obsessive Cookie Monster to the almost fanatically conservative

Bert—conveying the heart of each of them in gestures that can move you from laughter to tears to astonishment and back again in the blink of an eye.

Even when Frank wasn't being taped, he was often puppeteering.

"A camera was down or something, and Frank was lying on his back with his legs crossed, and the sole had come loose from his shoe so it flapped," Executive Producer Jon Stone once recalled.

"Frank had Cookie Monster on his hand, and he was talking

between Cookie Monster and his shoe, and he'd wiggle his toes to make the sole flap, and his shoe became a puppet. And then he got bored with that, so he made his shoe a ventriloquist's dummy for Cookie Monster. And Cookie would talk for the shoe and the shoe would flap back, but Cookie was a really bad ventriloquist, and his lips would move so that when the shoe would flap, you'd see Cookie's lips moving ever so slightly.

"Frank had no idea anyone was watching. I just happened to have a camera on him. We were all in the control room, just absolutely fascinated with this demonstration of brilliant puppetry."

What made Frank so brilliant?

"You don't have to sing a song and be a dancing rag to be a good puppeteer," says puppeteer Brian Meehl. "You have to totally personify and imbue your puppet with a life. And Frank did that with his characters. His brilliance as a puppeteer is that he brought acting into puppeteering, not just presentation. He brought out the inner life of the character. You knew there was something going on in that puppet's head."

Frank is also an excellent teacher.

"I make it tough for the guys," he says. "Because it's part of learning the craft; it's part of becoming part of the character." Frank pauses. "But," he admits, "it's also just to f**k around with them."

There isn't a hole in the puppet's mouth, so Cookie never gets to really sample his treats; he simply crumbles them in a feeding frenzy

NEWS FLASH Cookie Monster often "eats" real cookies. They're purchased at a supermarket conveniently located near the studio.

Dynamic Duo

"Performing the Ernie and Bert pieces with Frank has always been one of the great joys of doing the show. . . . It's really a unique way of working in television, because most of the time, you take a script and you're doing the lines, but about half the time when Frank and I are working, we decide not to use the script. Instead, we'll take the basic concepts of it and if it has a punch line or two, we'll circle around and hit those lines. But other than that, we'll just talk the piece, and so we're really working spontaneously and just sort of playing off of each other. It's a lot of fun."

—JIM HENSON

SEGMENT #0001-0286

Ernie: *(oblivious to Bert's attempts to get under his umbrella)* Isn't it interesting, Bert? Isn't it interesting that I can feel all three ways about the rain?

Bert: Oh, yeah.

Ernie: Because I can feel happy about it, I can feel sad about it, and I can feel very angry about it, too.

Bert: Yeah, angry. *Angry.*

Ernie: But what about you, Bert? How do you feel?

Bert: *(furious)* WET, Ernie. I feel very, very, VERY wet, Ernie!

Ernie: Well, of course you're wet. Where's your umbrella?

Bert: My umbrella? YOU have my umbrella!

Ernie: Oh. Well, gee, thanks, Bert. I'll see you around, huh?

Some of the very first sessions with the new puppets: in a short-lived experiment, Frank is performing Ernie and Jim is Bert

Jim and Frank (and John Lovelady as right-hander) clown around with prototype Ernie and Bert puppets, above, in 1968. Working in front of a mirror helps prep a performer for the disconnect of viewing a puppet's performance through a monitor once on set, where the action appears flopped on-screen. Many puppeteers are never able to master this aspect of TV and movie performance.

> "There are certainly elements of our own personalities in Bert and Ernie. We know each other's timing and we play off each other very well, and that's what a good comedy team does.

—JIM HENSON

> "Bert is a very boring facet of myself. I mean, I can be very boring. You can be very boring. Everyone in the world can be boring.

—FRANK OZ

A few classic segments between the perpetually sleepy Bert and his insomniac roommate

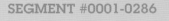

> "In the very beginning, we first built these characters and then we were trying to decide who should do which . . . I remember trying Bert, and Frank tried Ernie for a while, and then we settled on the present arrangement. I can't imagine doing Bert now, because Bert has become so much of a part of Frank.

—JIM HENSON

SEGMENT #0001-0286

Ernie: You know, it's just possible that my ol' buddy Bert here is asleep. For one thing, he is lying down, which he usually does when he is asleep. For another thing, his eyes are closed. Huh. For another thing, he's not answering me when I talk. So ol' buddy Bert is probably asleep, but I will check just to make sure. *Poke-poke-poke-poke-poke-poke-poke.* Note how I can poke ol' buddy in the stomach, and he doesn't complain. Now when ol' buddy Bert is awake and I poke him in the stomach, he complains. Hmmm. Oh lookee here. Note how floppy and soggy-like ol' buddy Bert's arm is. Yeah. When ol' buddy Bert is awake, he's not floppy and soggy-like, so I am quite certain that ol' buddy Bert is very definitely asleep. On the other hand . . . NOW his eyes are open! My ol' buddy Bert's eyes are usually open only when he is awake, so he's probably awake, but I will check just to make sure. *Poke. Poke-poke-poke-poke-poke-poke.*

Bert: Now cut that out!

Ernie: See, I was right. He's awake.

Question: Are Bert and Ernie gay?

Answer: "They are not gay, they are not straight, they are puppets," says Sesame Workshop President and CEO Gary Knell. "They don't exist below the waist."

Caroll SPINNEY

BIG BIRD, BRUNO, OSCAR THE GROUCH, OCCASIONAL ANYTHING MUPPETS

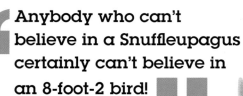

After five test shows were shot and screened with pre-schoolers in Philadelphia, the creators of the show discovered they had a problem.

Educators initially insisted that showing the fanciful Muppets on the street set would confuse children. The street was supposed to be the "real" part of *Sesame Street*, with puppets appearing only in interstitials, the brief commercial-like "bits" that interrupted the story. Testing soon demonstrated, however, that kids were most attentive and engaged when the Muppets were on screen.

That was the end of the Muppet-less block. Jim Henson began drawing sketches of a big bird who would live next door to 123 Sesame Street, a "wonder why" character suggested by advisors in the educational seminars. Soon after, a grouch and his trash can joined the mix.

The story goes that Jim originally offered the role of Big Bird to Frank Oz, but Frank had had an unpleasantly claustrophobic stint in the full-body La Choy Dragon Muppet and said no. (Frank doesn't remember this, but acknowledges that "If I were ever offered it, I *would* have said no.")

That meant Jim immediately needed a new member on the team.

Ultimately Henson chose Caroll Spinney, an artist and puppeteer who had been performing material at puppet festivals around the country, as well as puppeteering on local TV shows such as *Bozo's Big Top*.

Jim first spotted Caroll years before and then caught his act a second time. In that latter multimedia performance, the video part went "kaflooey," as Caroll describes it, forcing him to improvise madly. Jim was impressed by his spontaneity and ability to ad lib under pressure, and casually suggested that Caroll come down to New York someday to "talk about the Muppets."

Ironically, the ability to wing it had landed him the role of a bird. Because in 1968, they met again and, at that second meeting, Caroll learned that what he'd assumed was a casual suggestion had been Jim's way of offering Caroll a job. This time, Caroll accepted, despite some reservations about the potential success of the project. Caroll moved to New York, even though he was pretty sure a kids' show with a cast of zany puppets wouldn't last long.

No one thought it would . . . because no one expected what was about to happen to the experimental television show called *Sesame Street*.

Caroll Spinney rests here between takes inside Bruno, can-carrying trashman— a puppet no longer used because his foam literally disintegrated in storage

 Fans know that Caroll Spinney found Oscar's growl from an unlikely source.

"On the way to the studio to audition, I wondered . . . What am I going to use for Oscar's voice?" he says. "And I got into a cab, and the cabdriver said, 'Where to, Mac?' And then he talked about how this $&@! Lindsay is ruining the city. He went on and on like that. I got out of the cab, and as I walked to the studio, I kept saying, 'Where to, Mac? Where to, Mac?'"

Once on set, Caroll wiggled into the trash can and told Jim to knock on it. Oscar exploded out, and the first words out of his mouth are seen at left.

OSCAR
WEARS
ARMY
BOOTS

AB C D GOLDFISH

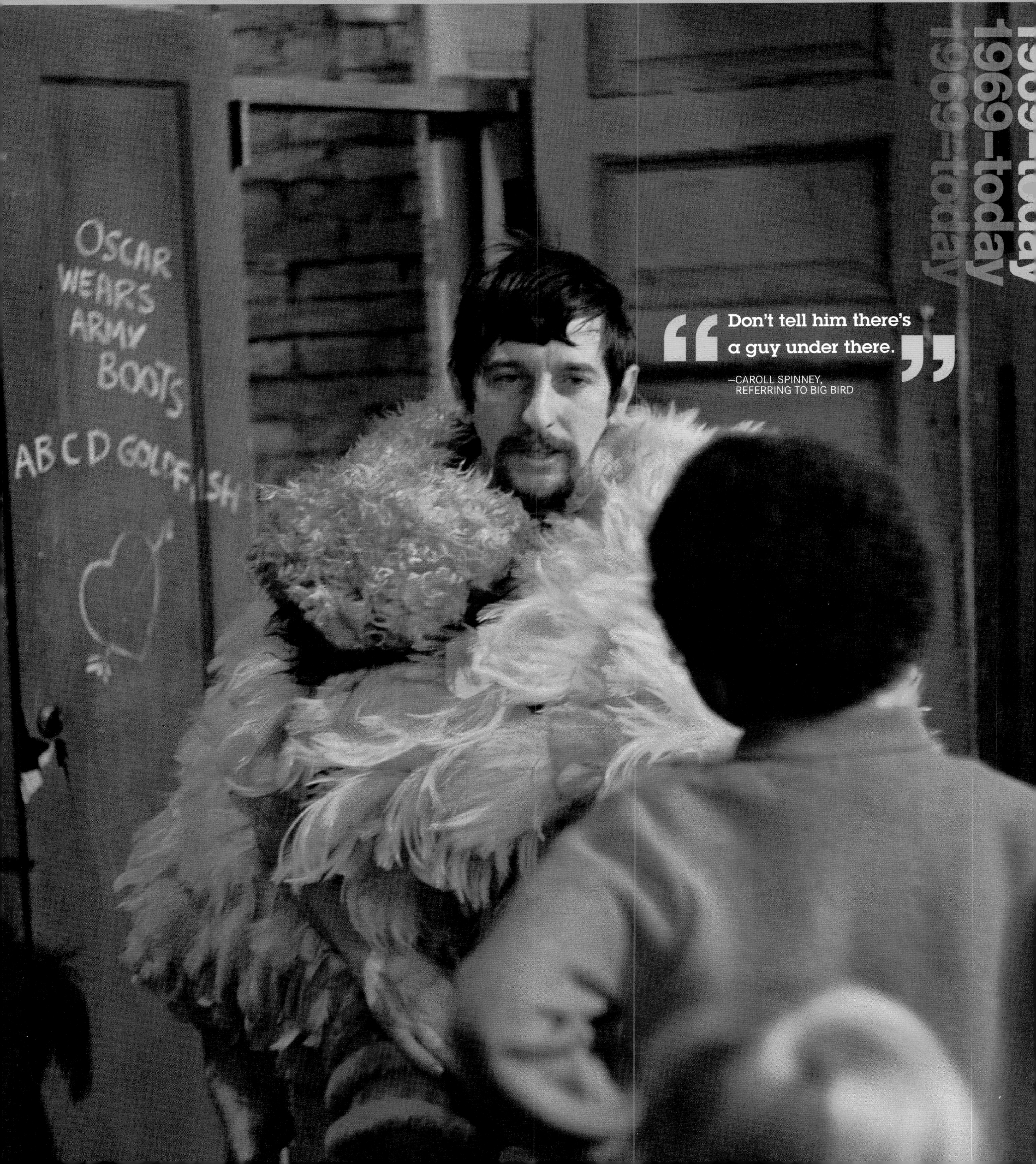

" Don't tell him there's a guy under there. "

—CAROLL SPINNEY,
REFERRING TO BIG BIRD

Muppets in the Making

Jim's original sketch for Big Bird was doodled during an educational seminar in 1969

Jim Henson originally told Caroll Spinney that in his mind, Big Bird was a kind of dim, walk-into-doors character. He envisioned a surrogate child who would get the answers wrong so obviously that kids watching would feel empowered by their own knowledge of the right ones. But somehow the balance was off. Big Bird was just a little too witless—as Caroll bluntly puts it, "A stupid kind of guy."

It didn't help that, until rehearsals for the pilot, the writers had never even seen the actual Muppet, just a rough sketch drawn by Jim. So they had little idea of how to develop him as a character in early scripts. But one day, a story line came in that placed Big Bird in a day-care center. That's when Caroll had a seminal idea.

"I thought maybe he shouldn't be a big goofy *guy*," he says. "Why would he want to go to day care if he wasn't a *kid*? He could be a *kid*—naive and learning."

In Big Bird's voice he adds: "I was never that stupid. I'm just six years old. Lots of people don't know a lot of stuff when they're just six years old!"

Feathers were added to the original pinhead shape, making Bird look less goofy.

And Big Bird was reborn.

> **I'm not much like Oscar in real life, but everyone has contrary feelings occasionally, and that's why it's fun to be able to play someone like Oscar.**
>
> —CAROLL SPINNEY

The first generation of *Sesame Street* fans may remember that Oscar was once orange—a hue seen in early press shots. In fact, Jim Henson's initial sketches are of a purplish-red Grouch. But then Jim realized that early cameras muddied magenta shades. Oscar was orange in the first show.

Oscar underwent his final color change shortly before a guest appearance on *The Flip Wilson Show*, surprising Caroll, who discovered the change moments before stepping on camera. He quickly extemporized a Grouch's version of the story: a sojourn at Swamp Mushy Muddy turned him green.

> **I try to make Big Bird's reactions those of a youngster who often feels that everyone else seems to know more than he does.**
>
> —CAROLL SPINNEY

Ernie rarely had much privacy in the tub—sometimes the whole neighborhood crowded in—this very first Ernie appearance is unusual in that Rubber Duckie isn't sharing the bubbles

F~~inal Revisions~~

AIR: 11/10/69

AIRED AS IS

SHOW # 1

CHILDREN'S TELEVISION WORKSHOP   B63 6648

SESAME STREET

VTR: October 21, 1969

1. FILM:∧ Show Identification # 1

2. FILM: SESAME STREET OPENING

3. GREETING - MEETING

SESAME STREET. Gordon enters with child. Calls to Susan who appears at the window. She remarks that he's home early. He tosses her his brief-case and asks her to put it on his desk. He asks her to say hello to _____, who had her first day in the Sesame Street school today. She's new to the neighborhood, and he's going to show her around.

A child comes by. Gordon introduces the two. The Big Bird comes in through the construction doors, bumping his head as he does and mumbling. Gordon stops him and introduces the child. Because the child is standing so close to Big Bird, he can't see her, and says so. Gordon tells him to look down. BB does and still can't find her. Gordon lifts the child up in front of BB's eyes. BB shrieks!

BB: "She's eight feet tall!"

Gordon: "She's four feet tall. I'm holding her up, Big Bird."

BB: "Well, thank heavens. Don't scare me like that. I'm a very nervous bird."

He walks away, mumbling: "I almost laid an egg right on Sesame Street ..."

Ernie's voice is heard singing. Gordon tells the new child that that is Ernie, who lives in the basement apartment of 123 with his friend Bert, and whenever Ernie is singing, it's a good bet that he's taking a bath.

props: small, softleather briefcase.

Jim: Big Bird

Caroll (in the bird) with Big Bird builder Kermit Love, who designed costumes for Balanchine's ballets

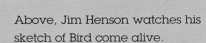

3.   (CONTINUED)

          Neil: pretape Ernie's singing

          Dulcie: child (girl)

4.   ERNIE BATHTUB BIT (LEADS SOLOMON GRUNDY) PRETAPE

Ernie and Bert's apartment. Ernie is in the tub.
Steam and bubbles. S.E. splashing. He calls to
Bert. From off, Bert calls back to ask what he
wants.

Ernie: "I'm out of soap. Will you bring me a bar?"

Bert enters, a bar of soap clutched in his hand.

Ernie: (taking the soap out of Bert's hand) "Just
throw it in to Rosie here."

Bert: "What?"

Ernie: "The soap." Just toss it into ol' Rosie
here."

Bert: "Who's Rosie?"

Ernie: "My bathtub. That's what I call it. I
call by bathtub Rosie."

Bert: "Ernie ... why do you call your bathtub
Rosie?"

Ernie: "Hmm?"

Bert: "Why do you call your bathtub Rosie?"

Ernie: "Because every time I take a bath, I leave
a ring around Rosie." (He does his inimitable
laugh.)

Bert: (after the take) "Ernie, get out of the tub."

Ernie: "Why?"

Bert: "Because there are a lot of people waiting
to take a bath."

Ernie: "Take a bath? In my Rosie? Who?"

Bert: "Well, Solomon Grundy, for one ..."

Above, Jim Henson watches his sketch of Bird come alive.

Puppet designer Don Sahlin, below right, created the original Ernie and Bert from Jim's sketches. Don was credited by Jim as best realizing his drawings, literally making them come alive.

The original Kermit was reconfigured by Jim with a collar and skinnier limbs for his debut on *Sesame Street* (facing page; note Jim's drawings for his animated number sequence for the show in the background).

Big Bird was assembled by master puppet builder Kermit Love; on the facing page, he lowers the first Bird onto a test subject in the Henson Workshop.

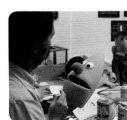

"There's an art to helping other people be funny."

—JERRY NELSON

Jerry NELSON

AMAZING MUMFORD, BIFF, COUNT VON COUNT, FARLEY, HERBERT BIRDSFOOT, HERRY MONSTER, MR. JOHNSON (FAT BLUE), SAM THE ROBOT, SHERLOCK HEMLOCK, SNUFFLEUPAGUS, TWO-HEADED MONSTER, ETC.

> ## Ah-ah-ah-aaaah!
> —COUNT VON COUNT

Soon after the first episodes of *Sesame Street* aired, it became apparent that Jim was going to need additional Muppet performers. Writers were beginning to get in the groove, writing new characters for each insert. A few associates—among them Muppet builder and old friend Bobby Payne—were helping out by performing miscellaneous characters and right-handing (performing the right hand of a Muppet while the other puppeteer does the head and left hand), but the cast needed to expand.

So Jim did what he and his wife, Jane, always did when they needed new puppeteers. They held a workshop.

A workshop was a trial by performance. You'd start the week with, say, fifty or a hundred talented actors, puppeteers, or wannabes. At the end of the day, only half would be invited back. The next day, the number would halve again, and so on. Few were left by the end of the week.

> ## Greetings! I am the Count von Count. They call me the Count because I love to count. That, and I inherited my father's royal title.
> —COUNT VON COUNT

Jerry Nelson was a star in Bil Baird's marionette theater when he first worked with Jim Henson on *The Jimmy Dean Show*, playing Rowlf the Dog's right hand. An actor and singer with incredible vocal talents, he then took off for California, only later returning to New York.

"One afternoon, I saw this truly unique TV program," he recalls. "It had advertisements for letters and numbers. And then these Muppet monsters were on and making me laugh out loud. I knew Jim Henson was doing a children's show, but this was beyond anything I could have imagined."

Jerry called Jim to congratulate him; of course, the topic of work came up, and Jerry was invited to a workshop in June 1970. He made it to the end of the week. Two months later, Jim asked Jerry if he'd like to come work on *Sesame Street*.

Jerry was ecstatic. "Would I?!" he remembers saying. He started taping the second season of *Sesame Street* with Jim and Frank in September 1970, and went on to create such indelible Muppets as Snuffleupagus, Herry Monster, and the Count.

How has he created such a disparate group of characters? "I think there are little parts of ourselves that go into each of the characters we do," he says. "And what are little parts of us, we then blow up into something larger or even consuming for each specific personality."

"As an actor, I've always been a student of human nature," he explains. It's this sensitivity to nuance that's allowed him to play the butt of a gag with such humor—and hilarious angst. "I'm especially fascinated watching the straight men in comic teams in old movies. They had great style and timing, an ability to set up a scene that I work to duplicate. I've learned a lot from them."

The first Snuffy puppet had crazy eyes—way too scary for kids

"In 1972," Jerry recalls, "head writer Norman Stiles came up to me on the set and told me about this new character he was writing named The Count, who was a Dracula type who had no interest whatever in things vampirish but who was fixated on counting things; and if he had counted it before, that was okay, he would count it again. 'He has a major jones for counting' was the way Norman put it.

"I went to Jim and told him about this new character and asked if I could do it. He asked me what he would sound like, [and] I gave him a voice that was probably a bad imitation of Bela Lugosi, and he said, 'He's yours.' That was the beginning of my involvement with one of my favorite characters, Count von Count. I especially love the pieces in his castle, or with the Countess (there were several)."

Jerry Nelson performs both the Count von Count (far left) and bumbling Mumford the Magician (left). Can you tell them apart? Sherlock Hemlock is at right.

Zoe, as the puppet appeared before a season 40 "miniaturization" to Prairie Dawn size

Fran BRILL

BETTY LOU, LITTLE BIRD (IN EARLY YEARS), PRAIRIE DAWN, ZOE, ETC.

> "Oh welcome, dear viewer, to our little play. We're ever so glad you could join us today."
>
> —PRAIRIE DAWN

Fran Brill, a talented actress and voice-over performer, was hunting for any kind of theatrical work when she spotted an ad in *Variety* offering to train puppeteers in an Ed Sullivan Christmas special. She called immediately, figuring she might be able to do voices for the show. But that wasn't the way Jim worked.

If you were going to do the voice, you had to perform the Muppet, too.

"After the phone call, I had a meeting with Jim and Frank," Fran recalls, "and there was a trunkful of puppets and a floor-to-ceiling mirror, and they said, try to come up with some characters. I'd never played with a puppet in my life. But Jim was a self-taught puppeteer, so that's probably why he was open to the fact that I was walking in without any training. I think he liked the fact that I could come up with characters right away, that I could do voices and accents, and I could sing."

She, too, was invited to that June 1970 workshop, making it through until Friday, after which she was offered a job as the first major female puppeteer on *Sesame Street*.

"All these guys were tall, and I'm five-four," Fran says. "So the only way for me to even come close to their height if I was right-handing or puppeteering was to wear these boots. They were regular boots, like you would wear in the winter, and then they glued on about four to five inches of a platform.

"It was not easy. The worst was running, or moving very fast. In musical numbers, when we would be constantly going from upstage to downstage and right  to left, you have to be very careful, because all it took was for you to twist your ankle and you'd fall. Knock on wood, I have never fallen, which I find amazing."

Fran established herself swiftly, creating, among other indelible characters, Prairie Dawn (child of hippies) and the indefatigable Zoe. And if Fran looks familiar, that's because she's also starred in motion pictures, such as *What About Bob?* with Bill Murray, and in a host of TV shows and commercials. Already a gifted actress and voice artist, she was a perfect apprentice puppeteer. "It just seemed like a good fit," she says, her eyes twinkling. "The only missing part was the fact that I wasn't, uh, what's the word? Good."

She is now. Cast members like Roscoe Orman, who plays Gordon, have nothing but high praise for her skills. "Fran is, to my knowledge," he says, "the most accomplished performer in the fields of *both* puppetry and character acting, ever."

Richard
HUNT

DON MUSIC, FORGETFUL JONES, GLADYS THE COW, PLACIDO FLAMINGO,
TWO-HEADED MONSTER, SONNY FRIENDLY, ETC.

Another puppeteer to make it out of that June 1970 workshop was Richard Hunt. Gregarious, generous, and outgoing, Richard was an aspiring actor when he answered the same ad that had attracted Fran.

"Richard knocked on the Muppets' door," Caroll Spinney recalls. "He had been doing puppet shows as a kid . . . doing birthday shows and stuff. Jim could identify with him, because as cool as Jim was, he was pretty much a nerd. Often the clever ones are. So Jim instantly could connect with Richard."

Richard became a huge asset to *Sesame Street* and to the Muppets in general. "Richie was the heart and soul. He had a sense of abandonment . . . the spirit of no-holds-barred, irreverent, and anarchic," recalls Frank Oz. "He was a spirit that was amazing for us . . . besides being a wonderful performer."

Richard created an atmosphere of barely controlled hilarity on the set. He was always on, full of life. Perhaps more than anyone, he made the set the joyous, relaxed, and goofy place it became.

"When Richard Hunt showed up, the energy of the room would go up noticeably," says puppeteer Marty Robinson. "Every time Richard marched onstage with his big, huge, brash self hiding all of his insecurities, it would just fill the room—everyone would respond."

Once on the set, though, Richard's dedication to his craft took over. In an interview during season thirteen (the year his blind Muppet, Aristotle, was introduced), Richard describes that effort: "We are totally locked into producing the right image for a TV screen, crouching in a half-sitting position, twisting and stretching our bodies and muscles, striving for just the right angle for the camera. You're always watching that monitor, seeing how the puppet looks, how much of it belongs in the picture, and which angles make it funniest—always trying to do better. Making the characters believe-

able on television is a constant challenge. It never gets easier."

Then again, sometimes he simply fell asleep.

"Muppet performers spend a lot of time waiting around," recalls the show's designer/director Victor DiNapoli. "They have dollies that they lay down on to perform. Richard would be lying on the dolly, reading the newspaper, and essentially, he would fall asleep under the paper. But somehow . . . when they were ready to shoot— boom!—just like that, he'd pop up and perform. It never failed. He never blew a shot."

Richard performed on *Sesame Street* until his death in 1992. At that time, his major characters were retired.

A prop bust of "Bill" Shakespeare oversees Don Music's attempts to write the tune "Yankee Doodle" —songsmith Joe Raposo's bust appears in later bits

The First
Ten Years

> " Puppeteering was not even a job opportunity . . . because nobody thought about puppets. It's really Jim Henson and the Muppets that brought puppetry to the forefront of everybody's consciousness. Where kids growing up on the show said, 'I could make my own puppet at home,' like Kevin [Clash] did. Nowadays, it's definitely a career path. "

–Fran Brill

Aloysius Snuffleupagus first appeared on *Sesame Street* in the first show of season three, on November 9, 1971. He was performed by Jerry Nelson, with Richard Hunt in his back half.

Dick Cavett once asked Jim about Snuffy. "Do they get along, the two guys?" he said.

"They have to," Jim replied dryly.

SEGMENT #0001-0404

Kermit: Now, I get MAD when people do things I don't like. Like when a monster eats my picture, I get MAD. You can tell I'm mad by the things I say to the monster, like this: You're a big, dumb, rotten, stupid monster and you make me so mad I don't believe it! You are without a doubt one of the nastiest people I've ever met, and I'm going to tell your mother on you, and she's never going to let you come here again because I don't like you! That's what I'm like when I'm MAD!

SEGMENT #0008-0079

Grover: . . . Nine.

Echo: Nine.

Grover: Ten!

Echo: Ten!

Grover: Oh, wasn't that wonderful?

Echo: Oh, wasn't that wonderful?

Grover: Uh, okay. That . . . that is enough there . . . uh . . .

Echo: That is enough there . . . uh . . .

Grover: Alright . . . uh . . . we've had our fun.

Echo: Alright . . . uh . . . we've had our fun.

Grover: Come on, will you knock it off?!

Echo: Come on, will you knock it off?!

Grover: Please stop it! [silence] Huh. Well, thank you.

Echo: You're welcome!

> **I'm Guy Smiley. They call me Guy Smiley because I changed my name from Bernie Liederkrantz.**
> —GUY SMILEY,
> FROM THE COUNT'S APPEARANCE ON GUY'S SHOW, EPISODE 1845

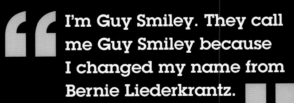

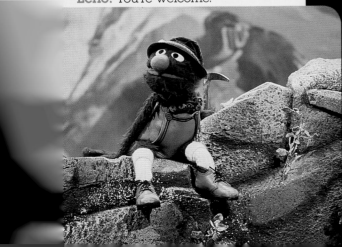

THIS CHAPTER HAS BEEN BROUGHT TO YOU BY THE LETTER H AND THE NUMBER 2.

The letter H is for the Henson Workshop, who made it all happen, Muppet-wise. The Street would never have been the same without them. **The number 2** is for Jim and Frank, who established the kind of brilliant comedic camaraderie that would define the Muppets for decades to come.

3

THE PEOPLE IN YOUR NEIGHBORHOOD

CHILDREN'S TELEVISION WORKSHOP

EPISODE
4156

Chris Knowings stands quietly on the side of the *Sesame Street* set, studying his script. He is seemingly oblivious to the swirl of activity around him, focusing on his work amid the bustle as the crew gets busy setting up the next shot. Tech crew member Chuck Tutino wrestles a large monitor stand into position. His job is to make sure everyone in the video area has everything they need, the moment they need it.

Chuck is an old-timer. He's been with the production from its first days in 1969. Chris, on the other hand, is new to the show. Four thousand one hundred and forty-five episodes have been taped without him. Today, his char-

acter, Chris, is being introduced into the *Sesame Street* family.

"Here we go," calls stage manager Shawn Havens from behind his portable podium, where he puts his script and other odds and ends. Chris quickly takes his place behind the convincingly weather-worn door of 123 Sesame Street.

"Four, three, two . . . " says Shawn, and a beat later, the door opens and Chris bounds out. Everyone on set watches just a little more closely than usual. Even though Chris has already been on set once before, shooting another episode, this show will mark the first time kids at home will see him. And when a new character debuts on *Sesame Street*, it's an important moment. After all, Chris not only is joining the Sesame family. In a very real sense, he's joining the families of all the preschoolers watching as well, kids who consider the neighborhood here a second home.

Chris plays Gordon and Susan's nephew (also named Chris), whose backstory is that he's moved in with the couple while attending college nearby. In this episode, he's on the hunt for a part-time job, and he's about to answer his first help-wanted ad, placed by the Count von Count. First, though, he launches into a verse of the classic *Sesame Street* song, "The People in Your Neighborhood," written by Jeff Moss, the composer/lyricist of some of the show's most enduring tunes—and for a time its head writer. New verses have been added by scriptwriter Joey Mazzarino for Chris's version:

Oh, a gym teacher should win a prize
For teaching how to exercise.
He teaches you to play and run,
And makes being healthy lots of fun.

Even the newspaper prop is customized for the show—note that Grouch on the back page story

on the set
on the set
on the set

As the familiar tune comes up over the sound system, arranged and recorded by then Director of Music Operations Danny Epstein, Chris waits patiently for his cue. Later, describing the moment, he shakes his head in wonder. "If you don't know that song, you've been under a rock for forty years," he says.

Even if Chris had never heard the song before, by the end of the day, every note would be burned into his brain. In the next eight hours or so, he'll be singing it again and again and again as he interviews with the Count, Cookie Monster, and Horatio the Elephant for a part-time job. Each Muppet will do what Muppets always do—be silly, goofy, and, ultimately, totally lovable. Chris's job—and, essentially, the job of every human being on the cast of *Sesame Street*—will be to hold his own, to deliver the straight lines, to react honestly to the Muppets, no matter what they ask him to do . . . starting with endless numbers of jumping jacks for the Count (so they can be counted, of course).

Chris next interviews with Cookie, a puppet originated by Frank Oz but currently performed by David Rudman. Sadly for Chris, it's a job selling cookies, and Cookie comes to the realization (surprise!) that he doesn't want to off-load any of his inventory. Then the script calls for Chris to interview for a dancing position with Horatio the Elephant, performed by Joey Mazzarino.

"I was so impressed," Joey says. "Chris reminded me of Northern Calloway." This reference to a former human performer beloved by fans is high praise. "He's right there with you . . . he doesn't miss a beat. He's so funny . . . and so natural when he talks to camera. I told him, 'You are the future of *Sesame Street*.'"

It turns out Horatio is paying peanuts—literally—which means Chris (the character) can't afford to take the job. But luckily, in the last scene of the episode, Alan Muraoka—proprietor of Hooper's—offers him a job behind the counter of the neighborhood store. Chris gratefully accepts the position, and the scene is in the can.

> "There's a powerful chemistry that evolves over a period of time among all of the cast and crew," says Roscoe Orman (Gordon), "creating a close-knit 'family' feeling." Chris Knowings, entering the set at the top of the stoop, is one of the recent entries into that genealogy.

"That's a wrap," director Ken Diego calls. "Chris Knowings, everybody."

There is a round of applause. Chris has accomplished the difficult feat of helping to make the Muppets completely believable, as real and "human" as he himself, a feat that enables kids at home to connect so strongly with the *Sesame Street* family.

"It's been a baptism by fire." he says wryly as he leaves the set.

Baptism by fur, that is.

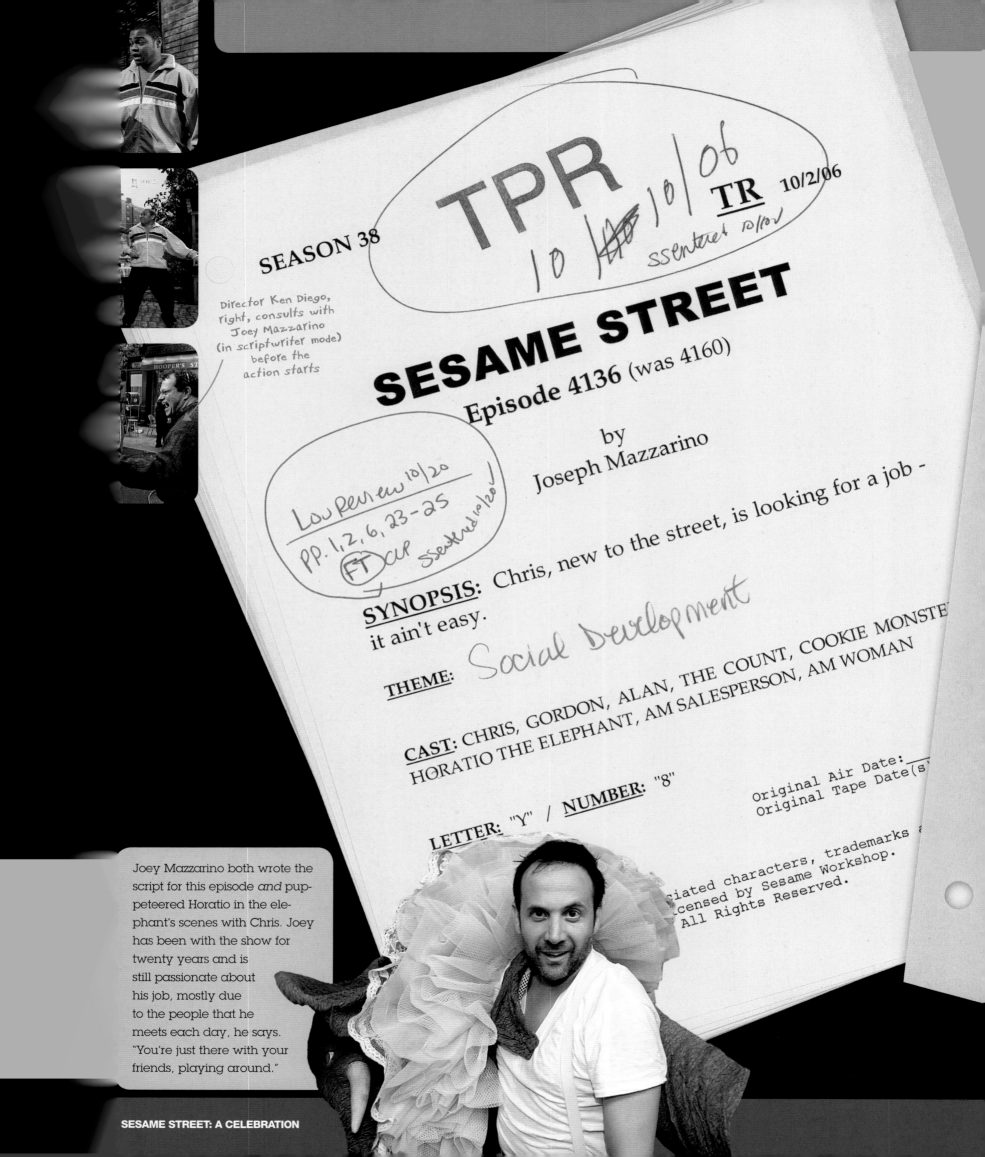

SEASON 38

Director Ken Diego, right, consults with Joey Mazzarino (in scriptwriter mode) before the action starts

TPR
10/ ~~HB~~ 10/06
TR   10/2/06
ssentreet 10/04

SESAME STREET
Episode 4136 (was 4160)

by
Joseph Mazzarino

*Lou Review 10/20
pp. 1, 2, 6, 23–25
(FT) CLP   ssentred 10/20*

SYNOPSIS: Chris, new to the street, is looking for a job – it ain't easy.

THEME: *Social Development*

CAST: CHRIS, GORDON, ALAN, THE COUNT, COOKIE MONSTE[R], HORATIO THE ELEPHANT, AM SALESPERSON, AM WOMAN

LETTER: "Y" / **NUMBER:** "8"

Original Air Date:
Original Tape Date(s)

...ciated characters, trademarks a
...icensed by Sesame Workshop.
...All Rights Reserved.

Joey Mazzarino both wrote the script for this episode *and* puppeteered Horatio in the elephant's scenes with Chris. Joey has been with the show for twenty years and is still passionate about his job, mostly due to the people that he meets each day, he says. "You're just there with your friends, playing around."

AM WOMAN: You know what? If it's not too much of a bother, I think I'd like two more cookies.

CHRIS: Not bother at all! Two more cookies coming up.

CHRIS TAKES TWO MORE COOKIES FROM THE TRAY.

COOKIE MONSTER: (A LITTLE PANIC) Wait! Wait! Where you going with cookie?

CHRIS: I'm selling them.

COOKIE MONSTER: But... there were 5 cookies left and now you taking away 2 more cookies to sell and that MELDS leaves... (COUNTING) only 1, 2, 3 cookies. left! Oh my, who knew subtraction could be so painful.

CHRIS: Am I missing something here?

COOKIE MONSTER: No, no! You cookie salesperson so sell cookie!

CHRIS: Right! (TO WOMAN) Here are two more cookies.

CHRIS PUTS THE TWO COOKIES INTO THE BAKERY BOX.

AM WOMAN: Those cookies look so darn good, you know I think I'll take three more.

CHRIS: Great! Three more cookies! 1, 2, 3.

CHRIS TAKES THE THREE REMAINING COOKIES OFF THE TRAY.

COOKIE MONSTER: (UPSET) Whoa! Whoa! Whoa!

CHRIS: Whoa what?!

COOKIE MONSTER: There were three cookies and now you selling the three cookies so there... are no cookies left at all! Zero cookies...?!

CHRIS: Right! I sold them all! Pretty impressive, huh? What do you think?

COOKIE MONSTER: Me think... Me think... Me think me can't do it! Forget job! Me can't sell cookies!

COOKIE MONSTER GRABS THE COOKIE BOX FROM THE LADY.

CHRIS: What? Why not?

COOKIE MONSTER: 'Cause me love cookie! Cookie!!!

COOKIE MONSTER TAKES THE BOX OF COOKIES AND POURS IT DOWN HIS GULLET, CHOMPING HUNGRILY AND NOISILY.

Also in this show when it airs: Worms in space shape the letter Y; guest Norah Jones sings "Don't Know Why"; and Clay-mation icon Cecille the Orange croons "I Want to Be Me"

(CONTINUED)

On the Block

After the decision had been made to place *Sesame Street* in an urban environment, the show's creators needed to figure out what types of locations would be incorporated in the set—places where both the human cast and the fuzzy one could easily and naturally interact. A kind of combination diner/corner store seemed a perfect gathering spot. They were common in cities at a time when no one thought twice about sending kids out to the corner store on their own for candy and groceries. Veteran actor Will Lee, the first actor in the *Sesame Street* family, was hired to run it.

Soon after, Bob McGrath and Loretta Long joined the cast, Bob as a music teacher from Indiana who lived above Hooper's Store.

Loretta created the role of Susan, a homemaker, later a nurse, married to Gordon, a teacher (that latter role would soon change hands).

Four shows were taped to research the show's concept with kids and educators. These pre-pilot shows, never aired, were shot in the now-defunct Reeves Videotape Center studios on 67th Street, around the corner from Broadway on New York's Upper West Side.

The Workshop planned on shooting the entire first season at Reeves. But before any episodes taped, something potentially catastrophic happened. Studio technicians went on strike, shutting down the studio and the production.

"It was our first reading, and we had no place to go, so they rented the ballroom of the Dixie Hotel, on 43rd Street in Manhattan—really seedy—and we were sitting in there and I met Bob McGrath for the first time, and I thought, 'What a fine guy; there are nice folks on this show!'"

—CAROLL SPINNEY

Dr. Loretta Long credits Will Lee with teaching the cast how to act in the early years

> " People always ask me, 'Are you really as good friends as you appear on the show?' And I say, 'Absolutely.' It's quite amazing, actually. "
>
> —BOB MCGRATH

Joan Ganz Cooney and Jon Stone quickly went to work. Against all odds, they found a new home in time at Teletape Studios, just a mile or so north on 81st Street. Walt Rauffer, who went on to become manager of technical operations for Sesame Workshop for many years, was given the job of prepping the studio. It was no easy task. In order to accommodate the show's unique needs, Walt and his crew had to rebuild the studio's technical facilities. Editing rooms had to be constructed. The studio had to be rewired.

During the summer of 1969, the *Sesame Street* set was quickly dismantled and moved into its new home. Luckily for the production, stagehands were willing to cross picket lines to load the set into a truck. Luckily, too, the original set was a lot simpler than it is today, with only four main structures: 123 Sesame Street, Hooper's Store, the Fix-It Shop, and the carriage house. The rest were all painted backdrops.

Once the set was housed in its new studio, production quickly began on the first season of the fledgling show. No one, least of all the actors and actresses hired to play the roles, suspected how many seasons it would eventually run.

In early testing, the very young kids watching liked the human talent very well, but the long narrative segments with them couldn't hold kids' attention as powerfully as cartoon segments set up nearby to distract them. Only Susan's singing had the same instant appeal. She was an immediate hit.

Small but essential details, like the weathered stoop and this hand-lettered sign in Hooper's Store, helped set the stage and create a real-feeling physical world for the humans; the original sign, seen here, attests to today's inflation rates

Will LEE

MR. HAROLD HOOPER

Mr. Hooper's first name was revealed in episode 871, when he got his GED

The first *Sesame Street* "neighbor" hired, Will Lee was perfectly cast as curmudgeonly Mr. Hooper, original owner of Hooper's Store. He had plenty of experience as a serious actor on TV; in films, including Alfred Hitchcock's *Saboteur* and the cult film *Little Fugitive*; and on the Broadway stage. He was a respected teacher as well, mentoring performers such as James Earl Jones, who would appear on the show partly in tribute to Will. He served in World War II, entertaining troops and leading acting classes as a distraction for fellow servicemen in the Army Special Forces. He received two citations for that war work.

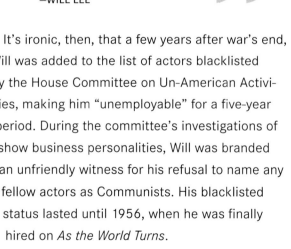

> ## Apart from the joy of knowing that you are helping so many kids, the recognition outside is very heartwarming.
>
> —WILL LEE

It's ironic, then, that a few years after war's end, Will was added to the list of actors blacklisted by the House Committee on Un-American Activities, making him "unemployable" for a five-year period. During the committee's investigations of show business personalities, Will was branded an unfriendly witness for his refusal to name any fellow actors as Communists. His blacklisted status lasted until 1956, when he was finally hired on *As the World Turns*.

Cast members today applaud Joan Ganz Cooney's "fearlessness," as Roscoe puts it, in casting formerly blacklisted performers such as Will and folksinger Pete Seeger. Since the show's early funding came partly from government sources, it was a gamble. But it was also a risk for the veteran actor who, once released from blacklisted status, undoubtedly had many other options besides an untested "experiment" in children's television.

Will's Broadway and film resume might suggest that working on a children's show was an aberration, even a step down. But Will felt otherwise. In *Sesame Street*'s early years, Will spoke lovingly of the show as giving him "the sense you sometimes get from great theater, the feeling that its influence never stops."

"Will had a broader dimension to his character than perhaps the rest of us did," recalls Bob McGrath. "He convinced me that no matter how simple the scene was with a child, you had to bring a tremendous integrity and an honesty and credibility to it."

This honesty and credibility was no better realized than in the relationship Mr. Hooper developed with Big Bird, who would often come into the store for a birdseed milkshake and a chat, although he never could get Mr. Hooper's name quite right.

Will brought great integrity and credibility to his work on *Sesame Street* until his universally mourned death in 1982.

Attesting to the power of television in general and Sesame Street in particular is this surreal moment in 1970 when, less than 15 years after being blacklisted for being "un-American," Will Lee is invited to the White House—yes, the NIXON White House—to help host their Christmas event

Bob McGRATH

BOB JOHNSON

> ❝ We really want all of you folks to be yourselves. ❞
>
> —BOB, RECALLING EARLY DIRECTION FROM SHOW WRITERS

was a fan.) The U.S. television show *To Tell the Truth* even did an episode on Bob's unguessable stint as Japan's American tenor.

He changed his mind about *Sesame Street* when Dave called a few months later and Bob finally saw Jim Henson's work for the first time.

"I thought, oh my God, this is—this is not like *anything* I've ever seen before, and this is very innovative and very exciting, and I want to do this more than anything I've ever thought of."

He's been doing it ever since starring in the show's pilot episodes in 1969, and he's been able to leverage his resulting star status to support the work of organizations like the American Lung Association, children's hospitals, and Christmas Seals.

Bob takes his work seriously—even taking an intensive course in sign language so his conversations with actress Linda Bove would be accurate. He brings that dedication to every aspect of his role, even (or especially) when it involves outrageous silliness. "He is the most fearless among us at self-parody—don't forget 'Sponge Bob Triangle Pants!'" Roscoe Orman, who plays Gordon, says with a laugh.

"Bob is a very warm and giving person," says Sonia Manzano (Maria), echoing the words of everyone in his *Street* family. "Bob and his wife will come over to my house for dinner, and we'll talk about things, and Bob's eyes will water at least two or three times, whether we're talking about something our children did or something the show was doing. He's a man of great feeling."

While Will Lee was immediately interested in working on *Sesame Street*, hiring Bob McGrath to play the role of Bob proved a little trickier. In fact, when Bob's former fraternity brother and Executive Producer Dave Connell ran into him on the streets of New York one day and asked him if he wanted to audition for a new kids' TV show, Bob's immediate response was, "Not in the least."

Bob was already a successful singer. His first important television work had been a lengthy stint on *Sing Along with Mitch*, a popular program in the late 1960s.

He was also a vocal superstar in Japan.

Bobu Magulath—Bob's name in translation—sang classic Irish ballads like "Danny Boy" in Japanese to hordes of adults and teens from Kyoto to Tokyo. (Prime Minister Sato's daughter

"He is a wonderful character to play off of," says Bob of Big Bird. "You know that if a six-year-old bird can understand . . . you are doing it credibly."

Dr. Loretta LONG

SUSAN ROBINSON

Loretta and Bob are the only current cast members who were also in the first pilots

Loretta Long was perhaps the most unlikely of the early cast members. It was the sixties, and the producers' original idea for the Street's resident den mother was something more along the lines of a long-haired folksinger. With her short Afro and flaming red nails, Loretta wasn't exactly what the Workshop people had in mind, she recalls. In fact, one of the first things they asked her during her audition was, "Where's your guitar?"

"They were thinking about a Joan Baez type," she laughs. "I looked like Angela Davis." And she couldn't play guitar, either.

They asked her to wait. She waited . . . and waited . . . and waited.

"I'm standing in the corner, everybody's playing their guitars," she remembers. "Finally everybody's getting ready to leave. So I said, 'Now, wait a minute. I came to sing for you.' I wasn't letting them out of the room." She sang "I'm a Little Teapot," unaccompanied, just as she might sing it to a child. It was immediately obvious that Loretta's delivery would captivate the show's audience. "It was all that babysitting," she says, smiling.

She won the role and originated the character of Susan.

It's difficult to imagine a time when simply including Loretta and Matt Robinson in a cast with Caucasian actors could be controversial, but the happy mix of races on the Street inspired Mississippi public TV stations to ban the show. When the cast visited the state to argue their case, they were escorted by the National Guard (the only incident: Big Bird was plucked for souvenir feathers by some guardsmen fans). After a year, the show's popularity forced Mississippi stations to carry it. These days, the state is a major supporter.

"There were no other black married couples on TV in those days," Loretta says. "We were also the landlords; 123 Sesame Street belonged to us. So we were married, landlords, and we had a career. It was heady stuff. Such an opportunity to be role models."

Loretta was also involved in another cultural breakthrough. Initially, the character of Susan was a stay-at-home housewife. But this didn't reflect the concerns of the women's movement at the time.

With Loretta's encouragement, writers scripted Susan's decision to go back to nursing. "That was a big deal in those days," she recalls. And speaking of careers—the *Dr.* in front of Loretta Long's name is for her Ph.D. in education. Loretta maintains a second career as a teacher and lecturer.

In 1979 Loretta toured Africa as a cultural ambassador for the State Department

Loretta's influence as a cultural icon—a woman in a mixed-race cast—was immense. Women's groups pleaded for her character to be given a career during the liberation movement, so Susan shifted from homemaker to nurse.

DEPARTMENT OF STATE

May 19, 1977

Dr. Loretta Long
6040 Boulevard East
Apt 10C
West New York, New Jersey 07903

Dear Dr. Long:

I am very pleased to learn from Ms. Sharon Wilkinson of your willingness to lecture in Africa this summer under the auspices of the Department of State's American Specialist Program.

I understand that your visit to Africa will begin June 20th and will include programming in Ghana, Nigeria, The Cameroons, Kenya and Zambia. Given your demonstrated talents as an educator and an entertainer there is no doubt in my mind of the excellent effect your visit will have on our African audiences.

Please accept my personal thanks and appreciation for your support of this important program. The combination of your warm and open personality, your academic background and your skills as a performer will undoubtedly make your visit to Africa a significant event in the furthering of African-American communication.

Sincerely and best wishes

James F. Relph, Jr.
Director
Office of African Programs
Bureau of Educational and
Cultural Affairs

"Bob and I teased each other about our common roots. We'd gone from being farm kids from the Midwest to being on a mythical inner-city street.

–DR. LORETTA LONG

Matt
ROBINSON

GORDON ROBINSON

Matt spoke the very first words on the show; here he and Sally meet the original (orange) Oscar →

(Loretta voiced Roosevelt's harried mom.) This was something very rare in Muppetdom. Puppeteers almost always provide voices for their own characters.

"Matt was one of a kind, really terrific," recalls Bob McGrath. "A very, very different approach to the part of Gordon . . . Matt had a little bit of an edge, he was very "street," and at that time, he had big lamb chops [sideburns] down to here."

"He was also a wonderful writer," Bob adds. Matt wrote for *The Bill Cosby Show*, among others.

> " The Gordons changed so many times . . . little kids used to ask, 'What happened to the last Gordon?' I felt a little bit guilty, as if I'd buried a bunch of them under the stoop. "
>
> —DR. LORETTA LONG

Despite initial reluctance to take the part, Matt proved to be a perfect Gordon. He preferred behind-camera roles, however, and gave up the part, leaving big shoes to fill. Actor Hal Miller stepped in for a year, but the fit wasn't quite right.

That's when Roscoe Orman came along.

Which Gordon you know instantly dates you: Roscoe Orman wasn't the first actor to take on the role of Gordon, although he's the Gordon most people remember today. The test-show Gordon didn't make that critical connection with audiences, so producers searched for a replacement. No one who auditioned proved the perfect conversational foil to both children and Muppets, so just before the first true episodes of the show were due to be taped, they turned to Matt Robinson. Matt was already in place as a writer and producer on the show and had proven a natural with kids on the set.

Matt accepted the role, taking it on for two years despite maintaining his behind-the-scene roles. He also created the character of Roosevelt Franklin, for whom he provided scripts and a voice.

Hal Miller stepped in when Matt left the role of Gordon, playing him for two seasons, from 1972 to 1974

 The name of the actor, right, who played Gordon Robinson in the four unaired pilot episodes has been lost to history. If you can identify him, please contact Sesame Workshop!

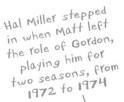

Roscoe
ORMAN
GORDON ROBINSON

A working actor and writer who continues to do additional television and stage work, Roscoe leapt at the chance to audition for *Sesame Street* when Stan Lathan, who was one of the show's directors, told him about the Workshop's search for a new Gordon. From the moment he stepped onto Sesame

Street, he felt at home. "The set reminded me of the neighborhood I lived in during my early childhood in the Bronx," he says.

After doing two scenes—one with Oscar the Grouch (his first time ever working with a puppet) and one with the delightful John-John Williams (a youngster famous for his legendary counting segment with Herry Monster)—Roscoe did the usual thing that actors do after

auditions: he sat staring at the phone, willing it to ring, alternately convinced he'd gotten the role, then sure he'd blown it.

"Dulcy Singer, the show's producer, finally called me at home to give me the news that I had been selected. I was ecstatic."

In those early days as Gordon, Roscoe sensed what he calls "the enormous responsibility" of being on the show and its impact on children—as well as on parents and educators. "They express genuine appreciation," he noted in interviews at the time he was first cast, "and talk about *Sesame Street* in tones that are different than when they talk about other programs."

One of his favorite moments on the Street remains the show's 1978 holiday special, with its multilayered stories showing the *Sesame Street* cast sharing the gift of love, friendship, and respect for one another's beliefs—no matter how childlike.

"I thought that was the best of what we'd become."

> **Sesame Street has kept the child in me alive and well.**
> —ROSCOE ORMAN

Matt Robinson's Gordon reflected common concerns of many men of the era when their wives joined the job market. Roscoe's Gordon is more unreservedly delighted by his marriage partner's every move. "I couldn't have imagined a better TV wife," Roscoe says. "Loretta, from day one, made me feel welcomed, appreciated, and loved."

Roscoe's Trash Gordon persona is a spoof of '30s superhero Flash Gordon

Sonia MANZANO

MARIA RODRIGUEZ

Sonia Manzano got her acting start in the seminal production of *Godspell* at Carnegie Mellon University. When the show transferred to off-Broadway, she went with it. After performing in the hit on Broadway, her agent suggested she leverage her success with a round of auditions.

The first one was for *Sesame Street*.

"The brilliant Jon Stone auditioned me," she remembers. "And he asked me to explain the sorting song—'one of these things is not like the other.' It was one of the early conceptual exercises on the show. And then he said, 'Make believe that you're walking down the street and somebody is following you.' He just wanted to see if I could make believe and act a little bit. And that was it.

"The next day, my agent called and said, 'You got the job.' Jon knew what he wanted. He wanted someone that the kids in the inner cities could relate to . . . luckily for me."

> **I never realized how much I missed seeing people of color on television till I actually saw *Sesame Street*.**
>
> —SONIA MANZANO

Finding the character of Maria was a bit more of a challenge.

"It's much easier to act if you're performing someone else," explains Sonia. "Jon once told me, 'I just want you to be yourself.' When I became comfortable with being myself was when I sort of let Maria be."

Learning to work with Muppets was also a challenge.

"I remember working with Frank Oz's Grover," she recalls, "and Grover was talking to me, but I kept looking down at Frank. Finally, Grover said, 'Don't look at that man down there! I'm talking to you!'"

Sonia has gotten to know those furry personalities well in her years on the show, years during which she's metamorphosed from young woman to wife and loving mom, sometimes in episodes she wrote herself.

"There were no Latin writers, and I remember kvetching about the Hispanic segments," she says. "And [executive producer] Dulcy Singer said, 'You know, why don't you try writing some yourself?'

"I was flabbergasted," Sonia goes on. But she did try it—and became a regular show writer. Now, in addition to *Sesame Street* segments, she has a number of successful children's books to her credit that draw from her experiences in a vibrant family of Puerto Rican descent.

The show traveled to Maria's hometown in Puerto Rico in 1979

Sonia's written several scripts that showcase her love of humor, and mentions her slapstick impersonations of Charlie Chaplin as among her favorite performances, like this one with Linda Bove.

Emilio
DELGADO

LUIS RODRIGUEZ

Emilio really is playing the trombone in episodes with the instrument, and plays the guitar in shows airing in season 40

> They asked, 'Would you be willing to shave off your mustache?' And I'm looking at my first unemployment check . . . my son needs milk . . . I'll shave anything!
>
> —EMILIO DELGADO

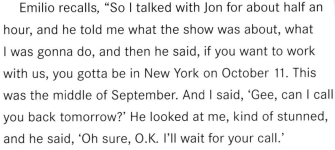

In 1971, when the *Sesame Street* team decided to look for a Hispanic actor to take on the new role of Luis Rodriguez, they cast their nets wide—all the way to Los Angeles, in fact. That's where Emilio Delgado had just returned to college, studying acting at CalArts after having spent nine years auditioning and then, in 1968, winning roles on both public and network TV as well as in the theater.

Sesame Street executive producer Dave Connell initially flew out to California to talk to him. But after their conversation, there was no callback. Emilio figured he wasn't right for the part.

A few months later, he got another call. Jon Stone was going to be in Los Angeles and wanted to speak to him.

> From very early, I knew I was going to be an actor, because where I grew up, there was just nothing but imagination.
>
> —EMILIO DELGADO

Emilio recalls, "So I talked with Jon for about half an hour, and he told me what the show was about, what I was gonna do, and then he said, if you want to work with us, you gotta be in New York on October 11. This was the middle of September. And I said, 'Gee, can I call you back tomorrow?' He looked at me, kind of stunned, and he said, 'Oh sure, O.K. I'll wait for your call.'

"I called my former wife and I said, 'Hey, guess what? I think I got a job in New York on this show called *Sesame Street*.' I had never seen the show before. I didn't even know it existed. And she said, 'Well, did you take it?' I said, 'Well, I don't know,' and she said, 'Take it, you fool!'

"So I called Jon back that same day and said, 'Oh, Jon, I'm so sorry. Yes—I'll take the job.'"

When Emilio got to the airport, the first thing he did was hail a cab to drive him to the studio.

"I got in this cab, and the guy . . . he got lost," says Emilio. "He and I just kept looking at the meter, and the meter was going click, click, click. And I think when we finally found the corner of 81st and Broadway, the meter was $25. Back in 1971, that was like $75 today. I said, 'How much do I owe you?'

"And he looked at the meter, he looked at me, and he said, 'I got lost. You don't owe me anything.'

"Can you believe it? Isn't that amazing? It was like magic. And when I walked into the studio, I met everybody, and they were all so nice. It was immediately like family." Since joining the *Sesame Street* cast, Emilio has gone on to perform onstage and in numerous television shows. He also teaches other talented young actors.

In an intriguing departure from the simplicity of adult relationships normally depicted on kids' programs, the wedding of Maria and Luis showcased *Sesame Street*'s respectful understanding of the complexity of grown-up feelings. In the climactic song, viewers are given glimpses into the thoughts of characters as they take part in the ceremony:

Best Man Bob and Maid of Honor Linda wonder if someday they, too, might wed (they never do), while David has feelings of longing as his old flame gets married.

Luis's uncle, played by actor José Ferrer, is proud, while Maria's mother's joy is tempered with sadness that her husband hadn't lived to see his daughter wed.

In Jeff Moss's "Wedding Pictures" song, bride and groom express uncertainty before they exchange vows—"It's altogether possible I've made a major error/My hands are cold, my forehead's hot/It's either love or terror"—before rediscovering their bond.

SESAME STREET   -15-   SHOW 2485

24. FILM: HEART SHAPED SUN   04-0105-0:48

25. VTR: BERT TEACHES CHECKERS (B/E)   10-0075-0:41

26. FILM: (LA) THE DOCTOR FLIES INTO TOWN (ALASKAN)   18-0798-2:53

27. FILM: MADRIGAL ALPHABET   05-0281-1:32

28. CEREMONY   19-0537-7:09
(FAMILY)

KIDS:
  KIRA DELGADO
  MARLENY DELGADO
  STEVEN VIDELA
  RALPH MERCADO
  CADESA RAMHARRACK
  SHARD RAMHARRACK

PRIEST:
  EDWARD DE SOTO

EXTRAS:
  MR. MACINTOSH
  CHET O'BRIEN
  MARTHA O'CONNOR
  RICHARD TERMINE

SCENIC: ROOF SET UP FOR WEDDING
TALENT: CAST, MUPPETS, PRIEST, EXTRAS, KIDS
PROPS: PILLOW, RINGS, BASKET OF FLOWER PETALS
SFX: ECHO
LIGHT: SUNSET
COSTUME: EVERYBODY DRESSED FOR THE WEDDING
MUSIC: SONG: WEDDING PICTURE

ROOF, SET UP FOR WEDDING: CHAIRS, FLOWERS, "ALTAR" AREA, ETC. EVERYBODY IS THERE. A QUIET MURMUR AS PEOPLE WHISPER TO ONE ANOTHER FOR A FEW SOUNDS UNTIL THE MUSIC STARTS 'THE WEDDING MARCH'. EVERYONE QUIETS DOWN AS A LITTLE BOY AND GIRL EACH CARRYING A BASKET OF FLOWER PETALS AND SPRINKLE THEM AS THEY WALK DOWN THE AISLE. THEN MARIA AND LUIS COME DOWN THE AISLE. AS THEY GET DOWN FRONT, LINDA TAKES HER PLACE AS THE MAID OF HONOR AND BOB TAKES HIS PLACE AS BEST MAN. THEN ELMO COMES DOWN THE AISLE AS THE RING-BEARER, CARRYING THE RINGS ON HIS PILLOW.

ELMO REACHES HIS SPOT. BOB AND LINDA TAKE THE RINGS AND STAND ASIDE. THE PRIEST ENTERS AND BEGINS THE CEREMONY. (MUSIC OUT.)

PRIEST: We're here today to celebrate the marriage of Maria and Luis. When two people get married, what they do is make a promise to each other. Luis and Maria are making a promise today — a promise to share their lives together, a promise to help one another and care for each other and love each other for the rest of their lives. They are celebrating this promise in front of the people they love most, their friends

SESAME STREET   -17-   SHOW 2485

28. (CONT.)

MARIA: Look at him, isn't he wonderful

JOSE: Me sobrinito
Se ha covertido
En un verdadero hombre, Luisito
Now when I look at you I see
The handsome young man I used to be, Luisito

BOB: Sometimes I wonder how I would feel being married
If I were married, would it be to someone like you?

LINDA: Sometimes I wonder how I would feel being married
I wonder if you ever wonder, too

LINDA/BOB: I wish I knew

ELMO: Don't drop the rings, Elmo
Please, Elmo, don't drop the rings

MRS. M.   I wish her father could have lived to see this day
He's have been so proud

OSCAR: I wish they'd let that lousy organ music play
It was nice and loud

SUSAN/GORDON: Look at him, isn't he wonderful?

MARIA/LUIS: Look at her (him), isn't she (he) wonderful?

PRIEST: (BEAT) ...Do you, Luis, take Maria to be your wife in good times and bad, to love her and care for her always?

LUIS: I do.

LUIS TAKES RING FROM BOB AND PUTS IT ON MARIA'S FINGER.

PRIEST: Do you, Maria, take Luis to be your husband in good times and bad, to love him and care for him always?

MARIA: I do.

MARIA TAKES RING FROM ELMO AND GIVES THEM TO LUIS

SESAME STREET   -18-   SHOW 2485

28. (CONT.)

ELMO: Don't drop the rings, Bob.

PRIEST: I now pronounce you husband and wife

MARIA AND LUIS KISS...

BB: Yay!

THE CROWD BREAKS INTO APPLAUSE AND CHEERING AS LUIS AND MARIA HUG EACH OTHER...

FREEZER FRAME AS THE CHEERING CONTINUES FOR A FEW SECONDS, RECEDING ON ECHO...

29. FILM: SONG: LITTLE THINGS   20-0016-1:35

30. GOODBYE
(FAMILY)   19-0538-4:07

SCENIC: ARBOR, FULLY DECORATED
TALENT: BIG BIRD, GORDON, SUSAN, MILES, AND EVERYBODY, KIDS
SFX: FREEZE FRAME
LIGHT: EVENING

ARBOR FULLY DECORATED FOR PARTY. THE PARTY IS IN FULL SWING. FOOD, MUSIC, DANCING, CONVERSATION. MARIA WANDERS FOR A FEW SECONDS, BEING SURE TO INCLUDE LUIS AND MARIA. THEN MARIA CUTS THE CAKE. THEY BOTH TAKE A BITE. THE DANCING RESUMES AS MARIA CLIMBS THE STAIRS AND THROWS THE BOUQUET. LINDA CATCHES IT. EVERYONE THE MUSIC STARTS AGAIN AS THE SHOW ROLL OVER THE PARTY.

SPECIAL CREDITS

CREDITS   01-0578-0:30

CREDITS

Here Comes the Bride

Maria's friendship with Luis became the focus of a falling-in-love storyline in Season 19. Head writer Jeff Moss wrote a script in which the couple found a kitten, and Luis was so tender to it that Maria began to notice him in a whole new way. Maria and Luis speedily courted and were married just in time—Sonia's frothy wedding gown disguised the fact that the actress was actually four months pregnant.

The producers, cast and crew of
Sesame Street
Cordially invite you and your readers to the Wedding of Maria and Luis, Friday, the thirteenth of May, nineteen hundred eighty-eight on your local public television station. *

* *Check local listings.   Limited.*

The press announcement for the episode was designed and printed like a formal wedding invitation

" Emilio and I were together somewhere, and a woman comes up and she says, 'Oh, it's Luis and Maria, I'm so happy that my child saw real love on television and not this fake sitcom love, but real affection between two people.' Emilio and I decided to tell her the truth, and we said, 'You know, we're not really married.' And she said, 'Well, as long as you really love each other.'

—SONIA MANZANO

Northern
CALLOWAY
DAVID

O ne more key person to join the *Sesame Street* cast in those early years was Northern Calloway.

Just two days after graduating from the High School of Performing Arts in New York City, Northern was hired by the

Lincoln Center Repertory company. It was the start of a stage career that saw him appearing in such diverse works as Shakespeare's *Midsummer Night's Dream* and the Broadway musical *Pippin*. *New York Times* critic John Simon cited Northern's "ironic flexibility, that mercurial resilience that I have never seen so well translated into song and dance." A few years later, that charisma was spotted by *Sesame Street*'s producers.

On the show, Northern's alter ego, David, became a helper in Hooper's Store. When the character of Mr. Hooper died, he left his store to David in his will. In addition to making birdseed milkshakes, David's role expanded to include a stint as a law student and, eventually, Maria's boyfriend. Sonia and Northern had known one another at the High School of Performing Arts, establishing a camaraderie that no doubt inspired their spontaneous decision to create a deeper on-screen relationship. As Maria puts it, "We just decided that ourselves. I loved to be around him. And so we were kind of 'the couple.'"

> **I gave a speech a couple of years ago at a university, and this woman came up to me and said, 'My God, you and David were the J-Lo and P. Diddy of my generation!'**
>
> –SONIA MANZANO

In fact, Maria and David shared an on-screen kiss that's still fodder for fan gossip decades later. It was in a script written by Sonia. "I was trying to write some bits for Telly," she explains. "I was explaining emotions—love and anger. And I actually had me and Northern Calloway kissing in the tenement doorway. Telly comes by and embarrasses them by saying, 'This is an example of love.'"

In 1988, Sonia's real-life marriage to Richard Reagan spilled over into the show when she became pregnant. On screen, the role of Maria's husband was naturally first offered to Northern. He had to turn it down—and eventually leave the show—to allow him to obtain treatment for a long-standing and debilitating illness.

After the wedding of Maria and Luis, David remained for the season, running the store until his character left the Street to move in with his grandmother. The talented actor and composer (one of whose songs was recorded by Lena Horne) taped his last episode of *Sesame Street* in 1989. Tragically, he passed away shortly afterward of stomach cancer, at age forty-one.

"My performances are most influenced by Northern J. Calloway," says Roscoe Orman of his own role as Gordon. "He was an extraordinarily gifted performer who made everything he did seem effortless."

Northern cracks up off camera with Clarice Taylor, who played his grandmother in a number of appearances in the '70s and '80s

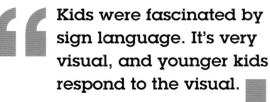

linda

"" **Kids were fascinated by sign language. It's very visual, and younger kids respond to the visual.** ""

—LINDA BOVE

Linda
BOVE

LINDA

L inda Bove first performed as a guest star on *Sesame Street*, in an appearance by a group of actors from the Little Theatre of the Deaf. She was already an established TV performer, juggling stage performances as a member of National Theatre of the Deaf with a featured role on the daytime soap *Search for Tomorrow*. In 1976, she became a full-time member of the *Sesame Street* cast but, even then, she moonlighted as a guest star on other series, like *Happy Days* (playing one of Fonzie's parade of girlfriends), and as a stand-in in Broadway's *Children of a Lesser God*. Each of her characters shared messages of tolerance and diversity. Her role on *Sesame Street* proved to be no different.

"I was invited to share my ideas with writers and producers," she reports. "If my character was to be portrayed correctly, that was important. The goal was to show how I could be part of the community without focusing on deafness. At other times, it became important to give information about deaf culture—not focusing on the disability, but on how I lived, how I answered the phone, how I went shopping, accomplished the things I needed to accomplish."

In fact, a segment in which her character learned to use a telephone typewriter, allowing her to see phone messages for the first time, unleashed a flood of viewer mail to Linda and the producers. People in the deaf community actually learned about the technology for the first time while watching the show with their children.

Initially, Barkley the Dog was Linda's pet. She was the only one who could control the rambunctious canine.

"They put Linda and Barkley together because—since Barkley couldn't understand language—they could have a physical relationship, a chance to sign," recalls Brian Meehl, who performed the puppet in those first years. "The irony was, I didn't have a camera [inside Barkley, a full-body Muppet], and I could only see out of Barkley's mouth. If Barkley was next to someone, he couldn't see above that person's waist. So if Linda wanted Barkley to do something, she would do the sign but also have to tap her foot, so I could see it."

"Linda and I have had some fantastic scenes together," Bob McGrath recalls. "And some heartwarming stories came back about kids' attitudes." He tells of a deaf man whose young relatives avoided him, until they watched the show. "It just changed the attitudes in that whole family," he says, "because they finally understood what it meant to be deaf."

"Bob was a great sport," Linda says. "He took a quick course on sign language, poor guy."

NEWS FLASH In her first season on the show, Linda's character was an actor, mirroring her real life. But the staff at the Workshop soon discovered that being an actor was not concrete enough for a young child to understand. So the writers came up with the idea that Linda would be a librarian. "I loved it," Linda says. "I enjoy books and reading. And it's a good way of storytelling—of using American Sign Language."

Linda uses American Sign Language on the show

Alison was the first Sesame "kid" to literally grow up on the show

Alison
BARTLETT-O'REILLY

GINA JEFFERSON

DR. GINA JEFFERSON
VETERINARIAN

Alison Bartlett-O'Reilly was brought up watching *Sesame Street.*

"I remember wanting to rip my hair out because no one else saw Snuffle-upagus," she says of her early days as a fan. "I was viscerally affected. I'd be screaming at the TV, 'He's right there! Don't you see him?!'

"They were my entire world," she goes on. "We have home movies of the Thanksgiving Day Parade in 1973 or '74, and you see me dressed up in a little muff and a long coat, and the *Sesame Street* float comes by, and Will Lee jumps off the float and shakes my hand. I get chills talking about it."

By age fifteen, Alison already had professional acting credentials. That's when her agent informed her about an audition for a day's work at *Sesame Street* and encouraged her to try out for the job. She needed to get something more "lightweight" on her resume, the agent advised; previously, she'd been taking on tough-girl Broadway roles.

"I was going to LaGuardia High School," she recalls, "so I literally walked across the street for the audition. I looked around, and I did a lot of those negative messages to myself: 'There's no way I'm going to get hired for this. Why am I here?' And I was going to just walk out when they called my name."

She got the job—for a brief stint on the show—during which time she met and worked with some Honkers and their prankish puppeteers one day, Kevin Clash and Marty Robinson.

> **You know, thumbs aren't very pretty, but they sure are useful.**
>
> —ALISON, AS GINA

"It's something Kevin and Marty still like to talk about," she says, laughing. "Jon Stone said, 'Action.' And whatever was on the page that day, they decided to just poke at me . . . pull my hair . . . honk my head. And I just had to go with it. I didn't realize it, but I think I was still being auditioned. The test was getting by the Honkers and Frank Biondo [a cameraman infamous for his teasing from the sidelines].

"I was from Brooklyn." She grins. "You couldn't wear me down. I wasn't going to have the Honkers and Frankie beat me to the punch."

A few weeks later, Alison got a second call. They wanted to keep her on the show. And so she became the first of a generation of human cast members who grew up on the Street.

Gina worked at Hooper's for a while and then went to veterinary school and became owner of the neighborhood pet clinic. Her role evolved to include a storyline about her adoption of an infant from Guatemala.

"What an incredible actor Alison is," says Emilio Delgado (Luis). "I was always amazed, because she was young—so young. A heart of gold. And then watching her grow up and get married and have children. Now I just see her as this spitfire mom. She's a wonder, she's a true wonder."

Alison rehearses early adoption episodes with a doll stand-in

Alan
MURAOKA

ALAN

Alan Muraoka was seven years old when *Sesame Street* premiered, and even though he was a bit older than the target audience, he was drawn to its humor and music. "I absolutely loved the baker who would sing, 'Ten chocolate cream pies!!!' and then fall down the stairs. Hilarious!" he recalls.

After 1982, Hooper's was run by a variety of owners, including retired firefighter Mr. Handford. But when that character left the show in 1998, the Workshop needed to find someone new to run the neighborhood's central meeting place, an actor who could generate the same chemistry with an audience that Will Lee did.

By that time, *Sesame Street* fan Alan was in the midst of a successful Broadway career that included playing the lead role of the Engineer in *Miss Saigon*. But in 1997, he got a call for something a bit different: an audition for a part on *Sesame Street*.

"My agent told me that they were looking for a new character to take over Hooper's Store," he says, "so of course I was interested. I knew how important Hooper's Store was to the fabric of the *Sesame* community."

Alan was faxed the scene for his audition, which included Big Bird in a dither over losing his teddy bear, Radar. Alan's role

in the scene was to calm him down.

"They didn't know what they wanted, so they saw a variety of people," Alan recalls. "Most were older and more grandfather-ish, so I was hoping that they were looking to go in a new direction."

By his third callback, the producers had decided that they wanted Asian Americans represented on the show. "There were ten of us. . . . It was very nerve-racking, but at the same time, I knew that I was a good fit for the show. I had done a lot of children's theater in the past, and I love kids. So it seemed like a natural. They thought so, too, and I got the part."

Alan started polishing the counter at Hooper's in 1998.

"I remember walking through the studio door," Alan goes on, "and then through the swinging door, which is the subway entrance on the set. I was filled with such awe and wonder, actually being on the set of a show that I grew up with. I remember seeing the steps of 123, and then seeing the awning of Hooper's Store, which was now *my* store. It was exhilarating and surreal.

"So I'm sitting at one of the outside tables in the arbor area of Hooper's Store, going over my script, when suddenly every Muppeteer on set runs up to me. They get into a single-file line, and one by one they introduce themselves to me, shake my hand, and welcome me to the set. I was so amused and touched."

Chris
KNOWINGS
CHRIS ROBINSON

hris Knowings has been acting professionally in movies and on TV since he was a kid; his first big job was in 1994, when he was fourteen and appeared in Spike Lee's *Crooklyn*. So you'd think he'd be pretty blasé about another acting gig.

But Chris grew up watching the show. That's probably why the actor remembers "every word, every moment, every mistake, every mess-up, every boom shadow on my shoulder—EVERYTHING" about the first day he appeared on *Sesame Street*.

"I made sure I got here extra early," he says of that first morning, "so I could walk around by myself. I remember I walked in and saw a PA coming in, so I walked right back out again. Because I wanted to be there alone the first time.

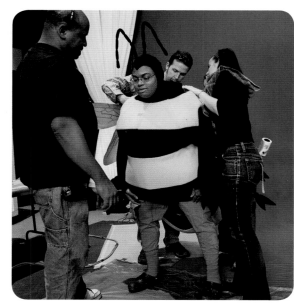

"When I walked on the Street," he goes on, his eyes glowing, "it was like, 'Am I really here? Is this for real?' I started sitting on the steps and opening doors. Lifting things off the shelves in Hooper's Store. I don't know how you're going to top this moment. I was five all over again."

Chris's new job assisting at Hooper's puts him in good company. It was previously filled by a long line of *Sesame Street* cast members, including David, Gina, and Gabi—even Bert and Cookie Monster.

> "Afterward, I called my parents and best friend. I shouted, 'I just met Gordon from *Sesame Street*!'"
> —CHRIS KNOWINGS

Nitya
VIDYASAGAR
LEELA

n a show that's an ongoing "experiment," as its creators call *Sesame Street*, there's always something—and someone—new. No sooner did Chris settle into 123 when a Laundromat opened down the block and another new face showed up there: Leela, played by actress Nitya Vidyasagar.

Nitya, a theater and film actress who recently graduated from NYU's Tisch School of the Arts, didn't grow up with *Sesame Street* in her childhood home of South India. But it didn't take her long to become comfortable with the Street and its Muppet denizens.

"I think it's easy for everyone if they just take a little leap of faith," she says. "It's obviously to the credit of the puppeteers. They know what they're doing. In the hands of people like that, it doesn't take a lot to make them real."

Keen-eyed viewers of season 40 will spot puppeteer Richard Hunt's name on the cover of Leela's book

Nitya should know. She's puppeteered herself, playing a monkey in a production of a play she also wrote, called *Serendib*.

Prepping for this new role in an unfamiliar series, Nitya studied *Sesame Street* intensely after she got the part. But she was still overwhelmed by what she describes as "the complete magic that goes on when the cameras are off . . . all the complicated processes. My first day was with two of the biggest puppets, Snuffleupagus and Big Bird, and just the technical operation of those things is unbelievable."

"It's an enormously important institution, a cornerstone of American culture," she says. "I know that without even being a part of it in the same way most people here are. It's an honor to be part of that."

Nitya's role wasn't originally written for a actor of Indian descent. "It was incidental," she says. "The casting notices said nothing of ethnicity."

Ruthie

Angela, Jamal, and Kayla

Comings
and Goings

Posing with Celina is David Smyrl, the first of two Mr. Handfords. "Kids didn't seem to mind the change," says fellow actor Roscoe Orman, "but then, they didn't notice the two Darrins on Bewitched either"

When *Sesame Street* introduced an expanded "around-the-corner" set in 1993, new actors joined the cast, including Ruth Buzzi as Ruthie, owner of secondhand shop Finders Keepers. Also populating the new set were dance instructor Celina (Annette Calud) and Angela (Angel Jemmot), a day-care worker, whose family included park-ranger husband, Jamal, performed by Jou Jou Papailler, and baby Kayla, played by twins Rachael and Syvae McDaniel. The expansion proved too much of a good thing, however. Follow-up research indicated that children were having trouble navigating the crowd of new faces. So in season 30, the extended set was dismantled and the show went back to focusing on the core *Sesame Street* family. Only Ruth Buzzi stayed on for another year, also appearing in the film *The Adventures of Elmo in Grouchland*.

The around-the-corner actors were not the first short-term additions to the show. As early as 1970, producers began experimenting by adding a variety of new "neighbors" to the Street. Some, like Buffy Sainte-Marie (played by her namesake) and Olivia Robinson (Alaina Reed), stayed for some time, becoming fixtures for fans growing up in the late '70s to '80s. Olivia appeared as Gordon's sister, a photographer. Buffy, already a noted folksinger, was joined on screen by her real-life husband, Sheldon Wolfchild, as well as infant Dakota, called Cody on screen. Together, as Crees, they broke ground as the first regularly appearing Native American performers on a kids' show; Buffy also challenged TV conventions in an episode where her character breast-feeds her infant on the street.

Alaina's character, Olivia, was a photographer—and Gordon's sister

Buffy (here with her on-screen and real-life husband and son) went on to write "Up Where We Belong," the Academy Award–winning theme song for the film *An Officer and a Gentleman*

NEWS FLASH

Why did Ruth Buzzi's character stay on even after her locale vanished? "She's hilarious," says Sonia Manzano. "She'll do anything. And it's interesting that she should be on the show, because *Sesame Street* used to be compared to *Laugh-In*." Ruth starred in that groundbreaking variety show, which pushed humor and political boundaries in the '60s. "She's like a Muppet herself," says Caroll Spinney, fondly.

Jaime Sanchez appeared as the first Latino cast member, for one season in 1970; Raúl Juliá followed in 1971 as Rafael, who partnered with Luis in the L & R Fix-It Shop

Charlotte Rae debuted in season 3 as Molly the mail lady, later starring in the sitcom The Facts of Life; aproned Larry Block joined as store helper Tom from 1977 to '78; and Bill McCutcheon's Uncle Wally spanned seasons 16 to 23

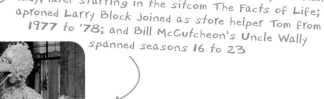

Stage manager Chet O'Brien stepped in front of the camera in 1971 as fruit peddler Mr. MacIntosh and was soon joined by another backstager, bearded Kermit Love, performing Willy the hot dog man; in the row below them, Leonard Jackson held the role of Hooper's Store owner Mr. Handford for a year in 1989, before David Smyrl assumed the role for eight years; in 1989, Ward Saxton debuted as Fix-It Shop worker Mike; Sixteen Candles alum Gedde Watanabe played artist Hiroshi from 1988 to 1991; and tap dance phenom Savion Glover starred for four seasons, starting in 1990

Family and Friends

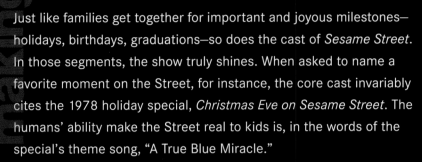

Just like families get together for important and joyous milestones—holidays, birthdays, graduations—so does the cast of *Sesame Street*. In those segments, the show truly shines. When asked to name a favorite moment on the Street, for instance, the core cast invariably cites the 1978 holiday special, *Christmas Eve on Sesame Street*. The humans' ability make the Street real to kids is, in the words of the special's theme song, "A True Blue Miracle."

> *Christmas Eve on Sesame Street* . . .
> Jon Stone wrote, directed, and produced it, an incredible vision. It was a wonderful tribute to the spirit of what we'd created.
>
> —ROSCOE ORMAN

Coproducer Dulcy Singer consults with writer/director Jon Stone; their work together on the Christmas Eve on Sesame Street special will earn them both a 1979 Emmy Award for Outstanding Children's Program

Sesame Street has always demanded a wide range of crazy roles and stunts from its human cast. Here, Northern shows off his comedic chops in a Grover-like spoof of superheroes. Loretta musically challenges Kermit to guess which thing is not like the other, while Emilio magically subtracts some friends.

Finally, Sonia and Bob take a dive off a pier into the cold, cold waters off City Island, New York. Just a few of the countless pratfalls and high jinks that the writers routinely put the cast through when they're not making monsters and grouches seem plausible.

Jon watches the obviously amusing playbacks of segments with Alan Arkin and his wife, Barbara Dana—fans have re-created some of their segments in online videos

During its early seasons, the show features duos of talented comics who created slapstick routines in the classic Laurel and Hardy, Stan and Ollie tradition. In season one, kids laughed as Buddy and Jim, played by Brandon Maggart and James Catusi (top right) try to hammer a nail with a balloon. Alan Arkin and Barbara Dana "acornatrinner" (cooperate) in season two. Next season, Wally and Ralph, played by Joe Ponazecki and Paul Price, carry the torch (and try to figure out how to paste a label on a bottle of glue).

> ## Now you know the difference 'tween loud and soft.
> —ROOSEVELT FRANKLIN

THIS CHAPTER HAS BEEN BROUGHT TO YOU BY THE LETTER L AND THE NUMBER 9.

The letter L is for Mr. Looper, just one of the *many* rhyming mispronunciations of Hooper's name by Big Bird. It's also for Leela. Welcome to Sesame Street! **The number 9** is for the current role call of grown-up people in the Street's neighborhood. In season 40, that cast includes the characters of Alan, Gina, Bob, Chris, Gordon, Leela, Luis, Maria, and Susan.

4

"Each Muppeteer lends an enormous amount of personality to the various Muppets. . . . Each character has developed more fully—growing out of the personality of the Muppeteer and becoming more and more alive each season."

—JIM HENSON

SOMEBODY
COME
AND
PLAY

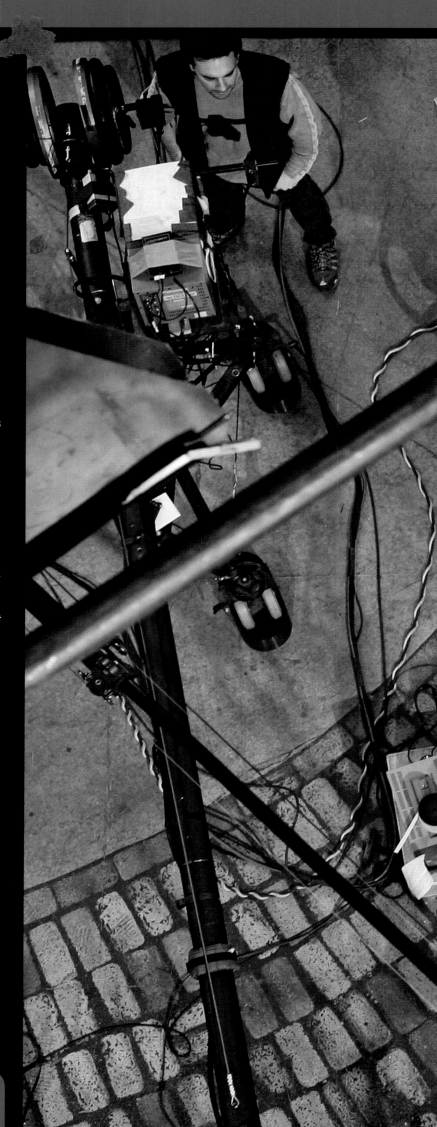

EPISODE
4149

This morning's taping has hardly begun when there's a pause in the action. Kevin Clash—head puppeteer, co-executive producer, frequent director, and performer of Elmo—has an idea.

The strains of a song he'll be performing with Big Bird fill the studio. It was originally written by composer Jeff Moss for Ernie and Bert, a celebration of friendship that also provides a lesson in early math skills. Elmo and Big Bird prerecorded the lyrics a few days ago. But Kevin thinks that something can make the execution even stronger. He confers with Director Emily Squires, who agrees.

Caroll Spinney can't easily sing live from inside the full-body Bird costume, so he'll stick with the pre-record. But Elmo will sing the song live.

Emily murmurs the necessary instructions into her headset. Like the show's other directors, she encourages puppeteer input on set; no one knows characters better.

Gordon Price (audio) makes some last-minute adjustments to the microphone hookup for Kevin. Vocal coach Dave Connor is called to the set in case the switch means that Kevin needs help with the song. Everything is ready. Kevin reaches for Elmo.

The small red puppet is a simple, lightweight Muppet with rodded hands. Next to the large and far more cumbersome Big Bird, he looks tiny and vulnerable. Elmo slips onto Kevin's hand like a well-worn glove, and as soon as the puppet is settled, he—Elmo, that is—absently begins to hum the *Sesame Street* theme song.

A woman visiting the set stares at Elmo with a mixture of awe and affection. "My daughter came from China," she confides. "At eighteen months, she still wasn't talking. I'll never forget one day, she looked at the TV and said clearly, 'Elmo.' It was her first word."

Nearby, Caroll suits up. In an instant, the Bird towers over Elmo. In response, Elmo shoves his little round bullet of a head into Bird's armpit and gags. Then he tries to push his way under the Bird. "Elmo wants to puppeteer Big Bird!" he cries.

"Bad, bad monster," Big Bird says solemnly, shaking his head.

Emily stifles a laugh. "Count down," she warns, then faces a bank of monitors, following the script, quietly calling the shots. Music comes up, faint and tinny, through everyone's headphones. Big Bird's head bobs happily to the music as the two friends walk together. Elmo sings, his voice sweet and high.

No matter how many times that pure falsetto is heard from the baritone performer under the red puppet, it's always a surprise.

Emily smiles as she watches the monitors.

"Lovely," she says.

on the set
on the set
on the set

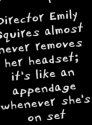

Director Emily Squires almost never removes her headset; it's like an appendage whenever she's on set

NEWS FLASH

Whether standing next to each other or on opposite sides of the set, the performers and most of the crew—including the people in the control room—use microphones and headsets to communicate. This has the advantage of making the crew's conversations audible to everyone else with headsets, including those not in the room.

There is a downside, however.

Puppeteers use headsets with attached microphones not only to communicate but also to record their characters' voices. (That way, they get a clear and crisp sound.) But if you're a puppeteer and you forget to turn your own mike off between takes—say, while you're exchanging gossip or on a break—everyone on the headsets can hear everything you say or do. Toilet flushings are a frequently shared occurrence . . . along with everything else that happens in a bathroom.

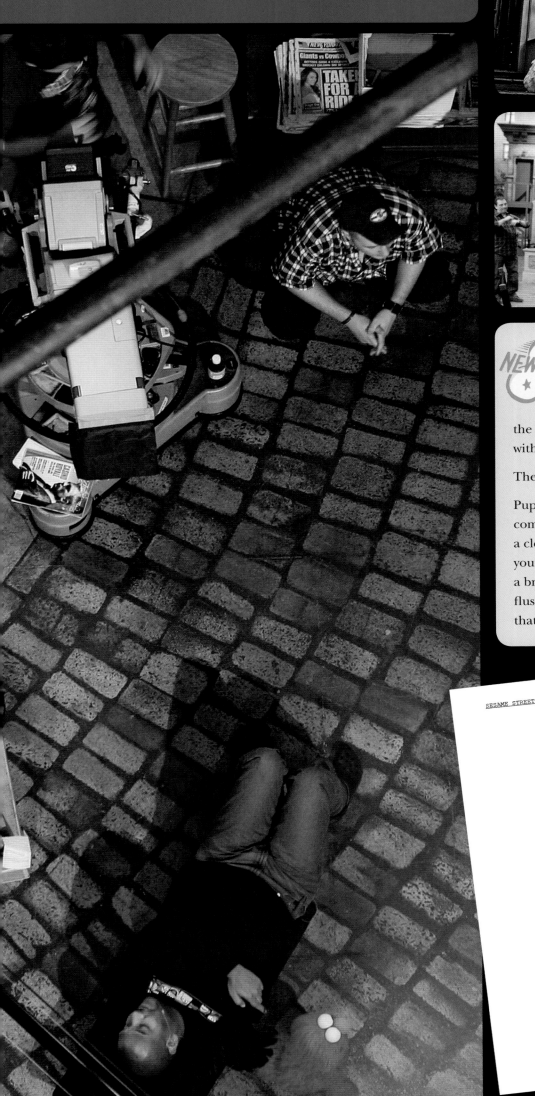

PRODUCTION MEETING COPY - BOYLAN
SHOW 4149
1

SESAME STREET

1. ALL FOR A SONG
(COUNTING, ADDITION, ENTERING SOCIAL
GROUPS, CRITICAL THINKING,
VOCABULARY, MUSIC: CREATE)
38-0142-0:00

SCENIC: ARBOR
TALENT: GABI, BIG BIRD, ELMO, ABBY, (3) AM
LITTLE PIGS, AM BIG BAD WOLF, AM BOY,
GRANNY BIRD (IN THOUGHT BALLOON)
PROPS: ABBY'S WAND, WATCH FOR GABI,
PHONE
SFX: ABBY'S WAND EFFECT, ELMO'S BUMP
(MID-RANGE BOING!), ABBY'S BUMP (HIGH
BOING!), BIG BIRD'S BUMP (LOW BOINK), TAXI
WHISTLE, REVELATION DING, SPEED DIAL,
ZOOM, SCREECH
TECH: FAIRY EFFECTS (PER SCRIPT), SPLIT
SCREEN, THOUGHT BALLOON, ABBY FLOATS
MUSIC: OPENING THEME, SONG: "ONE AND
ONE MAKE TWO, " SONG: "THREE," BUTTON

UP ON BIG BIRD AND ELMO IN THE ARBOR.

BIG BIRD: (TO CAM) Hi, welcome to
Sesame Street! You're just in time to hear our
song!

ELMO: (TO CAM) It's a special song for two
friends to sing together.

BIG BIRD: Which is perfect because that's
what we are, Elmo, two great friends!

ELMO: Wait... is Big Bird sure there are two
of us?

BIG BIRD: (SUDDENLY SERIOUS) Good
point, Elmo. We better check and see. It always
pays to do the math.

(CONTINUED)

New Kids on the Block

> **Perfect! Beautiful! I mean, Kermit, the sound of your heart is music to my ears.**
>
> —ANYTHING MUPPET, "HEART OF A FROG"

Sesame Street was in its sixth season when a pilot titled *Sex and Violence* aired on ABC TV on March 19, 1975. It was outrageous, funny, and, according to each and every U.S. network that turned it down, unproduceable.

Sex and Violence was created by Jim Henson.

Long before he joined *Sesame Street,* Jim had won recognition as a puppeteer for adult-targeted material through appearances in the early '60s on talk and variety shows, hosted by the likes of Steve Allen and Jack Paar. With the success of *Sesame Street*, Jim remained determined to spread the gospel of the Muppets as more than just preschool entertainment. He dreamed of a show starring his Muppets—Kermit, Rowlf, and a whole new crew—that would be broadcast on commercial television, watched by viewers of all ages.

To further that dream, Jim created a Valentine's Day–themed special in 1974, as well as the *Sex and Violence* follow-up. (The pilot was introduced by a Muppet proclaiming, "Ladies and gentlemen, presenting the end of sex and violence on television!" as he explodes foam letters spelling out those key three words.) Together, these two shows formed a pitch for a series that would ultimately be called *The Muppet Show*. But for some time it looked as if the series would never see the light of prime time.

Finally, Jim got the call from British producer Sir Lew Grade to come to the U.K. and produce the show there. Offered unrivaled artistic freedom, Jim jumped at the chance, along with longtime partner-puppeteers Frank Oz, Jerry Nelson, and Richard Hunt.

There was only one problem: The performers of *The Muppet Show* would have to live in London for most of the next six years. They might return for weeks at a time, long enough for *Sesame Street* insert segments, but they wouldn't be available to take on the new Muppet characters that show writers were creating daily.

This became an opportunity for more puppeteers, a whole new generation of performers and puppets, to step into the spotlight.

Behind the scenes at season 18's taping of the "Boston T Party" segment, then–rookie puppeteer Marty Robinson pops in Muppet eyeballs to mug for the camera, along with Jim Henson, Kevin Clash, Richard Hunt, Jerry Nelson, Pam Arciero, and David Rudman

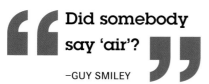

> **Did somebody say 'air'?**
>
> –GUY SMILEY

> **Who was that guy?**
>
> –ANYTHING MUPPET,
> "AIR" SONG

Ray Charles in a
fan-favorite performance,
singing the ABC song
in season 22;
Bryant Young performs
the right hand for Marty
Robinson on Telly, while
Pam Arciero (hidden in the mob)
right-hands for
Kevin Clash on Elmo

Brian MEEHL

BARKLEY THE DOG, TELLY MONSTER, GRUNDGETTA, DR. NOBEL PRICE, SAM THE ROBOT, SNUFFLEUPAGUS, CLEMENTINE (FORGETFUL JONES'S GIRLFRIEND), CAPTAIN BREAKFAST, ETC.

> " Like I said, the man marches to the beat of a different drum. "
>
> —CLEMENTINE

Brian Meehl (sometimes credited as Muehl) was already a gifted actor when he joined the *Sesame Street* team in 1978, taking on the full-body role of Barkley the Dog.

"I think I nailed the role," Brian says, "when during the audition, I was wearing the head [of Barkley] and a feather fell off, and I started doing a whole thing with the feather. I ended up getting the job and kind of reconfigured the character."

In early scripts featuring the oversized pup, the writers had created the character of a pretty savvy canine. Barkley knew how to count and had an almost human intelligence. But Brian thought this was a mistake. "I went in and said, 'Look. This thing was built to look like a dog. Let's play it like a dog. It's the goofy puppy that can't learn a thing, and it doesn't know how to count.'"

Brian had a cameo appearance as a human visitor on the show, playing skywriter Alphabet Bates

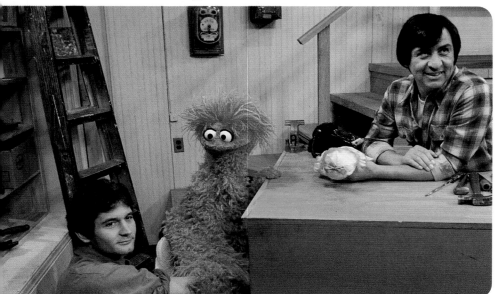

Many of the other personalities Brian created took the idea of expected norms and flipped them on their heads. His Dr. Nobel Price is an eager learner but a less-than-brilliant doctor. The supposedly perfect Sam the Robot (SAM is an acronym for Super Automated Machine) was prone to goofy mistakes. None of those roles took Brian as far as Barkley, though . . . literally. Playing the dog, Brian traveled to China as Big Bird's companion for the 1983 NBC special *Big Bird in China*.

Brian left the show after season 15 to focus on his young family and writing career, later penning scripts for *Between the Lions, The Wubbulous World of Dr. Seuss, The Magic School Bus*, and PBS's *Eyewitness*. Before his departure, however, he created one of his most enduring characters: Telly Monster. Brian wasn't the puppet's first performer, but his portrayal helped shape the character as viewers know Telly today.

"The original concept of Telly Monster . . . had swirling eyes, and he was glued to a television, really close, and he just liked to watch TV," Brian says. "Puppet builder Bobby Payne played him. And I think everybody on the set took a look at it and said, 'Oh, my God. This is the worst role model in the world.' So they completely dropped it; they removed his swirly, whirligig eyes, put normal eyes on him, and he became a monster."

The way Telly was elevated to Muppet stardom is a story straight out of Hollywood. "One day Caroll Spinney had a little bike wreck coming to the set and sprained his ankle," Brian recalls. "So in a panic, they had to completely reconfigure the show. They threw Telly in to do the Big Bird part. Suddenly, we had a new character."

NEWS FLASH

Telly shares the monomania that compels Cookie Monster, though for TV instead of cookies. The media obsession gave him his name, the British slang term for television: Telly.

Barkley was performed by Brian Meehl in the 1983 TV special Big Bird in China, shot on location; one of the first U.S. programs allowed into the country after the nation's Cultural Revolution, the show was unfamiliar to the Chinese, and Big Bird's giant size sent some locals fleeing in fear

A lot of people are surprised to find out that Barkley the Dog, despite being a very large Muppet, is performed by just one puppeteer.

"The genius part of it," explains Brian Meehl, "is you have about an eighteen-inch stilt on each arm, which equalizes the length of your front legs to your back legs. The tough part is you have to get at least half if not more of your body weight on your arms, because a dog is mainly tilted forward. And if you move too much weight back on your legs, where all your muscles and your support is, you end up looking like an orangutan."

Making Barkley bark is another ordeal. Bruce Connelly, the actor/mime who plays the role today, explains that the puppeteer holds a trigger cable mounted on the stilt, which closes the mouth. To open the mouth, Bruce tosses the head, built on an eight-pound helmet, to drop the jaw. Then he has to remember to bark.

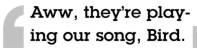

Martin P. ROBINSON

SNUFFLEUPAGUS, BUSTER THE HORSE, TELLY MONSTER, SLIMEY THE WORM, MONTY, ETC.

> " Aww, they're play-
> ing our song, Bird. "
>
> —ALOYSIUS SNUFFLEUPAGUS

Marty Robinson joined the *Sesame Street* cast in the role of Aloysius Snuffleupagus, sometimes known as Mr. Snuffleupagus, a puppet with a rather checkered past. After Jerry Nelson hurt his back in the vertebrae-challenging costume, Richard Hunt took over the puppet, with Jerry still doing the voice and Bryant Young manipulating the back end of Snuffy.

Then performer Michael Earl Davis took over the role for two years, with Jerry still doing the voice. When Michael left, it was time for yet another new Snuffy—one who could reunite the performance and the voice once again.

Marty, like Jerry, had learned puppeteering from Bil Baird. One weekday in 1981, he found himself in an audition with about 300 other hopefuls. On Friday, only a handful were left. All were six feet tall—a requirement for performing the giant, shaggy Muppet.

The weekend came and went. A few months went by. Then, one day, Marty opened his mail to

find a shooting schedule for *Sesame Street*.

"So I call up the office and say, 'I got this thing in the mail about the *Sesame* schedule,'" Marty remembers, grinning.

"'Oh, didn't anyone call you?' the guy says. 'Yeah, yeah, we want you to do Snuffy.'"

Marty studied Jerry Nelson's performance of Snuffy assiduously before even attempting the role. But when they finally spoke, Jerry gave him only one piece of advice.

"He said to start drinking and start smoking," Marty says dryly.

Marty didn't take up any bad habits, but he understood the advice. He pitched his voice low to nail Snuffy's husky, growly tones.

"I was really excited," Marty says. "I'd never had any money in my life. And working that first year at *Sesame Street* . . . all of a sudden, I had a salary. I could eat. And pay rent."

But Marty did much more than that. When Brian Meehl left *Sesame Street*, Marty took over Telly Monster and Buster the Horse. Oddly, Buster, first played by Frank Oz, outlasted both his owner, Forgetful Jones, and the cowboy's girlfriend, Clementine.

Also among Marty's characters is Slimey the Worm. Performing Slimey gives Marty the distinction of portraying both the largest (Snuffy) and the smallest character on *Sesame Street*. It also adds to the list of characters that Marty has made his own after taking over for other puppeteers. (Slimey, too, was originated by Jerry Nelson, then handed off to Michael Davis from 1978 to 1980.)

Marty's warmth, generosity, and comic talent have put a distinctive spin on them all. Snuffy remains Big Bird's stalwart and sympathetic friend. Telly is one of the more delightfully neurotic monsters on the Street. Slimey is enormously popular with show writers. Marty's skill at shaping characters like these is put into constant practice as he trains the casts of *Sesame* coproductions worldwide.

In addition to performing, he is also a builder. His most famous off-Street creation? Audrey the Plant for Broadway's *Little Shop of Horrors*.

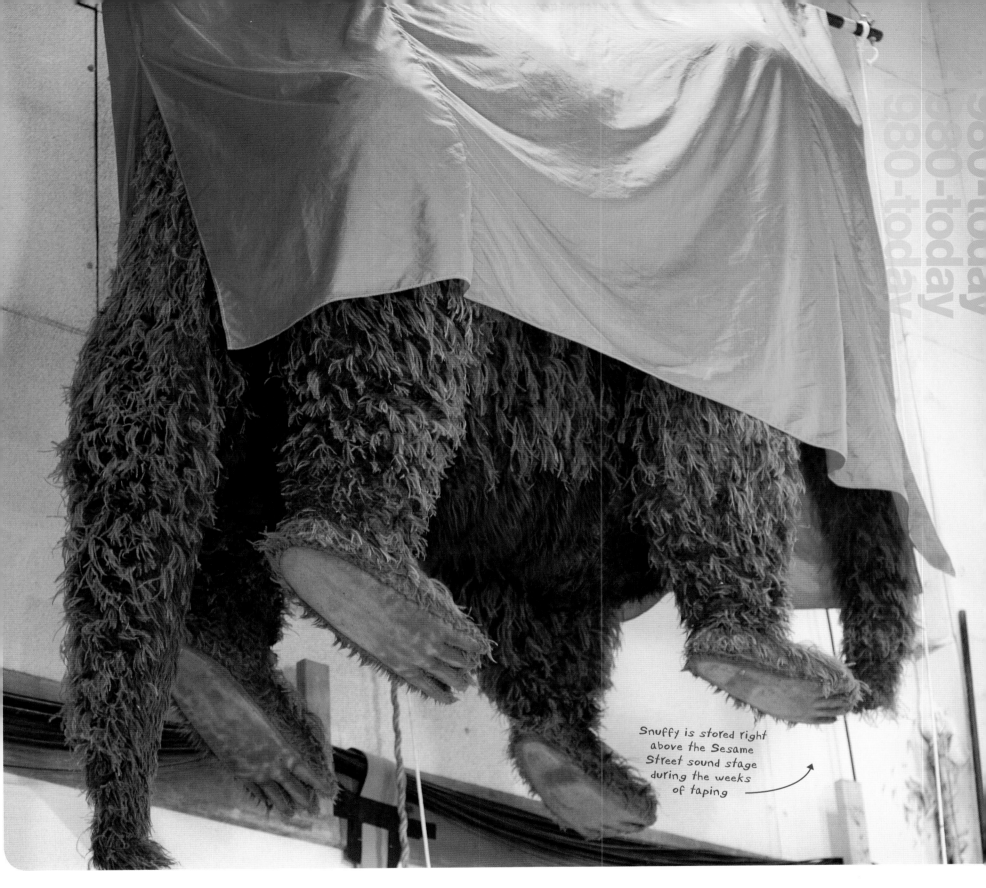

Snuffy is stored right above the Sesame Street sound stage during the weeks of taping

" A puppeteer's job is to translate everything that they know as an actor or as a human being into the tool that they're given . . . into the little communications tool. And whether that's a Snuffleupagus or a hand puppet or a shadow puppet or a marionette, it's, 'How do I communicate the human experience and reflect something meaningful back to humanity?' "

—MARTY ROBINSON

Marty signs autographs during a rare Snuffy appearance in the real world, in and around New York's Central Park in 1988

Snuffy first appeared in 1971 (episode 276), but only to Big Bird

29. (CONT.)

MUSIC: SNUFFY THEME

BB: Oh! Here he comes, Snuffy. This is it! Now remember we have to cooperate.

ELMO: Cooperate, yes!

BB: You hold Snuffy's snuffle and make sure he doesn't go away and I'll yell the secret word "food".

ELMO: Elmo hold snuffle!

BB: And don't let go until all the grownups come and see Mr. Snuffleupagus.

ELMO: Don't worry. Elmo not let go.

SNUFFY ENTERS.

SNUFFY: Hello Bird!

BB: Hi Snuffy. Say hello to my little friend Elmo.

SNUFFY: Hello, Elmo. Pleased to meet you. (EXTENDS HIS SNUFFLE TO ELMO)

ELMO: Same here. (HE POUNCES ON THE SNUFFLE AND HOLDS ON WITH BOTH ARMS AND WITH HIS HEAD PRESSED AGAINST IT.) Go Big Bird!

BB: FOOD! FOOD! FOOD! (RUNS OUT ON TO THE STREET, YELLING OFF CAMERA) FOOD! FOOD! Etc.

SNUFFY: Oh, that means Bird's friends are going to come and meet me now.

ELMO: Yes! Now!

SNUFFY: Oh boy! I better go home and brush my fur. I want to look good for them.

ELMO: No. Can't go! (HOLDS TIGHTER)

SNUFFY: Yes. I have to go. Let go of my snuffle.

(STARTS TO PULL AWAY)

snuffy revealed
snuffy revealed
snuffy revealed
snuffy revealed
snuffy revealed
snuffy revealed

Snuffy was originally envisioned as Big Bird's invisible friend—the Bird passionately believed in him, but the rest of the cast questioned his existence. Eventually, advisors theorized that this might suggest to kids the idea that grown-ups won't trust the word of a child—an alarming prospect in cases of potential abuse, a subject just becoming openly discussed in the eighties. Snuffy was then "revealed" to all, but only after a scene where Big Bird's adult friends ultimately decide to accept Big Bird's word, even before seeing Snuffy.

SESAME STREET   -15-   SHOW 2096

29. (CONT.)

ELMO: (STRAINS HARD) Uhhgh. No! Stay!
SNUFFY SLOWLY PULLS ELMO OUT OF FRAME...THEN AFTER
A BEAT ELMO PULLS SNUFFY BACK INTO FRAME.

ELMO: Elmo strong monster.

(SNUFFY PULLS HIM OUT OF FRAME AGAIN)

CUT TO: STREET

EVERYONE IS ASSEMBLING ON THE RUN IN FRONT OF 123
AS THEY ARRIVE THEY ASK WHERE SNUFFY IS.

BB: He's right through those doors.
(POINTS TO CONSTRUCTION DOORS) But hurry, I don't
know how long Elmo can hold him.

THEY ALL RUSH OUT OF FRAME. WE SHOULD NOT SEE
THEM GOING THROUGH THE CONSTRUCTION DOORS. BIG
BIRD IS LEFT ALONE IN FRONT OF 123.

BB: (TO CAMERA) I can't look. Yes I
can...no, I can't...I can...no, I can't. I can.
I have to. (HE GOES TO THE CONSTRUCTION DOORS.
HE LISTENS. ALL IS QUIET.) I can't look!
(STARTS TO WALK AWAY, THEN STOPS AND TALKS TO
CAMERA) What do you think? Should I open this
door and maybe see the grownups face to face with
Snuffy or not? I should? I shouldn't? Well,
which is it? Should! Right! Of course! It's
about time! Let's get this over with! (REACHES
FOR DOOR BUT STOPS) I don't know why, but I feel
like I'm saying goodbye to an old friend. (BIG
SIGH, HE OPENS THE DOOR VERY SLOWLY. OVER HIS
SHOULDER WE SEE WHAT HE SEES: THE FULL CAST
STANDING AROUND SNUFFY WITH MOUTHS AGAPE, BROADLY
STUNNED LOOKS ON THEIR FACES. IT IS STRANGELY
STILL AND QUIET.)

BB: (ALMOST A WHISPER, WITH A SIGH) At
last! (FADE OUT VERY SLOWLY)

THE SCENE IS AS BEFORE. ALL IS STILL QUIET. THE
CAST NOW QUIETLY CIRCLE SNUFFY EXAMINING HIM WITH
REVERENCE AND BARELY A SOUND.

SCRAM

Kevin CLASH

ELMO, BABY NATASHA, HOOTS THE OWL, DR. NOBEL PRICE,
WOLFGANG THE SEAL, ETC.

When Kevin Clash was a teenager, he saw a show on Maryland Public Television, *Call It Macaroni*, that would change his life. Each week, the show shadowed someone in a different profession. One week, it traced the footsteps of Muppet designer Kermit Love.

Kevin had watched *Sesame Street* avidly as a child and, as a teenager, already had a burgeoning career in his hometown as a puppeteer, with two local TV shows under his belt. "So I asked my mom to call the local PBS station, to see if I could meet Kermit," he recalls. "And she did."

Amazingly, Kermit invited Kevin to visit his workshop if the young man ever visited New York. Perhaps the puppet builder had an inkling of Kevin's talent, or maybe he was simply being nice to an interested kid. But Kevin wasn't just any kid. And when a school trip brought Kevin to the city, he knocked on Kermit's door.

Kermit was impressed by the persistence.

"If anything comes up with my production company," he told the twelfth-grader, "I'll keep you in mind. And I'll definitely tell them about you for *Sesame Street*."

↑ Kevin with Jim Henson in 1986

Kermit was as good as his word, giving Kevin a number of small jobs and finally recommending him to Jim at the Workshop in 1980.

"It was phenomenal to be around them," Kevin reports. "To watch Jim Henson and Caroll Spinney perform, and watch Richard Hunt and Jerry Nelson and everything. Amazing."

Initially, Kevin performed a number of small characters, among them Warren Wolf (formerly a Jim Henson creation) and the jazzy owl, Hoots. But then, magic happened.

"It's the stuff of legends," Marty Robinson says of that day on set in 1984 when the Street would move into a new era. "I remember Richard doing the puppet for a couple of episodes and complaining about it. He just didn't like doing cutesy characters.

"Richard came to the Muppet room, and he had Elmo in a ball," says Marty. "He threw it into Kevin's lap and said, 'You do this f***ing thing.'"

"Richard was Big Brother," Kevin recalls. "We all looked up to him. And so I felt that if he couldn't do anything with it, what the hell could I do with it? Anyway, I got through that season, and thought about it over the summer."

The next season, the first Elmo script up was about the young monster's wanting to go on vacation.

"He was at the fix-it shop," Kevin remembers, "and Emilio, who plays Luis, was there, and Elmo was packing to go on vacation. But it was all imaginary. There was no suitcase, no clothes, but I had to make it look like he was packing. And everybody started laughing. That's when I knew."

The Cookie Monster–like staccato speech patterns of the original Elmo voice took a subtle shift that day and suddenly emerged as the voice of an eager and ebullient child.

Just as he does with his other roles, Kevin gave the character great charm and a sly humor that's a hallmark.

"Elmo was just an Anything Muppet, a little red AM, and all of a sudden Kevin gave this character such personality," Sonia Manzano says. As one of the humans playing off the puppet, she's in an ideal position to witness the performance from every perspective. "And his manipulation is just perfect."

Evolution
OF ELMO

What makes him a breakout star? Some say it's Elmo's vivid color; others cite his perfectly proportioned googly eyes, which director Jon Stone appears to find mesmerizing

> **Elmo thinks Whoopi's skin is a very pretty brown. Elmo's fur is furry all right. But it's not like Whoopi's skin.**
>
> —ELMO

There can be different reasons to create a Muppet. In the Count von Count's case, the puppet embodies a celebration of the show's math curriculum. His creation began when then-head writer Norman Stiles came up with the character's essential fixation, and continued with Jerry Nelson's astonishing performance; it was he who discovered the Count's Dracula-like personality. Additionally, Muppet designers crafted the Count's distinctive look. The Count was envisioned as a featured character from the start, and a great deal of team thought was put into his development.

In other cases, characters are the creation of a performer who takes a bundle of fur originally destined to be a background character and gives that character an especially winning brain and heart. But even that takes a team. In fact, Brian Meehl describes the process as something like "three legs to the stool. You have a writer providing a script and a concept for the character; you have the puppet itself, which is a visual force; and then you have the performer."

Elmo was one of a host of random monsters who populate *Sesame Street*. He was first performed by Brian before being briefly taken over by Richard Hunt. He might have remained in the background forever. But the writers found him appealing and started to write for him specifically, originally as a way to introduce a bit of Spanish into the show.

"Everything was, 'Elmo do this, yes, yes, yes,'" Kevin recalls. "There were three yesses all the time. Elmo was always going to be a young monster, so they wanted the dialogue to be very, very primitive. I think that's why he talked in the third person. Brian did a really whispery, sweet, 'Yes, yes, yes.' Richard was yelling all over the place. I came up with the falsetto, and it stuck."

"This is a medium for children," Kevin goes on, "but we don't talk down to them. That's why *Sesame Street* plays on so many different levels. You have to create personalities that a child can connect to, and that an adult can connect to. It's also about how beautifully designed these characters are . . . this rainbow of monsters and Anything Muppets that you can use for any role—a bird one day, a mailman the next. It was so smart of Jim Henson . . . and cost-effective, too."

NEWS FLASH Kevin Clash credits show writer David Korr with helping to keep the Elmo character alive long enough for the red puppet to finally find his voice. "David just liked writing for him," Kevin reports. "Even when everyone else was saying 'who is this red monster you keep putting in here?'"

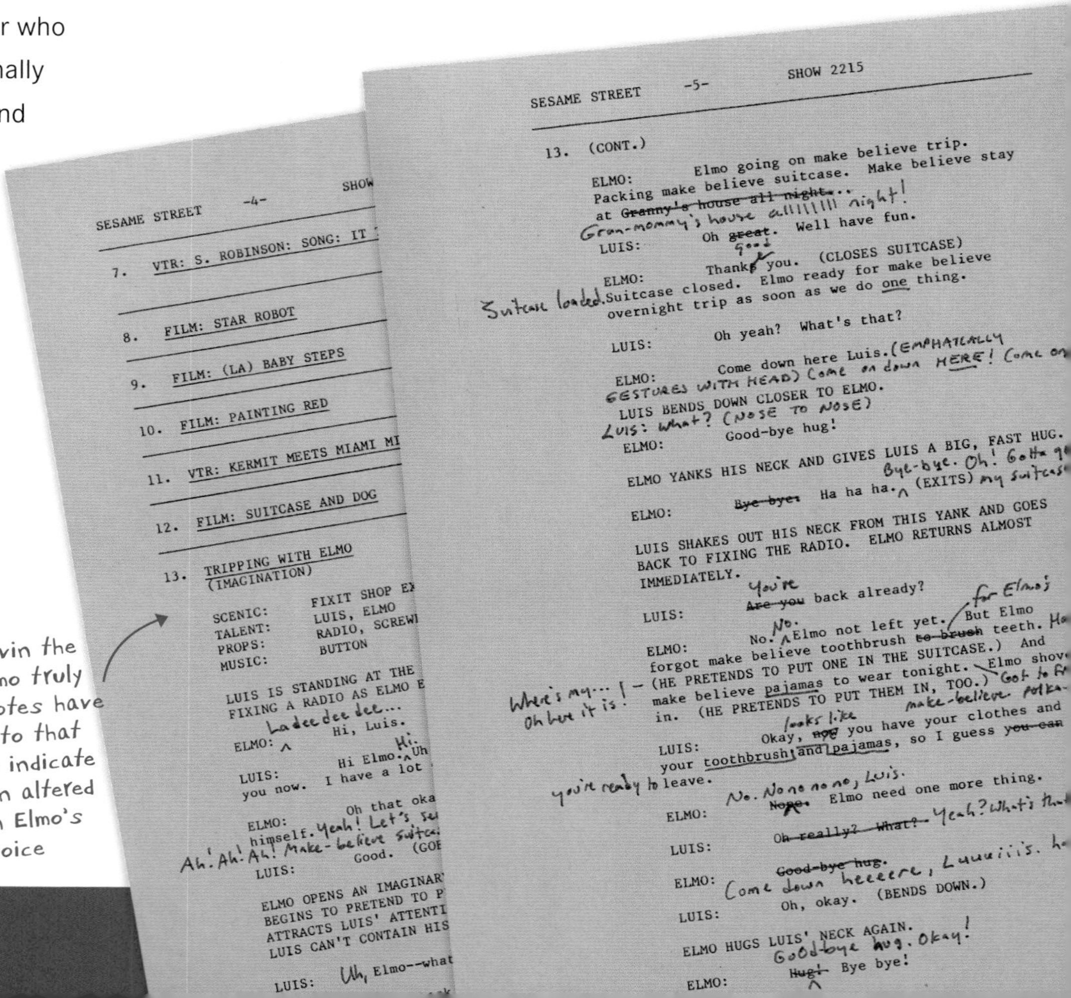

Considered by Kevin the episode where Elmo truly found his voice—notes have been added here to that original script to indicate lines where Kevin altered the phrasing in Elmo's newfound voice

[Script pages reproduced on right side of page]

SESAME STREET   -4-   SHOW

7. VTR: S. ROBINSON: SONG: IT

8. FILM: STAR ROBOT

9. FILM: (LA) BABY STEPS

10. FILM: PAINTING RED

11. VTR: KERMIT MEETS MIAMI MI

12. FILM: SUITCASE AND DOG

13. TRIPPING WITH ELMO
    (IMAGINATION)

SCENIC: FIXIT SHOP EX
TALENT: LUIS, ELMO
PROPS: RADIO, SCREW
MUSIC: BUTTON

LUIS IS STANDING AT THE
FIXING A RADIO AS ELMO E
La dee dee dee...
ELMO: Hi, Luis.
             Hi Elmo. Uh
LUIS: I have a lot
you now.

ELMO: Oh that oka
           himself. Yeah! Let's se
Ah! Ah! Ah! Make-believe suitca
LUIS: Good. (GO

ELMO OPENS AN IMAGINAR
BEGINS TO PRETEND TO P
ATTRACTS LUIS' ATTENTI
LUIS CAN'T CONTAIN HIS

LUIS: Uh, Elmo--what

SESAME STREET   -5-   SHOW 2215

13. (CONT.)
ELMO: Elmo going on make believe trip.
Packing make believe suitcase. Make believe stay
at ~~Granny's house all night~~.
Gran-mommy's house allllllll night!
LUIS: Oh ~~good~~. Well have fun.
             Good
ELMO: Thank you. (CLOSES SUITCASE)
Suitcase loaded. Suitcase closed. Elmo ready for make believe
overnight trip as soon as we do one thing.

LUIS: Oh yeah? What's that?
ELMO: Come down here Luis. (EMPHATICALLY
GESTURES WITH HEAD) (come on down HERE! come on
LUIS BENDS DOWN CLOSER TO ELMO.
LUIS: What? (NOSE TO NOSE)
ELMO: Good-bye hug!

ELMO YANKS HIS NECK AND GIVES LUIS A BIG, FAST HUG.
                          Bye-bye. Oh! Gotta g
ELMO: ~~Bye-bye.~~ Ha ha ha. (EXITS) my suitcase

LUIS SHAKES OUT HIS NECK FROM THIS YANK AND GOES
BACK TO FIXING THE RADIO. ELMO RETURNS ALMOST
IMMEDIATELY.   You're
LUIS: ~~Are you~~ back already?
             No.
ELMO: No. Elmo not left yet. But Elmo
forgot make believe toothbrush ~~to brush~~ teeth. H
(HE PRETENDS TO PUT ONE IN THE SUITCASE.) And
Where is my... ! — make believe pajamas to wear tonight. Elmo shove
oh here it is!   in. (HE PRETENDS TO PUT THEM IN, TOO.) Got to fi
                               make-believe polka-
                          looks like
LUIS: Okay, ~~now~~ you have your clothes and
you're ready to leave. your toothbrush and pajamas, so I guess you can

ELMO: No. None no no, Luis.
             Nope. Elmo need one more thing.
LUIS: Oh ~~really? What?~~ Yeah? What's that
ELMO: ~~Good-bye hug~~. Come down heeeere, Luuuiii's. h
LUIS: Oh, okay. (BENDS DOWN.)

ELMO HUGS LUIS' NECK AGAIN.
                Goodbye hug. Okay.
ELMO: Hug? Bye bye!

The much shaggier
original Elmo

SEGMENT #0017–1024

Elmo: Green frog no play with Elmo?

Kermit: Well, no, Elmo, not right now.

Elmo: Oh, Elmo sad. Green frog no play with Elmo.

Kermit: Yeah, but . . .

Elmo: Make Elmo very sad. Elmo very sad, very very sad.

Kermit: Okay, Elmo, I'll tell you what, hold on, uh uh, don't cry now. I will play with you, but . . .

Elmo: Green frog play with Elmo. Oh, make Elmo very happy, very happy happy happy happy. Oh, you make Elmo very happy, green frog. Play with Elmo make him very happy, happy happy happy.

Pam
ARCIERO

GRUNDGETTA, ASSORTED ANYTHING MUPPETS, ETC.

Pam Arciero was in the same Muppet audition that Marty Robinson attended when *Sesame Street* was looking for a replacement performer for Snuffleupagus. She vied for the role and, although she didn't get it, she became one of the few women who works at *Sesame Street* day in and day out—"a work-horse," as she describes herself, wryly.

Pam's journey to the show, like many of the puppeteers', didn't take a direct path; she first became a puppeteer because of an injury. While studying dance and drama at the University of Hawaii, Pam fell and damaged her knee, putting her in a cast. Not content simply to choreograph dances

> ❝ **Aw, get lost!** ❞
>
> —GRUNDGETTA

for one leg, which she did ("Because that's who I am," she says, laughing), Pam followed the suggestion of a few friends who were studying puppeteering, and took a class.

Kermit Love happened to be teaching, and the class changed Pam's life. She began her hands-on training in the Muppet style. In 1980, while she was a graduate student in puppetry at the University of Connecticut, she heard about the weeklong audition for Snuffy.

She lost out to Marty—they really needed a six-footer to hoist the basketball-hoop-height Muppet—but she was one of the last few performers still standing by the weekend. She impressed everyone enough to be called back a few years later when Brian Meehl was leaving and *Sesame Street* needed someone to take over Grundgetta the Grouch. (Pam had finished her degree and was working on *The Great Space Coaster* with Kevin Clash at the time, forging yet another connection to the *Sesame Street* show.)

There was still one more hurdle to tackle, though: a three-month-long workshop in puppeteering that functioned like a kind of boot camp, whittling out performer after performer until only two were left. On her way out that last day, not sure she'd done well enough to make the cut, Pam paused to talk to producer Dulcy Singer.

"Should I show up again next week?" she remembers asking.

"Oh, no, no," said Dulcy. Pam's heart sank. But then Dulcy added: "Just show up in September. We'll send you the dates."

Pam's first day on set, she was handed a new female character the producers wanted to try out, an assistant for David in Hooper's Store. This was an unexpected development. Normally, new performers are assigned only right-handing duties.

"It was incredibly fun, incredibly challenging," she recalls.

David RUDMAN

COOKIE MONSTER, TWO-HEADED MONSTER, BABY BEAR, FLO BEAR,
SONNY FRIENDLY, ETC.

> **I love listening to this painting.**
> —BABY BEAR

David Rudman fell in love with puppets when he first saw *Sesame Street*. "It was everything that I liked," he recalls. "I liked art and sculpture. I liked television. These works of art coming to life . . . it was something I'd never seen before."

His feelings solidified when, while watching a Muppet special, he saw the camera pull back to reveal the puppeteers. "That was when I first realized, wait a minute," he says. "This is a job!"

David taught himself to build puppets and began performing, eventually at high school and on local TV shows in his hometown of Chicago. In 1981, after a lot of harassing phone calls to the Jim Henson Company and a visit to New York during his spring break, he landed a summer job building Muppets. Just before returning to college, David made an audition tape of his work to show Jim, using the red Muppet that would, years later, become Elmo. To his astonishment, David got a call a few months later from Jim's secretary with happy news:

"Jim loved your audition tape and he wants to meet you."

David raced right back to New York.

David performs one half of the Two-Headed Monster, along with Joey Mazzarino

"I'll quit college and just come to work for you!" he told Jim. But Jim wouldn't let him. "Stay in college," he advised. "But you can work for us during the summer."

David headed off to the University of Connecticut, coming back at intervals to perform in a variety of Muppet projects, including the movies *Labyrinth* and *The Muppets Take Manhattan*. After his graduation in 1985, he was invited to join *Sesame Street*. "It was a whole different thing," he recalls of those first days on the Street set, "very intimidating. . . . It was like a family. It had a flow."

Richard Hunt stepped in to help. On David's first day on set, the new puppeteer was supposed to right-hand for Richard on two segments. Instead, Richard offered him the role of primary puppeteer.

"I said, 'Are you sure? Can you just do that?'" David recalls.

Always a champion of the underdog, Richard waved away David's concerns. "Everyone will know who you are," he said.

David took on Sonny Friendly and the horns-down half of the Two-Headed Monster in 1992, after Richard passed away. "I worked with Richard for so long . . . I knew where those characters came from," David says. "I knew what his face and body would be doing, how he would physically perform those characters."

Later, he became the stand-in whenever Frank Oz wasn't available to perform Cookie Monster, trying to tap into the subtleties that Frank brought to the character—"the things that he would do between the lines," as David puts it. He continues to study tapes of Frank's performances to this day.

> **It's fun to wonder.**
> —BABY BEAR

Around the same time, David originated the character of lisping comic book artist Baby Bear. After noticing a lot of *R* words, like porridge, in a script, he got the idea to lisp the letter. The character quirk made everyone laugh, so writers developed Baby Bear scripts.

"David is different every take," says performer Matt Vogel. "I love watching and assisting David. He makes it fresh every time . . . living in the moment of the character, right then."

Colorful Characters

The expanding cast of *Sesame Street* puppeteers in the show's second decade on air meant a correspondingly larger crew of characters, many of them mind-bendingly nutty. A parade of Honkers and Dingers, who communicated only through noises, made their debut, along with a nonstop parade of Anything Muppets and monsters. Some made only fleeting appearances in a single segment, while others, like Dr. Nobel Price, stuck around long enough to become cemented in the minds of fans who grew up in the '80s. The misguided inventor, played first by Brian Meehl and later by Kevin Clash, became the bane of reporter Kermit's existence with his assortment of inventions, all of which were recognizable to giggling preschoolers under much more familiar names: talking stick (microphone); page-rememberer (bookmark); hoopy toss (basketball); handy-dandy-you-are-herezit (map); hoppity-hop (frog); foot snuggies (socks)—even gravity, which Nobel "discovers" after dropping his teddy bear 10,963 times.

> **Sesame Street News takes you once more to the far-off island laboratory of Dr. Nobel Price.**
>
> –ANONYMOUS ANNOUNCER

The briefly glimpsed, scene-setting painting that opened most Nobel Price segments

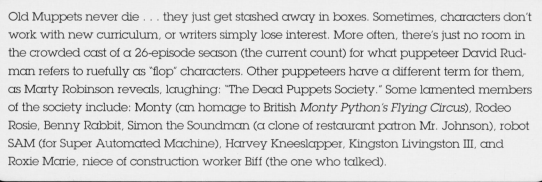

Old Muppets never die . . . they just get stashed away in boxes. Sometimes, characters don't work with new curriculum, or writers simply lose interest. More often, there's just no room in the crowded cast of a 26-episode season (the current count) for what puppeteer David Rudman refers to ruefully as "flop" characters. Other puppeteers have a different term for them, as Marty Robinson reveals, laughing: "The Dead Puppets Society." Some lamented members of the society include: Monty (an homage to British *Monty Python's Flying Circus*), Rodeo Rosie, Benny Rabbit, Simon the Soundman (a clone of restaurant patron Mr. Johnson), robot SAM (for Super Automated Machine), Harvey Kneeslapper, Kingston Livingston III, and Roxie Marie, niece of construction worker Biff (the one who talked).

making magic making magic making magic

> "Hi there, kid, I'm Captain Breakfast!"
>
> —CAPTAIN BREAKFAST

In episode 1836, Snuffy ran the New York City Marathon. These "remote location" scenes with Big Bird, Snuffy, and the Count were shot at daybreak on the Verrazano-Narrows Bridge. In another remote, in season 10, Oscar jogs in Central Park. That's shot during normal hours, but nonchalant New Yorkers don't even do a double take as they jog along beside the Grouch around the reservoir in the city's famous park. No one says a word.

> "Yip-yip-yip-yip-yip-yip! Ummmm. Ooooh! Uh-huh-uh-huh-uh-huh. Yip-yip-yip-yip-yip-yip!"
>
> —THE MARTIANS, AKA THE YIP-YIPS

Oscar's legs (appearing here in the jogging episode) are rarely seen—the last time they showed up, a child actor was inside the puppet

THIS CHAPTER HAS BEEN BROUGHT TO YOU BY THE LETTER Y AND THE NUMBER 26.2.

The letter Y is for **Yip-Yips**, the nickname used for the Martians who, since their first landing in 1974, irregularly visit Sesame Street. **The number 26.2** is the mile distance of the marathon Snuffy and Gordon run. Snuffy comes in last, after all the humans have gone. Oscar doesn't clock his mileage during his jog.

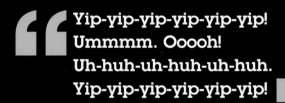

5

"When I saw James Earl Jones and the children, I knew that this was going to make contact educationally . . . and I wanted to volunteer. I called them.

—BILL COSBY

SESAME STREET

STICK OUT YOUR HAND AND SAY HELLO

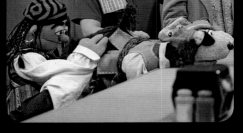

EPISODE
4135

Comedienne Tina Fey—star of *Saturday Night Live* and *30 Rock*—is surrounded by about twenty adults and children, three cameras, two large monitors and a scattering of small ones, lights, reflectors, a boom, and two teleprompters, all crammed into a small insert stage at the back of the *Sesame Street* set that recreates the interior of a snug little library.

It's early evening, and everyone on the set is a little tired. They've been working since 9:00 A.M., and there's still one more

scene to shoot. But Tina remains good-natured and focused. How could she not be? She's surrounded by a crew of puppet pirates who are about to discover the joys of taking out books from the library rather than hijacking them.

Today's episode is about Elmo's adventures with these Bookaneers—pirates who love to read. Tina is their swashbuckling captain. In addition to performing Elmo, Kevin Clash is directing; at the moment, he's conferring with Ken Diego, his assistant director, about the upcoming shot. Puppeteers drift in, including Joey Mazzarino, performing Salty Dog, and Tyler Bunch, First Mate, with Matt Vogel on right hand. Carmen Osbahr is there to handle puppet props.

Two child extras sit at a library table; two adults chat with each other. The set doesn't feel busy enough (populating the Street is a constant challenge), so Kevin ropes in another extra, hands him a book, and seats him at a table—but the extra's too

A fake facade and a few quickly assembled props create a whole new location on the Street: the library, where the pirates discover they can borrow books

tall, and now he's messing up camera op Frankie's shot. So the extras are repositioned.

Puppeteer Paul McGinnis scoots over on a round brown rollie, holding the fuchsia Anything Muppet who's playing the part of the librarian in the scene. Other Muppets get handed out. Soon the library looks crowded and cozy, a nice place to end the day. As the tech stuff gets worked out, Tina passes the time quietly talking to one of the kids, who's unmoved by Tina's fame but clearly delighting in the attention and the puppeteers' good-natured horsing around as they wait. Salty Dog nestles into Tina's side, and she absentmindedly scratches him behind the ears.

"Nice and quiet," says stage manager Shawn Havens. "Here we go. In five, four, three, two . . . "

Soon, one more scene is in the can.

The children are let go after a thank-you from Kevin and hugs from Elmo. The last shot of the day will be a close-up of pirate captain Tina, and Kevin decides not to rehearse. "Let's just shoot it, please," he suggests, hoping for a feeling of spontaneity.

Kevin's instincts are solid: the performances are perfect. "It's

When Tina Fey made an appearance on Conan O'Brien's late-night talk show in 2008, it was a meeting of minds—and of *Sesame Street* alumni. (In one of Conan's *Sesame Street* guest shots, he coincidentally played a late-night talk show host.) The two chatted about wanting to limit their children's television exposure, but Tina admitted that her daughter, Alice Zenobia—then 19 months old—was a fan of the Street. "She wakes up in the morning and goes, 'TV? Elmo? Elmo? TV? TV?' " Tina said.

Many celebrities bring their children to the set when taping an episode of the show. Tina Fey was no exception. Alice got to meet her favorite, Elmo, and some of his neighbors when her mom was taping. Tina would later tell *Parents* magazine that Alice appeared unfazed by the behind-the-scenes glimpses of puppeteers, "She just thinks, 'Okay, there's monsters here. That's real.' She met Elmo and spoke to him and never once remotely thought to look at the gentleman who operates Elmo."

Even celebrities—and busy parents—with very full calendars are easily recruited as guests. "Having grown up watching the show, you don't think twice," Tina said. "If they call and ask if you want to be on *Sesame Street* . . . 'Absolutely! When and where?' And when I got to the set, I found out what a juicy part I had: a pirate captain. Just the coolest."

a wrap!" someone calls. "Let's hear it for Tina Fey!" Kevin says. There's a round of applause and some cheers.

Yawning and stretching, pirate captain Tina leaves the puppet world behind, leading a ragged parade to the exit as everyone heads home.

Well, not everyone.

Art Director Victor DiNapoli's staff will stay to work on new sets into the night, to be ready for another day . . . another guest.

> **I was excited when I heard I was going to be with Elmo. Elmo's a rock star!**
>
> —TINA FEY

Most scripts for a season are written before the final guest stars have signed on, so this script lists only an anonymous pirate captain, Tina Fey's role on the show

SESAME STREET   REVISED #1 — MAZZARINO
                          6   SHOW 4139

THE AM SALTY DOG HOLDS UP A CAN OF BEANS WITH A LABEL ON IT THAT READS "LIMA BEANS." **(RESEARCH NOTE: THE "L" AND THE "B" SHOULD BE UPPERCASE, THE REST OF THE LETTERS SHOULD BE LOWERCASE)**

AM PIRATES SING:

Read, read, read, read,
We're pirates who love to read.
Read, read, read, read,
We're pirates who love to read!!!

<u>MUSIC</u>: ENDS.

CAPTAIN: Now that you know who we are, hand over the book!

ELMO: But Elmo loves his book.

CAPTAIN: You say you <u>love</u> your book, lad?

ELMO: Oh yes!! Elmo loves to read the stories in his book, and Elmo loves to look at the pictures in his book.

AM FIRST MATE: Why Captain, the little, red, furry, fella sounds like one of us.

AM SALTY DOG: He's a regular Bookaneer, he is!

ELMO: Yes! Elmo's a Bookaneer!

ELMO SINGS:

Read, read, read, read,
Elmo's a pirate who loves to read!

CAPTAIN: Calm your oars, laddie, you're not a Bookaneer yet!

(CONTINUED)

Bill Cosby and his young friends

NEWS FLASH

The slow, measured pace of James Earl Jones's famed recitation of A to Z was largely an accident—the actor was waiting for the animated letters to pop up in the on-set monitor before naming them. But those dramatic pauses ended up giving savvy kids at home the chance to shout out the sequence after repeated viewing. Show researchers named this kind of empowering cadence "The James Earl Jones Effect," and it became a convention for other shows that encouraged kids' participation.

May I Have Your Autograph?

Hundreds of guest stars have shown up on *Sesame Street* over the years. The show has long been a preferred destination for actors, athletes, astronauts, broadcasters, critics, musicians, politicians and presidents' wives, authors, super-heroes, talk show hosts, and United Nations secretary generals.

Some appear on the Street playing characters, as did comedi-enne Lily Tomlin or actor Neil Patrick Harris. Stars, such as Lena Horne, also act in Muppet inserts with puppet characters. Others perform solo, reciting the alphabet, counting, or defining the "Word on the Street," like NBC anchorman Brian Williams, model and reality-show host Heidi Klum, or actors Bill Cosby and James Earl Jones. (The latter actor's segments were included in the unaired test shows, technically making his the first celebrity appearance, although Carol Burnett's bit, taped in the studio where she filmed her own show, aired first.)

Judging from their on-screen enthusiasm, the performers all seem to love being dressed up as shoe fairies or elephants, dressed down by Elmo or Oscar, or simply pelted with puppet monsters.

"Hey, they're on *Sesame Street*," cameraman Frankie Biondo says. "They're happy to be here. They have an up attitude. I mean, you've got Elmo . . . Bert . . . Big Bird. That's why they took the job."

Many guest-star performances, especially those involving musi-cal numbers, are produced with an audience of children on the set because children have been as essential to the Street as celebrities ever since that first episode, where Gordon introduced a small girl

named Sally to his neighbors.

"I think the charm of the show comes from the children—that kind of dangerous conversation that you can have with a kid," says Sonia Manzano, who plays Maria and is also a scriptwriter. During taping with one famous singer, she recalls, a child extra interrupted the song to ask, "How come you sweat so much?"

Children's flubs and non sequiturs provide essential windows into the thinking of the audience. And in the end, kids' responses are the final arbiter. Cofounder Joan Ganz Cooney remembers some educational advisors warning against the use of some adult per-formers like James Earl Jones. "This great bald head fills the screen doing nothing but reciting the alphabet, with dramatic expression," she says. "Adults warned us kids would be scared out of their wits, but instead they loved it and shouted the letters along with him."

No official photos exist of Carol Burnett's segments—they were shot in California, in a quick break from taping "The Carol Burnett Show"

James Earl Jones stopped by the Street again in 1979, to host the show's tenth anniversary special (and pick up some coffee from Hooper's Store)

Arts
and Letters

Joan Ganz Cooney's original pitch for the show, a report titled "Potential Uses for Television," first suggested the idea of using recognizable faces in the entertainment industry to attract children. The initial production team and researchers concurred—anything that kept parents in the room as they watched with their kids would help the learning process of the show. But the question remained: Would celebrities want to be on an experimental kids' television program?

It turned out they did—even before the show was a proven hit. Happily, Joan's previous work in documentary filmmaking and Executive Producer Dave Connell's wide-ranging contacts in the media made their initial approaches successful. Even in its first season, *Sesame Street* attracted top talent—James Earl Jones and Carol Burnett were both major stars by then. Carol's cameo aired nationally first; her only line: "Wow, Wanda the Witch is weird."

It turned out a lot of celebrities were ready for the challenge of playing against a puppet. Many turned out to be superb at it—or at least willing to give it a try. Jackie Robinson and Lou Rawls quickly followed Carol Burnett during that first year. Bill Cosby had no problem appearing on the show in its infancy either. And those appearances encouraged other celebrities (five hundred and counting) to agree to visit whenever their agents called. It's for a good cause, after all—helping to educate young children.

NEWS FLASH

Noted film and music-video director Spike Jonze credits *Sesame Street* with cementing his decision to cast James Gandolfini for a lead role in Spike's filming of Maurice Sendak's *Where the Wild Things Are* (2009): "I was thinking about him for the main character, and I knew his work from *The Sopranos*. Somebody mentioned to me, 'Have you seen him on *Sesame Street*?' So we got a copy of it and it sort of just sealed the deal. It was like 'He is everything I'd want. He has all of the emotionality, and also he's just so endearing when he is with the kids. That's a great clip.' "

Show-off.

—GROVER TO MADELINE KAHN AFTER HER MAD CRESCENDO OF FIDDLE-DIDDLE-DEES

Madeline Kahn's guest spots have achieved legendary status—it's almost impossible to imagine a puppeteer concealed behind her during her charming duet, "Sing After Me"

Some of the show's guests listed in the Workshop's database

AARON CARTER
AARON NEVILLE
ALADDIN
ALEC BALDWIN
ALEX TREBEK
ALICE WALKER
ALICIA KEYS
ALISON KRAUSS
ALLAN HOUSTON
ALLISON JANNEY
ALVIN AILEY DANCERS
AMY ACUFF
AMY BRENNEMAN
AMY SEDARIS
AMY TAN
ANDERSON COOPER
ANDREA MARTIN
ANDY GARCIA
ANDY RICHTER
ANDY RODDICK
ANGEL CORELLA
ANGELA LANSBURGY
ANN CURRY
ANNE HATHAWAY
ANNETTE BENING
ARRESTED DEVELOPMENT GROUP
ARTE JOHNSON
ARTHUR ASHE
ARTHUR MITCHELL
ARTOO DETOO
AWADAGIN PRATT
B.B. KING
B.D. WONG
BACKSTREET BOYS
BARBARA BUSH
BARBARA WALTERS
BATMAN-ANIMATION
BELA FLECK
BEN GRAHAM
BEN STILLER
BENJAMIN GRAHAM
BILL COSBY
BILL IRWIN
BILL NYE
BILLY CRYSTAL
BILLY DEE WILLIAMS
BILLY JOEL
BLAIR BROWN
BLAIR UNDERWOOD
BO DIDDLEY
BO JACKSON
BOBBY McFERRIN
BONANZA
BRAD PAISLEY
BRANDY
BRANFORD MARSALIS
BROOKLYN YOUTH CHORUS
BUDDY & JIM
BURT LANCASTER
C3PO
CAB CALLOWAY
CANDIAN BRASS
CAROL BURNETT
CAROL CHANNING
CAROLINE KENNEDY
CARLY SIMON
...
CHER
CELINE DIONNE
CHAD PENNINGTON
CHAD PENNINGTON — MY JETS
CHARLENE FOSTER-GAULT
CHARLES GRODIN
CHARLIE GIBSON
...

DANNY GLOVER
DAVE WINFIELD
DAVID ROBINSON (BASKETBALL)
DAVID SCHIENEN
DEADLY NIGHTSHADE
DEBORAH STARR
DEBRA WINGER
DENNIS FRANZ
DENYCE GRAVES
DENZELL WASHINGTON
DESTINY'S CHILD
DIANA KRALL
DIANA ROSS
DIANE SAWYER
DIXIE CHICKS
DIZZY GILLESPIE
DOMINIQUE DAWES
DON McLEAN
DONNY OSMOND
DORIS ROBERTS
DOROTHY DONNICAN
DOUBLE DUTCH JUMPERS
DOUG E. DOUG
DR. JOHN
DR. JULIE BROWN
DR. PHIL McGRAW
ED WINTERFEART
EDGAR KENDRICKS
EDIE FALCO
ELLA MITCHELL
ELLEN DEGENERES
EN VOGUE
EMERIL LAGASSE
ENRICO IGLESIAS
ERIC MANGINI
ERYKAH BADU
ETHEL KENNEDY
EVELYN GLENNIE
FAIRY GODPLANT
FAITH HILL & TIM McGRAW
FLIP WILSON
FOUR TOPS
FRAN DRESCHER
FRED NEWMAN
FRED WILLARD
GARTH BROOKS
GARY CARTER (METS)
GEENA DAVIS
GEORGE BENSON
GIGI JIANG (CHORAL HALL)
GIAN CARLO ESPOSITO (MICK)
GIANTS KNIGHT & THE PIPS
GLEN CLOSE
GLENN CLOSE
GLOBETROTTERS
GLORIA ESTEFAN
GOO GOO DOLLS
GREGORY HINES
GREGORY KIMBS
HARRY BELAFONTE
HARVEY FIERSTEIN
HEATHER HEADLEY
HELEN REDDY
HENRY WINKLER
HERBIE HANCOCK
HILLARY CLINTON
HOLLY NEAR
HOOTIE & THE BLOWFISH
INDIA.ARIE
ISAAC STERN
ISIAH THOMAS
ITZHAK PERLMAN
JACKIE JOYNER-KERSEE
JACKIE ROBINSON
JAIME LEE CURTIS
JANE FOX
JAMES BLUNT
JAMES EARL JONES
JAMES GALWAY
JAMES GANDOLFINI
JAMES TAYLOR
JAMIE LEE CURTIS
JANE CURTIN (CINDERELLA)
JASON ALEXANDER
JASON BIGGS
JAY LENO
JEFF GOLDBLUM
JENNIFER BROWN
JENNIFER NETTLES
JERRY ORBACH
JESSYE NORMAN
JILL SCOTT
JIM CARREY
JIM HABOR

JOAN CUSACK
JOAN RIVERS
JOCK SOTO
JODIE FOSTER
JOE MANTH
JOE PERCI
JOE SILVER
JOE TORRE
JOE WILLIAMS
JOHN CANDY
JOHN GILLESPIN
JOHN GOODMAN
JOHN LEGEND
JOHN LEGUIZAMO
JOHN McEHEN
JOHN MORIETTA
JOHN POPPER
JOHN STEWART
JOHNNY CASH
JOSE CARRERAS
JOSE FELICIANO
JOSE PERSER (LUIS'S UNCLE)
JOSEPH ESTATE OF WILLIAMS
???
JOSHUA BELL
JUDY COLLINS
JUGGLERS
JULIA LOUIS-DREYFUS
JULIA ROBERTS
JULIANNE MOORE
JULIUS ERVING (DR. J)
KAREEM GARDISON
KATHLEEN BATTLE
KATHLEEN TURNER
KATHY LEE GIFFORD
KATIE COURIC
KEISHA KNIGHT-PULLIAN
KEISHAWANNA (METS)
KEITH LOCKHART
KELLY RIPA (LETTER CARRIER)
KELSEY GRAMMER
KEN JENNINGS
KEVIN JAMES
KEVIN KLINE
KID N' PLAY
KNICKS
KOFI ANNAN
KRISTI YAMAGUCHI
KRISTIAN BUSH
L.T.O.D.-TIM SCANLIN
LADYSMITH
LANCE ARMSTRONG
LANG LANG
LARAINE NEWMAN
LARRY KING
LASSIE
LAURA BUSH
LAURENCE FISHBORNE
LAVERNBRUE COLES
LEA SALONGA
LEE ANN WOMACK
LENA HORNE
LIAM NEESON
LILY TOMLIN
LINDA RONSTADT
LISTEN MY BROTHER GROUP
LITTLE RICHARD
LITTLE THEATRE OF DEAF
LORETTA LYNN
LOS LONELY
LOS PLENEROS
LOU DIAMOND PHILLIPS
LOU RAWLS
LOUISE GOLD (OPERA DIVA)
LOUREEN LOPEZ
LUCKY PETERSON
LYNNE THISPER-BABA PENSON
MADELINE KAHN
MAGALIA JACKSON
MALCOLM JAMAL WARNER
MANDY PATINKEN (POLICEMAN)
MARGARET CHO
MARIA CONCHITA ALONSO
MARCHITIS
MARILYN HORNE
MARILYN SONGS-AGNT MAE
MARISA TOMEI
MARK LINN-BAKER
MARSAILS
MARTIN SHEEN
MARY HART
MASALA MATLIN
MARLEE MATLIN
MARTIN SHORT

MARTINA NAVRATIL
MARY ALBERT
MARY CARPENTER
MARY LOU WILLIAMS
MATT LAUER
MAX ROSENKRON
MAX ROACH
MAYA ANGELOU
MAYOR DINKINS
MEL GIBSON
MELISSA ETHERIDGE
MELVINA REYNOLDS (?)
MENUDO
MEREDITH VIERA
METS
MICHAEL CHANG
MICHAEL COONEY
MICHAEL DAVIS
MIDORI
MIKE MEYERS
NIKI BEN-ARI
MOOKIE WILSON
MOLLY SHANNON
MORGAN FREEMAN (season)
MR. ROGERS
MRS. BUSH
MS. GOOSE
NADIA-SALKONO-SCHESINE
NANE ANNAN
NAMRATOR (TIM CURRY)
NATALIE MERCHANT
NATALIE PORTMAN
NATHAN LANE
NATEN
NEVILLE BROTHERS
NEW YORK CITY BALLET DANC
NATEN
NEW YORK GIANTS
NEW YORK JETS & KIDS
NICK CARTER
NINA SIMONE
NOAH WYLE
NORAH JONES
NONOKOTO KERNER (ORTIZ)
NY JETS — ERIC MANGINI
NY JETS — LAVERANUS COLE
NY TYO BEN GRAHAM
OONITA
OOKIE DAVIS
ORPHAN
P. PIPER
PAT TROLSEN
PATRICK STEWART
PATTI LABELLE
PAUL SIMON
PAULA POUNDSTONE
PEE WEE HERMAN
PEGGY FLEMMING
PETE SEEGER
PETER JENNINGS
PHIL DONAHUE
PHIL SIMMS
PHOEBE CATES
PHYLLIS DILLER
PICABO STREET (SKIER)
PILOBOLUS DANCE GROUP
POINTER SISTERS
QUEEN LATIFAH
R. FURGASON
RACHAEL RAY
RALPH NADER
RANDY TRAVIS
RAVEN SYMONE
RAY BARRETTO
RAY CHARLES
RAY ROMANO
REBECCA LOBO
REGIS PHILBIN
REM
RENEE FLEMING
REV. JESSE JACKSON
RHEA PERLMAN
RICHARD BELZER
RICHARD KIND
RICHARD PRYOR
RICHARD STELMAN
RICHIE RAVENS
RITA DOVE (POST LAUREATE)
RITA MORENO
ROB GOTTFRIED

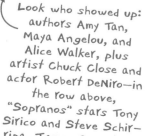

Look who showed up: authors Amy Tan, Maya Angelou, and Alice Walker, plus artist Chuck Close and actor Robert DeNiro—in the row above, "Sopranos" stars Tony Sirico and Steve Schirripa, James Gandolfini, and Edie Falco

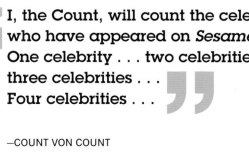

I, the Count, will count the celebrities who have appeared on *Sesame Street*! One celebrity . . . two celebrities . . . three celebrities . . . Four celebrities . . .

—COUNT VON COUNT

Anthony Daniels's own Polaroid from one of the days of taping—in all, they taped 15 segments

When *Star Wars* characters C-3PO and R2-D2 landed (literally) on *Sesame Street*, the smaller robot was manipulated via remote control (including during the scene in which he falls in love with a fire hydrant). But Anthony Daniels, the actor behind the iconic, irascible C-3PO, was on hand to re-create his role on the Street.

"I spent about a week in the studio, and I didn't want to leave," he says now. "For the first time I was with people who understood people in costume. And the human characters interact so well with the creatures; they make you believe [that the puppets are real,] just like Mark Hamill made you believe, in a nonhuman entity." Anthony reveals that R2-D2's beeping dialogue is looped in later, so movie scenes together were usually "silent and quite lonely—I was going mad talking to myself, really." He adds: "On *Sesame Street*, everyone babbles along all the time, though in a hugely professional way. The atmosphere was one of almost permanent joy. I was thrilled."

Another "Star Wars" veteran, Natalie Portman, also guested on the show

Jamie Foxx, Jimmy Fallon, Adam Sandler, Christopher Reeve, Carol Channing, Sarah Jessica Parker, Denzel Washington, and Patrick Stewart are some of the diverse stars that can label themselves Sesame Street alumni

Some familiar actors show up in the personas they play on television, like Fred Rogers of "Mister Rogers' Neighborhood," Lassie, and Henry Winkler's Fonzie character next to Ron Howard's Richie

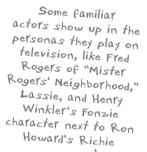

Neil Patrick Harris, far right, and Paul Rudd take breaks during taping to act as puppeteers

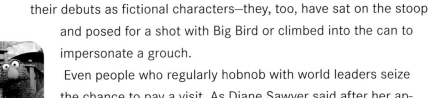

News
Makers

Brian Williams charms the cast and crew—he also hosted the Workshop's 2009 fundraising gala; Katie Couric, Phil Donahue, and Kofi Annan are also show veterans

They are the newsmakers and newsbreakers . . . the people that you often see on your television sets, newsstands, or newsfeeds every day. Politicians, astronauts, news anchors, first ladies—sometimes appearing as themselves but often making their debuts as fictional characters—they, too, have sat on the stoop and posed for a shot with Big Bird or climbed into the can to impersonate a grouch.

Even people who regularly hobnob with world leaders seize the chance to pay a visit. As Diane Sawyer said after her appearance on the show, "They called, that's all. It's the equivalent of winning the Nobel Peace Prize."

In 2009, First Lady Michelle Obama, who just a few months before had stood beside her husband as he was sworn in as America's first African-American president, had a similar reaction. Meeting United Nations delegates for the first time just hours after taping her segment for the show, she told them, "I'm thrilled to be here, but I was just at *Sesame Street*. I never thought I'd be on *Sesame Street* with Elmo and Big Bird, and I was thrilled. I'm still thrilled. I think it's probably the best thing I've done so far in the White House."

Moon walker Buzz Aldrin and shuttle crew member Sally Ride on the show

Anchors and talk show hosts, such as Anderson Cooper or Barbara Walters (who appeared in *Stars and Street Forever!* and *The Sesame Street Special*), often spoof their on-screen personas. But like Diane Sawyer, Barbara also unexpectedly broke out into song for the celebrity chorus of "Put Down the Duckie." Kelly Ripa, meanwhile, has played a character (in "Elmo's World") and also appeared as herself, in "Word on the Street" segments.

Jesse Jackson was one of the first political icons to appear as a guest star on *Sesame Street*. In 1971, he read children a poem he'd authored: "I Am Somebody." Later, the cast, including Bob, Loretta, Will, and Matt, made a special appearance at a community center in Chicago, Jesse's home base.

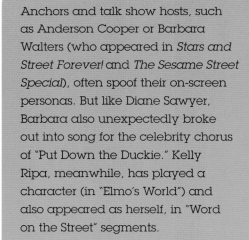

Joan Ganz Cooney met Bill Clinton at a summit about children's issues, and Hillary Clinton visited the Street in season 25

Amy Carter climbed into Oscar's can on a visit to the set of "The Electric Company" and called it one of her best days ever

The cast was asked to do a guest stint at the White House Christmas party for kids during both the Nixon and Ford administrations

Seen here backstage, Ethel Kennedy, Robert Kennedy's widow, made a cameo on the show in its very first season

Nearly every White House administration since 1969 has had a *Sesame Street* experience. At times, the show's cast pays the visit, as they did to the Ford and Nixon families, but first ladies Hillary Clinton and Barbara Bush, above, and Laura Bush and Michelle Obama, below, have brought their senses of humor to the Street, appearing in show segments.

Laura Bush read aloud from a prop book based on the song "Monster in the Mirror"

SESAME STREET — 43 —
SANTEIRO
SHOW 4032

22.   L. BUSH READS W/ELMO AND BIG BIRD

TITLE: L. BUSH READS W/ELMO AND BIG BIRD   TIME: 1:56
PRODUCTION# 34-0280   SHOW/ITEM #: 4032-22
WRITER: FERRARO   DIRECTOR: DINAPOLI   AD WILLIAMS   PA ROSA
AUDIO IN: AUDIO OUT:
VIDEO IN: VIDEO OUT:
PROD DATES: 9/19/02   VT 1: 34121   VT 2: 34122   BETA# 114119
                      VT 3: 34123   VT 4: 34124   CASS:
                      VT 1:   VT 2:   CASS:
                      STEREO 8 TRACKS   P/B: RECORD:
GOALS   READING FUNDAMENTALS: BOOKS, CULTURAL APPRECIATION
SCENIC: ARBOR
TALENT: MRS. BUSH, BIG BIRD, ELMO, (3) KIDS
GRAPHICS: BOOK: "WUBBA, WUBBA, WOO"

MRS. BUSH IS SITTING AT A TABLE WITH A BOOK IN FRONT OF HER. ELMO, BIG BIRD, AND A FEW KIDS ARE GATHERED AROUND ON EITHER SIDE OF HER, BEHIND HER, ETC., SO THEY CAN READ ALONG.

BIG BIRD AND ELMO LAUGH.

BB: (TO CAM) Oh, hi! We're here with our friend, Laura Bush!

MRS BUSH: (TO CAM) Hello!

BB: (TO CAM) ...And she's going to read a book to us!

MRS. BUSH: That's right. This is a fun book called... (SHOWS BOOK TO CAM) "Wubba, Wubba, Woo!"

Good Sports

The Harlem Globetrotters, top, make an early appearance—Grand Slammer Arthur Ashe comes by later, above

The Knicks, above, show up; Martina Navratilova, right, sings with Bob; and Rebecca Lobo promotes the letter O, below

Few guests could appreciate the deliberate teamwork of the puppeteers and cast better than the sports stars that have popped up on the show. A dizzying array of athletes have fielded all the craziness that a day on set throws at them. Former Los Angeles Sparks' center Lisa Leslie has been watching sports stars' appearances on the show for years, first as a kid, then as a sports giant herself (four-time winner of Olympic gold and three-time Women's National Basketball Association MVP), and finally as a parent to her daughter, Lauren.

At 6 feet 5 inches, Leslie says, "I totally identified with Big Bird." But now she's learning to love Elmo, Lauren's favorite.

"Elmo has taught her so much," Leslie reports, "She knows all her ABCs and her numbers up to thirty, and a lot of that has come from *Sesame Street*."

A woman making groundbreaking moves on the court—she was the first to dunk in a WNBA game—Leslie appreciates the show's dedication to featuring sports stars, and especially women athletes. "I think it's awesome that we introduce sports to kids at that young age," she says, "And I can say from a female perspective, it helps to break down that gender barrier that we experience later. I think it's important for boys to see that, too."

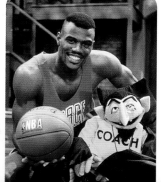

David Robinson, of the San Antonio Spurs, gets coached (and counted) in season 29

> **They have a miniature Kobe! We can play one-on-one on *Sesame Street*.**
>
> —KOBE BRYANT

Tennis pro Venus Williams teams up with Elmo in an imaginary game, above, and the 76ers' All-Star Julius Erving battles Oscar's No-Stars, right

David Beckham gives (and gets) a lesson in persistence, above; the Redskins' Jason Taylor receives a cow, right; and Tim McCarver rewards Slimey's persistence, below

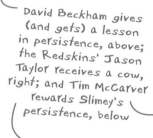

Olympians visit, like Picabo Street, left, and Dominique Dawes, below (an advisor on the Workshop's healthy habits initiative)

Local teams, like New York's Giants and Jets, stop by, as do players such as famed Jets quarterback Joe Namath, top, and multisport player Bo Jackson, left

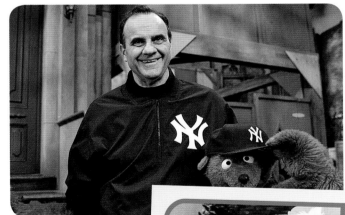

New York's rival baseball teams, the Yankees and the Mets, both hit for the Sesame team: coach Joe Torre, above left, Keith Hernandez and Mookie Wilson, below, and Dave Winfield and Ron Darling, left

Workshop cofounder Joan Ganz Cooney (second from left) and its outreach coordinator, Evelyn Davis (center, in glasses), meet with former Brooklyn Dodgers' second baseman Jackie Robinson in 1969. Jackie, center, screens the pitch reel here and agrees to appear on the show. He recites the alphabet in season one.

SESAME STREET
123
Ron Darling

SESAME STREET
123
Dave Winfield

Play It Again

When she was growing up, singer Leslie Feist envisioned herself as a puppeteer one day; as a kid, she'd crafted puppets named Rat-Fink and Smurfy that she used in local performances.

"How surreal is this?" she told *Rolling Stone* magazine during a taping with the Muppets. "There was a moment when I stood at the crossroads and decided between puppets or music. Today almost sparked a tear in my eye, seeing things come full circle."

The Canadian singer is one in a distinguished line of musicians who have appeared on the show in its curriculum-enhancing musical numbers. Spike Jonze, whose music videos launched an acclaimed film-directing career, was inspired by those segments.

"When I first started doing music videos, I would go back to *Sesame Street* and *The Electric Company* in terms of just how simple they are . . . . They would take an idea and make this little short film or even music video that had such simplicity and charm," he says. "You can imagine

Lena Horne's appearance on the show is one that tops most hit lists for kids who grew up to become the show's first generation of fans. Her rendition of "Bein' Green" is deeply soulful and helped the song become a civil rights anthem.

Journalist Chuck Klosterman says of *Sesame Street*'s young audience: "When R.E.M. goes on *Sesame Street* and a little kid is watching that clip and starts dancing, it's not because he is trying to illustrate that he is interested in alternative music. That might be the only time that R.E.M. can perform in a situation where their audience is solely interested in the sonic quality of what they're creating."

them making it in an afternoon . . . it's not tortured in any way."

Chuck Klosterman is a journalist and author known as a pop culture and music guru. He has an extensive knowledge of musical performers, and he can't imagine anyone who would turn down a guest slot.

"No one is going to say no to this," he asserts. "Slayer would go on *Sesame Street*. And Slayer would smile, and they would be nice, and they would do a funny version of 'Raining Blood.' "

Same-day rehearsals lend spontaneity to star turns by R.E.M., Gloria Estefan, Tim McGraw and Faith Hill, Herbie Hancock, Johnny Cash, above, Queen Latifah, and Wyclef Jean, below

Behind the scenes, Lena Horne gets up close and personal with costar Grover, with whom she sings "How Do You Do?" in one of several guest shots on the show

Victor Borge, on piano, entertains director Jon Stone

Sheryl Crow also supported the show by making an appearance at a Workshop fundraiser in 2009

> It was the best day of my life . . . the Muppets trump everything!

—LESLIE FEIST

NEWS FLASH

Leslie Feist's appearance on the show was one of the first to be impacted by viral media. The singer's whimsical homage to her single "1234" triggered an explosion of interest. Soon after a clip was released online, it generated tens of thousands of hits on YouTube and was passed along all over the Internet. The power and passion of fans—not only of the show but also simply music fans—continue to shape the way the Workshop promotes the show in an increasingly digital world.

Virtually every musical genre has gotten its due on the show over its forty years, from opera to reggae to pop—including appearances by, to name a few, the legendary Victor Borge, Destiny's Child, Marilyn Horne, Randy Jackson, Harry Belafonte, Sheryl Crow, India Arie, Jason Mraz, above, Paul Simon, left, Ray Charles, and dancers with the Mark Morris and Alvin Ailey companies, below. And as the contract here attests, guests all appear on Sesame Street at scale rates, for love of the show and to support Sesame Workshop's not-for-profit educational mission.

See You on the Street

From day one, part of what made the show and set resonate with kids at home were the kids on the screen. Whether they're swaying lazily on a tire swing or rolling by on a trike or sharing an adventure with one of the Muppets, the naturalistic performances of the show's enormous cast of child guests have helped define the you-are-there experience of *Sesame Street.*

No one knows the impact that these largely nameless characters have had on the audience at home more than Polly Stone, Director/Producer/Head Writer Jon Stone's daughter. Preschooler Polly made an appearance on the show in a bit with Grover. Years later, when she was in her thirties, a four-year-old who knew the adult Polly called her at work one day to say he'd seen her on *Sesame Street.*

"His babysitter was the one who dialed the phone and she said, 'Would you please explain to this child that he's wrong? He's determined that he saw you on *Sesame Street*, and I'm tired of this argument,' " Polly recalls wonderingly, "So he got on the phone, and said, 'You were saying the alphabet to Grover, but you left out M and you stopped at V. You weren't very good at it.' "

" 'You know, you're right,' " Polly told him. " 'You saw me on *Sesame Street.*' "

Director Jim Martin says one reason for the show's success is the *set's* success. "I love the *Sesame Street* set," he reports, "because you have this sense of theatricality and film meshed into one. I think that's what makes the show so real for kids. When Big Bird sits on the steps, you know he is really on the steps. When Oscar comes out of the can, you know he is really in the can. Wasn't that the reason *Sesame Street* was created? To ground the show in an urban setting that kids could relate to? It wasn't a fantasy show as much as a reality show with a sprinkling of fantasy."

Jim Henson's son Brian makes an appearance counting peas and other foods; he also starred in a short film in which he digs in a sandbox, pretending to be a fleet of trucks

NEWS FLASH The *Sesame Street* audience was treated to a performance by Jim Henson's oldest son, Brian—now co-chair and co-CEO of the Jim Henson Company—on November 10, 1969, during episode one. Six-year-old Brian's one line was, "Three peas?" Cheryl Henson, Jim's daughter, who worked as a liaison between Sesame Workshop and the Jim Henson Company after her father's death, didn't actually appear on the show until she was an adult. "I was in a crowd scene when Slimey came home from the moon," she recalls. "I happened to be out at the studio, so I got to be in the background as a person."

Sonia Manzano—Maria on the show—describes why casting kids is so important. It lets the cast see a child's viewpoint. "You'll do a scene where the kid will say, 'What can you do with your hands?'" Sonia explains. "You wave, point, all the things that you can think of, and then the kid says, 'You forgot one thing. You could check your tooth to see if it's loose.'"

Demand to visit the Street is consistently high, so casual guests are rarely admitted to the set. But staffers' family members, guest stars' kids, and children sent by the Make-a-Wish Foundation are often nearby.

"I love to see kids react to the puppets," Sonia Manzano says. "One time, I was standing by a four-year-old when Caroll Spinney took the top half of his Bird suit off. The kid turned to his mother and said, 'Mom, does Big Bird know there's a man in him?'"

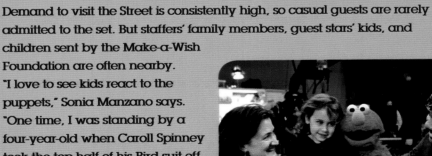

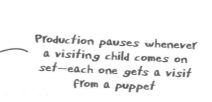

Production pauses whenever a visiting child comes on set—each one gets a visit from a puppet

First Comes Love . . .

Sonia Manzano, playing Maria, was already pregnant here, so writers created a romance between Maria and Luis

Sonia Manzano's real-life child played the role of Gabi for two seasons . . .

Children love watching other kids interact with *Sesame Street*'s Muppets and cast, and research supports the notion that children can learn more readily when they watch their youthful on-screen counterparts tackling problems. So it was always a priority for the show to feature children learning and growing on the street, both as occasional guests and as long-term residents.

But the introduction of young cast members on *Sesame Street* embodies something more: the show's commitment to reflecting the diversity of the families watching it. When the character of Maria gave birth to Gabi on the show, it launched stories about the joys of family and also about responsibility and trust. And later, when Susan and Gordon adopted their son, Miles, it created a situation that was groundbreaking at the time. Adopted families were far less prominent in media at that point, and African-American families created through adoption were virtually invisible.

More recently, the show's resident vet, Gina, has become a single mom, adopting a child of another ethnicity: Marco, who is from Guatemala. Baby Marco's continuing story arc will provide show writers with opportunities to tackle issues of diversity and nontradi-

tional families at a level appropriate for preschoolers.

Because of the power of these storylines, the children starring in them have become fixtures on the Street and beloved of the show's second and third generation of viewers.

The role of the Rodriguez's baby, Gabi, was first played by Gabriella Rose Reagan, the real-life infant of Sonia Manzano (Maria), beginning when Gabi was ostensibly born, in 1989. When it became clear that toddler Gabriella didn't love the spotlight, Sonia took her off the show, and the role has been played ever since by Desiree Casado, who has quite literally grown up on *Sesame Street*.

Miles has gone through the same growing pains. He was first performed by the young son of actor Roscoe Orman (Gordon), also named Miles. After seven years in the role, the real Miles was ready for

. . . Then Desiree took over as Gabi

The show expanded on Miles' adoption storyline with later segments, including one where Susan and Gordon share family pictures with their son, at the time played by Imani Patterson. Elmo's puppeteer, Kevin Clash, played the role of their grown-up son in a season 18 dream sequence, but the adult Miles has been played by Olamide Faison since 2003 (seen left).

Desiree Casado and Olamide Faison

Desiree Casado and Miles Orman

↑ Nathan Zoob, Desiree, Tarah Schaeffer, Imani, and Lexine Bondoc, circa 1993— below, Carlo Alban and Joey Calvan →

Marco's homecoming was greeted with a visit from Big Bird and his squadron of Birdkateers. Many kids have acted in the role of the Bird's fan club of brightly feathered friends.

a change, and Imani Patterson stepped in for the next decade. Next to assume the role was Olamide Faison, who continues as the grown-up Miles today. He and Gabi have grown up together, playing on the Street with other kid guests; they're now old enough for their characters to go off to college. In fact, some of the Miles and Gabi generation of viewers are starting to have kids of their own, who now watch the show and will be growing up alongside baby Marco.

A day in the life of one of the child actors on the show—like Joey Calvan, seen above with Executive Producer Jon Stone—is pretty standard for the industry: tutored on location, their hours on set are limited. On *Sesame Street*, where many scenes are worked out on the fly and must be adapted to its unique production issues, the young actors become part of the directorial team, meeting up with puppeteers and producers, then watching instant playback to help refine their performances.

Sesame Street's most famous young graduate has to be John Williams III, better known as John-John. John-John won a place in viewers' hearts with his effortless connection to the Muppets and the bold confidence of his delivery in numerous seg-

ments. The bit most commonly cited by fans: counting to 20 with Herry. John-John stumbles a bit but then gamely continues to a triumphant finish. The show's research team is adamant about keeping in the hesitations and flubs by child actors—those teach-by-example moments serve as excellent models for viewers at home. The grown-up John-John, an Air Force graduate with a family of his own, remembers the show fondly.

Star Turns

What happens when you put a comedian in the same room as a Muppet? Both get a little funnier. And what's the result of mixing world-class musicians with an audience of kids too young to know they should be awed? Magic. It's a testament to the performers' skill that the interaction looks so effortless, though, because *Sesame Street* demands an imaginary leap from its guest stars and child actors.

"People can be very uncomfortable talking to a puppet," explains Fran Brill, who performs Prairie Dawn and others. "They're looking at Ping-Pong balls and a bag of fleece. Some people are really good at it and treat the puppet as a person, and some are not."

While the Workshop's lips are sealed about any guests who struggle, there's no denying the chemistry during moments as diverse as Stevie Wonder's nearly seven-minute "Superstition" jam,

or comedienne Jane Curtin's rapport with the Two-Headed Monster, or Comedy Central talk-show host Jon Stewart's banter with Prairie in *Sesame Street*'s 30th-year special, *Elmopalooza*.

> **"You know what, Grover? You did it better than me."**
>
> —STEVIE WONDER TO GROVER, AFTER THEIR SCAT-SINGING SESSION

A trooper, Stevie Wonder taped five segments in a single day, including a funk version of the "Sesame Street Theme" with his band

Sesame Street writer Jim Thurman also supplies jokes for Bob Hope—Big Bird's stint on the star's 1979 "Road to China" special inspires the Bird's own excursion, for "Big Bird in China."

Lily Tomlin appears in five segments, sometimes in her famous comic persona, childlike Edith Ann.

Jane Curtin tapes this segment with the Siamese twin monsters, as well as the 25th-year special and "Put Down the Duckie."

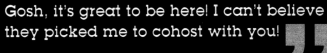

"Gosh, it's great to be here! I can't believe they picked me to cohost with you!"

—STEPHEN COLBERT AS THE LETTER Z, ON "ALL-STAR ALPHABET" (WITH NICOLE SULLIVAN AS THE LETTER A)

An astonishingly star-studded array of comedians have done funny stuff on the Street, as this small collection of appearances shows: Ben Stiller, Bob Hope, Lily Tomlin, Jane Curtin, Richard Pryor, Ellen DeGeneres, Martin Short and Billy Crystal, Jon Stewart, Margaret Cho, Andrea Martin, Rosie O'Donnell, Amy Sedaris, Wayne Brady, Ricky Gervais, John Candy, and Conan O'Brien.

THIS CHAPTER HAS BEEN BROUGHT TO YOU BY THE LETTERS AND NUMBER C-3PO.

The letters and number C-3PO are for Anthony Daniels's character in the *Star Wars* films. After his stint on *Sesame Street*, Anthony "wished they'd asked me to stay." One reason? He cites "this huge sense of love all around—not in a horrible Pollyanna way but in an inventive, fun, and protective way." He says of his own character, "He's very caring, and so are the characters on the Street. It's a very socialized world, a very good paradigm ."

6

"Here I was, working next to my heroes. That's all I ever wanted to do, since I was a small child . . . work for the Muppets on *Sesame Street*."

—PETER LINZ, PUPPETEER

EPISODE
4149

Abby Cadabby sits quietly on the wrangler's table along with a purple monster and Prairie Dawn, waiting for her cue. Today, Big Bird, Elmo, and Abby—a fairy-in-training and the Workshop's latest major Muppet character—will be singing about their still-new friendship.

Leslie Carrara-Rudolph, the puppeteer who performs Abby, enters wearing a black and green Count von Count T-shirt—puppeteers frequently sport clothes with one another's characters. Leslie hunkers down on the floor beside Kevin Clash, Caroll Spinney and director Emily Squires perch nearby on some apple boxes, and the four quickly go over the next scene.

At 10:45 a.m., there is a full rehearsal. Puppeteer Matt Vogel becomes welded to Leslie's side like a Siamese twin. He will help her perform Abby, occasionally working the rod that moves the puppet's right hand and magic wand, as well as handling the big black radio-control box, complete with antennae, that enables Abby to flap her wings and "fly." The wing mechanism, or "mechie" as it's often called, is in a heavy backpack that Leslie normally has to wear. But Kevin volunteers to shoulder it in this scene.

The only person not performing a Muppet is Caroll Spinney; he simply holds his naked arm in the air as he recites Big Bird's lines.

When Leslie mimes Abby's exit—being a fairy, Abby simply waves her magic wand and disappears—a tinkly sound is heard on set in playback. Even during the rehearsal, somebody in audio is paying attention.

Whenever Abby magically appears or disappears, it also requires a stop tape. Everyone and everything in the scene has to freeze while Abby ducks in or out of the frame, resuming movement in sync after a countdown. That tinkling sound of Abby's wand is also everyone's cue to freeze.

Big Bird has just suited up when a baby and its mother, guests on the set, wander by. Everyone is instantly distracted. ("Things stop for every guest," cameraman Frank Biondo explains, "bigwig or not.") Pictures are taken as Elmo nuzzles the baby, who seems delighted. "That baby looks real!" says Abby Cadabby in surprise, and everyone laughs. After a moment, the group breaks up, and then it's back to work.

This time, Abby pops up too early. "There's no excuse, stupid-head," says Elmo to Abby. Abby bops Kevin on the head with her wand.

Tape is rolling. Shawn Havens counts down. "Five."

"Six!" Elmo pipes up.

"Four," Shawn says, valiantly ignoring him.

"Twelve," Elmo says.

Stage Manager Shawn Havens appears amused by Elmo's antics

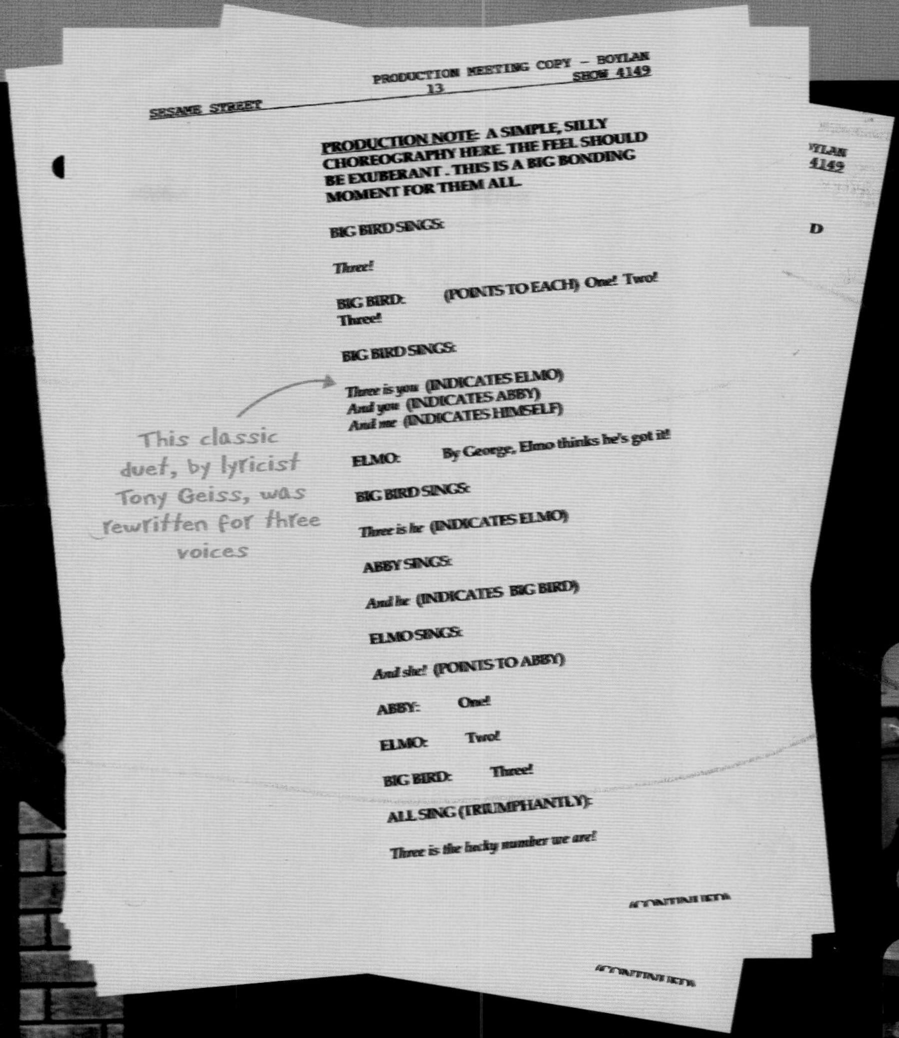

PRODUCTION MEETING COPY – BOYLAN
13   **SHOW 4149**

SESAME STREET   BOYLAN
                                                 4149

PRODUCTION NOTE: A SIMPLE, SILLY
CHOREOGRAPHY HERE. THE FEEL SHOULD
BE EXUBERANT . THIS IS A BIG BONDING
MOMENT FOR THEM ALL.

BIG BIRD SINGS: D

Three!

BIG BIRD: (POINTS TO EACH) One! Two!
Three!

BIG BIRD SINGS:

Three is you (INDICATES ELMO)
And you (INDICATES ABBY)
And me (INDICATES HIMSELF)

ELMO: By George, Elmo thinks he's got it!

BIG BIRD SINGS:

Three is he (INDICATES ELMO)

ABBY SINGS:

And he (INDICATES BIG BIRD)

ELMO SINGS:

And she! (POINTS TO ABBY)

ABBY: One!

ELMO: Two!

BIG BIRD: Three!

ALL SING (TRIUMPHANTLY):

Three is the lucky number we are!

(CONTINUED)

(CONTINUED)

*This classic
duet, by lyricist
Tony Geiss, was
rewritten for three
voices*

"Three," Shawn says very firmly.
"Twenty-four . . . hike!" Elmo shouts in reply.
Leslie cracks up. Her laughter is as girlish and infectious as her puppet's, and it quickly ignites giggles from everyone on set.
Elmo turns to her. "What are you—new?" he says disdainfully.
By now, Shawn is laughing too hard to finish the countdown.
Just as the snickers are dying down, Matt gently touches his radio-controlled machine, and Abby's fairy wings open and close, sparking another riddle of laughter.
Things finally settle down, and the threesome quickly nail the scene.
"Kill take," says Shawn. Time to move on.

*Thanks to clever edits and
camera angles, viewers
don't seem to notice that
Big Bird's height difference
would leave smaller
characters hovering in
midair for shots like this*

A New Generation

A good puppeteer is hard to find. Discovering one who can tackle the multiplicity of skills needed to perform expressive puppets on television—that's priceless.

"What no one realizes about working with puppets is how hard it is," explains Alan Muraoka, who should know. In the character of

Alan, proprietor of Hooper's Store, he's witnessed a parade of Muppets troop through his shop. "The puppeteers are often on the floor or rolling around on their backs, while they are acting, manipulating the puppet, watching their monitors to make sure that the puppet is looking in the right direction and performing up to their satisfaction, and reading off the script. It's a very complex process, and it always amazes me how easy they make it look."

It takes training to achieve that level of ease and skill and so, despite the additions of Kevin Clash, Marty Robinson, and other esteemed puppeteers to

the fold, by the mid-'80s it became clear that *Sesame Street* producers had to address an issue that became more pressing with each year—the need to recruit talent to sub for Jim Henson and Frank Oz in their roles as Ernie, Bert, Grover, Cookie Monster, and other iconic characters in the neighborhood. There were too many projects vying for Jim's attention, and Frank was ramping up a directorial career that began with *Little Shop of Horrors* in 1986. Both men were itching for more freedom from *Sesame Street*'s intensive taping schedule.

"I had four kids who were growing up, and I was directing, and I just couldn't do everything," Frank says. "It was only fair to let it go, so that's what happened.

"It was hurtful at the beginning," he says, describing the handing off of the bulk of his puppeteering of Grover, Cookie Monster, and Bert, "because the characters are so much a part of me; they're still in my heart, and I know them inside out. But at the end of the day, just because I can't work, they can't stop working."

Other puppeteers had come and gone over the years; voices and characters continually changed as some characters were being developed. Snuffy, Telly, Elmo—these Muppets evolved over time as different puppeteers took over a role. But what about a character that was already fully established and beloved? No one knew how successfully the show could replace the human talent behind (and under) the original *Sesame Street* icons.

Today, the answer is clear.

Caroll Spinney is currently mentoring Matt Vogel in the role of Big Bird. The role of Cookie Monster is performed maniacally and almost exclusively by David Rudman, as Frank's career more frequently takes him away from the Street. And Bert and Grover have been handed off to Eric Jacobson, who has perfected the two very different personas of those puppets, uncannily mimicking Frank's brilliant puppeteering.

"Eric Jacobsen and those guys have been very respectful," Frank says of the transition process. "They've done a great job, and I'm just pleased that they're there."

> **Caroll is amazing . . . just fearless. He just trusts and goes for it. They actually asked me one season, 'If Caroll can't do it, can you roller-skate?' And I said, 'Uh, no. I'll walk, I'll dance, I'm happy to do it, but I can't get on roller skates.'**
>
> —MATT VOGEL

Finally, Steve Whitmire has delicately placed his own stamp on the characters of Ernie and Kermit. These transitions, the source of intense adult-fan scrutiny, appeared undetectable to the preschoolers watching the show. They were the result of patience, practice, and great sensitivity to each of these characters. They also were the result of heartbreak and, ultimately, healing . . . because they were triggered not by Jim's new work in other fields but by the tragic news of his death on May 16, 1990.

While traveling to promote his wide range of media projects, Jim left untreated a bacterial infection he thought was a nagging cold or flu. Pleas by family finally sent him to a hospital for care, but it was too late. The infection, later diagnosed as streptococcal toxic shock syndrome, attacked his system and eventually shut it down. Suddenly, shockingly, Jim Henson was gone.

That's Steve under the puppet, on his first tentative test as Ernie; he's assisted by puppeteers Paul McGinnis and Frank Oz here and, below right, director Jon Stone

NEWS FLASH In Steve's first segment as Ernie, Bert is envious of his buddy's success on a fishing trip. Ernie suggests Bert call for them: "Here, fishies, fishies, fishies!" It works for Ernie, who attracts a boatload of dinner-size fish. Bert attracts a shark. As always, kids giggled along with Ernie's signature snicker, cementing Steve's assumption of the role.

The world, and especially his Muppet family, reeled from the news. More than one of them, even in the midst of grieving, must have wondered: What would become of the Muppets Jim left behind?

Jim Henson's own family and local *Sesame Street* legend concur that Jim himself was already thinking of the up-and-coming young puppeteer named Steve Whitmire as his successor to the roles of Kermit and Ernie. Still, even with Jim's tacit approval, it was enormously wrenching for everyone to contemplate the switch during those dark days. Ernie, especially, existed in a symbiosis with Bert; Jim and Frank had honed a rapport that was indescribable.

"There were quite a few years when they didn't do Ernie at all," puppeteer Peter Linz recalls. He was one of the few people on the set one quiet day in 1993 when Ernie finally reappeared. In fact, it wasn't the normal set at all, but a corner of the Henson Carriage House, normally used by the Jim Henson Company as offices and a photo studio. "It was all hush-hush," Peter explains. "A test. It was the first time Steve was doing Ernie, and Frank was great. He is always so gracious and giving. He has a wonderful sense of humor, even with something delicate like that."

Taking on these characters requires respect from both sides. Matt, who will be Big Bird when Caroll retires, says of the shift to come: "The character may be a little bit different from Caroll, just like Kermit is a little bit different now than he was with Jim, but you make it your own. You'll have to, really. There's kind of an evolution that happens when somebody takes over for someone else. My starting point has to be Caroll, because he is the character. But then I try to make it fresh and real and in the moment."

With so many sensitive puppeteers willing to help carry the torch, the Muppets will be around for a long, long time to come.

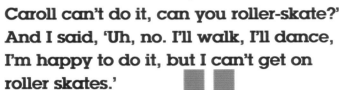

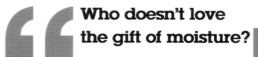

Joey and Davey made their first appearance in season 24—the two monkeys are the alter egos of Joey and partner-in-crime David Rudman

Joey MAZZARINO

MURRAY MONSTER, HORATIO THE ELEPHANT, STINKY, COLAMBO, JOEY MONKEY, ETC.

> **" Who doesn't love the gift of moisture? "**
>
> —STINKY THE STINKWEED, ARTICULATING THE SHOW'S "GREEN" CURRICULUM

1967–today 1987–today 1987–today

Joey Mazzarino was at Fordham University when puppeteer Camille Bonora came to teach a comedy improv class. He'd been working at a day care in his free time, so he was familiar with *Sesame Street*. When he found out that Camille performed Meryl Sheep, he flipped.

"I said, 'That was hilarious!'" Joey recalls. "'Because I loved the accent you did, just like Meryl Streep.'" Camille was flattered and issued an invitation to the set. When Joey finally took her up on her offer, it was a day Jim Henson was performing. "I was just flabbergasted to meet him," Joey says. "I didn't know what to say."

But the most pivotal moment that day came when Joey saw Richard Hunt perform. "If I remember correctly, he was doing a waiter puppet. . . . He cracked up the crew off camera, he was so funny. And I said, 'I want to be that guy. I want to do that.'"

"I didn't even know this was a job, you know?" Joey continues. "So I went back to Fordham, and I went to the costume shop, and I said, 'Do you guys have anything I can make a puppet out of?' And I went home and I kind of got obsessed."

For the next year, he built puppets in his basement at night. "And during the day, if I wasn't at school, I was training in front of a camera," he says. "My parents thought I was nuts. They said, 'What are you doing? You don't see your girlfriend anymore. You're going insane.'" But it paid off. A year later, Camille asked Joey if he wanted to join a Muppet workshop. Soon after, he was hired.

It was just two years after *that* when producer Lisa Simon suggested that Joey take a look at some of the unused Muppets at the Muppet workshop to see if he could come up with any ideas for segments. It was an offer made to all the puppeteers when they achieved a high level of expertise, and Joey seized the chance. He found a lamb Muppet and developed a Columbo parody called "Colambo," in which the lamb solved nursery-rhyme crimes. Joey expected to be performing the lamb. But producers Lisa and Dulcy Singer surprised him by suggesting he write the sketch as well.

At first he was terrified. But one sketch and a show later, he officially joined the show's writing staff. That was followed by opportunities to produce and direct the show and home videos. Joey is now head writer, and still puppeteers and directs. He marvels, "It's the greatest company in the world. It lets you grow."

> **" What's the word on the street? "**
>
> —MURRAY MONSTER

Carmen OSBAHR

ROSITA, OVEJITA, ASSORTED ANYTHING MUPPETS, ETC.

Little lamb Ovejita accompanies Murray on his expeditions to schools of all kinds, beginning in season 39

Carmen Osbahr, a talented puppeteer from Mexico City, first watched *Plaza Sésamo*—the Latin American version of *Sesame Street*—when she was seven or eight.

"It blew me away," she recalls. "I remember Ernie and Bert, and Cookie Monster, and Kermit . . . I remember all the characters. It was just a world that I never experienced in my mind, and suddenly it was right there, and I loved it."

Carmen went into acting and then communications. But one day, she saw a notice on a bulletin board for a television show starring puppets on Televisa, a Mexican network.

"The short story is, I went to the audition," she says with the lilting accent that lends such charm to her performances. "The first day, I got the puppet in my hand and I started playing, and I thought, This is what I want to do all the rest of my days."

A few years later, Kermit Love was trolling for talent for an all-new *Plaza Sésamo*, and Carmen requested an audition. But the roles for female puppeteers were already filled.

Carmen was devastated. But she convinced Kermit to look at her puppeteering work on Televisa. After he did, he hired her to help train puppeteers in her native city. He also invited her up to New York to meet the *Sesame Street* cast.

She ended up staying for six months, studying and observing. Carmen became a quiet fixture on the set.

"I talked to Jim Henson," she says, "and I said, 'Will you adopt me? Do you think that you will need a character like me one of these days?' And he said, 'Yes, yes. But, you know, step by step. Let's see, you know? I always audition puppeteers; we have workshops, and let's see what happens.'"

What happened is obvious. Jim eventually asked Carmen to join the Muppet family.

Sadly, Jim died within the year. Kevin Clash took Carmen under his wing and, after a few years of right-handing, Carmen's persistence paid off. Together with head writer Norman Stiles and Executive Producer Dulcy Singer, she and Kevin created Rosita, a bilingual cave bat. Her wings (evident in her first season) have disappeared, but the Muppet remains a hugely successful addition to the cast.

Carmen's biggest challenge, though, was her struggle to master the English language.

"She had a heck of a time," says Sonia Manzano. "She once said to me, 'When you guys used to improvise, I would go nuts . . . because I would practice my English, the exact lines, and then you guys would throw in a joke and I couldn't respond.'"

Sonia adds, smiling, "But now she can."

Can you spot Carmen back there against the blue screen?

> **Kevin Clash found me crying . . . sweet Kevin . . . And he said . . . I'm not Jim Henson, but I'll guide you.**
>
> —CARMEN OSBAHR, MOURNING JIM HENSON

NEWS FLASH

Sonia Manzano was in Cancun in 1986 when she was recognized by a young woman. "She said that her dream in life was always to work with Jim Henson," Sonia recalls. "And I said, 'Oh, that's nice,' thinking, How is this going to happen!? You don't speak English, you live here, forget it.

"Next year she's around the set. The year after, she's still around the set. She is finally hired, and three years later, she's got her own character."

Stephanie
D'ABRUZZO
CURLY BEAR, HONKER, ASSORTED ANYTHING MUPPETS AND MONSTERS

Workshop, where Stephanie was snapped up as a right-hander and ensemble puppeteer. With the female puppeteer family slowly growing, she was among those tapped to develop new girl characters.

Elizabeth was one of Stephanie's favorite experiments during that period, debuting in season 29. A facility with character voices inspired the pigtailed Muppet's Brooklyn-inflected accent. "She was unlike your typical little girl characters," Stephanie says of Elizabeth, known for a love of the number 732 and her cat, Little Murray Sparkles. Ironically, though Elizabeth was short-lived, the cat earned a recurring role and is now played by Stephanie. Curly Bear is another of her spotlighted roles.

But her favorite puppet performance on the Street isn't either of these puppets. It is, Stephanie says, "Get this—a little pink jacket. Her fur-lined hood was her mouth, her eyes were on top of the hood, and her sleeves were her arms." Stephanie invested the unusual puppet with so much character, the writers developed a show around it, as Zoe's jacket come to life.

When not on the Street, Stephanie has originated characters and voices on other shows, such as *The Wubbulous World of Dr. Seuss*, *Oobi*, *Sheep in the Big City*, and *Jack's Big Music Show*. Although unseen on these or *Sesame Street*, she became visible to fans through her work on *Avenue Q*, a *Sesame Street*–inspired Broadway spoof that situates its adult puppets in a far edgier milieu. Stephanie's "Kate Monster" in that hit is a grown-up homage to the Anything Monsters seen on the Street. Her lusty songstress "Lucy the Slut," though, is a creation unique to that Avenue.

These characters won Stephanie numerous theater awards and a Tony Award nomination. But her flourishing career never keeps Stephanie away from *Sesame Street* for too long.

It was Jim Henson's first fantasy film, 1982's *The Dark Crystal*, that inspired Pittsburgh native Stephanie D'Abruzzo to pick up a puppet. Since that time, she's created more than 200 characters, many who share her own upbeat personality and quirky humor.

Among the first generation of puppeteers to grow up on the show, by the time she was in college Stephanie had amassed a library of Muppet videos that she watched obsessively. It was this Muppet fascination—and a bad hairdo—that Stephanie credits for her first foray into puppetry. The idea of disappearing not only into but also behind a character was the force that motivated her role in a puppet-based college television show called *Freeform*, which earned her The National College Emmy award.

The production also nabbed her an audition with the Henson

Steve WHITMIRE

ERNIE, KERMIT

> **I feel absolutely certain that I couldn't have even done anything I've done with any of Jim's characters had I not known him.**
>
> —STEVE WHITMIRE

Steve Whitmire recalls that he knew the Muppets "my whole life—when I was five years old, I used to ask if I could stay up late to watch Rowlf [the Dog] on *The Jimmy Dean Show*," he admits.

When he was ten, he wrote Jim Henson a letter. "I said, 'I'm a ten-year-old guy in Atlanta, love the Muppets, and have you written any books on puppet-making?' And he wrote back. I got this letter from Jim Henson saying, 'I haven't written any books on puppet-making, but I encourage you to try to make them.'"

Steve shakes his head in wonder. "He put me onto these patterns he had published in a *Woman's Day* magazine. . . . I got these things and I started making puppets. . . . That's how I got into it all."

Although it would be years before Steve worked on *Sesame Street*—he began as a puppeteer on *The Muppet Show* in 1978, going on to create the role of Rizzo the Rat in a successful comedy partnership with Dave Goelz, who performs Gonzo—it was Caroll Spinney who actually "discovered" him.

"It was at a mini puppet festival down in Atlanta," Caroll recalls. The day after catching Steve's act, Caroll met up with Jim and Jane Henson. One of Jane's responsibilities was scouting for puppeteers and leading tryouts for Muppet workshops. Caroll mentioned the marvelous young puppeteer. "I think he's exactly what Jim needs," Caroll told her.

Those words turned out to be more prophetic than anyone could have imagined.

On any given day, Steve may perform with right-hander Paul McGinnis, above, or Matt Vogel, seen at right in the home video "Counting on Sports"

Soon after Jim died, Brian Henson invited Steve to meet him in Los Angeles. Jane Henson and Frank Oz were there, too. Brian asked Steve if he wanted to try taking over Jim's characters. Stunned, Steve agreed and first performed Ernie in 1993. Although Kermit wouldn't appear on the Street until season 28, Steve's frog debuted earlier, in a television tribute to Jim. Announcing the new performer, Jane told reporters, "Kermit won't come back so strong at first. Then little by little, he will get his whole personality back."

Thinking of that transition now, Steve remembers how staggered he was by that meeting with the family and the responsibility.

"I was in shock," Steve says. "I said I'd love to try to do it, and we'll see how it goes." It turned out to be harder than even Steve anticipated. When he first received Kermit, he didn't touch the Muppet for almost a month. It was even longer before he tried Kermit's voice—on the song "Bein' Green."

"It was not very good," he reports, "but it was a start."

When scenes like this call for many characters, the right-handers step up to the plate . . . a half dozen more are in there somewhere, buried under all that fur

"We're lying in a heap, arms and legs all over each other, in a big ol' clump. *Every race, every ethnicity is on this set,* I remember thinking. *This is what the world should be like—everybody's somebody . . . this is a microcosm of what the world should be.*"

—FRAN BRILL,
PUPPETEER

Fran Brill and Jerry Nelson are joined by a friendly crowd—and a new generation of puppeteers—for the debut of the "Around-the-Corner" set in 1993 (episode 3136)

Right Hand, Left Brain

Bryant Young teams with Marty Robinson to perform Snuffy—the two are literally inseparable

Birds, bees, bears, and chickens. Doctors, lawyers, bus drivers, and beatniks. Beat cops and Canadian Mounties. Super-heroes and schoolkids. ETs, oak trees, and letter *P*s. Plus, all the people in your neighborhood. The list of extras on *Sesame Street* stretches the limits of the imagination and continues to expand.

At a recent production meeting, where one episode's cast list was being discussed, a writer rattled off the list of vegetables appearing in a proposed dance number: tomato, radish, broccoli, peas, potatoes. There was a pause as the group digested the list. Then Creative Workshop Supervisor Jason Weber asked the obvious: "What kind of potato?"

All of which begs another question: Who animates all these species, potentially lifting a simple Yukon Gold to prominence?

The answer is a group of talented puppeteers employed by Sesame Workshop to perform one-off characters as well as do right-handing. Right-handing?

"Assisting is sometimes referred to as 'right-handing,'" explains puppeteer Paul McGinnis. "This is because, often an assist performs the puppet's *right* hand while the principal puppeteer performs the puppet's head and *left* hand."

"The main goal," he explains, "is to make it look as natural as possible, as if one mind is controlling both of the puppet's hands.

"I watched the first episode in my house when I was three years old," Peter Linz reports

"A right-hander should never lead the performance of a character," says John Kennedy. "If you draw attention to your hand, then the audience will miss what is happening to the character."

"I'm not what you'd call a small person," says Tyler Bunch, "so size has actually prevented me from right-handing. I get the one-off characters who have to hit the ground running."

"When performing as right-hander, never, ever move right when you're supposed to move left," says Alice Dinnean. "The puppet looks like he's on a rack, stretched in the weirdest way."

Ruby, Meryl Sheep, and Countess von Backwards (one of the Count's several girlfriends) were given their quirky personalities by puppeteer Camille Bonora

"To assist is to be a part of a team. When the team works in synchronicity to breathe life into a puppet, it's a feeling like no other," says puppeteer and right-hander Paul McGinnis

When done correctly, your work is paid no attention. When done incorrectly, it sticks out like a sore thumb . . . or hand."

"Pretty much every puppeteer starts out as a right-hander," says puppeteer Fran Brill. "It takes a certain amount of sensitivity to the primary puppeteer to know what they want to do with both hands. I remember when I first started and was doing right hands, and I was just *dragged* around the set trying to keep up . . . trying to figure out: Oh my gosh, what is Jim or whoever going to do with the hands right now?"

In the course of their work, they're asked to do mind-boggling feats of coordination. Puppeteer John Kennedy names one: "Juggling is the trickiest thing to master. It's hard enough to learn to juggle on your own . . . to juggle over your head while wearing puppet hands is beyond difficult."

Each of these intuitive puppeteers performs an incredible dance with his or her primary puppeteer, providing characters with believable movements. And when they're not right-handing, they may be performing anything from a humanoid character to a carrot, a bath towel, or a spoon.

"The hardest thing about right-handing," reports Jennifer Barnhart, "is not having an extra joint between your elbow and your wrist"

One of Lara MacLean's early jobs on Sesame Street was sorting Big Bird feathers. A fan from way back, she says she probably "watched Sesame Street way longer than you're supposed to"

When John Tartaglia paid his first visit to Sesame Street at fourteen, "My mom said my eyes were glazed over. It felt like a dream to me." Two years later, he was performing there

Performer Cheryl Blaylock joined the cast in 1978. "Jim, Frank, Jerry, and Richard . . . they were my fab four," she recalls

"I remember being as young as four when I really started loving puppets," says John Tartaglia of his road to *Sesame Street*. A letter to Jim when he was nine or ten, a missed opportunity to meet Jim on a TV show before he passed away, and another letter—this time to Kevin Clash—got him there. "You know, 'Hi, my name is John Tartaglia, and I'm fourteen years old and I've always wanted to be a puppeteer.'

"A few months later, I got a call," he goes on. "I was watching television, and my stepfather, he yells, 'John, there's a call for you.' So I pick up the phone, and I hear this deep voice, and he says, 'Hey, Johnny, this is Kevin Clash.' And he basically said, 'Why don't you come on down to the studio?' Then he got on the phone with my mom and they arranged it."

Eric
JACOBSON

BERT, GROVER, ASSORTED ANYTHING MUPPETS, ETC.

Eric Jacobson feels like he grew up on *Sesame Street*.

"It was on when I was born," he says. "I don't have any recollection of the first time I sat down in front of the set and watched it. But it was there for me. And in a way, I felt like I was there for it and for Jim . . . to be his audience."

Eric kept pace with Jim's work, starting off with *Sesame Street* then graduating to *The Muppet Show* and movies. Always attracted to performance media, he then went to prestigious film school New York University to study directing.

Jim Henson's death, while Eric was finishing up his freshman year, was a defining moment for the student. Before then, Eric had been contemplating a behind-the-scenes career.

"I realized how much this one man had meant to me growing up," he says. "I realized I should be doing something to help continue his legacy. I didn't know exactly how, but . . . I started seeing in hindsight all these signs."

Eric found a job with an upstart puppet company that he located through the Yellow Pages. He became an intern at Jim Henson Productions. Then, one day, Jane Henson held a small Muppet workshop. Eric asked if he could sit in, and Jane said yes. Then he asked if he could officially attend a workshop. Jane said yes again.

"I kept going and kept improving—my goal was to just be the best puppeteer I could," Eric says. "And if I did that, then there was no way that they could turn me down. They'd *have* to use me."

During this time, Eric made a videotape of his puppeteering work and sent it to Kevin Clash. A year later, Kevin invited him to observe on *Sesame Street*.

"That first time, I'm early," Eric recalls, "and I see Kevin . . . and the first person after Kevin who walks in the door is Frank Oz. And I was like, 'Oh my gosh.' Then Kevin turned to Frank and said, 'I want to introduce you to one of our new puppeteers.'"

Eric's amazed reaction: "'Wow. Did I really just hear that?'"

> ❝ **I started seeing all these signs that seemed to be pointing me toward performing.** ❞
>
> —ERIC JACOBSON

Currently, Eric fills in for Frank as Bert and Grover. But he—along with David Rudman, who performs Cookie Monster—still thinks of them as Frank's characters, and considers that he's simply "holding the fort" when Frank can't perform. His humility disguises the fact that he has also assumed key roles in the cast of non-Sesame Muppets, characters like Miss Piggy, Fozzie Bear, Sam the Eagle—even scenery-chewing Animal, a surprising role for the quiet-spoken puppeteer. More recently, back on the Street, he's taken on another chatterbox: everybody's favorite talk-show host, Guy Smiley.

Eric and Muppet wrangler Andrea Massey inspect Eric's puppet sunny-side-up egg on toast for any necessary touch-ups

Matt VOGEL

BIG BIRD, HERB THE DINOSAUR, ASSORTED ANYTHING MUPPETS

During Matt's audition, Caroll Spinney talked about thinking of Big Bird as a child. "It helped him, and . . . it helps you perform it, too," reports Matt

Actor/singer/producer Matt Vogel is in line to take up the role of Big Bird should Caroll Spinney ever decide to retire. "I was a big fan of *Sesame Street* and *The Muppet Show*," he says, "and in fact, the thing that really interested me about them as a child of seven or eight was not the characters, although those were very interesting to me, but how they were being operated, who the guys were underneath." He spent hours poring over puppetry books at his local library. "I would look up books on the Muppets or Jim Henson, and there would be pictures that would show how they were operated. And when I was watching *The Muppet Show*, I would look for the rods, or I would look for where the live hand was coming from."

Matt built and performed puppets when he was younger, but decided in junior high school that puppeteering might be "uncool." So he turned to acting. Senior year in college, he returned to his first love, however, and made a puppet video, sending it to the Jim Henson Company, but he wasn't asked for an audition. Then one day, on a drive, his wife noticed an ad in *Backstage*, an acting trade publication.

"There was a drawing of Kermit the Frog, and the caption, 'Do you measure up to be a Muppet?'" Matt remembers. "She just happened to see it—we were looking for audition notices as actors. They were looking for, literally, somebody my height, my weight, my build for a costumed puppet."

As it turned out, the Jim Henson Company was recruiting for a replacement for Jim's younger son, John, who had been performing a Coca-Cola polar bear at live events. The first day Matt returned to New York, he found himself having lunch with John after what turned out to be a successful audition.

Following a series of polar bear appearances, Matt shipped off another video to Henson. This time, he was asked to puppeteer

> **I wasn't the cool person that played the bass, or the guy that sang the Journey song . . . I was the puppet geek.**
>
> —MATT VOGEL

on the *Sesame Street* float at the Macy's Thanksgiving Day Parade.

In 1996, he attended a Muppet workshop along with future Muppet performers (and, later, *Avenue Q* stars) John Tartaglia and Stephanie D'Abruzzo. Then he was asked to audition for Big Bird.

"Caroll Spinney didn't want to have to do every public appearance that was coming down the pike," explains Matt, "but they didn't want to just send a silent puppet or a walk-around. I was thrilled, I was terrified. I'd never ever thought of trying to imitate Big Bird. So I bought a bunch of CDs and videos and listened over and over to Caroll to see if I could be somewhere in the ballpark."

The morning of the audition was the first time Matt met Caroll.

"We shook hands," he recalls, "and as we did, Caroll Spinney said, 'You know, Vogel means bird in German. This may be just the job for you.' It completely floored me."

"Matt is one of the very best lip-syncers on *Sesame Street*," says Caroll, who assumed the role of Big Bird around the same age as Matt. "He's just a natural, awfully good puppeteer. I think that Matt isn't at all vexed by the fact that you can't see where you're walking.

"He does a wonderful job. He'll be fine when he does it full time. He's just a good soul."

Leslie
CARRARA-RUDOLPH

ABBY CADABBY, ASSORTED ANYTHING MUPPETS, ETC.

When Abby Cadabby kisses her prince doll, he becomes a frog doll

Sesame Workshop has been trying to create strong female characters for a long time, and up to a point, they've succeeded—witness Prairie Dawn, Rosita, and Zoe. But none of the female characters has the same kind of sky-high popularity as do Big Bird, Elmo, or the other iconic male Muppets.

One of the reasons, according to *The New York Times*, is that "a show as politically sensitive as this one has an added challenge: finding female characters that make kids laugh, but not laugh at them as female stereotypes."

So when three-year-old fairy-in-training Abby Cadabby was created for season 38, producers decided to find a puppeteer to literally embody the new character they had in mind, hoping that the investment in a personality, rather than a quality like self-confidence or grit, would turn their latest creation into a star. They were eager to provide girls with a strong role model and writers with more options to add to the current feminine roster of Rosita, Zoe, and Curly Bear.

They found Leslie Carrara-Rudolph, a creative dynamo.

A job in an after-school theater program had first led to Leslie's self-discovery that she had a gift for reaching children. At college, she designed a major in child development through the arts. Her goal? No less than to become the ultimate entertainer for kids. She also put in time on comedy specials before winning an audition to work on *Muppets Tonight*, a *Muppet Show*–like live-action comedy developed by the Jim Henson Company in 1996. That's where she was introduced to Kevin Clash. At the time, she says, laughing, "I was a terrible puppeteer. I was relegated to the back."

Leslie shows off her puppet-building skills horsing around on set

She became good enough, just a few years later, to be asked to perform on *The Wubbulous World of Dr. Seuss*, another Henson production, where she met Marty Robinson, Pam Arciero, and a number of other *Sesame Street* performers.

At first, she wasn't even going to audition for the part of Abby. She already had a role on a Disney show, and she thought the two characters might be too similar.

But friends on *Sesame Street*—including Kevin and Marty—insisted that she try for the part.

"I made the callbacks," she says wonderingly. "Sixty percent of our audition was improv, so I'm—" Leslie's own bubbly tones shift slightly into the even more ebullient voice so recognizable as Abby's, "'My favorite cookies are, um, fennel cookies because my dad is part gnome and he gets gas and fennel is good for gas, and I have a pet squirrel named Doyle. . . .'"

"I just started rambling," Leslie marvels, "and I thought, 'Wow, she's coming through.'"

NEWS FLASH Abby Cadabby hit the big time . . . quite literally . . . when she was only two years old, debuting as a balloon in the 2008 Macy's Thanksgiving Day Parade. Leslie calls it "a thrill beyond words."

Girls
IN THE 'HOOD

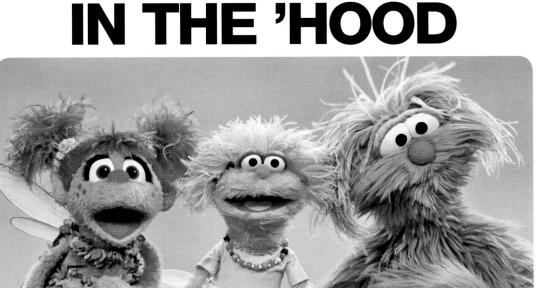

The "Sesame Beginnings" video series starred baby characters and caregivers, like infant Prairie Dawn and her mom, seen here

> **If Cookie were a female character, she'd be accused of being anorexic or bulimic. There are a lot of things that come attached to female characters.**
>
> —CAROL-LYNN PARENTE,
> EXECUTIVE PRODUCER

The smaller Zoe puppet introduced in season 40 appears here

Scott Preston directs Fran, Pam, Carmen, and Leslie in season 40; below, season 39's last appearance of the larger Zoe puppet

So why is it so hard for female Muppets on *Sesame Street* to break into the top five?

The show's struggle to find a female character whose traits will catapult her to stardom has mistakenly been referred to as a drought of female characters on the show. That's not the case. Over the course of forty years, the producers have introduced many extremely funny and appealing female characters. The lack of a major female "celebrity" Muppet may have less to say about the show than about the instincts of viewers: ratings studies make it clear that girls become invested in boy characters they enjoy, but boys rarely form the same strong attachments to girl characters.

Anything Muppets and monsters added over time, like Elizabeth, Ruby, Lulu, Roxie Marie, and Zoe, all had strong appeal but weren't able to cross the gender divide with great success, although their characters were deliberately not too girly. Carmen Osbahr's Rosita was one of the few to stick; a strong characterization as a Latino monster helped her stand out. But for a long time, there were no female juggernauts on the level of a Big Bird or Elmo.

In fact, originally, there were few female *puppeteers*. When asked why, Jim Henson occasionally blamed the deficit on his own not-inconsiderable height. When performing side by side, with arms stretched overhead with a Muppet, he'd explain, it's easier if the puppets are all on the same level.

Jane Henson worked with her husband in the early years of Jim's commercial work, but in the seventies, she opted for time at home to raise their children. So when Fran Brill came on the Street full-time, she essentially integrated a boys' club. Gradually, more women joined up, like Pam Arciero.

Happily, these days Fran and Pam have plenty of company in the high-soled boots that many of the women wear to make them tall enough to perform next to the male puppeteers. The latest addition is Leslie Carrara-Rudolph, whose Abby seems poised for that elusive superstardom that has evaded other female Muppets on the Street. Perhaps truly embracing her feminine side—Abby is flaming pink, sassy, and wildly girly—will finally fill the bill. Abby's character is as fully rounded as Zoe's, but also as easy to categorize and as primal as Elmo—after all, she's a fairy-in-training—all of which help to make her highly memorable for kids.

Abby's "Mom," her builder, Rollie Krewson

Some early concept sketches for Abby, done by art directors Janis Beauchamp, Nancy Stevenson, Evan Cheng, and Kip Rathke, plus master puppet designer Ed Christie's final drawing

Not long after Jim was gone, his *Sesame Street* friends gathered some of Jim's most personal songs from the show into a tribute album because, even as they grieved, everyone felt the need to honor Jim's request to celebrate his life and work. When the tribute was released, Joan wrote of him: "Jim Henson was an authentic American genius. He was our era's Charlie Chaplin, Mae West, W.C. Fields, and Marx Brothers—and, indeed, he drew from all of them to create a new art form. . . . We feel lucky that he left us so much of himself to go on sharing with the world."

Puppeteer Frank Oz has said: "Jim was not perfect. But I'll tell you something . . . he was as close to how you're supposed to behave toward other people as anyone I've ever known."

Fran Brill, one of the first *Sesame Steet* puppeteers mentored by Jim, compares Jim's role in her life to that of a parent, "in terms of learning how to be a good person. Even today when I'm in a very difficult situation, I ask myself, 'How would Jim have handled this?' Because that's the person I want to be."

Brian Henson visits his dad on set in the '70s

It's a Good Life

"I've lost my voice"

No one wore black, because that's how he wanted it. It was a celebration, not a funeral, and you don't wear black to a party. You wear white. Or red. Or Kermit green. Jim Henson's memorial services, one at the Cathedral of St. John the Divine in New York City on May 21, 1990, and another in his adopted city of London at St. Paul's Cathedral, were treated as celebrations. The overwhelming gathering of friends, family, and fans in both cities marched together (to "When the Saints Go Marching In," because Jim had specifically requested a jazzy New Orleans funeral procession) and sang together ("The Rainbow Connection" and Harry Belafonte's "Turn the World Around," among others). And they cried together when Caroll Spinney, as Big Bird, performed a solo of "Bein' Green," singing with characteristic sweetness and unfamiliar longing. Celebrities were there but, more important, so were thousands of regular fans, including tiny kids waving foam butterflies. In tribute to Jim, his staff had worked nonstop for days making hundreds to pass out to the crowd.

> ## My hope still is to leave the world a bit better for having been here.
>
> —JIM HENSON

Jim had formed that loving and expansive creative team because he envisioned so much good work ahead of him, and he knew he had to maintain the Muppets on *Sesame Street* while that work was being done. Sure enough, after *The Muppet Show* ceased taping in 1981, new projects arose, such as *The Great Muppet Caper* (1981) and *The Muppets Take Manhattan* (1983), sequels to 1979's hugely popular *The Muppet Movie*. In the mid-eighties Jim produced his first fantasy film, *The Dark Crystal;* his second, *Labyrinth,* followed

in 1986. These two films represented a new direction for Jim, with puppets built to tell darker, more adult stories, like those in his innovative *Storyteller* series.

In 1990, not long before his illness, Jim produced a pilot for a reality television series that followed two guys on a road trip shooting tape of themselves guerrilla-style, a filmmaking style that anticipated the reality-television revolution still a decade in the future. In the pitch, Jim hoists a weighty video camera, grinning. "In the years to come," he says, "the television people and filmmakers, they're going to be coming out of a time of watching MTV and using Handycams, and I think we're going to see a whole new and different kind of television."

These days, the technology in which Jim always delighted is making it much easier to track down clips of this pitch, as well as his Oscar-nominated *Timepiece* short film, *Jimmy Dean Show* appearances, and early *Sam and Friends* footage, featuring Jane Nebel, who became his wife and longtime puppeteering partner.

Jim's five children—Lisa, Cheryl, Brian, John, and Heather—are also active in the arts, performing (sometimes with puppets) or producing in a variety of media. Lisa and Brian run the Jim Henson Company, which creates original series for children and adults, as well as manage Jim's groundbreaking series, *Fraggle Rock*. The Jim Henson Foundation headed by Cheryl sustains puppetry worldwide with creative encouragement and financial support. The Hensons also contribute toward the Jim Henson Legacy, a personal archive of Jim's creations and photographs, which travels to museums in a series of exhibits that aim to spark creativity in a new era of fans.

Generously, at the memorials in 1990, Jim's family shared a letter he left behind for them, voicing the message he wanted to leave to the generations to follow:

"Please watch out for each other, and love and forgive everybody. It's a good life, enjoy it."

Fairy tales and nursery rhymes are repeatedly skewered on the show, like Humpty Dumpty here (season 38)

Goofs
and Spoofs

Bob gets the yucky treatment in the Queer Eye for the Straight Guy spoof "Grouchy Eye for the Nice Guy," seen in season 36

Parodies—of fairy tales, game shows, musicals, or any pop culture icon—are staples on *Sesame Street* and have been since the earliest days, thanks to directives from Joan Ganz Cooney and Lloyd Morrisett to pull in parents as coviewers. They often require "builds" of both sets and new Muppets, plus a lot of puppeteers to embody those newly hatched characters. Principal puppeteers usually take on the major roles, but these segments provide a venue for new puppeteers to sharpen their skills, shine, and, hopefully, explode out from the ranks.

Season 38 was an inspired year for parody mayhem. In a series of "Dinner Theatre" spoofs, musicals like *Hair* and *Annie Get Your Gun* became "Pear" and "Annie Get Your Gumbo." Oscar impersonated Donald Trump. And guest star Shirley Jones, as the straight man in the crowd, brought ineffable comic timing to her homage to Mother Goose.

The blue screen is filled in with a view of the ship's surroundings when the "Star Trek" spoof, "Starship Surprise," airs in season 15

Grover, reprising Marlon Brando's Stanley Kowalski, spoofs the movie "A Streetcar Named Desire" with a familiar, plaintive cry in the night—only to discover that Stella lives on the next block

" **Stella!!!!!** "
—GROVER

These popular segments spoofed the Indiana Jones movies (season 39) and eighties television detectives ("Miami Mice" in season 21)

ER series star Julianna Margulies studies an x-ray of Big Bird's wing

SEGMENT #0023-0895

Cookie Monster: Dis Alistair Cookie, welcoming you to "Monsterpiece Theatre." Today, me proud to present modern masterpiece, a play so modern and so brilliant, it make absolutely NO sense to anybody, including Alistair. Okay, maybe you can figure it out: the puzzling story of two monsters waiting for their friend, a play called "Waiting for Elmo."

[in the following scene, Telly and Grover endlessly bemoan the fact that Elmo has not arrived at their rendezvous, until the nearby tree suddenly bursts out in a rage]

Tree: Okay, that does it! I've been standing out here waiting for this play to make some sense. I don't get it! It's the most ridiculous thing I've ever seen. I'm outta here. Why couldn't they do *Oklahoma*? I understand *Oklahoma*. *[exits, singing]*

Telly: *(frantic)* The tree is leaving, and Elmo said to wait for him by the tree!

Grover: We will have to follow the tree! Wait, tree! Wait, wait! *[all exit]*

Cookie Monster: That deep, deep stuff. Now for something that make a lot more sense. Ah-ha-ha-ha. COOKIE! Ah . . . num-num-num. Ummm num-num-num . . . oh yeah, four stars.

Bad-modeling issues led to the disappearance of Cookie Monster's pipe in later episodes, like this one, of Monsterpiece Theatre

The "Wing in a Sling" storyline from season 40 helped send off landmark series *ER* in style (the medical drama aired its fanfare episode just weeks after the taping), the latest in a long line of witty spoofs pushing the curriculum. *Sesame Street* has "Muppetized," in Workshop parlance, films and shows as diverse as Ingmar Bergman's *The Seventh Seal* (season 21), *Singing in the Rain* (season 23), *Twin Peaks* ("Twin Beaks," in season 22), and *Desperate Housewives* (season 36).

Announcer: Coming soon to the Bloom Network, the show everyone's talking about, "Desperate Houseplants." It's the story about some houseplants that were *not* getting what they needed.

Houseplant: Oh, I can't take it anymore! I've lost my bloom. I haven't been watered in days!

THIS CHAPTER HAS BEEN BROUGHT TO YOU BY THE LETTERS A AND M, AND THE NUMBER 4.

The Letters A and M are for the Anything Muppets, a.k.a. AMs, a rotating repertory company of humanoid Muppets who fill the roles of everything from irate restaurant patron to dinosaur fairy.

The number 4 is how many puppeteers it can take at times to operate a full-body rod puppet—one primary, one right-hander, plus one to operate each leg.

7

"It's not whether children learn from television, it's *what* children learn from television, because everything that children see on television is teaching them *something*."

—JOAN GANZ COONEY, COFOUNDER

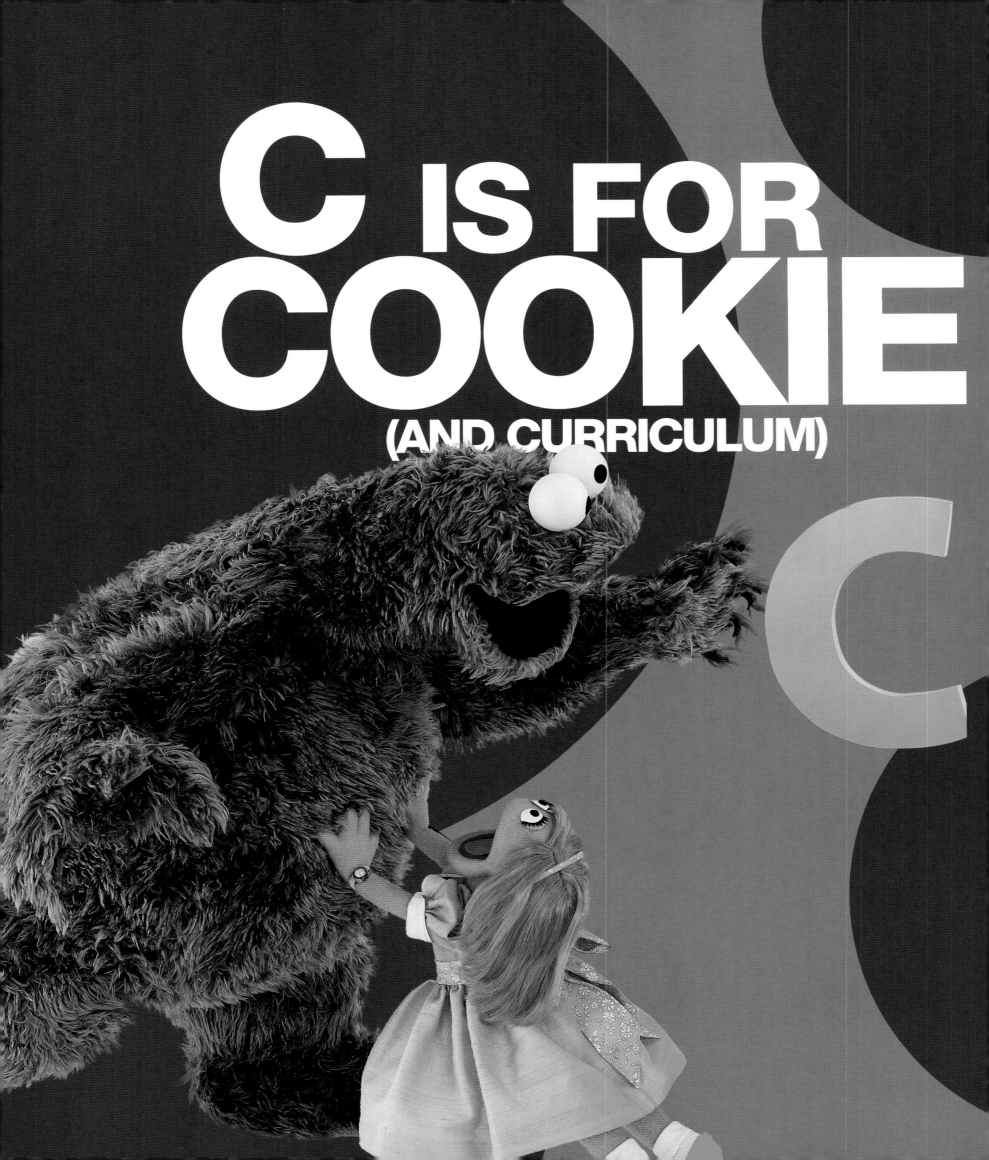

Word on the Street

Murray reflects the comic chops of puppeteer Joey Mazzarino, here cracking up soundman Chuck Tufino, with help from right-hander Matt Vogel

Murray and David are talking. They talk about libraries, then about how it feels to be angry. "So, what do you like about school?" Murray asks with lively interest—he really wants to know—and the conversation flows along a new route. David isn't naturally chatty, but Murray, master of the ad-lib, nudges the conversation this way and that. Soon the two are yakking like old friends bellying up to the bar.

David is a little boy and Murray is a monster. But during their conversation, David never once glances down at Joey Mazzarino, the puppeteer crouched below the boisterous flame-colored Muppet. And during their chat, David is never once aware that he and Murray have touched on a half dozen predetermined curriculum goals that are targets of the show. What he may realize is that he's just heard some new words that he can use himself, an empowering moment for a preschooler just learning to communicate in a big world. What's more, Murray's given these key vocabulary words a context and offered them with a frequency in their brief talk that will anchor them in the minds of kids watching at home.

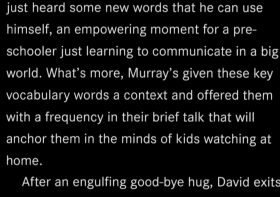

After an engulfing good-bye hug, David exits stage left. Talent Coordinator Carrie Haugh escorts another child over, past the small crowd gathered to watch the interaction. Carrie talks softly and reassuringly to the new preschooler, Michael, as he's introduced first to Joey, then to Murray.

Michael instantly pops his hand in Murray's smiling mouth. Then he pokes Murray's nose. (To be fair, the egg-yolky blob presents an irresistible target.) When he's gently reminded not to touch Murray—in hi-def any damage to the susceptible fur leaps into focus—Michael giggles helplessly, then becomes owlishly mute, too overcome by the distractions of the puppet to respond to Joey's banter. The perfect rhythm of kid and puppet just never materializes. The tiny actor is hugged and reassured but finally led away.

"Not every child will talk . . . even to a Muppet," director Jim Martin murmurs into his mike.

"He was just overwhelmed," Murray says wisely, as Joey remains in character. In a moment, another child is brought in.

For *Sesame Street*'s "Word on the Street" segments, production crews like this one take the show to the real city streets. "We get permits to shoot in Washington Square Park or Brooklyn," says Joey Mazzarino, puppeteer of "Word" star Murray Monster. "Some kids are brought in and some kids are just there on the scene. We say, 'Do you want to talk to this Muppet?' and Murray asks, 'What is . . . say . . . pumpernickel?'" When the segment airs, it will work as an episode's cold opening, a kind of teaser that jump-starts the show—the moment when parents might still be in the room. The segment also was designed to provide those watching parents with strategies for starting their own vocabulary-building conversations with their kids.

> **How do you get one of these mustaches? Can I grow one right now? What if I water it and keep it out in the sun? What do I do to speed up the process? I really want a mustache!**
>
> —MURRAY, ON THE WORD OF THE DAY: MUSTACHE

Murray knows a lot about talking to children. His "Word on the Street" segment finds him roaming the set and the sidewalks of New York City, improvising dialogue with children about vocabulary. And not just words you'd expect kids to know—Murray stops traffic by using jargon like "predicament," "glockenspiel," and "mustache," words that delight preschoolers with their mouthwatering sounds. There's a frisky, ad hoc feel to the bits that even the youngest viewers appreciate.

Five words are tackled per day when these improvs are taped; often, ten hours of taping—the kids are reliably unpredictable—ends up as just a few moments on air. Joey recalls one girl who surprised the director and coordinators.

"They said, 'I don't think we're going to get anything. She's four, she's too young.'" Joey recalls. "We talked for twenty-five minutes and got so much material. I could have done a whole series with this girl. She totally believed the Muppet. Some kids get that it's a guy underneath, but that kid was just right there."

Some of the most memorable segments on *Sesame Street* have involved one-on-one interactions between a Muppet and a child. These segments are not strictly scripted.

First, the research department weighs in with questions tailored to spark discussions about the target curriculum issues. Then performers are prepped on key messages. The Muppet has to go along with kids' conversational gambits, responding and refocusing on the fly.

"The performers deviate from the script a lot," says producer Ben Lehman, who supervises the script department. "The kids are totally unpredictable, which of course is what makes these great."

A typical "Muppet Insert" script has blanks for improvised moments, like this one for segments with other puppets, like Bert and Grover

SESAME STREET   - 2 -   SHOW WILD

--Wow, so there you have it, family dinner time together. I can't wait!

"FAMILY"

SCENIC: ULTIMATTE W/ STOOL (FOR PUPPETEER) AND STEP-LIKE SET-UP (FOR CHILD TO SIT ON)
TALENT: GROVER, KID

--I'm here with my good friend _____ and she's going to tell me about her family, right, _____?

--So tell me, who's in your family, _____?

THE KID RESPONDS.

--What a great-sounding family! And tell me, what does your family do together?

THE KID EXPLAINS ACTIVITIES.

--That sounds terrific... It's so nice to be a part of a family!

"SCHOOL"

SCENIC: ULTIMATTE W/ STOOL (FOR PUPPETEER) AND STEP-LIKE SET-UP (FOR CHILD TO SIT ON)
TALENT: BERT, KID

--I'm here with my good friend _____, and she's going to tell us all about school, right, _____?

THE KID ANSWERS, "RIGHT."

--So, tell me... do you go to school?

Bean Counting

CHILDREN'S TELEVISION WORKSHOP
BUDGET OF EXPENDITURES
APRIL 1, 1968 to JUNE 30, 1970

SUMMARY

	Total	Start-Up	First Year	Second
Direct Program Costs:				
Production -				
Broadcast Cost	$4,685,000	$ —	$ —	$4,685,0
Executive Producer	177,300	12,100	79,100	86,1
Production Unit #1	206,700	16,900	94,400	95,4
Production Unit #2	175,500	12,700	78,600	84,2
Production Unit #3	160,600	—	65,700	94,90
Production Unit #4	141,900		58,200	83,70
Total Production	5,547,000	41,700	376,000	5,129,300
Program Support:				
Executive Director	202,900	20,800	90,800	91,300
Office Service	751,800	4,800	566,500	180,500
Public Information	154,800	11,500	67,900	75,400
Administration, etc.	436,500	8,800	205,600	222,100
Research, Development & Evaluation	657,000	11,000	570,600	75,400
Total Program Support	2,203,000	56,900	1,501,400	644,700
TOTAL	7,750,000	98,600	1,877,400	5,774,000
Public Information Materials	250,000	—	50,000	200,000
TOTAL	$8,000,000	$98,600	$1,927,400	$5,974,000

Divide that by 130 episodes!

When *Sesame Street* flickered to life on November 10, 1969, it didn't exist in a vacuum. There were other children's television shows competing for kids' attentions at the time, some likewise featuring puppets, music, and amiable hosts. But *Sesame Street* had something none of the others did: research and testing. Setting aside the cast's enormous appeal and the scripts' abundant humor, it is the show's experimental curriculum that sets it apart.

The origins of the so-called Sesame model—a research process that continues today—can be traced to the intersection of the cofounders' vision of the show as a laboratory for evolving educational ideas and the funders' insistence on testing at critical stages to evaluate its ultimate success.

How did bean counters become the impetus for the show's rigorous research standards for teaching letters and counting? It's another of the unique elements in the show's history.

"Television for Preschool Children: A Proposal" was cowritten by Joan Ganz Cooney and freelancer Linda Gottlieb in 1968 as a follow-up to Joan's original feasibility study. That earlier document had answered the question, "Can television be used to teach young children?"—yes!—but this latter one was a full-on television show pitch for what Joan described as a season-long on-air "experiment," one that needed to be "slickly and expensively produced" in order to lure young viewers away from rival commercial networks.

When Joan formally presented the proposal to public broadcaster NET (now PBS), she had every expectation that the public broadcaster, which had produced her documentaries and public forums in the past, would fund and air the show.

She was wrong.

A young woman at the helm of an $8 million "experiment"? Public-television executives balked.

Luckily, Joan had a powerful advocate. Lloyd Morrisett, as VP of the Carnegie Foundation, had secured a commitment to partially fund the project from that grant-making entity. It was Lloyd who, in the yearlong quest for the remainder of government funding and sponsorship, brought the show to U.S. Department of Education (DOE) head Howard "Doc" Howe II and convinced him to support it.

Doc pushed the show through his department's budget by

Lloyd Morrisett

> It never occurred to us that we couldn't change the world. Part of it was our youth, and part was the times.
>
> —JOAN GANZ COONEY

NEWS FLASH Public broadcasters initially said no to *Sesame Street*, fearful that they would end up funding the entire project. Undaunted, Joan and Lloyd pitched *Sesame Street* to the three major networks: NBC, CBS, and ABC. But none of the Big Three, as the all-powerful networks were known at the time, believed that an overtly educational show could have the same appeal as their existing kids' programs. Without the support of "Doc" Howe, *Sesame Street* might have ended right there.

Joan's careful attention to detail is evident in this draft of a speech, complete with notations

I appreciate the opportunity to meet with you today and describe our experiment in educational television. In the next few minutes, I would like to give you a little background on the ~~projected development~~ *development of the Children's Television Workshop* and show you a ~~brief~~ *short* film that explains more fully what we are all about.

I might say that we are openly soliciting your approval and support ~~of this project~~, in hopes that you will help us reach our maximum potential audience of about 12 million.

In terms of *commercial* television ratings, reaching 12 million viewers won't sell much soap or toothpaste, but we're after a very specific -- and possibly much more discriminating -- audience. It is the 12 million three-, four- and five-year-old children living in the United States today.

What we're "selling" is education -- a product not as easy to *sell* ~~peddle~~ as Bosco or Barbie dolls, which is ~~why~~ *one of the reasons* we call the program "an experiment." It will have all the elements of commercial television that are known to be attractive and enjoyable to children, yet will be designed to teach them certain basic skills. Fast action, humor, plenty of animation, lively music, and easy-to-memorize jingles, a la Madison Avenue *commercials* -- these are some of the things we'll use to ~~sell our product~~ *motivate children to learn from our show.*

We began planning the program in 1968 -- and have a budget of $8 million dollars, to research and design the show, and see us through our first season of broadcasting, which begins in November. The primary financial backers are Carnegie Corporation, the Ford Foundation, and the U.S. Office of Education.

A basic question we have to answer is: "Why spend $8 million dollars to help

(more)

With funding in place, one of Joan's jobs was to initiate testing efforts and convince PBS stations—which independently chose what to air locally—that they should carry the show. Equally critical was the need to inform community organizers in the stations' districts about it, so they could rally viewers. This speech was one of dozens Joan gave across the country to such groups.

---

insisting that it could be categorized as a research project. Joan's "experiment" language came in handy in this respect. Doc's own assistant initially advised against the partnership, arguing that more money would be needed to compete effectively with commercial broadcasting's cartoon lineups. Ironically, the assistant's comments caused Joan and her team to up their budget from $6 million to $8 million.

Once the DOE was on board, the Ford Foundation was persuaded by Lloyd and Doc to join the party with the majority of the show's funding. With this promise of financial backing in hand, the team went back to the public-broadcasting network for its support, and the show was given a green light. Together, Carnegie, Ford, the

DOE, and public broadcasting would sponsor the show. The funders agreed to Joan's proposal for "an experimental year of production and broadcasting in order to ascertain what techniques of entertaining and educating are most popular and effective with young children." Amazingly, they committed not only to an intensive development phase and the "experimental" first year but also to a second season. In return, though, they insisted on one thing: The show must document and measure the success of its techniques—no mean feat.

What would eventually become a decades-long experiment was about to begin.

The New York Times announces the formation of the Children's Television Workshop in 1968

In a recent post to women's group blog wowowow.com, Joan revealed something that had proved helpful in the show's research phases: "When I was in college, my mother worried that her daughters would be widowed, as her own mother had been when she was two, and have nothing to fall back on. She convinced us that we should major in education so that we could teach if we had to. . . . Years later, I was doing the research that led to the creation of *Sesame Street*. I needed to talk to very high-powered academics at Harvard and other universities who were experts in child development. Each of them always asked rather haughtily what my credentials were for doing the study I was doing, and when I answered that I had majored in early-childhood education, they immediately warmed up and became very helpful. So I bless my mother's wisdom."

What to Teach

Those first years on the air, when government funding briefly provided a hefty part of the program's price tag, the question would be asked: Is *Sesame Street* a successful use of taxpayer dollars? From the beginning, Joan's pitch for the show urged that testing be done to measure the success of the series and recommended that the show change over time as a result of research findings. With government oversight, her inclination toward continuous testing became an imperative.

Another research imperative shaped by the funding source? The show's special attention to the needs of the urban poor. Joan's original pitch talked mainly about teaching children as a mass audience—only briefly did she call out lower economic populations as being a special focus. Even then, she only mentioned the possibility that the show, if appealing enough, might be able to cut through the "din" of media exposure that children in poor urban areas often encountered in their homes, where more formal child-care options were beyond the means of working parents. The government funders, however, saw a greater need for the show among this challenged segment of preschoolers. Gradually, the series' focus narrowed in on these kids within that broader circle of viewers.

The urgent question was what, precisely, to teach them.

Enter Harvard professor Gerald Lesser.

Gerry was an expert on children and media who had previously consulted on a short-lived kids' show, *Exploring*, which established a model of teamwork between TV producers and academics. He decided to expand on that model in the development of a curriculum for *Sesame Street*—that is, a list of educational goals for the show. Over the summer of 1968, he convened five seminars to help determine those goals. Educators, animators, pediatricians, psychologists, children's book authors, and TV producers and writers

Gerry Lesser, wearing his signature glasses

were invited to an exchange of open dialogue. Gerry hoped that by the end of the five seminars, Joan and the Workshop would have the beginnings of a curriculum, one that would work for both scriptwriters and researchers.

Everyone expected there would be some inherent tension between the two camps. The surprise was the friction among the educators themselves. Getting a roomful of them to agree on a single philosophy proved daunting. Happily, Gerry was brilliant at resolving these differences—or, at least, taking responsibility for some unilateral decisions.

"I'm not sure all the educators ever really agreed," says Chris Cerf, who came on to run a publishing division and became one of the show's premier songwriters. "But Gerry made them think they did. He ran meetings better than anyone I've ever seen. He made everybody feel like they were important, that they got listened to, and that their work ended up in the final product."

One subject of contention was the alphabet.

Some educators argued that simply memorizing the A-to-Z sequence was a useless recitation skill that didn't really help children learn to read. Others cited valid reasons to teach the alphabet—not the least of which was the sense of accomplishment it gave children to recite it, generating feelings of pride that motivated further learning. Perhaps equally important, knowledge of the alphabet was something that could be concretely measured, providing much-needed data to funders who demanded visible results. The success of the show at communicating other goals,

Joan meets some early advisors—from left, Jane O'Connor, Joan, Dorothy Hollingsworth, Allonia Gadsden, and Gwendolyn Peters

such as cooperation and entering new social groups—or even certain cognitive skills, such as problem solving—although critical to a child's achievements in school, would be more difficult to assess and report.

Given the importance of successful testing to the future of the show, Frank Pace, chairman of the Corporation for Public Broadcasting, suggested that the show zoom in on only four or five educational goals that it could measurably accomplish. These goals ultimately became symbolic representation (letters and numbers), cognitive processes (things like size relationships and ordering), the physical environment (e.g., city and country, plants and animals), and the social environment (including interactions like cooperation and appreciating differing perspectives). The numerical goal of counting from one to ten turned out to be so easy for preschoolers to master that within a year or two, the show bumped the count up to forty.

In the show's final program proposal, Joan described the end goals as the promotion of "intellectual and cultural growth of preschoolers, particularly disadvantaged preschoolers."

"Not only will it attempt to teach specific information, such as language and mathematical skills," she wrote, "but it will strive for the broader aim of getting children to learn how to think for themselves."

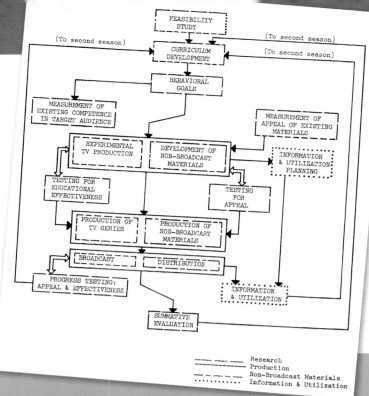

"The CTW model" was a term coined for the multiple layers of testing—before, during, and after the taping of every episode—that helped to shape the show's content. This diagram, adapted by National Center for Educational Technology consultant Herman W. Land from early production documents, outlines the various stages at which this testing occurred. The current research team has modified the process of preparation and evaluation, and the cycle now follows the pattern seen in this recent PowerPoint slide.

Wild Things

Maurice Sendak consults with Joan, Dave Connell, and Matt Robinson, at that time in writer/producer mode, before he stepped into the role of Gordon on the show

Invited to the *Sesame Street* educational seminars was writer and artist Maurice Sendak, today famous for his brilliant children's books. During the seminars, he sketched a number of funny and irreverent doodles reflecting his take on what he saw and heard.

Sendak eventually produced two animated segments for *Sesame Street*, becoming just the first of many now-famous children's book illustrators, like Gahan Wilson and Mo Willems, with *Sesame Street* animation credits. Sendak's best-known short, about the number nine, featured inebriated monsters attending a hapless boy's birthday party. Another counted off seven enormous monsters.

Unfortunately, the Workshop started getting reports that children were, as Joan Ganz Cooney put it, "freaked out" by them. The Workshop tested the pieces in day-care centers and discovered that the depictions of monsters and mayhem were indeed scaring kids, and they were pulled from the show's lineup. It's perhaps no surprise, though, that Sendak's anarchic "Bumble Ardy #9" is still vividly remembered by adult fans.

> **Bumble Ardy had a party when he was nine, which isn't bad, in fact it's fine, except he asked nine groovy swine to come for birthday cake and wine.**
>
> —FROM "BUMBLE ARDY #9," SEASON 2

The sweet but addled Adeline, Bumble's put-upon mom

The original smudgy carbon copy of the invitation to Maurice Sendak

Another Sendak short, "Monster Number 7," is less well known but every bit as subversive and wonderful

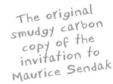

We will meet at noon on the 26th and probably talk generally that day through dinner. The following day we'll try to reach some kind of consensus on the kinds of social, moral and affective issues that the program might try to present; and on the 28th, we'll work until about 3:00 p.m. on how these things might be done on television. You should be back home by late afternoon, the 28th.

You will be hearing from us soon ... ... tel arrangements
and suggested flight ti ...

I do ...

May 23, 1968

... se and that things

... rdially,

Dear Mr. Sendak:

I cannot yet give you full details about the Social, Moral and Affective Development Seminar which we are holding in Cambridge, Massachusetts, June 26, 27 and 28, but I can give you an idea of who is coming:

Dr. Leon Eisenberg, Chief of Psychiatry
Massachusetts General Hospital
Boston, Massachusetts

Dr. Keith Conners, Dr. Eisenberg's Assistant

Lawrence Kohlberg, Psychologist
Harvard University
Cambridge, Massachusetts

Annemarie Roeper, Head of
Roeper City & Country School
Bloomfield Hills, Michigan

Paul Ritts, Puppeteer

Fred Rogers, Star of
"Misterogers Neighborhood," a NET children's show

Hylan Lewis, Urban Sociologist
Brooklyn College

Paul Taff, Head of Children's Programming
NET

Dorothy Hollingsworth
Seattle HeadStart

Father John Culkin, Head of Communications
Fordham University
New York City

... Ganz Cooney,
... utive Director

Breaking New Ground

"When we first began," the show's original head writer, Jon Stone, once remarked, "and they told us that we had to incorporate all this education into this format, I was convinced that it would be impossible to do. But we tried it. And I almost immediately did a 180-degree turn in my attitude about the curriculum.

"Instead of being a millstone around our necks, it was really a backbone, a spinal column that we could build the show around. No longer as a comedy writer were you starting with that terrible blank piece of paper in the typewriter. It was a tremendous help."

With the curriculum established, writers banged out the first scripts, and it became the research department's job to test the early segments as they were assembled into five test shows. Could producers deliver as promised? Was the show actually teaching?

The producers had already hired someone to direct this testing phase: University of Oregon professor Ed Palmer. In the summer of 1969, just months before the show was scheduled to air, Ed's research revealed something that stopped production in its tracks. One hundred families had been recruited to watch five pilot episodes in Philadelphia. It was hot. Children were fidgety and distracted. Reception of the broadcast's frail UHF signal wasn't great.

Researchers watched attention plummet among antsy preschoolers during human-only scenes, spiking only when Muppets appeared.

The idea that Bert and Ernie were not intended to appear out and about in the neighborhood seems alien now, but educators at the time were concerned about children's ability to distinguish between reality and fantasy. The Street was "real." Muppets were not. But testing made it abundantly clear: without that mix, kids would not watch. The thought is frightening: the show came that close to failing.

> Barbara Fengel conducts tests in Philadelphia

> **Stating a curriculum goal did not limit creativity, because there were still an infinite number of ways in which to express it on the screen.**
>
> —ED PALMER, HEAD OF RESEARCH IN 1969

"If we hadn't been in that mode where it was all an experiment and where we tested everything, it would have been terrible," says Dr. Lewis Bernstein, the VP of education, research, and outreach at the Workshop today. "That really helped save the show."

Jim Henson was charged with enlarging the family of Muppet characters who would make that transition to the Street locale.

Bert, Ernie, and Kermit were already "cast" for those earlier test shows, but now Big Bird was added. His emotional foil, Oscar, was written into the show because educators agreed that it was important to give kids permission to feel grouchy—and to demonstrate differing viewpoints. Interactions with him would model the ways people adapt to the quirks of others. Dr. Loretta Long (Susan on the show) has her own view of that character's surprising success: "The kids who like Oscar really would love to slam a door in grown-up faces."

> **On *Sesame Street*, the monsters that we do are soft and cuddly and fuzzy. To an adult they might not look a bit scary, but for a three- or four-year-old child, they might be rather frightening things. For those kids who see this rather frightening thing and then get to know that it is not something to be frightened of, I think there's a catharsis.**
>
> —JIM HENSON

Writer/actor Matt Robinson is seen here with the earliest Big Bird. Harvard professor Sheldon White, one of the summer of '68 advisors, was among those who first suggested adding a character, whom he dubbed "Mr. Fluster," that could make the same frequent mistakes as the watching audience when tackling new experiences. Jim Henson took note and dreamed up Big Bird, whose very size, he reasoned, would present the opportunity to see any problem or question "from a different perspective."

Minor Distractions

Field researcher Sharon Lerner tests the show before its debut, using techniques created by her boss, Ed Palmer

A new kind of television show demanded new methods for testing its success. Ed Palmer's job at the Workshop was to figure out whether the *Sesame Street* programs both engaged and educated its audience. To do this, he invented ways to test television that had never been applied before. One that became extremely important to the Workshop was dubbed "the distractor technique."

Researchers on the Workshop staff lugged a giant tape recorder to children's homes and preschools, where they screened tapes of individual segments or whole episodes. They soon discovered what they ominously referred to as "the zombie effect." Researcher and longtime staffer Sharon Lerner explains.

"When kids are watching television, very often they will disconnect, and it's impossible to really see what they are attending to," she says. "It turned out that the only way to find out if something was really compelling was to distract them."

Shots of ice cream and puppies might make them look away. The question was, Lerner recalls, "What would make them look back?"

A slide projector and screen were set up next to the TV monitor. During the airing of a test show or segments, slides would be flashed on the screen at eight-second intervals, a soft click alerting kids to the changes. Watching researchers noted if the child's eyes wandered off the television screen and onto a slide or elsewhere in the room. Each time a slide changed, there was the same clicking sound, which reminded kids that there was a new slide on the screen and tempted them to look at it.

Researchers depressed a button whenever the child was watching the episode and released it when the child's attention wavered. Data recorded the percentage of time per eight-second intervals that children stayed glued to *Sesame Street*.

The CTW model of monitoring was applied to other Workshop shows at the time; here, researcher Hylda Clarke tracks data for The Electric Company using the distractor method

> ## Children won't learn from TV if they don't watch and listen to it.

—DR. LEWIS BERNSTEIN, EVP EDUCATION, RESEARCH, AND OUTREACH, 2009

The resulting data were painstakingly analyzed; and the resulting graphs made it painfully clear when things worked—or didn't.

This testing method proved so precise in identifying and shaping successful content that every succeeding season of the show—as well as other Workshop programming—would be tested as well.

As a result of all this formative research, Workshop staffers learned an enormous amount both about how children watch television in general and how they watched *Sesame Street* in particular. "What we have to do first is engage the child," says current head of research Dr. Lewis Bernstein, who was also there in the early years. So episodes were reorganized to provide a variety of fast and slower material so that the show was paced appropriately.

Music became not simply an adjunct to the show but an essential attention getter and punctuator; surprise became a

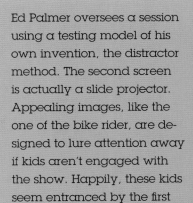

Ed Palmer oversees a session using a testing model of his own invention, the distractor method. The second screen is actually a slide projector. Appealing images, like the one of the bike rider, are designed to lure attention away if kids aren't engaged with the show. Happily, these kids seem entranced by the first episode's "J Jive" animation.

critical element in segments, and characters (both human and fuzzy) were added or eliminated from the show.

This careful and thoughtful response to testing continues today. Every show is tested with children. That's a hallmark of *Sesame Street* that few other TV shows can hope to match.

> ## The writers and producers eventually had to turn directly to the audience for answers: Would their ideas work? Would they be effective in attracting an audience? Would the audience learn what was intended?

—LLOYD MORRISETT, COFOUNDER

New Goals

Dr. Valeria Lovelace tests the race-relations curriculum with schoolkids in New York City

The review of *Sesame Street*'s educational effectiveness continued under the stewardship of Dr. Lewis Bernstein, who first served as director of research under Ed Palmer. When Lewis shifted his focus to international production in the eighties, Dr. Valeria Lovelace took over as head, continuing in that role until 1996, after which she brought her experience on the Street to bear as the educational consultant on shows like *Blue's Clues* and *Dora the Explorer*. During Lewis's and Valeria's tenures, the distractor method evolved into an eyes-on-screen method of testing that has become archetypal in educational television. Instead of testing just one or two children at a time, in this new model groups of as many as fifteen preschoolers were tested simultaneously. This was not a focus group, since children were still interviewed individually to find out what they'd learned, but the slide projector was replaced with the natural distractions that adding more children brought to the mix. Researchers noted children's attention to the show every five seconds, recording their eye movements at more than 700 selected observation points to graph when children were attentive to the screen.

Valeria's research indicated that children were having trouble remembering the letter and number of the day. So the show consulted with renowned psychologists Dr. Thomas Armstrong and Dr. Howard Gardner, proponents of the "multiple-intelligence theory," which postulated that children assimilate knowledge in many ways, including linguistic, musical, mathematical, and interpersonal experiences. This led to a decision by the *Sesame Street* team to cluster the show's short films, animations, and inserts around a single topic, rather than scattering them throughout the hour-long program.

Subsequent testing led by Valeria changed as well, employing what was dubbed "the engagement method," a system that measured not only visual attentiveness but other behaviors, such as moving along to a song. Shalom M. Fisch was vice president for program research at the Workshop during the transition to the next phase of testing, a methodology that elaborated on the idea of measuring all kinds of participatory "watching" attitudes. "It was state-of-the-art research design at the time," he says. "It built on the behaviorism concept that you don't try to measure stuff you can't see—what's going on in people's heads, that's a black box."

Dr. Valeria Lovelace, prepping a session of "engagement method" testing

Dr. Ed Palmer's original "distractor method," which tested the show's appeal and takeaway messages on one child at a time, was eventually replaced with the grouped-child "engagement method"

Keith Mielke became executive director of research in 1977 and, during 30 years with the Workshop, he assisted in the creation of an automated system for collecting data, called Program Evaluation Analysis Computer (PEAC). He also commissioned a new wave of evaluations of the show, the first since the original ETS testing in 1970.

Model Behavior

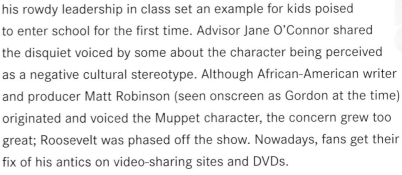

> **If you won't play with my friend Snuffy, then I can't play with you.**
>
> —BIG BIRD, TO A GULL ACQUAINTANCE, GULLIVER, WHO DISPLAYS BIRD BIGOTRY TOWARD SNUFFLEUPAGUSES

Sesame Street's willingness to discard segments that could net high ratings but that don't succeed at teaching kids is unprecedented on television. This dates back to the very first season, when testing showed that kids didn't absorb the goal of one animation where an offscreen voice interrupted a child's recitation of the alphabet. Kids lost track of the A-to-Z sequence.

"The intended humor," Gerry Lesser would later write, "apparently interferes with the intended instructional message."

"Bad modeling"—showing inappropriate behavior—explains the disappearance of other segments. Don Music's comically escalating frustration in Muppet skits cracked kids up, but when they started copying his head-banging at the piano, it was nixed.

"Puppets have limited expressions," puppeteer Fran Brill acknowledges wryly. "We'd bang heads against walls or show surprise by falling backward. It turns out that wasn't good modeling. We don't do that or toss Muppets around so much anymore."

The fate of viewer favorite Roosevelt Franklin was partially dictated by similar concerns. Staffers and teachers grew worried that

his rowdy leadership in class set an example for kids poised to enter school for the first time. Advisor Jane O'Connor shared the disquiet voiced by some about the character being perceived as a negative cultural stereotype. Although African-American writer and producer Matt Robinson (seen onscreen as Gordon at the time) originated and voiced the Muppet character, the concern grew too great; Roosevelt was phased off the show. Nowadays, fans get their fix of his antics on video-sharing sites and DVDs.

One entire episode famously went unaired. Developed to help children of divorcing parents cope with their fears and sadness, a story where the Snuffleupagus parents of Snuffy and Alice reveal that they're separating upset children more than it supported them. "It was just devastating for test groups of kids," actor Bob McGrath reported later in an interview. "So they just threw the whole thing in the garbage and never tried it again." It was too difficult a concept for a three-year-old to grasp in the limits of a one-hour show.

Other episodes met the same fate. The day after the terrorist attacks of September 11, 2001, as the writers were wrapping up work on season 33, Dr. Lewis Bernstein led the research group's plea to co-executive producer Arlene Sherman: "We have four more shows to write. We have to do something." One segment that emerged was a show intended to model peaceful conflict resolution. But it turned out that Telly Monster's argument with a bullying cousin proved more memorable to children than the antifighting message. It, too, no longer airs. Happily, another tolerance-themed segment, where Big Bird confronts the racism of a new friend, a gull named Gulliver, was far more successful. It aired in episode 4021, just five months later.

> **Who says I can't teach?**
>
> —ROOSEVELT FRANKLIN

A rare shot from an unaired episode, including a one-time-only appearance on-screen by Snuffy's dad (actually performed by the Snuffy puppet—the two never shared a scene)

More Eyes
on Screen

When it debuted, *Sesame Street* was greeted with almost overwhelming love and praise by both the commercial and educational media. But the honeymoon couldn't last, not with the ambitious goals and radically new educational approach of the show.

Like even the best-loved child, it faced increased scrutiny and scolding from both the press and child-care experts in its tween and teen years. It was criticized for being too urban and integrated and, alternatively, for presenting a world where there were "no cross words or conflicts," according to Urie Bronfenbrenner, former founder of Head Start—despite Mr. Hooper's often-ascerbic asides, Kermit's meltdowns, and Oscar's put-downs (all calculated to support social-emotional curricular messages).

One educational professor accused the show of a "hard sell" of its educational goals; others saw little educational content but, instead, in the words of a columnist for *Childhood Education* magazine, "phony pedagogy, vulgar side shows, bad acting, and layers of smoke and fog to clog the eager minds of small children." Most famously, in the mid-eighties, NYU Media Ecology professor Neil Postman derided the show's appeal as presenting a rival for formal education, stating, "*Sesame Street* encourages children to love school only if school is like *Sesame Street*."

To those who worried that the show's quick pace would contribute to, as one educator phrased it, "shortened attention span and a lack of reflectiveness," Professor of Psychology Daniel Anderson countered with a belief that the show encouraged an engaged response. "Children are intellectually active when they watch television," he argued.

"The Workshop kept track of these criticisms," wrote Gerry Lesser in his 1974 book, *Children and Television: Lessons from Sesame Street.* Despite debating the value of critiques that tended toward opinion rather than quantifiable and validated research, he acknowledged that the Workshop monitored its criticism "partly in the hope we could discover ways to improve *Sesame Street*."

> ❝ **We wanted to make sure we were still doing the right thing . . . that we were still on target.** ❞
>
> —DR. LEWIS BERNSTEIN, DIRECTOR OF RESEARCH IN 1972, CURRENTLY EVP EDUCATION, RESEARCH, AND OUTREACH

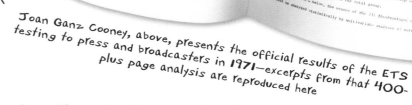

Joan Ganz Cooney, above, presents the official results of the ETS testing to press and broadcasters in 1971—excerpts from that 400-plus page analysis are reproduced here

"How do we define engagement?" asks Dr. Rosemarie Truglio, who directs current testing. "It's visual attention plus participatory behavior, like clapping hands along to a song."

When Sonia Manzano and Emilio Delgado were added to the cast in answer to criticism from the Spanish-speaking community, Spanish became an innate part of the show.

"Counting on the show was a favorite thing with fans," says Emilio, who plays Luis, who began introducing Spanish organically by calling Big Bird *pajaro*, Spanish for "bird." "I remember all these little kids would come up and say, 'I can count in Spanish: *Uno, dos, tres . . .*' And all the way to ten."

Susan went from homemaker, as seen here, to nurse after informative talks with the National Organization for Women

> **❝ . . . The impact of early educational TV viewing was so evident a dozen years later. I was surprised that the effects were mostly attributable to watching *Sesame Street*. ❞**
>
> —DANIEL ANDERSON, PROFESSOR OF PSYCHOLOGY, UNIVERSITY OF MASSACHUSETTS AMHERST

In fact, that's exactly what happened. Among the voices raised in the earliest years were groups representing what they considered underserved minorities on the show. African-American groups derided some puppets they perceived as representing stereotyped racial constructs, such as Roosevelt Franklin. Some minority groups thought Oscar could be seen as a negative racial stereotype . . . though this caused surprise in the Workshop offices, where the Grouch had never been envisioned as any one race.

When the Latino population asked for a quality presence on the show, a conference was convened with community leaders in 1971. The Workshop was startled when the invited group met behind locked doors, then issued a press release calling for better representation on the block. Criticisms were silenced when Maria and Luis were cast.

A similar tack was taken by the National Organization for Women (NOW); its New York chapter proposed a boycott of sponsors unless the show created more appealing female images. NOW representatives were invited to the offices to make their case, an experience that writer Jon Stone said raised the consciousness of the staff.

"They weren't angry, just factual," Dr. Loretta Long recalls of the discussions around her own character's role as homemaker on the show. "They thought it was a lost opportunity."

As a result, the character of Susan left her kitchen and took up an earlier career as a nurse, to husband Gordon's initial discomfort.

Despite the show's continuing commitment to meet children's needs, some still found room to debate its efficacy. One educator, Dr. Herbert A. Sprigle, argued that "there are simply no shortcuts through the problems of educating poverty children," and called shows like *Sesame Street* "easy answers to a complicated problem." That may be true. Ed Palmer himself called the show a bandage on the larger economic and social problems faced by children in poverty. The Workshop must live with the reality that the show can't be all things to all people . . . especially critics. But that didn't

stop the show's researchers from meeting the critics head-on with documented studies that spoke to these concerns.

Thirty years after its debut, the show's researchers participated in an independent study. Daniel R. Anderson, professor of psychology at the University of Massachusetts Amherst, together with associates Wright, Linebarger, and Schmidt, aimed to discover if the show's long-term goal of giving kids a leg up in school had been met. "The Recontact Study," as it was dubbed, located 87 percent of the child subjects from the original ETS testing; interviews with them and school records were collected to track any measurable long-term effects of watching the show. The study concluded that "Adolescents who often watched *Sesame Street* as preschoolers, compared with those who rarely watched . . . had higher grades in English, mathematics, and science; spent more time reading books outside of school . . . and expressed lower levels of aggressive attitudes."

The study acknowledged that it was possible that children attracted to the show were inherently more inclined to these behaviors, but the study's control groups helped negate that conclusion. Its data also "contradict the hypotheses that the show's pace or content had negative impact on attention or creativity," read the report.

Even its authors were surprised by the definitive results, and the show's beneficial impact comparable to other educational programs. Only *Mister Rogers' Neighborhood* could boast similar results, and those primarily indicated its viewers' increased interest in the arts. Professor Anderson believes the study, published in 2001, did much to silence critics in the show's later years. "I think almost all knowledgeable academics changed their view about the potential of television to do good for children," he notes.

Eyes are always on *Sesame Street*. As recently as 2009, teachers and their students gathered for a panel discussion of the show at the annual Pop Culture Conference in New Orleans. One of the conference's organizers, an educator with a focus on children's media, had this to say about its impact on viewers: "Programs such as *Sesame Street* help children establish their own self-identity, and even adults continue to interact with the show and its characters," says Richard Graham, media services librarian and assistant professor at the University of Nebraska-Lincoln. "YouTube, blogs, and other viewer-generated content clearly demonstrate that viewers interact and feel a sense of personal ownership with *Sesame Street*, long after they're regular viewers of the show."

Season 40: Hour Testing: Cowmonster Pair 4196 #202401
April 16th and 17th 2009

SEX F AGE 4 Ethnicity L

						Telly: We can help because...We're the Cow monster Pair!								
Smile	Laugh	Counts/ ABCs	Sings	Rep to ?	Char ID	Screen Related Pointing	IMI Action V/P	Clap	Moves to music/ Dances	Verb-Label	Predict	Post. comm	Neg. comm	

Researcher Jen Kotler explains that this "coding" sample of recent testing with kids indicates moments of high (and low) attention—as Joan Cooney herself once stated: "Every segment is evaluated by the toughest critics of all . . . the children themselves."

Meet the Need

Sonia Manzano wrote the lyrics for the song she dances to here in 1984

Through the years, *Sesame Street* has endeavored to help kids cope with the realities of their remarkably complex worlds, in episodes that tackle correspondingly weighty topics. There have been story lines, carefully scaled to preschool proportions, that deal with race relations, birth, death, adoption, sibling rivalry, and frightening events, such as fires and hurricanes, that can change a child's life. Each year a specific curriculum goal is given primary focus and, occasionally, a particular challenge preschoolers face is integrated into a series of special episodes.

Often it's not a specific event but a larger social issue that's addressed in the show's "affective"—that is, emotion-based—curriculum goals. Sometimes the addition of these goals is fluidly introduced through casting. Although showing and celebrating diversity certainly was a rudimentary focus on *Sesame Street*, it wasn't until Sonia Manzano and Emilio Delgado came on board that Hispanic and Latino viewers could truly identify with the show.

In fact, Sonia became a principal scriptwriter because of her interest in accurately portraying the Latina point of view. Writer Luis Santeiro also brings a sensitive and authentic Latino voice to the show. The puppet character of Rosita, played by Carmen Osbahr, was introduced to lend a Mexican flavor to the melting pot of monsters.

Race relations gets the fuzzy treatment and, above, Cookie Monster helps spread the word about healthy habits for life—but, yes, he still eats "sometimes food" (cookies)—just lots of anytime foods, too

> " Latins from Queens and the hip Argentines / Say *hola* when greeting each other / We know the way, we can all say / *Hola*, what's happening, brother? "
>
> —MARIA & LUIS, SINGING "YOU SAY HOLA, I SAY HOLA"

Care is likewise taken to address other protocols of the larger world outside the Street. The female characters on *Sesame Street* continue to reflect the changing roles of women in society and the addition of curricula centered around career opportunities and self-esteem. Sonia recalls how Maria initially ran a library on the Street and, over thirty-plus years, went from being a teenager to "a bit of a hippie to a feminist," and eventually became a wife and mother.

"It's a pretty impressive fictional biography," Sonia laughingly says of Maria's resume. "Not many other TV characters have gone through so many phases of life in 'real time' like that." And Alison Bartlett-O'Reilly's character, Gina, now runs a veterinary clinic and is a single woman who chose to adopt a child on her own.

Researchers seized on the opportunity presented by cast member Buffy Sainte-Marie's newborn baby by bringing him on the show in 1977 to help writers tackle issues of sibling rivalry. In a script by Tony Geiss, Buffy reassures Big Bird when he worries that she doesn't have enough love left over for him. She explains that there are different kinds of love but always plenty to go around, so she can love her baby *and* Big Bird.

"That issue of sibling rivalry was too powerful a subject to leave in one Street scene," says today's research head, Dr Lewis Bernstein. So in season 34 writers give Baby Bear a sister, Curly Bear.

> " I have Big Bird love for you. "
>
> —BUFFY SAINTE-MARIE, COMFORTING BIG BIRD

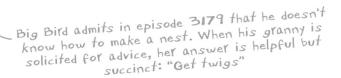

When the four-part hurricane-themed story line (episodes 3177 to 3180) was first broadcast, a swinish architect from the firm of I.M. Pig, roped in to help rebuilding efforts, references New York's "Twin Towers." He suggests Big Bird relocate to twin beds there. After the tragic events of September 11, 2001, the line was redubbed with the phrase "a new hotel at the Best Nesters." The episodes then became an element of the Workshop's Community Outreach efforts after the events of September 11 and 2005's Hurricane Katrina, demonstrating how lives and homes can be rebuilt after emergencies . . . with help from friends.

Big Bird admits in episode **3179** that he doesn't know how to make a nest. When his granny is solicited for advice, her answer is helpful but succinct: "Get twigs"

The research team is especially proud of the show's response to the cataclysmic events in children's lives, like the rebuilding episodes that aired following Hurricane Katrina and, a few years earlier, show number 3981, which was taped not long after the events of September 11, 2001. After asking rescue workers what the show could do to help in cases of emergency, researchers learned that kids are sometimes too frightened of firefighters in full gear to react quickly, so Elmo tackled his own fear in a story line where Hooper's Store catches fire. New York City Fire Department Ladder Companies 58 and 26 dedicated their appearance on the show to fallen comrade Lt. Robert Nagel, lost on September 11.

"You're right, Big Bird, it's not all right . . . but it *will* be all right."
—GORDON, EPISODE 3977

New Ways to Teach

Dr. Rosemarie Truglio, on the set with Elmo and her son, leads a team that vets each script, song, and animation

D r. Rosemarie Truglio took over in season 29 as vice president of education and research. It was a critical time for the show. Increased competition was making itself felt, with whole cable channels now dedicated to children's programs and high numbers of preschool shows being introduced on the standard channels. More options meant viewership was spread thinner. Ratings were naturally affected, and the show's demographic was skewing younger than at its debut, with a core audience that averaged three years of age.

Rosemarie instituted a series of studies to explore what made this new generation sit up and watch. What she found was that *Sesame Street* had become "a magazine format, hour-long show in a narrative half-hour world."

In a sea of shows dominated by animations, some broken up into even briefer 15-minute nuggets, the show struggled to hold its audience. *Sesame Street*'s original construct had been designed to mimic an adult's hour-long dramatic story line (in show parlance, the "Street stories"), interrupted by brief "commercials"—the short segments shot off the Street. That no longer met children's needs.

"It was around the 45-minute period that children were beginning to lose attention," says Rosemarie, summarizing the findings of research done at the time. "You had them at the very beginning, because they're interested in the story; but then you keep breaking up the story, so you see their interest level drop."

> " Sometimes people ask, 'Why are you changing my show?' It's not about a parent saying 'This is my *Sesame Street*.' This is *Sesame Street* for the child. "
>
> –DR. ROSEMARIE TRUGLIO, HEAD OF RESEARCH

This was a real problem. No matter how many times the show was tested, the results came back the same: at forty-five minutes, the children's attention lagged.

Together, research and the writers decided to shorten the core show by fifteen minutes and add a new, independent piece to round out the hour. The new segment would be specifically oriented to the younger audience that the show now attracted. A "science of discovery" curriculum had proved quite popular in an earlier season, so it was decided to build on that theme of asking questions to find out more about the physical world.

Field researchers Carly Shuler, Mindy Brooks, Jessica DiSalvo, Jennifer Schiffman, Leslie Fleming, and Andy Chen visit the New Rochelle Day Nursery to conduct testing of season 40 episodes; the diverse population makes it a favorite testing site

The current method of testing moves children out of classroom chairs and onto the floor for an experience that more closely simulates how they'd be watching in a home's less formal setting. Instead of the more arbitrarily regulated five-second intervals used previously, researchers monitor closely during whole scenes to identify visual attention and other behaviors, like talking to the screen or singing along, that indicate which moments are most engaging. Later, one-on-one interviews reveal if children took away the intended messages.

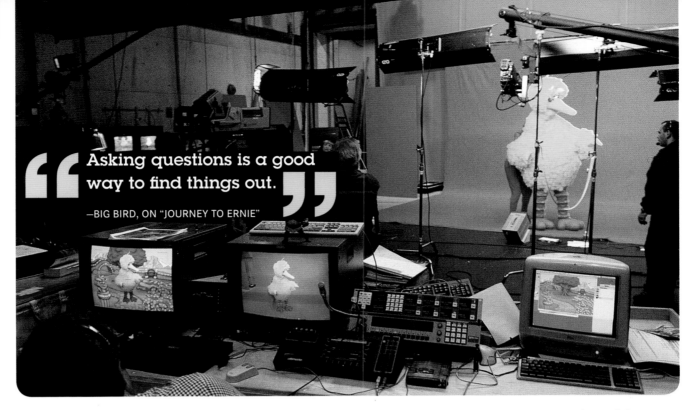

> **Asking questions is a good way to find things out.**
> —BIG BIRD, ON "JOURNEY TO ERNIE"

Journey to Ernie was one of the show's first forays into computer-generated animation for a segment with Muppet characters—here, Matt Vogel wears the Big Bird suit

Next, the creative team had to decide which character would drive the segment. That was an easy one. By now, Elmo was enormously popular, and he was three and a half years old—closest in age of all the core characters to the target audience. That was how "Elmo's World" began, and it was an instant success.

The show continued to adapt to the audience's environment. During season 33, viewers tuned in to see a radical change. "That was the year that we didn't break up the story," Rosemarie recalls. For the first time, the Street story ran uninterrupted; the collection of theme-related Muppet inserts and films were in a cluster, followed by "Elmo's World."

There were more experiments. "Muppet Clubhouse," mimicking preschool, had nap time, snack time, and circle time, plus a segment designed to get kids moving. It was an inspired idea, but kids didn't know the new Muppets and became confused, and the frenetic pace of the segment raised concerns. The puppets Mooba, Mel, Narf, and Groogel literally bounced off the walls. So it was abandoned after just two seasons.

"Journey to Ernie" was the next experiment. "That came about when we were trying to focus on thinking skills," Rosemarie explains. "I felt sequencing was really important for children. They're told to do a series of three things on IQ tests, for instance, such as 'go to the desk, pick up a crayon, and bring it to me.'" That prompted her to wonder, What if Big Bird were in a maze where he had to do different tasks? Each task could be an interactive moment.

"It was very popular, especially among the younger children," Rosemarie says. "They loved the game of hide and seek." But however popular the segment was, writers and the producers felt it wasn't 'Sesame' enough and wasn't a comfortable fit. The look and feel of the animation was too similar to other shows on the television schedule and, while funny, it didn't mesh with the whole show. The team learned from the experience and, for season 40, developed an animation that seemed more true to the show's signature Muppety look and feel: "Abby's Flying Fairy School." Time will tell if it joins the lists of classics or drops off to make room for new experiments. Regardless, the continual evolution of the show through the partnership of researchers and writers is assured.

The most current show breakdown, seen at right beside the season 40 curriculum, differs considerably from the previous structure, seen in an example from 1994, far right. The show has moved from its classic magazine format (interrupted by many curricular "commercials") to fewer segments arranged in a more predictable pattern—a friendlier format for younger viewers, who find comfort in routines.

SESAME STREET

Curriculum Document
Season 40
Statement of Educational Goals
2008 – 2009

sesameworkshop.
The nonprofit educational organization behind Sesame Street and so much more

WORKSHOP EDUCATION & RESEARCH

SHOW BREAKDOWN GRID: Season 40

Word on the Street
00:30
New Opening
00:50
Street Story
10:00-12:00
Celebrity Vocabulary Word
Murray Tune-In
01:00
Letter Film
01:15
Abby Fairy Flying School
08:30
Murray Tune-In
01:00
Number Film
01:15
B/E Claymation or
Murray has a Little Lamb
05:00-6:30
Murray Tune-In
01:00
Music Video/Curriculum Spot
02:15
Elmo's World
17:00
Murray Close
00:30
Closing Credits
00:45

The "Elmo's World" set is real, but some effects, like dancing tables, opening drawers, and snapping window shades, are added digitally

Kevin Clash holds his nose to get the distinctive squashed-schnoz voice of Elmo in this shot

Using Our Noodles

> **" Dorothy has a question, Mr. Noodle! "**
>
> —ELMO

O n November 16, 1998, an unusual visitor showed up on *Sesame Street*. More accurately, he showed up outside the window in Elmo's room on the show-within-a-show segment "Elmo's World." His name was Mr. Noodle, a role played by renowned actor/mime Bill Irwin. The Tony Award–winning performer was already a noted Broadway and stage star, familiar to the show's preschool parents from roles in the movies *My Blue Heaven* and *Popeye*; he's since appeared in dozens more films and shows.

Irwin's mastery of mime work presented a perfect interactive element for the segments: his mistakes empower viewers, who call out instructions that allow them to feel smarter than the adult.

In 2000, Mr. Noodle was all too briefly joined by his brother, the other Mr. Noodle, played by actor Michael Jeter with great humor and warmth. Sadly, Michael died in 2003, but children can still get to know his character, since his segments continue to air.

The Noodles are apparently a dynasty of mimes. When Elmo asks them about something he's interested in, they physically (and hilariously) act out their replies, in the tradition of great silent-film comedians like Charlie Chaplin, Buster Keaton, and Harold Lloyd.

"It comes out of that same idea that adults who are bungling give kids the opportunity to figure it out before they do," notes vice president of education, research, and outreach Dr. Lewis Bernstein, who lead the "Elmo's World" creative team. "Kids are empowered to say 'I know more than he does. I'm a learner.'"

All of the Noodles make mistakes, but, urged on by enthusiastic kid voice-overs, they "use their noodles" and figure out a key element of the segment's curriculum goal.

Another star of "Elmo's World" is Dorothy the goldfish, Elmo's pet, an equally silent confidante who provides another way to invite responses. Kids instinctively fill in the blanks. By making Dorothy an insatiably curious goldfish in Elmo's imagination, the research team was given a tool that allows for many comic but also curriculum-based opportunities. Neatly avoiding didacticism, Dorothy can "ask" Elmo about whatever the research team wants kids to learn.

Kristen Chenoweth, who won a Tony Award for her role as the good witch, Glinda, in Broadway's Wicked has appeared multiple times as a Noodle sister

> **" Oh, it's Mr. Noodle's brother, Mr. Noodle. "**
>
> —ELMO

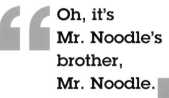

Tony Award-winning Michael Jeter, as a Noodle brother, was familiar to fans from the film The Green Mile

When a fish is needed for taping, props buyer Keith Olsen acquires as many as nine, so one may be swapped for another depending on the liveliness of its performance. Like all goldfish, they often are not long for this world, so several are needed throughout the season. At the end of the season, surviving Dorothys are sent to good homes. Heather Dixon, unit manager, reports that there are currently around twelve former Dorothys living in her parents' pond.

Making Magic

To this day, the goals developed for the *Sesame Street* curriculum are still the heart and soul of the show. The "Season 40 Curriculum Document: Statement of Educational Goals" has transformed the old language—it's been rephrased to identify the writers' goals rather than the child's—and messages have changed over time. But it remains that "backbone" that underpins everything *Sesame Street* is built upon, from the television show to outreach projects, from the website to the books and imagination-promoting plush that help to fund the show. And still, teams of researchers and writers continue to work together. "Joan built this forty years ago," says Dr. Rosemarie Truglio, vice president of education and research. "She came up with this model of research: the developmental psychologists and the early-childhood teaching experts working hand in hand with the creative folk. It creates a healthy tension. I think the reason why the model works is that everyone who is a part of the model really, truly cares about children."

The new language seen in season 40's "Statement of Educational Goals": "Present letters in context through multiple exposures. . . . This repetition can help children develop richer understandings of each letter"

> " Given a set of symbols, either all letters or all numbers, the child knows whether those symbols are used in reading or counting. "
>
> —CURRICULUM GOAL I, INSTRUCTIONAL GOALS, 1969

> " The child recognizes that a single event may be seen and interpreted differently by different individuals. "
>
> —CURRICULUM GOAL IV.B.1, INSTRUCTIONAL GOALS, 1969

Season 40 language: "Model strategies for handling conflict in responsible and appropriate ways, such as sharing and taking turns. This involves taking on others' perspectives, identifying the problem and generating solutions"

Season 40 language: "Encourage children to observe and sort objects according to one characteristic at a time"

> " One of these things is not like the other. "
>
> —SUSAN, SINGING THE SONG BY JOE RAPOSO, JON STONE, AND BRUCE HART

> " Given 4 objects, 3 of which have an attribute in common, the child can sort out the inappropriate object on the basis of: Size, Form, Function, Class. "
>
> —CURRICULUM GOAL II.C.1, INSTRUCTIONAL GOALS, 1969

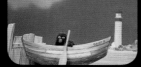

Season 40 language: "Help children sustain and develop their innate sense of wonder and curiosity about the natural world"

> " The child can label the physical world around him: Land, Sky, and Water. "

—CURRICULUM GOAL III.A.1,
INSTRUCTIONAL GOALS, 1969

Episode #0877

Grover: Okay, now this time, remember—do not all go up to THAT end of the boat, okay? Because if you go up to THAT end, up to the tip, we will fall into the water like we did before. Right? We do not want that, do we? Okay, guys, come on in. C'mon, let's go. Let's go! Okay, over here. Somebody over HERE. Hey, guys. Uh . . . Guys? Guys. Hey. *[As the boat sinks]* Oooooooooh.

These snapshots from season 40 show the latest segments illustrating some of the core goals, plus the current "green" focus

> " The child can identify himself and other familiar individuals. . . . He comes to see situations from more than one point of view. "

—CURRICULUM GOAL IV,
INSTRUCTIONAL GOALS, 1969

Season 40 language: "While celebrating differences, we can also highlight the many ways we are all the same"

Bert's relative, Brad, looks just like his uncle except for one very important thing: he has red hair. Recognizing family units is a curriculum goal

NEWS FLASH

Over the years, many things have changed on *Sesame Street*. But the basic process by which the show is created is still heavily informed by educational experts.

Once a need is defined, experts from a variety of fields—education and psychology, for example—are invited to a curriculum seminar to figure out what and how *Sesame Street* can teach to that need and where they should put their energy and efforts. Then a curriculum is created and disseminated. Each year's curriculum focuses on a specific area that the shows will highlight, but also updates methods of teaching old standbys, like letters and numbers.

As Rosemarie explains, "Every year, we reinvent ourselves . . . and that starts with the curriculum."

Prankster/ writer/director Jon Stone wears Bert during a pause in taping this segment in season 12

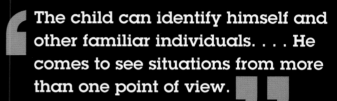

THIS CHAPTER HAS BEEN BROUGHT TO YOU BY THE LETTERS F AND S AND NUMBER IV.

The letter F is for formative research, undertaken before or during the creation of the show in order to shape its content. **The letter S** is for summative research, testing done after taping, to determine the success of the segment or episode—whether kids liked it and learned the take-home message. **The number IV** is for the number of broad goals first outlined for the show.

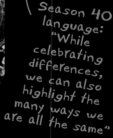

8

"**We're in the comedy business.**"

—JON STONE, ORIGINAL HEAD WRITER

IMAGINE THAT!

EPISODE
4157

Sesame Street is crowded this morning, with Abby Cadabby, Elmo, a Honker, a Dinger, Alan, and a chicken sharing the studio with two kids, the entire crew, and a medium-size Christmas tree, which sits off to the side beyond Big Bird's nest.

Taping is starting half an hour earlier than usual. There's going to be a Christmas party on set this evening, and the day has to end a little early so the crew can set up for the event. Meanwhile, in today's episode, Elmo is showing Abby the magic of pretending. Longtime *Sesame Street* scriptwriter Tony Geiss has written it, along with the music and lyrics to "Making Believe," a song embedded in the episode. A particularly gifted songwriter, Tony often includes a tune in his shows, and he's also credited with the invention of the musically inclined Honkers in one of his scripts; one is appearing today.

Puppeteers Tyler Bunche and Jen Barnhart, playing the Honker and Dinger, wait for Dean Gordon, the segment's director, to finish his consultation with Tony. Meanwhile, puppeteer Peter Linz wanders around the back of the set with a microphone on, bocking like a chicken. And inside Hooper's Store, Alan Muraoka chats up Abby. As rehearsals start, Alan leans across the shop's counter. "Good luck, Abby," he tells her. "Make some magic!"

Tony and Dean huddle together, discussing the first shot. There's usually a writer around the set—the writer of that day's episode or the head writer—because someone has to be available in case last-minute script changes need to be made.

At 9:10 A.M., they're ready to shoot. After only two takes, things are looking good. "I think that's a purchase," says Dean. "Very nice, everybody. My work here is done." That gets a big laugh.

Five hours and a lot more work later, in the nearby control room, Tony is having a discussion with Executive Producer Carol-

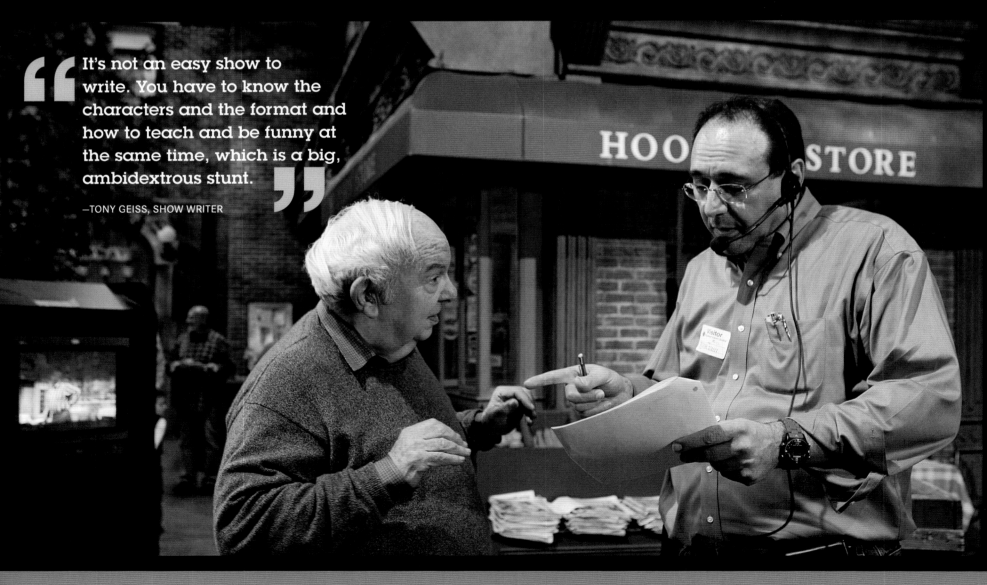

> It's not an easy show to write. You have to know the characters and the format and how to teach and be funny at the same time, which is a big, ambidextrous stunt.
>
> —TONY GEISS, SHOW WRITER

on the set
on the set
on the set

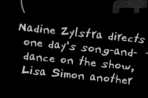

Nadine Zylstra directs one day's song-and-dance on the show, Lisa Simon another

Lynn Parente and Producer Melissa Dino about a problem he's having with the visuals for his tune. The song talks about pretending, and the diligent props department has provided a bowl of porridge and an oar, among other things referenced by the lyrics. Tony thinks this is too literal an interpretation, and he doesn't like it. When you're pretending, should you see the imaginary object? Tony thinks not.

"I wish someone had asked me for a rewrite if they thought it wasn't visual enough," he sighs. Scripts go through a number of revisions before taping. Even so, there's usually on-set finagling.

Melissa quietly sweeps the set of the unwelcome props. Tony has gotten his point across.

Back in the studio, Dean ignores the noisy Honker shadowing him and begins blocking the next scene. Guests are arriving for the Christmas party, but they're going to have to wait.

There's some more pretending to do on *Sesame Street*.

The first season of taping on *Sesame Street* was referred to as a "sausage factory" by the production crew, as they cranked out 130 episodes in a few brief weeks. That tradition of speed and efficiency continues today. Producers and directors are often called on to manage two or more complex shots in a single day, as evidenced in these images from season 40. Above, Director Nadine Zylstra guides her casts through a spoof of a popular TV show, then a green-screen shot promoting the letter H, and finally a song. At left, Lisa Simon directs a large cast for a Street scene, then shifts gears for a celebrity appearance with Julianna Margulies, in a spoof of her role on the series *ER*.

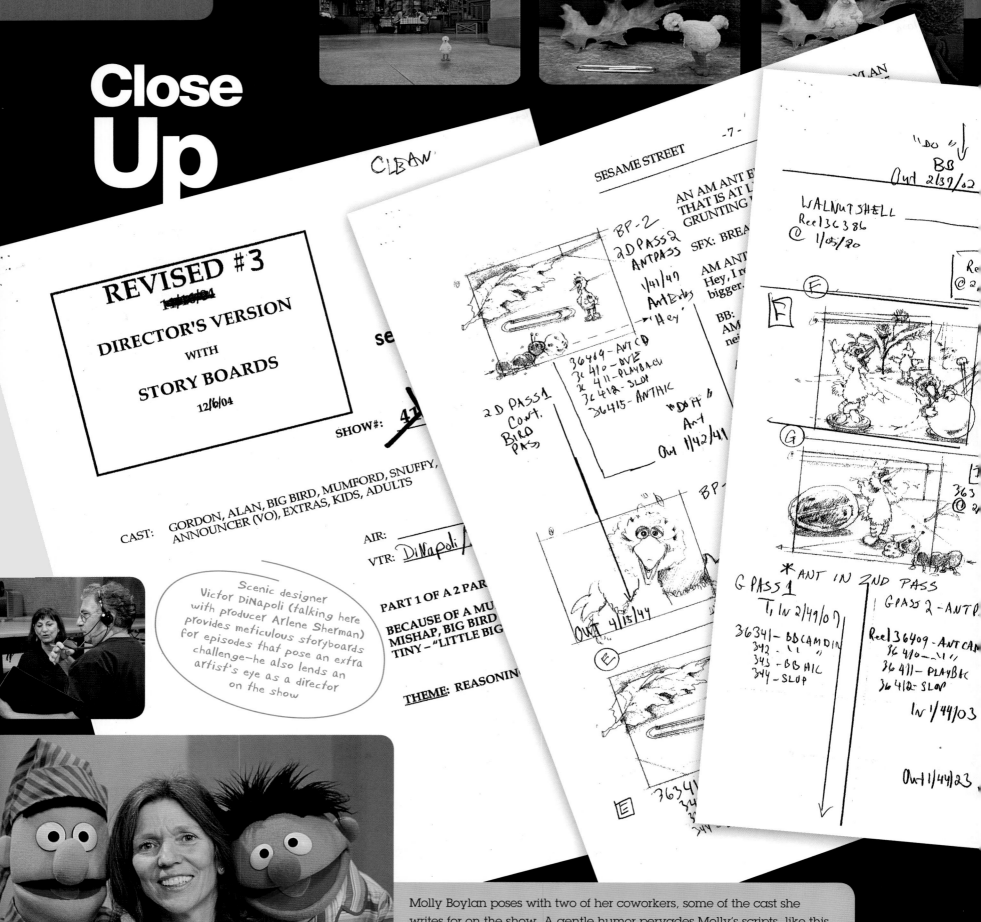

Molly Boylan poses with two of her coworkers, some of the cast she writes for on the show. A gentle humor pervades Molly's scripts, like this one, which showcases a rare mingling of elaborate animation effects with characters shot on the Street. The copious notes and detailed storyboard demonstrate how even details tackled in postproduction are thoughtfully planned together by writer, director, producer, and the production crew before taping begins.

Scenic designer Victor DiNapoli (talking here with producer Arlene Sherman) provides meticulous storyboards for episodes that pose an extra challenge—he also lends an artist's eye as a director on the show

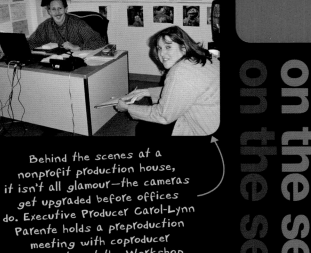

SESAME STREET   - 9 -

BOYLAN
SHOW 4105

SNUFFY 12/7

(AS BP-6) CUT UP TO: SNUFFY ENTERING FRAME.

SNUFFY: (CALLS) <u>Bird! Oh, Bird!</u> (STOPS
AND MUSES ALOUD) I wonder where Big Bird is?
He was supposed to meet me here for a playdate.

Reel 36337
36338
36339
36340

CUT DOWN TO: LITTLE BIG BIRD.

BB: (TO CAM) That's my friend, Snuffy. Wow!
Does he look big! (CALLS) <u>Snuffy! I'm here!</u>

Reels 36391 - BB CAM ON CU
36392 - BB CM OYR WIDE
36393 - BB WIDE HICU
36394 - SLOP
36408 HI CU BB CU   *12/7*

INSERT H-1

WE SEE SNUFFY FROM BIG BIRD'S POV.

BB: (CONT, CALLS UP) <u>Snuffy!</u>

SNUFFY: (OBLIVIOUS) Bird! Come on, Bird, I
want to play!

V1- Snuffy CAM D   36337
V2- Snuffy "   36338
V3- Snuffy HIC   36339
V4- SLOP   36340

BB: He didn't hear me. I'd better shout louder.
(AS LOUD AS HE CAN) <u>Snuffffyyyyy!</u>

BP-7

MUSIC: SONG END.

AS SOON AS BIG BIR
ROUND STARTS TO

CH: POST SHAKE.

X: BIG FOOTSTEPS.

UFFY IS APPROACHING AND LITTLE BIG BIRD
OSSED AROUND BY THE VIBRATIONS.
(STAGGERS) Whoa! What's going on?

on the set on the set on the set

Behind the scenes at a nonprofit production house, it isn't all glamour—the cameras get upgraded before offices do. Executive Producer Carol-Lynn Parente holds a preproduction meeting with coproducer Tim Carter at the Workshop

Months later, she's on set with writers and directors

Talent bones up on lines in corners

Teams consult behind the cameras

Taping feeds from the cameras to the control room

IMAGINE THAT!   177

The Write Stuff

Jon Stone was a huge hit with the kids on the show— "He never took himself too seriously and loved to be silly and outrageous," says fellow writer Chris Cerf

It only looks easy.

"Most everyone *thinks* they can write for children," Jon Stone once said. "But there are many more limitations than there are possibilities when you write for kids. It ain't that simple."

First, you have to know what kids like. For the show's original writing team, that meant going to the source: the kids themselves.

"We showed them everything," Jon Stone said, "from Walter Cronkite to soap operas to children's shows, anything that was on television. We studied their reactions using very sophisticated research methods; we quizzed them, talked to them, found out what they liked, what they didn't like. We found out what they retained, what they didn't, and tried very hard to assimilate all this knowledge," he elaborated. "Out of it came this potpourri . . . which all stuck together and became *Sesame Street*."

Just as critical, the show flouted convention by not hiring teachers to script shows, which was typical of educational television of the time. Project director Joan Ganz Cooney and the producers felt instinctively that it would be easier to teach writers how to successfully interpret curriculum than it would be to teach a theorist how to write "funny." And it was. Perhaps one reason Jon and later writers made it look so easy to find the funny in the curriculum is because comedy was simply a way of life for them.

Fellow scriptwriter Chris Cerf remembers, for example, that in the early years, Jon Stone would hack the lobby sign in the building where the Workshop had its offices. Every morning, just for fun,

The job of head writer (Jon Stone's role on *Sesame Street*) originated on soap operas and other series, where the work of many writers needed to be corralled into a cohesive "voice" for a television show.

When Jon began focusing on producing and directing the show, Jeff Moss took over as head writer, followed by Norman Stiles, Lou Berger, Tony De Sena, Lou Berger again, Belinda Ward, and Joey Mazzarino. Joey recently described the role he currently holds in an interview with Joe Henn for the in-depth fan site toughpigs.com:

"There are about nine other writers beside myself, and they're all given an assignment [and assigned characters]. So you might get Elmo, Snuffy, Big Bird, whatever. You can also trade, like 'I really want Telly for this one, can I have Telly?' Then they'll come and meet with me, and they'll have their curriculum laid out with the letter and number and pitch me a story based on the characters in their cast list, and we'll work on it from there."

> **Writing for children is not so easy.**
>
> —JON STONE

Jon would jumble the small white letters around on the felt board so that Children's Television Workshop was written as "Children's Television porkshoW." Invariably, some diligent staffer would correct it.

And the next morning, Jon would do it again.

Jon's death in 1997, after a long illness, was a tremendous blow for the staff. His whimsy on the set is still greatly missed. But happily for the show, the silliness didn't end.

Show writer Lou Berger recalls his first meeting with Norman Stiles, who became head writer in 1972.

"He looked very serious and shook hands with me and started walking me toward his office," remembers Lou. "And there was a security camera, and he broke into an insane Jerry Lewis dance. He said, 'I do that all the time for security.'"

You gotta laugh.

Puppeteers can tape scripts to monitors, so aren't required to memorize all their lines. The human actors (and full-body puppet performers) don't have a similar option—and often receive a final script from writers the day a scene is shot.

The Process

Writing for the show has followed a pattern through the years that originated with its first writing team. The typical process went something like this: Writers received an assignment sheet, a.k.a the show sheet, which described in general terms what they had to tackle in any given episode.

"On the top, it said who was in the show," recalls writer Tony Geiss. "In the left column were all the goals. We had specific research goals. You would choose from those what to write about."

Norman Stiles's twenty-five-year tenure as head writer began back in season four. Possibly his studies in the fields of zoology and chemistry, plus a stint in social work, came in handy for a job among the zany species behind and in front of the camera at *Sesame Street*. He explains what happened next: "Let's say you were supposed to spend six minutes on the letter of the day," he says. "The theory was that if the available animations totaled four minutes, you were supposed to write two minutes more on that subject, and that writing was probably going to be on the Street.

"Street segments at that time were not story-based," Norman continues. "They didn't even have a theme. It was all individual segments that were pegged directly to curriculum." The

Street segments were interrupted by the puppet "inserts"—bits that didn't happen on the Street—and the short films and animations assigned to outside filmmakers and animators, which each elaborated on a single curriculum goal. Pacing was key, because it would be easy to confuse an audience of preschoolers, who can swiftly lose track of what show they're watching.

Tony Geiss relates the next evolution in the show. "It wasn't until about fifteen to twenty years ago that it was decided that the Street pieces should tell a continuing story," he says. "It changed the nature of the show."

"It turned out that little kids can follow a story, and they loved it," adds former head writer Lou Berger. "We could write these wonderful one-act musicals, allowing all of the elements to be emphasized in a storytelling way. You can have more fun with characters . . . stretch those muscles."

In recent years, that story structure has changed again and again to meet the evolving needs of its audience. But one element has remained consistent: to appeal to the adult in the room in order to encourage co-viewing. Written into Joan Ganz Cooney's show pitch, this strategy was championed by Jon Stone. "The child can watch this fuzzy little puppet bobbing around and enjoy that while we're doing an inside, adult joke for the parent," he once explained. "That makes the show function on two levels. It was a very intentional move on our part, based on my personal aversion to kiddie shows that make me retch as an adult."

Current head writer Joey Mazzarino, along with a writing staff that includes Tony, Judy Freudberg, Molly Boylan, Annie Evans, John Weidman, Belinda Ward, and Luis Santeiro, has no problem following that lead.

"We've made a conscious decision that we're aiming for three-year-olds, because that's our target," Joey explains, "but I'm still pushing to get that comedy in there for adults."

Memos from 1974's director of research, Lewis Bernstein (now EVP of that department), outline content for the "Writer's Notebook," a resource for scriptwriters like Norman Stiles, seen above, clowning around with Oscar

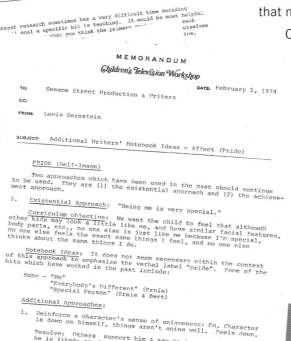

Director Jim Martin and Producer Tim Carter get a laugh from writer Belinda Ward's letter spoof: "A's Anatomy"

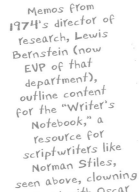

SUBJECT: (1) What's the goal? (2) the "Gon" family

Sesame Street research sometimes has a very difficult time deciding what instructional goal a specific bit is teaching. It would be most helpful to us if . . . what you think the primary goal . . . each . . . bit that . . . ourselves to indicate . . . ics,

MEMORANDUM
Children's Television Workshop

SUBJECT: Additional Wr

TO: Sesame Street Production & Writers   DATE: February 5, 1974
CC:
FROM: Lewis Bernstein

SUBJECT: Additional Writers' Notebook Ideas - Affect (Pride)

PRIDE (Self-Image)

Two approaches which have been used in the past should continue to be used. They are (1) the existential approach and (2) the achievement approach.

I. Existential Approach: "Being me is very special."

Curriculum objective: We want the child to feel that although other kids may look a little like me, and have similar facial features, body parts, etc., no one else is just like me because I'm special. No one else feels the exact same things I feel, and no one else thinks about the same things I do.

Notebook Ideas: It does not seem necessary within the context of this approach to emphasize the verbal label "pride". Some of the bits which have worked in the past include:

Song - "Me"
"Everybody's Different" (Ernie)
"Special Person" (Ernie & Bert)

Additional Approaches:

1. Reinforce a character's sense of uniqueness: Eg, Character is down on himself, things aren't going well. Feels down.

Resolve: Others support him & say he is special and that he is liked; or character himself remembers back to a friend or relative telling him he is special..!

2. Extinguish a character's . . .

Do the Write Thing

Emily Kingsley's son, Jason, communes with Cookie Monster

"I sometimes say that they hired me because it was the only way to get rid of me. I was such a pest," says frequent *Sesame Street* scriptwriter Emily Perl Kingsley. "I was determined that this was where I needed to be. It was just my kind of humor and whimsy, and working with children. It was a perfect match."

Emily, who was brought on board in 1970, has scripted segments and lyrics for everything from a barnyard of dancing animals to a cookie-obsessed monster. The curriculum area closest to her heart, however, and one she's become an expert at interpreting, focuses on tolerance, diversity, and inclusion—something that's become synonymous with the show.

The goal of segments like this is to show preschoolers that physical differences are less important than shared feelings and friendships

From the beginning, *Sesame Street* was all about inclusion, in the most natural way imaginable. Initially that simply meant including people (and Muppets) of all colors and both genders; the focus widened to portraying people and puppets with a variety of challenges and abilities. Early on, Emily Kingsley was particularly involved with, as she puts it bluntly, "all the disability stuff."

"In season two," she reports, "I was sent out to check out the Little Theatre of the Deaf to see whether they would be any good on the show. I loved them. They were absolutely magic. So I started writing some stuff for them on the show. I got friendly with the actors, and started taking classes in sign language. Because of my friendship with these people who were deaf, I got a little bit politicized about deaf issues—specifically, the lack of inclusion."

Deaf actress Linda Bove, a member of the theater company, was invited to become a regular cast member as a result, appearing on the show for nineteen years.

But Emily's interest in widening children's perspectives didn't end there; instead, it became far more personal. Because, in 1974, her son, Jason, was born with Down syndrome.

NEWS FLASH

Emily Kingsley worked in television for years before she heard about *Sesame Street*, but she knew the show was her destiny. She kept interviewing in department after department, not giving up until Jon Stone finally allowed her to audition as a writer. Emily rushed home, and that same day, she was back with writing samples. ("I lived only seven blocks away from his office," she admits.)

The next day, Jon called. "We've read your two pieces," he said, "and we've decided we don't want to put you in the writer's workshop."

Emily's heart sank.

"They can go on just as they are," Jon went on. "We want to put you on immediately."

Emily Kingsley at a writers meeting with, clockwise, Bob Abrams, Judy Freudberg, actress Buffy Sainte-Marie, Tony Geiss, John Brent, and Sarah Durkee

The casting of Linda Bove, who became a regular on *Sesame Street* in season four, enabled the show to weave exposure to deaf culture into routine segments, like the "One of These Things" game seen above, and story lines such as the episode in which the character of Linda demonstrates her new TTY telephone. After that episode aired, the show was flooded with inquiries from deaf viewers for information about the technology, many of whom were unaware it existed until they saw it for the first time on the show.

"In that one day, I was hit in the face in a very physical kind of way with the absolute absence on television and in the media of any families like my own," Emily says of that sudden insight. "As I started getting involved with other families, it became so apparent that kids are kids. In those days, they were segregated, but my kid was starting to learn like crazy. And it was all the same stuff we were doing on *Sesame Street*."

It became, as she calls it, "a crusade" to get people with a variety of disabilities on *Sesame Street*.

Emily and Jason would go on to cowrite books and be featured together in a documentary about growing up with Down syndrome. And Jason made several appearances on the show, the first when he was just fifteen months old. No special fuss was made; he was simply one of the kids on the block.

"I think that *Sesame Street* has a better record than any other

show in the history of television of doing this on a regular basis in a comfortable kind of way," Emily says. "There have been lapses, though. And so one of my jobs has been to keep constantly, year after year after year, reminding the filmmakers and the film producers: You've got a checklist. You check for racial balance, you check for gender balance, you check for ethnic balance, you check for everything else. Just put this on your list. It's not that big a deal."

It's no accident that the script Emily is the proudest of writing, "The Furry Little Red Monster Parade," is all about inclusion—in this case, the inclusion into a furry little red monster parade of everyone on *Sesame Street*—furry or not.

The Little Theatre of the Deaf, then and now

Inclusiveness on *Sesame Street* means that all kinds of abilities are seen in the neighborhood, in every way it's possible to integrate them: cast members, like child actor Tarah Schaeffer (a regular for seven years), who uses a wheelchair; Muppet characters (Aristotle, a blind puppet); and celebrity guests (such as musician Itzhak Perlman and singer Andrea Bocelli, above).

Good-bye, MR. HOOPER

Fans watching the Macy's Thanksgiving Day Parade in 1982 saw actor Will Lee portray beloved curmudgeon Mr. Hooper for the last time. The 72-year-old performer was already ill with heart disease; even twenty years later, the cast gets misty-eyed talking about his bravery in making that final appearance for the children thronging New York's streets. Days later, Will Lee would be hospitalized, and on December 7, 1982, the show lost one of its bulwarks.

Beyond the grief felt by the cast and crew, another burden weighed heavily on everyone—the question of how to tell the show's millions of preschool viewers why Mr. Hooper was not behind the counter at his corner store anymore.

Norman Stiles was head writer at the time. "We had to decide at that point what to do. We could just bring somebody else in, or just have him disappear," he recalls. "We said, let's look into the possibility of teaching something about death to our audience."

The first thing that was done was what's always done at the Workshop. Producers, writers, and on-staff researchers consulted with experts in the subject, in this case, child psychologists and educators. There were a variety of issues involved, writers learned. You shouldn't say that Mr. Hooper died because he was old, because to a child, his or her parents are old. You couldn't simply say he got sick, because children and parents get sick all the time, and the suggestion that sickness leads invariably to death would be a terrifying implication for a child. It was a delicate and emotional negotiation but everyone eventually agreed on the message. Interestingly, that message is an example of how well the writers had honed their own skills as educators. Expert advisors reviewing the proposed script objected to the explanation that writer Norman Stiles gives Big Bird for Mr. Hooper's death: "Just because." Roscoe says the line in a deliberate reflection of Big Bird's own explanation, earlier in the same episode, for why he's walking backward and upside down. There's no real reason Big Bird can think of, it's just something that happened, and that's the best answer he can offer.

The show's outside advisors didn't think the same open-ended explanation would be enough for children when given back to Big Bird as a reason for something as monumental as death. But in this instance, as in

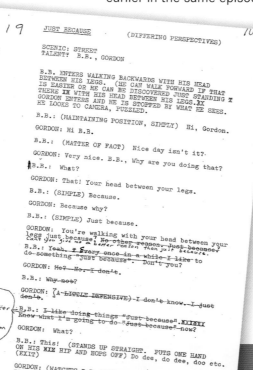

An advisor recommends that the episode's now-classic "Just because" line be replaced; Norman and producers will ultimately leave it in, with support from the show's own research staff

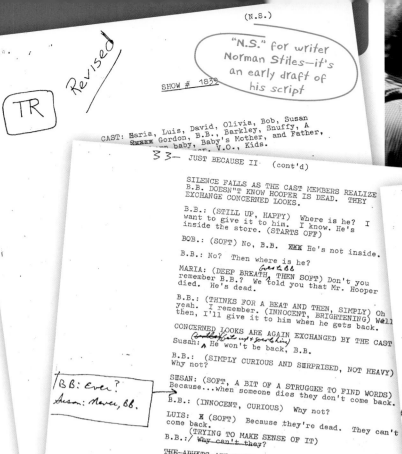

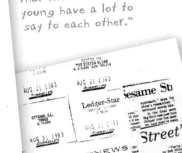

"N.S." for writer Norman Stiles—it's an early draft of his script

Speaking of Will Lee after his death, Joan Ganz Cooney praised the actor's ability to connect with the children who loved his curmudgeonly character: "He gave millions of children the message that the old and the young have a lot to say to each other."

others through the years, the writers—and *Sesame Street*'s own researchers, who ultimately approved the script—knew better. The line stayed in, spoken by actor Roscoe Orman with unfeigned emotion. It spoke to the needs of children because of the actor's sincerity and because his character, Gordon, along with all of Big Bird's adult friends acknowledge that it's *not* a good answer—there *isn't* a good one. It worked because they are able to reassure Big Bird that even in sad times he is surrounded by people who love him.

The tears of all the performers in this scene were genuine—both those that were visible and those unseen: Caroll Spinney reveals that he was "weeping freely" under the feathers. Most adult fans of the show, preschoolers at the time, remember the episode with vivid clarity.

Everyone felt strongly that children needed adults present when watching the episode. "We were very careful to do it over the Thanksgiving holiday, when there would be a lot of adults in the house to help the children," says Dr. Loretta Long, who plays Susan on the show. It was broadcast on Thanksgiving Day, 1983, in the first season of shows without Mr. Hooper. The segment was heavily promoted to ensure that parents would be aware of its content and plan on co-viewing.

The script Norman wrote became an extraordinarily moving television experience for preschoolers and their families. Heartbreaking yet affirming, the episode set a standard for the sensitive treatment of a powerful subject matter that has rarely been equaled. It remains one of the show's proudest moments.

"I wanted Will to be remembered," recalls the episode's scriptwriter, Norman Stiles. "So in the last segment of the show, Big Bird hangs Will Lee's picture in his nest area." (It's still there 25 years later)

Take Forty

Director Bob Myrhum, soon-to-be director Emily Squires, and producer Arlene Sherman at the control board, circa 1975—and Emily directing today

An episode of *Sesame Street* is a complicated animal to produce. The same show might have at least one large-scale musical number with set pieces and choreography that rivals anything in a Broadway Musical, sandwiched between Street scenes that could either bring you to tears or make you break out in giggles—maybe both in the same show. Add to that a cast of celebrities of every genre (complete with posses), preschool performers (many of them nonprofessionals), show regulars—both of the human and Muppet persuasion—and a roomful of union labor. The potential for chaos is almost unlimited.

Luckily, the Workshop's staff of directors and producers has grown in scope and size to meet these myriad challenges. Jon Stone was hired as a producer/writer, for instance, but eventually became the show's principal director and a creative guiding light. Lisa Simon, Emily Squires, and Ted May grew up on the Street in a variety of roles before becoming directors. Kevin Clash, Jim Martin, Joey Mazzarino, Matt Vogel, Carol-Lynn Parente, and Nadine Zylstra have all expanded upon their various original roles at the Workshop. And staffers such as Millicent Shelton, Scott Preston, Ken Diego, and Dean Gordon journeyed to the Street from other shows, but now consider 123 their home address.

> " If you never do anything but work at *Sesame Street* your whole life—there's nothing wrong with that. "
>
> —CAROL-LYNN PARENTE, EXECUTIVE PRODUCER

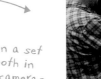

Producer Carol-Lynn Parente, center, meets each day with writers and directors

Laughter is frequent on a set where comedians are both in front of and behind the cameras

The director has a variety of responsibilities off and on set. Before a show is taped, decisions have to be made about props, lighting, sound, and the script. These happen in production meetings held by the director. Then there are a variety of on-set jobs. Some are very specific—keeping an eye out (along with everyone else) to make sure no Muppet performers are visible under their Muppets, for example. The director is also responsible for the quality of the performances, working with the actors and performers to get the feelings and delivery of the lines he wants. Sometimes, the director, with the writer, will change dialogue in order to enable a scene to play better, or to avoid confusion.

Then there's the actual directing part. *Sesame Street,* like many television shows, is shot using three cameras. One typically focuses on a close-up of the character currently talking; a second might pull back to show two characters; and another, called the master, usually frames the entire scene, with all the characters. On the fly, the director quietly instructs the control room to move from one shot to the other to create a rough edit of the show, which will later be refined and finalized.

Producers are responsible for a host of things, including overall oversight, mediating curricular/creative disputes, overseeing the writing, and generally making sure the days go smoothly on set.

Not surprisingly, a large team is needed on *Sesame Street*; in season 40 it included Executive Producer Carol-Lynn Parente and Co-Executive Producer Kevin Clash; producers Melissa Dino, Tim Carter, April Chadderdon, Stephanie Longardo, Benjamin Lehman, and Ronda Music; and associate producers Mindy Fila, Theresa Anderson, and Todd James. The relaxed, friendly vibe on the *Sesame Street* set is a credit to the producers and directors, and it's well known that the show has had some of the most talented directors and producers in the business—witness the record-setting number of Emmy Awards they've collected, including 2009's Lifetime Achievement Award for the show, an unusual honor.

Carol-Lynn Parente picked up her production skills from her predecessors. Producer Dulcy Singer was a mentor who helped her get over the initial hurdle of taking over the job of one of Carol-Lynn's heroes, Jon Stone: "They were pretty big shoes. I try not to think about that so much. It's an awfully important job, one that needs the heart of the show in mind at *all* times.

"From Dulcy Singer, I learned that if you have really talented people, you lead the way and then get *out* of the way."

> It's the best of the best. You're always not just aiming high, you're aiming the highest. It goes everywhere, this show. It's important you get it right.
>
> —CAROL-LYNN PARENTE, EXECUTIVE PRODUCER

Let's Work Together

Collaboration is routine on the show and off—Baby Bear and Mama Bear count polka dots together, while writers Molly Boylan (above, left) and Judy Freudberg, review a script with producer Ben Lehman

Where else could your wildest ideas become such hilarious reality? A hotel where every room is customized to the species of animal or alien that checks in? Marathon-running Snuffleupaguses? Worms in space? Only on *Sesame Street* would creative types be given the freedom for all of those zany concepts.

In this neighborhood, everyone gets into the act, from educators who work tirelessly with writers, to writers who freely collaborate with performers, to directors who add their own special spins to a script. Then there are the producers willing to take risks and the artists, builders, and musicians who realize them. What's more, some of these personnel tackle multiple roles.

Director Ken Diego, left, works out the details of a shot with the cast

"To me, the greatest joy . . . is working with the writers and working with the Muppeteers," says former head writer Lou Berger, who joined in 1989. He fondly recalls his earliest days, working alongside producers like Dulcy Singer and Jon Stone. Dulcy, who began as a production assistant on the show, became a producer and then executive producer for seasons 12 through 24. Dulcy's style was notably collaborative. During her

tenure, she often focused on stories that showcased the human cast, presiding over Gordon and Susan's adoption of Miles, as well as Maria and Luis's romantic story arc. The willingness to exchange ideas and the generosity of spirit that she and Jon established still flourishes and fosters a consistently upbeat atmosphere on set and in the writers' room, where ideas are born.

> **It's paradise for a writer. Because whatever you can dream of, if they like it, they'll get it on; it's one of the great production teams in the world. Everything you need—scenery, costumes, sound, characters—they'll build anything.**
>
> —TONY GEISS

NEWS FLASH

Dulcy Singer, pictured above watching video playback with mentor Jon Stone and puppeteer Jim Henson, became the first woman to serve as executive producer on the show, holding that role from 1982 until her retirement in 1993. She won Emmys for her team's work on the specials *Christmas Eve on Sesame Street* (1979) and *Don't Eat the Pictures: Sesame Street at the Metropolitan Museum of Art* (1984).

In the role of Buster here, Matt Vogel does the grunt work for Jerry Nelson, whose lung illness prevents him from performing the contortions needed for a scene like this one in season 40—though he does the vocal work off camera; writers and producers take these set-ups in stride to accommodate brilliant talent like Jerry

Kevin Clash, Elmo's puppeteer, wears many hats on the show—here he directs performers in an episode in season 40 that utilizes every back-up Elmo available and, as a performer, consults with Director Nadine Zylstra, near left; he's also the show's co-executive producer

The results are routinely playful and entertaining, but the process to get there varies. For example, six writers—Judy Freudberg, Molly Boylan, Tony Geiss, Emily Kingsley, Cathi Rosenberg-Turow, and Annie Evans—were given the challenge of expanding upon the original format of *Sesame Street* in late 1998.

"The first week we spent breaking down the show," recalls Judy, head writer of "Elmo's World" since its debut. "The second week we spent seeing what we could do to fix it. We broke up into four or five different groups, and a few of us talked about this Elmo idea. And within a very short time, we'd come up with the basic idea of what 'Elmo's World' would be."

"Everybody was just bouncing off everyone else, and there wasn't one person in the room who didn't contribute something major," Judy says. "It was just one of the most wonderful creative experiences."

> "I don't ever think of them as puppets. To me, by this point it's become so real . . . . I'm always surprised when I get to the studio to see the puppeteers."
>
> —BELINDA WARD, WRITER

Marty takes a break from puppeteering with writer Annie Evans—the two are newlyweds who first met years ago on the set

Show writers seem intent on a mission to constantly challenge the ingenuity of the set and prop builders—and everyone else behind the camera. In season 38, the script for episode 4168 called for Elmo and Zoe to compete in the senselessly silly "Who Can Wear the Most Hats on Your Head Day" celebrations by tying with a score of 30 hats each. The collection of 60 hats was the work of the prop meisters. The utility crew and puppeteers had to engineer a way to make the lids balance in a stack that allowed Elmo and Zoe to move freely. The final result: puppeteers Matt Vogel and Marty Robinson manned two mini cranes, controlling the towering caps like marionettes.

Writing for Yuks

Writer Lou Berger gets a laugh with David Rudman's Baby Bear, above; lunch fuels brainstorming at a writ- ers meeting, right, circa 1990

How do you write funny? As a children's show writer, especially on *Sesame Street*, you need to know.

"Comedy comes out of conflict," explains writer Belinda Ward, "as well as out of the obsessional quality of our characters. Certain behavior is going to come out of these obsessions. It's not just Cookie Monster wanting a cookie, or Telly with his triangles or his worrying. It's that each character has something that they're possessed by, and that sets up things. When you understand the characters, you understand that the comedy is going to come."

At times, conflict has come from unexpected places.

An animation was created for the show, in 1994, based on a Chris Cerf song that taught the idea of zero. It involved a goat eating objects until there were zero things left. Soon after the segment first aired, the Workshop received a letter from the Dairy Goats Association of America demanding that the segment be pulled from the airwaves. One of the things the goat ate was a pair of sneakers; dairy goats, the association asserted, never ate anything unhealthy, saying the show could damage the reputation of dairy goats, endangering sales of goat products.

A number of conciliatory letters went back and forth, but the association was adamant: the piece was misleading and should not air again. Norman Stiles was head writer at the time.

"By coincidence," Norman says, "Chris and I happened to be in Orlando doing another project, and we were at the children's zoo talking to the zookeeper, and Chris asked this woman whether goats will eat things other than corn,

will they eat clothing and stuff. And as the woman was saying, 'Oh, yes, they'll eat anything,' a goat was nibbling at Chris's sneaker."

"Maybe it's my *Sesame Street* training," Norman explains, "I still tried to see things from the Dairy Goat Association's perspective. I realized . . . you know, if you're eating some chevre, you don't want it to have any sneaker in it."

He decided to create an editorial reply by a puppet goat to add to future airings of the animation. The angry animal attests that dairy goats eat only good foods, and that's how they create delicious milk and cheese. Dairy goats "do not, I repeat do *not*, eat sneakers! I eat healthy food!" she adds emphatically, looking disparagingly at a pile of dirty sneakers in front of her.

"And then I had another goat come in and say, 'Are you gonna eat those sneakers?'" Norman laughs even years later as he delivers the punch line: "And she says, 'Certainly not!' And this other goat starts eating them, and says, 'Mmmm-mmmm, tasty! I'm glad I'm not a dairy goat.'"

It's through clever, complex scripts like these that *Sesame Street* has endeared itself not only to its young audience but also to their parents—something many children's shows have singularly failed to do. To further encourage parents to stay in the room, which boosts a kid's take-away from the show, the producers cast pop icons as guest stars and use them wittily, playing off their cult personas, like Sarah Jessica Parker's greeting to Big Bird: "Hello, Big."

"It is obviously for three- to five-year-old children," Jon would explain, "but we're constantly putting in inside jokes, puns, references to old Marx Brothers movies, things that go right over the children's heads."

No child smiling at the Muppets' antics will ever notice that they've missed a joke. Adults? Feel free to giggle.

> " I feel very proud to have been part of the line from John, to Jeff Moss, to Norman. All of us were very different people, but the baton that was handed down— Norman jokingly said, 'I'm passing you the torture'—was to a project that people care very deeply about. "
>
> —LOU BERGER, HEAD WRITER, 1998–2008

"Oh, yeah, sure, sure, now they want the frog back. Now that all the important stuff is over."
—KERMIT

Now I Know My ABCs

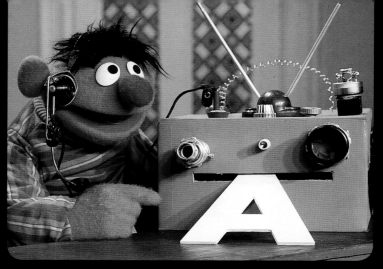

During the original educational seminars, there were many arguments about whether or not *Sesame Street* should teach the alphabet. Proponents won out. In the four decades since then, writers and composers have been taxed with figuring out ways to embody, explain, describe, and melodically represent each and every letter—over and over. What they've come up with—from a ditty about rebel L, to a segment featuring a salesman trying to sell the letter U to an uninterested Kermit, to a lament about a failed relationship between a woman and her X—highlights their rampant creativity.

That's Patti LaBelle singing writer Mark Saltzman's double-entendre-filled "Oh, How I Miss My X," and Norah Jones spoofing her hit song by transforming it into the wistful "Don't Know Y"

Just one of the show's Emmy Award moments, which Cookie Monster and Bob share with the production team, from left, of Lisa Simon, Arlene Sherman, Dulcy Singer, and Norman Stiles

THIS CHAPTER WAS BROUGHT TO YOU BY THE LETTERS ABCDEFGHIJKLMNOPQRSTUVWXYZ AND THE NUMBER 119.

The letters A to Z are highlighted by writers in their scripts, one per show these days. When PBS scaled back on the number of new episodes aired each year—preschoolers benefit educationally from repeated viewings—producers initially proposed doing only 25 unique shows a year. Writers insisted on 26. "Which letter do you propose we drop?" they argued. They won. **The number 119** is the latest count of Emmy Awards, including Lifetime Achievements, taken home by cast and crew—more than any other television show.

9

"People don't understand what's involved in putting on just one little hour of *Sesame Street*. I mean, the number of people that are involved in coming up with it—people don't realize. They just see the tip of the iceberg."

–EMILIO DELGADO

OVER,
UNDER,
AROUND
& THROUGH

EPISODE 4161

It's an insert day—a day of shooting off the main set of *Sesame Street*. The crew is busy setting up for Active Elmo, the name given to Elmo when he's performed full body. In order to operate Elmo's mouth and all four limbs, performer Kevin Clash is being joined by three additional puppeteers: Peter Linz, who will manipulate Elmo's right hand; Matt Vogel, who works Elmo's left hand; and Paul McGinnis, who controls Elmo's feet.

"I love Active Elmo," murmurs Judy Freudberg, head writer of "Elmo's World" and a longtime show veteran. "He blows me away. You see all that stuff—," she indicates the elaborate blue-screen set-up, "—and on TV, it's just Elmo." It's just one of the many miracles that happen behind the camera, the result of planning, work, and talent that viewers never guess at or see if it's done well.

A blue-screen shoot is just what it sounds like. Active Elmo will be performed against a scrim of bright blue fabric. (Sometimes, the screen is green, depending on the colors of the Muppet—the screen color can't be anywhere on the puppet.) Performers who want to disappear behind the puppet dress in a matching blue or green color, rendering them invisible on camera after computer tinkering.

Paul comes out on set wearing a long-sleeved blue turtleneck and blue tights. He tugs on a head mask with a net patch stretched across his eyes and nose so he can breathe. You can barely see his features through it. Paul pulls on two long blue gloves. Peter and Kevin also wear blue gloves and tunics cut to their knees; their lower legs will be off-camera. Matt has the easiest costume—only his arm could be seen, so he simply slides on a long blue glove.

Music comes up in the studio—an instrumental of the classic Chubby Checker song, "Limbo Rock." Elmo starts wiggling his hips. The limbo rig is a piece of wooden apparatus that was taped the day before. This image will now be fed into the video camera, along with another piece of art—a shot of a blue sky and sandy beach. All three will come together in the camera, creating what is called a composited image. It will look like Elmo is actually limboing under the rod, on a beach, the sun shining above him in the sky.

These shots are from the composited version of the limbo-dancing scene that's finally aired; below, the puppets for the week's shoot are arriving from storage and getting primed for their segments

> ## It would be better if you took your feet off.
>
> —KEVIN CLASH, DIRECTING ABBY CADABBY DURING TAPING OF A RECENT SCENE

In rehearsal, Kevin asks Paul to fix the placement of Elmo's feet. Then—as if concerned that Kevin has hurt Paul's feelings—Elmo bends down and asks, in an audible whisper, "Are you okay, Paul?" Paul snickers from his cramped position under the table.

After the next take, Elmo turns to Matt. "That was terrible, Mr. Matt Vogel," he says. Matt shakes his head and smiles. Elmo looks down. "I see puppeteers!" he shouts in surprise. A five-year-old boy, visiting the set with his father, giggles.

Camera operator Frankie Biondo struggles for a close-up of Elmo. "Move in the jib," Frankie suggests. That's a long arm that holds the camera, great for angling in to places to get shots that earthbound cameras can't. Kevin demurs at the change in camera rig . . . it'll take too long. "It'll take twenty seconds!" Frankie insists.

"Sure," says Kevin dryly. He's heard this before. "One, two, three . . . " he starts counting. The crew picks up the chant as Frankie races to get the camera in place. ". . . eighteen, nineteen, twenty!"

It takes a *little* longer than promised, but the shot is rigged and a costumed Elmo is ready for his close-up.

Some more of Elmo's blue-screen adventures, from "Elmo's World" episodes on the themes of jumping, under the sea, violins, and building things

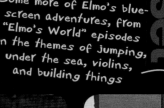

A Side of Silly

Whether the scene takes place against a blue screen, on the Street, or in one of the many, many "limbo" sets used on the show, producers and directors know that what the camera sees is the be-all and end-all of filming puppets and humans together—or simply puppets of varying sizes who share the same scene. Limbo sets can be as basic as a half wall or as elaborate as Alice's Wonderland, a lush semitropical swamp, or the authentic Russian restaurant, below. Frankie Biondo is the senior member of the team of keen-eyed camera crew, a team that somehow manages to properly frame the shots so that puppets (some with no lower extremities) appear to actually walk on the Street and across nonexistent limbo "floors."

Each shot may be planned out in advance by the director, but Frankie and the other camera ops always have to make adjustments on the fly, all of which they note in the margins of the scripts. Frankie has become so influential a part of the directing and producing team's decisions that his caustic comments from the sidelines carry weight, even while they're cracking up cast and crew. His voice is one of the many that shape every moment you see on screen.

Frankie Biondo mans the camera on a dollie that allows smooth tracking across the action

Puppeteers and crew run through the scene with director Victor DiNapoli, wearing the headset, right. Victor uses his experience as the production designer, managing the props and scenery, to bring a unique visual sensibility to segments like this one

SESAME STREET — 2 — GEISS SHOW 4123

MUSIC: OCHI CHORNIE, SONG: "THE STROGANOFF IS GONE," TA-DA CHORD, VERY, VERY SLOW INSTRUMENTAL OOM-PAH VAMP, KAZATSKY DANCE, BUTTON

10 ① PAN TO FAT BLUE @ TABLE ✱OPENING MUSIC SCORE

CHARLIE'S RESTAURANT DONE UP RUSSIAN-STYLE (THERE ARE LITTLE ONION DOMES ON THE POSTS OF THE SWINGING DOORS, ETC.). IDEALLY, A SIGN ON THE WALL SAYS "CHARLIE'S" IN CYRILLIC PRINT.

FAT BLUE, SITTING AT A TABLE WITH EMBROIDERED CLOTH, LOOKS AROUND, CONFUSED.

11 ② DOORS - GROVER +2 CARRY TO F.B, Ⓠ OCHI CHORNIE

PROP Q ON DOORS

CHOREOGRAPH MOVE TO TABLE

FAT BLUE: Waiter! Oh, waiter! DOORS FLY OPEN ✕

✱GROVER AND TWO AM MUSICIANS ENTER. GROVER WEARS A RED TUNIC WITH BANDOLIER, FROGS, TASSELED BELT AND A COSSACK HAT. THE AM ACCORDIONIST AND AM BALALAIKA PLAYER WEAR THE SAME UNIFORM.

✱MUSIC: OCHI CHORNIE. CONTINUES UNDER.

GROVER: Welcome to Charlie's Russian restaurant, sir, and may I add, zdrastvuyta! *(pron. ZDRAHSS-vweech-yĕh)* That is "hello" in Russian. This is Sasha and Masha! We will sing and dance for your dining pleasure!

12 ① CU F.B. MUSIC OUT

FAT BLUE: Forget the singing and dancing. I just want food! P/U

13 ② HOLD

GROVER: We cannot "forget the singing and dancing," tovarish *(pron. tōh-VAR-ish)*. It comes with the dinner!

14 ① F.B.

P/U

Frankie works camera one; generally two to three cameras will shoot different angles of each scene. Here a Jib, above Frankie, is also in place to zoom in and out

The segment's writer, Tony Geiss, follows along with the funny business he concocted

Jerry Nelson, as Mr. Johnson (aka Fat Blue), brings flawless comic timing to scenes with bumbling waiter Grover in this and countless other restaurants

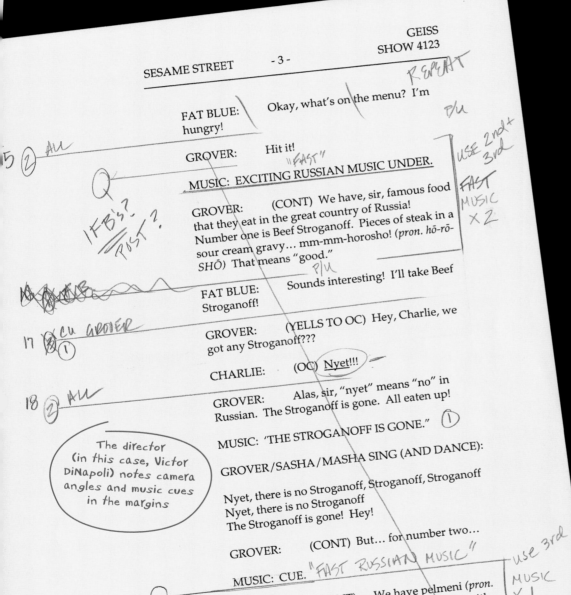

GEISS
SHOW 4123

SESAME STREET   - 3 -

REPEAT

FAT BLUE: Okay, what's on the menu? I'm
hungry!   P/u

GROVER: Hit it!

"FAST"

MUSIC: EXCITING RUSSIAN MUSIC UNDER.   USE 2nd + 3rd

GROVER: (CONT) We have, sir, famous food   FAST
that they eat in the great country of Russia!   MUSIC
Number one is Beef Stroganoff. Pieces of steak in a   X 2
sour cream gravy... mm-mm-horosho! (pron. hō-rō-
SHŌ) That means "good."

P/u

FAT BLUE: Sounds interesting! I'll take Beef
Stroganoff!

GROVER: (YELLS TO OC) Hey, Charlie, we
got any Stroganoff???

CHARLIE: (OC) Nyet!!!

GROVER: Alas, sir, "nyet" means "no" in
Russian. The Stroganoff is gone. All eaten up!

MUSIC: 'THE STROGANOFF IS GONE."

GROVER/SASHA/MASHA SING (AND DANCE):

Nyet, there is no Stroganoff, Stroganoff, Stroganoff
Nyet, there is no Stroganoff
The Stroganoff is gone! Hey!

GROVER: (CONT) But... for number two...

MUSIC: CUE. "FAST RUSSIAN MUSIC"   use 3rd

MUSIC
X 1

GROVER: (CONT) ...We have pelmeni (pron.
Pĕl-MAIN-ee)- cute delicious little dumplings with
meat inside...
MUSIC OUT

15 (2) ALL

IFB's?
POST?

17 CU GROVER
(1)

18 (2) ALL

The director (in this case, Victor DiNapoli) notes camera angles and music cues in the margins

Making Muppets

In the Muppet Workshops through the years—here, supervisor Caroly Wilcox meets with Bob Flanagan and Jim

When *Sesame Street* debuted, television shows utilizing puppets were still using centuries-old forms on conventional proscenium stages. Jim Henson used a visionary's eye to lose the puppet stage—the camera became the puppet's framing device—and modify puppet faces so that they could be expressive in television's tight close-ups. Kermit was already built when the show's development began, and Jim applied the same techniques he'd used for the frog, which he developed for commercials and films, to a new crew of puppets for the Street.

Currrent Muppet builder Rollie Krewson started in the puppet workshop as an intern in the seventies

"There are certain kinds of shapes that make much better puppets," Jim once explained. "One of the things I always look for is a kind of flexibility in the character, so he has a great range of expression. A lot of people build puppets that are very stiff, which means you can hardly move the thing. Your hand has a lot of flexibility to it, and you want to build a puppet that allows you to use all that flexibility. You're limited a great deal. But it's working within those limitations that makes it interesting."

Jim sketched many of the original *Sesame Street* Muppets with this in mind. But it was up to his team to figure out how to build them. Gifted Muppet designer Donald Sahlin joined Jim in 1962 after stints doing special effects for films like the 1960 classic *The Time Machine*. Don remained with the Muppets until his sudden death in 1978. He was perhaps most responsible for the signature Anything Muppet and monster look and is credited with building Bert, Ernie, Grover, and Cookie.

"Don Sahlin had an extraordinary essence about him," says puppeteer Frank Oz. "Jim could do a quick drawing of a character and Don could get the essence and would just build it."

Don wasn't just a consummate puppet builder. He was also an unmitigated practical joker. Bonnie Erickson, a fellow builder who headed up Jim Henson's Creature Workshop for a number of years in the eighties, describes one of Don's many, many stunts.

"I was experimenting with some really ugly treatments of foam, warts, and things like that," Bonnie recalls, ". . . and I had this head that had been flocked a sort of greenish color. I came in one day, and everybody who came out of the bathroom had a funny look on their faces." It turned out that Don had scrounged a dressmaker's dummy and dressed it in a trench coat, with Bonnie's monstrous head on top (complete with hat). He'd rigged it in the bathtub with an arm tied to the door, so that it sprang out at anyone who entered.

"Everybody would scream *Ahhh!*," Bonnie laughs, "and then swallow it because they didn't want to give up the joke."

Don Sahlin frames a shot for puppeteers Jim Henson, John Lovelady (who acts as right hand for Ernie, a live-hand puppet), and Frank, solo-performing Bert, a rod puppet

Ed Christie (seen here holding Aristotle) began working on *Sesame Street* in 1979. His first puppet was a generic tiger; he's happy to report that it's still being used today. He later supervised the Creature Workshop, designing Zoe, Rosita, and Abby Cadabby. Currently, he's in charge of designing Muppets for international use.

Just visible in this close-up, though not seen on camera, is the monofilament that is strung from one wing to the other through Big Bird's beak—the puppeteer has only one hand free for the Bird's wings, so this counterbalance creates a slight movement in the empty wing

"The magic triangle" is a phrase often heard when designers at Jim Henson's Creature Workshop talk about the Muppets.

According to Jason Weber, a supervisor at the Creature Workshop, you have to construct the eyes so the pupils focus slightly inward. The triangle this creates with the tip of the Muppet's nose makes the eyes appear as if they're focused directly on the camera—and the kids watching at home.

"If you were to place the eyes where you would if the character were flat," Jason explains, "it would have a kind of walleyed look, because the face and eyes actually curve outward a bit. You have to compensate for the curve."

> [Designers] think if they're doing a head, they have to put on ears and eyes and nose and mouth. And I always think, how really necessary are any of those things? To listen, you can cock the head. . . . I try not to have appendages. I get rid of everything I can.
>
> —KERMIT LOVE, MUPPET DESIGNER

Don was responsible for introducing Jim to designer Kermit Love, adding another integral member to the team. A soft-spoken man with a philosophical manner, Kermit affected a British accent, although he was actually born in New Jersey. He also sported a flowing Rip Van Winkle–like beard. (He was once cast as Santa for a magazine cover, but Caroll Spinney affectionately notes that Kermit's personality inclined more toward Grinch than Claus.)

Kermit was primarily involved with Jim's large-body characters. He designed Snuffleupagus and was instrumental in the design of Big Bird. He also served as the Bird's personal wrangler for many years, traveling with Caroll to ensure the puppet was in tip-top condition. For a number of years, he was also responsible for building Muppets for Sesame Street's numerous international productions.

It is the job of Jim Henson's Creature Workshop, active today with dozens of non-Sesame puppet projects, to maintain the Muppet cast of the show and assemble the myriad cameo

"performers" appearing on Sesame Street over the last forty years. Workshop Manager Caroly Wilcox headed that effort for many years. Her first association with the Muppets was in 1969, as a performer.

"I'm not a great ad-libber," she confesses. So she found herself shifting to work behind the scenes, constructing rather than puppeteering the Muppets, a stroke of luck for Sesame Street. Caroly was able to use her experience on the business end of the puppets to inform her work.

"I always simultaneously think of the materials I'm going to use, the type of puppet it's going to be," Caroly has said. For a puppet moving in real time, she explains, "we try to figure out the scale of a group of puppets, because a puppet is not usually alone."

Big Bird, traveling to Germany with his entourage—Jon Stone, Kermit Love, and Debbie Spinney—circa 1980 (Debbie met husband Caroll while she was working as a production assistant on the show)

Jason Weber, Creative Workshop Supervisor at Jim Henson's Creature Workshop, lends wrangler Michelle Hickey a hand to attach fine monofilament to Chris Knowings's bumblebee costume so the wings can flap

Performing Puppets

Scriptwriters and puppet builders provide the skeleton of a character, but it's up to the performer to fill in the blanks—to make a character come alive

Muppets can take many forms but essentially fall into three distinct categories: rodded, live-hands, or full-body characters.

A rodded Muppet, like Kermit the Frog, has slender yet stiff wires attached to both Muppet hands. The performer nimbly manipulates these rods with just one hand, making the Muppet's gestures look remarkably lifelike. The rods "disappear." The performer's other hand fits inside the Muppet's head to animate the mouth.

Muppets with live hands have sleeve-like arms and glove-like hands into which performers slip their own hands, giving puppets motor skills that rodded puppets lack. If performing alone, the puppeteer manipulates the character by placing one hand (usually the right) inside the Muppet's head and the other inside one of the character's hands. The other puppet hand is usually pinned to the Muppet's body in a Napoleon-like pose.

Both types of Muppets are performed over the puppeteer's head; the camera frames only the Muppet and not the manipulator. But hiding from the camera in tight quarters can be challenging.

"I was right-handing for David Rudman on Baby Bear," reports puppeteer Tyler Bunch, "and there was a point where . . . I'm trying to make my rather large frame as small as possible . . . and David turned around and said, 'I've never been so aware of a right-hand in my life.'"

Then there are other right-hand issues. Peter Linz, who's performed a variety of characters on the show since 1991, made the mistake of overplaying his hand one day while working with Jerry Nelson as the Count.

"The Count had this long page of dialogue. It was my second season, I'm twenty-four, and I was doing just

Before the common use of green screen shots, spotting Muppet feet was a rare treat that fascinated kids. Feet at that time were either operated by radio or just posed naturally

According to builder Caroly Wilcox, a performer's fingertip-to-head ratio limits the size that a puppet can be. Naturally. But if a puppeteer had no head to get in the way of a shot, this wouldn't be a problem. In fact, Caroly once drew a picture of the ideal puppeteer's body. She eliminated the head and gave him three hands.

> **The most important thing about puppets is that they must project their imagination, and then the audience must open *their* eyes and imagine.**
>
> —KERMIT LOVE, PUPPET DESIGNER

a little *too* much with that right hand," Peter explains. "And without any warning at all, the Count's left hand just smacked the heck out of my right hand.

"It was stinging for about ten minutes afterward," he says, laughing. "I never did too much with the right hand after that."

Then there are the full-body Muppets—like Big Bird or Snuffy—worn like costumes that fit over the puppeteer's body.

Bryant Young has performed Snuffy's back half since 1980, taking over from Frank Kane and, before him, Jerry Nelson. Bryant began his career as a professional ballet dancer, and his extraordinary partnering skills were

Caroll Spinney, rehearsing with Loretta Long, as Susan, in the very first Big Bird design, which separated the head and torso; this costume ultimately caught fire

One of many hurdles faced by the size of Snuffy—the need to airlift him into position for one of the location shoots for the series of six episodes (1090 through 1095) shot in Hawaii in 1977

"It takes so many years to learn to do what we do," reports puppeteer Pam Arciero. Perhaps that's because, as Jim Henson once explained, "You're actually performing and being an audience at the same time. We're seeing the same view that the audience is seeing. It's kind of a neat thing. No [other kind of] actor can see his performance the same way the audience does."

There's only one problem: Just like looking in a mirror, in the monitors the puppeteers' performances appear *backward*. Walt Rauffer, seen here helping Matt Vogel with his monitor rig, worked in technical operations right from the beginning and suggested early on that he could easily reverse the images so that puppeteers could see their actual performances. Once he made good on that promise, however, performers found it impossible to readjust to the new viewpoint. They were too used to working backward. Walt reverted the monitors, and everyone went back to their old habits. They've worked that way ever since.

put to the test when he took on Snuffy. Bryant had already learned how to make his ballerina partners stand out, he explains. "And as a supporting character in Snuffy, I was able to do the same thing. I was able to read exactly what movements Marty [the puppeteer], in front, was doing . . . to make Snuffy look much more believable."

When Bryant began, he didn't even have a monitor—until the decision was made to put Snuffy on a trampoline. "I said, 'I think I need to be able to see,'" he says, laughing. And this only begins to reflect the challenges associated with full-body puppets.

When the original Snuffy Muppet had to portray his cousin from Mexico, Señor Snuffleupago, he was given a fifty-pound sombrero to wear. During the performance, the entire Snuffy frame (a latticework made from lightweight wood) cracked under the hat's weight. Bryant and Marty Robinson crumpled to the ground under the strangling bulk of Snuffy's fur.

It was a dramatic moment.

An even more dramatic moment occured while Caroll Spinney was performing the first incarnation of Big Bird.

"One day, a klieg light crashed to the ground about a foot away from where I was standing," Caroll recalls. "It exploded and showered me with chunks of burning debris. It was everywhere. Then I realized that there were sheets of flame actually *inside* the bird. A cameraman patted it out, slapping at my legs to put out the fire. That's how we found out that the legs were highly flammable."

And that's when the costume changed.

Happily, puppeteers usually don't find

themselves in actual danger, although writers are constantly throwing creative hurdles their way. More often, the challenges are routine—as routine as television puppetry on a show like *Sesame Street* can be, that is.

And often, the challenges are shared.

As Bryant says, "Marty and I have been working together so long that I can pretty much anticipate what he's doing." The well-choreographed *pas de deux* between principal and supporting puppeteers is often more than just a performance—it's a partnership of friends.

Marty Robinson and Bryant Young rehearse a series of Snuffy antics. Bryant not only choreographs Snuffy's dances, but he's acted as choreographer for many of the other characters on the Street when they need complex moves

Stone's Street

> **I wanted a totally realistic set. . . . It might as well be shot on location, it is so solid.**
>
> —JON STONE,
> WRITER/DIRECTOR/PRODUCER

The team was in place, the mission was clear, Muppets were being built, and the cast was cast. But there was another important decision to be made. Where would they live?

"We didn't want another clubhouse or a treasure house or a tree house or a secret meeting place, or one of those local-kid-show kind of sets," Jon Stone would say later. And fellow producer Sam Gibbon recalled Jon was "bitterly opposed" to the idea of placing the action in a fanciful setting.

"It seemed to me that a street in an urban rundown area would give the children we were most interested in reaching a neighborhood to identify with," Jon declared. By setting the show in such a place, he reasoned, kids would be able to recognize the possibilities of their own situations.

"It came into focus for me when I saw a commercial for the Urban Coalition," Jon recalled in an interview with scenic designer and director Victor DiNapoli. "It was shot on location in Harlem out on the sidewalk, on the front stoop of a brownstone, and as soon as I saw it, I knew exactly where we ought to be." The crew created the lived-in neighborhood that small fans feel is just down the street from their homes. And that's where it remains to this day. "Because to the three-year-olds," Jon insisted, "cooped up in the room upstairs, the action is on the street. That's where the big kids are, that's where they're playing, they're jumping rope, they're running up and down."

NEWS FLASH

Caroll Spinney recalls that is was director Bob Myrhum's idea to add leaves to the set. Bob instructed the crew to scatter leaves along the bottoms of the painted flats and structures, to help conceal the clean lines where they met the floor. It added a surprisingly potent feeling of reality, regardless of the season. Bob also cast more kids as walk-ons, making the street come alive.

So how do you actually get to *Sesame Street*? Any local in the neighborhood will tell you: take the N or the R train.

The physical Street is located a quick subway ride five miles east of Manhattan, along that Broadway train line (take the N; it's the express). The set occupies most of the third floor of the fabled Kaufman Astoria Studios, a complex that sprawls across a full city block in Astoria, Queens.

The studios have been around since the early days of silent pictures, built by movie mogul Adolph Zuckor in 1920 as a home for Paramount Pictures, in an effort to lure movie-making to his home state. Over 120 films were produced there before the U.S. Signal Corps took over the building at the beginning of World War II. After the war, the mammoth building was left abandoned until it was reopened for the filming of the Michael Jackson musical *The Wiz*, in 1977.

In 1980, real estate developer George S. Kaufman was designated by the City of New York to take over the moribund studio after it was declared a national landmark. Today, it's home to a host of film and television productions . . . including *Sesame Street*, where the studio's high ceilings allow for the movements, lighting, and camera angles needed to make eight-foot birds and mammoth Snuffleupaguses look their best.

Joan Ganz Cooney consults with Jon Stone in the Children's Television Workshop offices—not far from the Harlem neighborhoods that help to inspire the set's locale

SESAME STREET

BUS STOP

" Jon Stone came to me at some point and had asked me if I would consider the set being an inner-city street. And, as he always said, I turned several shades paler. "

—JOAN GANZ COONEY

Yesterday's 'Hood

According to a line in one early episode, Mr. Hooper opened his shop in 1951

> "When I was a girl, they hardly had any images on television that were even the city—they were all suburban worlds. You never really saw the inner city, which is where I lived. You never saw immigrants, which is all I knew. And they presented a suburban lifestyle that you didn't even see, though I liked it. But I was always wondering—there was always this little fear, this little uncomfortable feeling about how was I going to contribute to a world that didn't see me? If you don't see yourself in the media, in magazines—or people like you—you really don't know where you're going to fit in."

–SONIA MANZANO,
SPEAKING OF THE CHILDREN'S TV WORLD
PRIOR TO *SESAME STREET*'S CITY NEIGHBORHOOD

Still called the "arbor area" by Workshop personnel, this seventies set was the only time there was an actual arbor there

Susan and Gordon's seventies-era kitchen, off-limits during breaks in taping so the meticulous props remain in place

Big Bird's nest area—the painted oil drums were familiar to seventies urban kids; the cans were recycled materials frequently found in playgrounds at the time

123

No detail was overloooked: watermarks graced the backboard of the typically net-less basketball rim; paint was layered to make doors look aged; even doorbells and mailboxes were given antiquing treatments to make the set look lived-in and gritty

Those iconic doors . . . the same doors and cement stoop have been used since 1969, and many of the elaborately painted background "flats" (an example is seen below) are also veterans

The repair shop location has been transformed a number of times—from a library and then a pet shop, to the L&R Fix-It Shop (it was co-owned by Luis and Rafael) to the plain Fix-It Shop to the Mail-It Shop and back to a repair shop again. There's currently a Laundromat on the site, and the Fix-It Shop has moved down the block, to the far side of the subway station

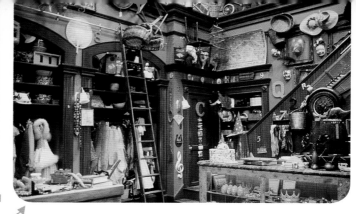

Jamal, Angela, and Kayla move in

The interior set of Finders Keepers, Ruthie's secondhand shop, is microscopically detailed

changes changes changes

Let's Move

At the Reeves Videotape Center studios on West 67th Street in Manhattan—where the test shows for *Sesame Street* were shot and the first season was going to be produced—the Street had been laid out in a straight line. But when a sudden strike cancelled production and the set moved to Teletape studios, only fourteen blocks north, director Bob Myhrum suggested that they lay the Street out in a right angle—turning a corner between Hooper's Store and 123 Sesame Street. This made it far easier to shoot. Bob suggested a few other improvements to the set as well.

The "Around the Corner" architect's model

"I remember when he was brought in as director of the second season," recalls Caroll Spinney. "He brought tremendous excitement to the show. That first season there was never anyone on the street in the background. Suddenly, all these incredible things were happening. He made the set so full of life, so gritty."

Sesame Street remained at Teletape until 1982, when it moved to Unitel Studios on 57th Street. It was produced at Unitel for the next eleven years, up until the show's twenty-fifth season.

That was when the Workshop decided to expand Sesame Street around the corner—which meant the set needed a larger home.

Teletape and Unitel had actually always been too small for the Street. The biggest problem was headroom.

Lights are hung primarily above sound stages on what's called a lighting grid, and they have to be high enough to cast the right kind of light on the production below. Because many Muppet sets are built up—so that performers can't be seen on camera—they need a lot of clearance. And at Teletape and Unitel, they weren't getting it.

In addition, Big Bird is so tall and so brightly colored that the lights on the grid tended to make his upper half glow, leaving his bottom half in shadow. Lighting him properly was really tricky.

The crew had dealt with these problems for twenty-five years. But now, with the expansion of the set, a move was imperative. So the Workshop decided to look for ceiling height as well as square footage, and the show was relocated to the Kaufman Astoria Studios in Queens, which has remained its home ever since.

Once the new studio was found, the writers and producers immediately began figuring out what they'd like to see around the corner of Sesame Street. Sketches were made and blueprints drawn. Many parts of the set that had originally been painted

NEWS FLASH

Do you know what's on the shelves at Hooper's Store? Well, here's a list of some of the items for sale:

Gid-De-Up Blazing Saddles Pork & Beans

Krinkle-Free Aluminum Foil, with Oven-Browning Regulator and Odor Blocker

Almost Famous Chocolate-Chip Cookies

Extra Tough Detergent

Hedda Cheddar Macaroni & Cheese Dinner

Birden Birdseed Snacks

Famous Ugottabe Nuts

Dooty Free Diapers (with Scent Guards)

HineePoo Bathroom Tissue

Angela, Jamal, and Kayla's apartment building

Celina's dance studio

The local subway station

Farther down the street is the entrance to the local park and playground

Baby Natasha's parents, Ingrid and Humphrey, manage the Furry Arms Hotel—a structure built to puppet scale—where Muppets' natural habitats are replicated in the rooms

Finder's Keepers, Ruthie's secondhand store

"Out of all the stuff we did, Jon Stone loved the Furry Arms," reports puppeteer/writer/director Joey Mazzarino. "The best thing about around-the-corner, I remember, was that Jon would ride his bike there, because it was so far around; he would take a bike from the control room all the way around the corner. I loved it. I miss Jon."

backdrops were now actually built, including the area behind the carriage house, which is currently Gina's veterinary office. Elmo's brownstone and a number of other building fronts were also created. And the backdrop that had always existed behind and around Big Bird's nest was built as well. In all, five or six new buildings or parts of the set went up.

The new set debuted in 1994. Not only did it include the new around-the-corner buildings and park; it also included the new people who lived and worked there. But the around-the-corner set was short-lived and was dismantled in 1998. The show had become too complicated; testing showed that there were too many new characters and too little time to develop them.

This was not the only change made to the *Sesame Street* set over the course of forty years. In 2002, in response to a desire by producers to update the Street, the Fix-It Shop became a Mail-It Shop, where residents of *Sesame Street* could mail and receive packages, make copies, send faxes, and the like. No mention of this change was made in the show; Maria and Luis simply became the proprietors of this new shop, helped by their daughter, Gabi. However, this change, too, was short-lived, and the shop went back to its former incarnation in 2004. Viewers easily accepted the changes, perhaps because the kids watching a preschool show are going through so many changes of their own.

Sherry Netherland (seen top right) owns the Furry Arms Hotel, where irascible Benny Rabbit is the bellhop (get it?); set elements that appear when the street expands are the playground and Gina's veterinary office behind 123, seen here

Century 21

Elmo's family lives in the second floor of the building behind 123. For Kevin Clash to puppeteer him in his bedroom window, he has to work on a crane-like platform, seen to the right

Over the years, *Sesame Street* has undergone a variety of changes. Most recently, when the set was moved from a first- to third-floor studio at Kaufman Astoria, the set had to be made a bit smaller to accommodate the new space. Additional realistic details were also added to the set to accommodate the demands of television's newest technological bell and whistle: high definition. Despite the alterations made over the years, the constantly renewing audience of preschoolers doesn't seem fazed, and the set retains its friendly neighborhood vibe.

Hooper's Store, below left, received a facelift for season 40. The Workshop felt that the old Hooper's belonged to a generation of emporia that no longer existed and decided to make it a bit more recognizable to modern kids by making it more like a convenience store. But the familiar green door of 123 is the same one that's always been there.

Some of the Fix-It Shop's iterations before its location became the Laundromat—the Shop has moved to a nearby street

Child-size clothes stand in for full-size garments on the clothesline, which helps to create an illusion of distance

Ernie's window box, below, must be in the back window of his apartment because his front window—hidden behind the short wall in front of 123, above—is clearly too shady to grow flowers (and in previous seasons, that's where the apartment deposited its garbage—the trash not going to Oscar, that is)

A rare look at what's on the shelves in the Fix-It Shop through the years

A combination of real structures, textured facades, and trompe l'oeil painted backgrounds provides the illusion of tremendous depth on what is actually a fairly small soundstage

The wall of doors has been spruced up with brighter paint but still gives Big Bird privacy in his nest 40 years later

The Hooper's Store facade from the nineties

This article in Time Out New York magazine, which ran in November 2008, identifies Sesame Street locations with their real-life New York City equivalents

NEWS FLASH

The doors that hide Big Bird's nest from Sesame Street are another realistic city touch. Set Designer Victor DiNapoli says that in the sixties, old doors were often installed around construction sites instead of fences. Danny Epstein, who worked on the show in 1969 in the music department, remembers that for a brief moment producers played with an idea of using the doors as a screen. "There was to be rear-projected curriculum, for the children to watch in front of the doors," Danny reports. "Jon Stone [took one look] and said, 'But preschoolers can't read.'"

Props and Scenic

Set designer Victor DiNapoli surveys his kingdom

The inner-city world of *Sesame Street*—along with its various insert sets—are kept fresh and up-to-date by Production Designer Victor DiNapoli, who is responsible for all the sets and props on the Street. He works with a department that includes an art director, graphic designers, prop builders, scenic artists, even a shopper, all of whom pitch in both to maintain old sets and construct detailed new ones on *Sesame Street*.

Fortunately, the show's basic setting remains the familiar and fixed-in-place street. The lighting grid is another fixed feature, because the lighting needs remain consistent on a fixed set. Usually, the only thing that has to be added on a daily basis is some fill lighting, illumination of focused areas of the set or specific characters. Fill makes Big Bird's orange and pink legs as vivid as his yellow top feathers.

Normally, a production meeting is held a month before a script will be shot. The producers, directors, and Victor decide if "limbo" sets (temporary, stand-alone sets) are necessary, such as rooms that aren't already in the basic Street set.

The design department sketches the additional set pieces, and blueprints are sped off to Gotham Scenic, a construction company in Manhattan, where they're painted and built. Later, they're trucked to the studio.

There, three crews are responsible for realizing the final vision of the Street. The electric crew deals with lighting, special electric needs, or effects—rain and snow, for example. The carpentry crew unloads sets from trucks and hauls them into the studio, as well as ensures that windows and doors open properly. Grover flying into a door may get a laugh, but it's better when it's intentional.

The props crew decorates the set; in this studio, they're independent Local 4 union crews. Currently, the head of props is Steve Dannenberg, who took over for his father, George, who was with the show at its inception.

The night before a shoot, the lighting and art departments stay late. First the basic lighting is hung for the new set—that has to be done before the set is built, while the floor is clear. Then Victor's department sets up the set. Anything that hasn't been done that night is finished at 8 A.M. the next morning. Pictures are hung, curtains are steamed and pressed, lighting is focused, and other tweaks are made. Everything has to be ready by 9 A.M. on the dot.

And it always is.

Props as well as Muppets and their costumes are built in Jim Henson's Creature Workshop, stored off-site, and then carted to the studio; here, wrangler Andrea Detwiler holds a chicken while the Creature Workshop's supervisor, Jason Weber, stands by

Nat Mongioi, art department mainstay from 1969 to 2008, holds an early Rubber Duckie, which he made famous by sourcing for the song

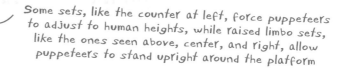

Building On Up

Some sets, like the counter at left, force puppeteers to adjust to human heights, while raised limbo sets, like the ones seen above, center, and right, allow puppeteers to stand upright around the platform

Unless the Muppet in question is a full-body Muppet like Big Bird, puppeteers basically perform their characters by holding their Muppets over their heads, using one hand to operate the mouth and the other to operate one or both hands.

On a normal set that's built on the ground, this can be a difficult feat. Performers must be completely hidden from the camera, so they often find themselves in tiny, cramped spaces, sometimes performing their Muppets through holes in fabric or wood.

If Muppets have to walk on the street or perform with people, the puppeteers may sit or even lie on rollies, a kind of rolling platform that resembles those used by auto mechanics to slide under cars. Wheels allow the puppeteer to follow humans across the set by propelling themselves crab-like with their feet at the same time they manipulate the puppet with their hands.

It isn't easy.

For this reason, Muppet sets are often *built up.* The floors of the set are raised so puppet performers can stand beneath them and hold their Muppets up through holes in the set's floor or simply walk in front of it. Often, most of the floor of a built-up set is removable, so that human actors can still walk on it but spaces can also be opened in the floor to accommodate one or more Muppet actors in a scene.

Even in 1969, limbo sets—like the simple wall on which Grover or Cookie often performed—were built up. But the actual Street set was built on the ground, so that adults and children could easily move around it. That was fine for them . . . but it made things hard for the puppeteers. And as more and more Muppets joined the cast on the Street, things became more and more difficult.

So when the set was moved upstairs within Kaufman-Astoria studios, it was rebuilt. It now contains many more built-up, puppeteer-friendly performing areas. All this has made it a little easier being green . . . and red, and orange, and purple.

NEWS FLASH

"When we first did the brownstones, we built the front steps out of wood because it was cheaper and the normal way to do it," Jon Stone once recalled. "When people ran up and down, you'd hear their heels hitting the wood and you'd say, That doesn't sound right! And we had the steps cast in concrete. The stagehands love us for it every time they have to load them in and out. And they're heavy as can be, but the sound is right." When puppets need to be performed while seated on the stoop, the concrete version is swapped out for a hollow stoop.

"To the millions of children who watch, it's a real neighborhood," Jon added with some pride. "When they come to visit the studio, they can't believe that *Sesame Street* is inside another building."

Reconstruction Era

Shortly before season 40 was due to tape, *Sesame Street* moved from the ground-floor stage G at Kaufman Astoria Studios to new digs in Stage J, up on the third floor. It was a challenging process: The Street set hadn't been disassembled since the show's move to Kaufman-Astoria in 1993. The relocation was overseen by Set Designer Victor DiNapoli and Art Director Bob Phillips. And it gave the Workshop a chance to make some upgrades.

A number of areas were built up so that performers could more easily puppeteer their characters. A Laundromat was added to the set: Writers felt that a host of subjects—size and shape comparisons and other math-curriculum goals, for example—could be tackled very naturally in a setting where clothes are sorted and matched. Like Hooper's Store, the Laundromat was also a location where characters had a good excuse to linger and chat. And as mom-and-pop repair shops increasingly vanished from city land-scapes, it felt more relevant than the Fix-it Shop locale . . . though the Fix-It Shop still exists nearby.

In addition, Hooper's Store was modernized, going from an old-fashioned soda shop to a more familiar convenience store. While adult fans might lament losing a set familiar to them, writers and producers were concerned that today's children wouldn't connect with the older location. After all, *Sesame Street* has to continue to evolve to meet the needs of kids today.

> **I wanted to keep the old-fashioned framework of the tenement building that housed the Fix-It Shop. If we lose that, we lose the Street.**
>
> —VICTOR DINAPOLI, PRODUCTION DESIGNER

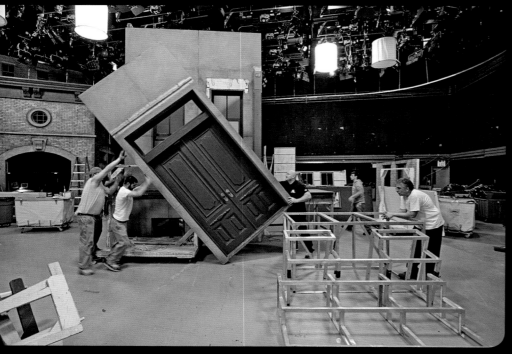

Far left, Victor DiNapoli supervises as the 123 door is raised; Victor reports that it was too close a fit to squeeze the previous set into the new studio, so there had to be some changes—the arbor area is slimmer, there's less space around Big Bird's nest, and there have to be four-foot fire aisles around the set

A glimpse at the cramped quarters where Caroll Spinney performs Oscar

It's a painstaking painting process to replicate New York's fabled cobblestones. Layers of paint are applied by sponge to create a dimensional and aged, mottled look

The new Laundromat set joins a renovated Hooper's Store in season 39

Centuries-old brickwork is recreated with painting techniques while greenery is "cultivated" by hand, leaf by tiny leaf

THIS CHAPTER HAS BEEN BROUGHT TO YOU BY THE LETTER L AND THE NUMBER 23.

The letter L is for the Laundromat—the latest location on Sesame Street, and **the number 23** is for the number of entirely new Muppets built for Season 40, according to Creative Workshop Supervisor Jason Weber. Currently, 26 new episodes are shot each season, so that's close to one new Muppet per show. With over 4,000 episodes of *Sesame Street* in the can, that means the puppet population through the years has to number in the thousands.

23

10

> " We don't play down to kids. We just have a very short audience. "
>
> —JOE RAPOSO,
> *SESAME STREET* SONGWRITER

WHAT'S THE NAME OF THAT SONG?

EPISODE
4143

Mike Renzi on piano; he also composes and arranges music for the show

At the same time the lights are coming up on the *Sesame Street* set for the taping of segment 4143, the first of the Sesame house band members step off the elevator on the 17th floor of the nondescript midtown Manhattan building that houses Nola Recording Studios.

Nola is cluttered and dimly lit, showing the wear and tear of years of recording history. It's also where magic happens on a regular basis: the location for much of the taping of *Sesame Street*'s iconic music and the site of today's recording session.

The first fifteen minutes of the day are spent catching up on the previous evening's antics, trading jokes even older than the paint on the walls. Another half hour is spent deliberating over lunch choices.

They settle on Chinese. But there's always someone who grumbles about the selection; today it's engineer and Nola co-owner Jim Czak, partner of John Post, who first engineered *Sesame Street* music back in 1970 ("a lifetime of fun" is how John describes his association with the show). Jim wants a burger and fries, but he's out of luck; lunch will be kung pao chicken.

When the band finally begins the actual music recording, the morning speeds by. Arrangements are ironed out on the fly and nailed after just two or three run-throughs. They include not just the "big songs"—the literally show-stopping, full-blown song-and-dance numbers that interrupt street stories—but also all the music cues: underlying music that establishes ambience during street and Muppet segments, lead-ins, even the melodies behind the animations and special effects on screen.

The music stops and starts erratically, as someone in the band hits a snag and calls out to ask for advice. Pens scribble notes in the margins of lead sheets. Music Director Mike Renzi, leading the session on keyboard, abruptly stops to make a suggestion for a tricky passage.

During a break, while Mike jumps over to the piano to work out a bit of business, horn player Glenn Drewes puts aside his trumpet to haul out a duffle, eager to show off the oddball collection of wind instruments he's concocted—a conch shell, a paper cup, something else—to create the unusual sounds the band is so often called on to produce.

Not to be outdone, Wally Kane, on reeds, demonstrates how to slide a dollar bill under a key on a sax to stop it from sticking. Meanwhile, Danny Epstein hunts in a huge canvas tote crammed with every conceiveable drumstick or mallet. Head of the music department for four decades until his retirement in 2009 and frequent percussion player, Danny's on the prowl for the precise pair that he needs to get a certain sound from the xylophone. He's found one mallet, but the other is elusive. He keeps rummaging.

There's a roar of laughter over by the workman-like partitions surrounding the drum set. Drummer Ricky Martinez has just told another joke, and bassist Ben Brown is cracking up. Steve Bargonetti grins across at them, then bends over his own guitar, tuning up for the next number. He finishes just as Danny finds the missing mallet. They're ready to tape the next song.

The music they're recording will eventually be utilized three and a

Steve Bargonetti plays a Street tune on his guitar

Jim Czak (at the console) and Bill Moss record the session—later, they'll "master" the audio for use on the show

Ben Brown makes a note on the lead sheets for "The Amazingly Awesome Seven Song"—debuting in season 40

half miles away, back on the *Sesame Street* set. In fact, a previously recorded track will be used today in the Queens studio. It's for the song "I Love Every Part of You," with music by Mike Renzi and lyrics by show writer Christine Ferraro. It's sung in English and Spanish by Gina and Rosita to Gina's adopted son, Marco.

As puppeteer Carmen Osbahr picks up Rosita, Gina asks to hear the song. The prerecorded track comes up on the loudspeakers. Gina and Rosita's voices have already been recorded; both performer and puppeteer will be lip-synching to the song today.

Baby Marco is brought on the set last, so he won't be tired and cranky when shooting begins. His cheeks are flushed and his nose is a little runny.

"Hi, baby!" says Rosita. Marco stares seriously at the Muppet, then makes a lunge for her turquoise fur and sticks his fingers in her mouth. Gina settles the restless toddler on her lap and starts to sing, with Rosita chiming in, translating.

The tune is light and lovely; the arrangement is perfect. Marco listens, wide-eyed.

"Pretty sweet," says director Emily Squires, after the final notes fade away. The playback confirms her judgment, and some applause breaks out.

Got it in one.

Carmen Osbahr and Gina (with a doll stand-in for baby Marco) prepare for "Roll tape"

Perfect Timing

Joe and a barely visible Danny, far left, with Joan Cooney, Dave Connell, and other members of the Street

Danny Epstein

Danny Epstein is a boy from Brooklyn who loves playing the drums. He played them throughout his high school career and then at Juilliard. Eventually, he played them on Broadway in the original production of "My Fair Lady."

It was Danny's skill on the kettle drums that first caught the attention of Joe Raposo. Danny was working at local New York TV station Channel 5 when Joe was hired to lead the band on conductor Skitch Henderson's *The New Yorker Show.* Joe introduced himself by paying Danny one of his rare professional compliments: "I really like the way you play timpanis."

That was the beginning of a life long friendship and partnership.

The two were friends working together on New York's Upper East Side when "lo and behold," recalls Danny, "one day, a car rolls up with arms and legs and eyeballs hanging out of it."

It was Jim Henson, setting up shop next door.

Joe and Danny began to team up with the puppeteer on a variety of projects: commercials, sales films for IBM, *The Ed Sullivan Show, The Jimmy Dean Show,* and a TV special called *Hey, Cinderella.* In one of the remarkable confluences that led to the creation of *Sesame Street,* they met Jon Stone while working on that fractured fairy tale. "One day," says Danny, "Jon appeared and said, 'Hey guys, I'm involved with something.' " That something was *Sesame Street.*

Weeks later, in June 1969, the musicians were already at work up at a studio in New York's Spanish Harlem. Their first piece? Joe's score for freelance producer Clark Gesner's "Dot Animation," which would eventually appear in episode one of *Sesame Street.*

Danny was, as usual, on percussion. "Whoever was sitting in front of me hit me on the head with a box of music," he recalls, smiling. "He said, 'Keep time! You're all over the place!' "

But others tell a different story about Danny's skill and flexibility as a musician.

"Danny's sense of timing is perfect," Joe said early on in the show's production. "I demand so much of the band . . . Epstein is the keystone." In marathon recording sessions that sometimes lasted three days, the musicians staggered breaks so they could keep recording, crashing on couches in the studio. "Joe would sleep under the [mixing] console!" Danny remembers. Danny was asked to play musical styles ranging from burlesque to Latin to classical.

"Danny was there for everything. He was one of the few guys my father trusted to always know exactly what to do in the studio," says Nico Raposo, Joe's son. He cites Danny's wealth of musical contacts as instrumental to the show's sound, recalling that Danny was responsible for bringing in famed jazz musician Toots Thielemans to play the iconic harmonica riffs in the theme.

Danny became *Sesame Street*'s music coordinator in 1970, which was an unforgiving task, says Nico, given his father's penchant for scribbling song arrangements on envelopes on the way to the studio. Danny would turn these ad hoc arrangements into comprehensible charts for the band, which he would keep up-to-date even when Joe made last-minute changes to the compositions. Danny not only played on virtually every track but provided sound effects for everything from Cookie Monster's stomach rumbles to breaking glass. Danny (and Joe) even appeared in early 16mm short films made by the Workshop, but music remained their mission.

"Music was the binder that held [the show] together," says Danny. "At the risk of sounding a little egotistical, we held it together pretty well."

Composers Joe Raposo and Jeff Moss meet up with the production team, including Joan Ganz Cooney and Dave Connell

Some songs, however deft, never make it onto the show, like this unproduced number by Jeff Moss

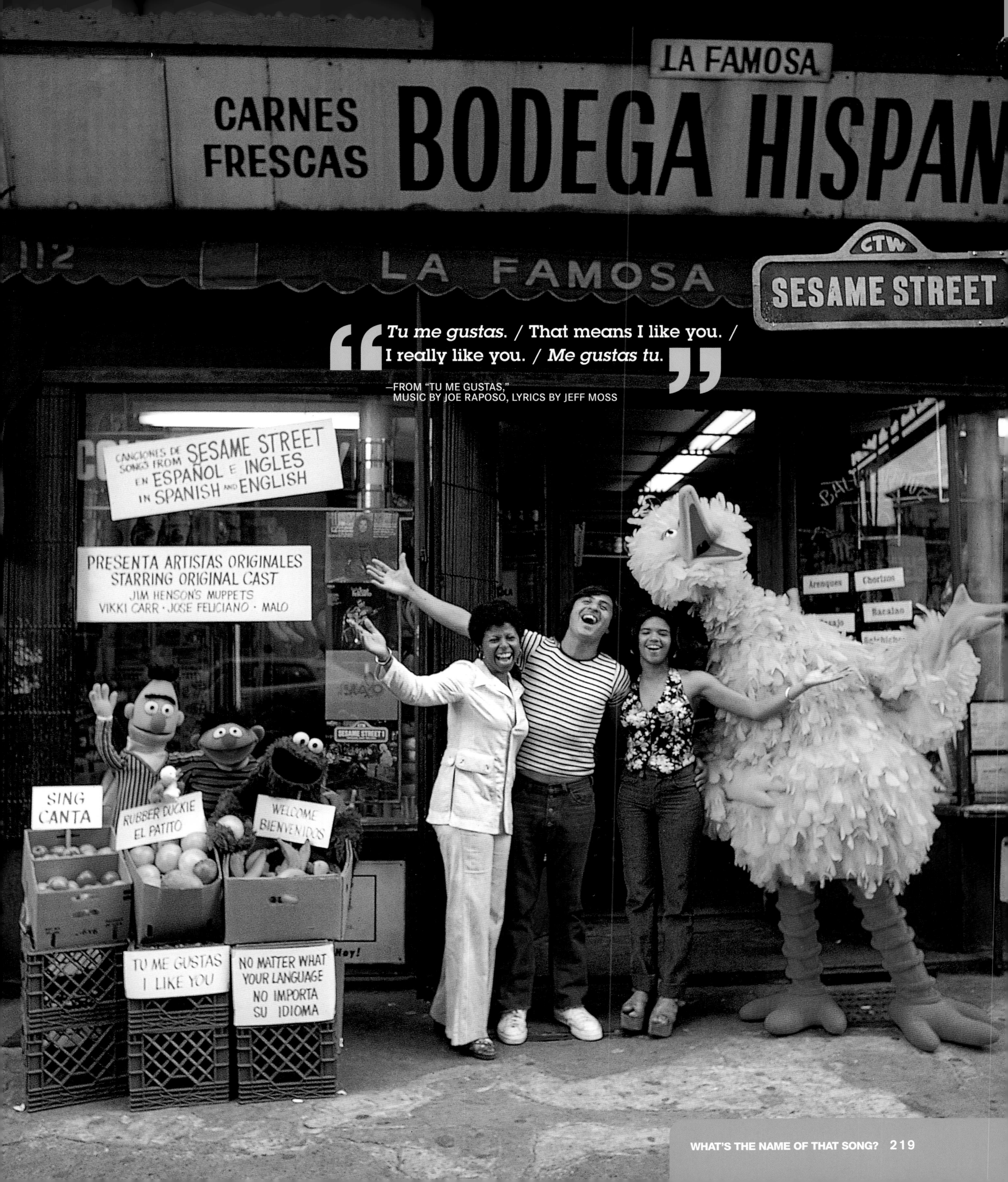

LA FAMOSA

CARNES
FRESCAS **BODEGA HISPAN**

112 LA FAMOSA

CTW
SESAME STREET

"*Tu me gustas.* / That means I like you. / I really like you. / *Me gustas tu.*"

—FROM "TU ME GUSTAS,"
MUSIC BY JOE RAPOSO, LYRICS BY JEFF MOSS

CANCIONES DE SESAME STREET
SONGS FROM
EN ESPAÑOL E INGLES
IN SPANISH AND ENGLISH

PRESENTA ARTISTAS ORIGINALES
STARRING ORIGINAL CAST
JIM HENSON'S MUPPETS
VIKKI CARR · JOSE FELICIANO · MALO

SING
CANTA

RUBBER DUCKIE
EL PATITO

WELCOME
BIENVENIDOS

TU ME GUSTAS
I LIKE YOU

NO MATTER WHAT
YOUR LANGUAGE
NO IMPORTA
SU IDIOMA

The Giant

Any fan can tell you that "It's Not Easy Bein' Green" or hum along to the melody of the "Sesame Street Theme." That's because composer Joe Raposo's music and arrangements have been wildly popular since *Sesame Street*'s first days on the air. Director/Head Writer Jon Stone once summed up Joe's impact by saying, "There was no other sound like it on television . . . the first few notes would bring [a child] running from wherever she might be at the moment."

But that sound wasn't originally part of the plan.

The initial vision of the show's producers was to use different composers and musicians to record the many songs and scores. But with a crushing schedule of 130 episodes a year, dozens of unique pieces of music needed for each show, and a tiny budget, Joe (brought on board as the show's first music director) soon realized there was no way to make that vision work. Instead, he suggested he and scriptwriter Jeff Moss do it all.

That boyish confidence and energy were characteristic of Joe. A graduate of the prestigious École Normale de Musique in Paris, Joe arrived in New York in 1965. In the brief interval before teaming up with *Sesame Street*, he'd worked as a composer and music director on theater works as diverse as Bertolt Brecht's *A Man's A Man* and Clark Gesner's musical comedy *You're a Good Man, Charlie Brown*. Tom Whedon, one of *Sesame Street*'s founding writers, knew Joe from their days at Harvard and the legendary jazz club Storyville, and Tom had no hesitation about recommending him to Jon.

Joe Raposo's son Joe, a musician himself, says ruefully, "From then on we never saw our father." For the next six years, Joe spent countless hours squirreled away in a recording studio or in the Workshop's offices.

Joe jokingly called his team's production style a "salami factory" because of the amount of music they had to produce. "You don't want to know what goes into the salami," he would add. Whatever the ingredients were, they worked. The show's original cast album went gold in 1970. Given an assignment by Jon to write a song for Kermit the Frog that engaged issues of race and self-acceptance, Joe produced "Bein' Green" virtually overnight. And then there's "Sing," which as many as four generations might know by heart. Longtime music coordinator Danny Epstein says, "That song is a monument."

And while that tune was hugely successful, it was just one of more than two thousand compositions Joe wrote for the show before succumbing to lymphoma at the age of 51.

As Frank Oz said, "He went right to the heart of things and made them simple and delightful."

NEWS FLASH Joe Raposo won three Emmy Awards and four Grammys for his work on *Sesame Street*. His songs from the show have been covered by Frank Sinatra, Ray Charles, the Carpenters, Barbra Streisand, Lena Horne, Van Morrison, Dizzy Gillespie, Paul Simon, and José Feliciano.

" We had films with animals in which a voice-over would be singing songs about the animals. That's all Joe. It's Joe's music, it's Joe's words, and it's Joe's singing—and singing in all different voices. "

—JOAN GANZ COONEY,
SESAME STREET COFOUNDER

" 'Bein' Green' was really strikingly personal to my father. "

—CHERYL HENSON, THE
JIM HENSON FOUNDATION

Music helped define characters such as Cookie Monster, seen here performing "C is for Cookie" live on tour, and Kermit

Will Lee, as Mr. Hooper, was famously unable to come in on cue during live performances. So music gurus Joe Raposo and Danny Epstein hid offstage holding one end of an invisible-to-the-audience piece of string tied to Will's leg. They pulled on the string to cue Will for his parts.

Prior to the taping of an *Evening at the Pops* televised special, Caroll Spinney rehearses his long walk down the aisle to the stage; he would walk up alongside Boston Pops Orchestra conductor, Arthur Fiedler, "helping" him lead his symphony orchestra. *Sesame Street* composers Joe Raposo and Jeff Moss, as well as then-Music Coordinator Danny Epstein, were on hand to help the cast, both human and Muppet, prepare for the big night.

The Street Hits The Road

Another "road" show: the "Sesame Street LIVE!" taping in 1973

Among his other accomplishments, Joe Raposo created what is called a house band for *Sesame Street*—a group of musicians that had a signature sound. In the original band were Danny Epstein on percussion; Bob Cranshaw on bass; drummer Ed Shaughnessy, from *The Tonight Show*; Jimmy Mitchell on guitar (who shared the chair with Bucky Pizzarelli); Bobby McCoy on trumpet; and Wally Kane, a reed player (the latter two also came from *The Tonight Show*). Joe was often on piano.

"It was instant magic," Danny recalls, "because Joe's arrangements were done in a style that made it possible for each player to do something major as part of his contribution."

"Joe had a very strong idea that you could do all kinds of music," says Chris Cerf, "all kinds of different cultures, and all kinds of different musical types, but he wanted a *Sesame Street* sound throughout. He was able to do that with the band.

"The band always sounds like *Sesame Street*," Chris explains, "whether it's playing rock and roll or opera."

The "sound" created by this house band was so consistent and recognizable that it was able to be successfully reproduced in places the band itself couldn't appear, such as when the show's stars toured for the "Sesame Street LIVE!" album, or even earlier, when the cast made a guest appearance on *Evening at the Pops: A Special Program with Arthur Fiedler and Friends from Sesame Street*, in 1971. That day, in Boston's Symphony Hall, conductor Fiedler's own Boston Pops Orchestra took over the band's duties.

A problem did arise, though, relating to Jeff Moss's song "Rubber Duckie." The intent had been for every member of the orchestra to squeeze a duck during the tune. But union rules dictated extra fees be paid for each new "instrument" played, making lots of ducks unaffordable. So a single duckie was classified as a percussion instrument, to be performed solely by the percussionist.

Record producer Arthur Shimkin, above right, with Will Lee (Mr. Hooper), supervised many of the show's album recordings

"There's always room for one more . . . but you better be good."

—DANNY EPSTEIN'S ADVICE TO UP-AND-COMERS

Joe Raposo, top left, rehearses with early band members. Dave Conner and writer/songwriter Jeff Moss, far left, work with Jim Mitchell, Danny Epstein, Bob Cranshaw, Steve Little, Mel Davis, and Wally Kane

The Gentleman

Over the years, a group of incredibly talented songwriters have penned unforgettable songs for *Sesame Street*, including Princeton grad Jeff Moss (a scriptwriter, composer, and lyricist who joined the team in 1969). At the time, Jeff was already a veteran of children's television—like Director/Head Writer Jon Stone and Producer Dave Connell, Jeff had been recruited from *Captain Kangaroo*.

Jeff, whom longtime music director Danny Epstein calls "a true gentleman," joined *Sesame Street*'s original writing staff and went on to compose numerous songs featuring a unique blend of poignance and silliness, including the immortal "Rubber Duckie," "I Don't Want to Live on the Moon," "Captain Breakfast," and "People in Your Neighborhood." He managed this while also penning three books of poetry—the classic *The Butterfly Jar*, among them—and numerous short stories beloved by children and adults.

"What makes kids laugh is the same as what makes us laugh," Jeff once said. "The key is to keep the vocabulary simple so children can understand it. That way you keep the kids watching and smiling, and it's something you watch yourself."

Danny Epstein believes Jeff accomplished that goal musically, describing Jeff's compositions as "simple . . . not simplistic."

Like so many of the talented team that helped shape the show, Jeff's personality combined the sensitivity of an artist—"heart of gold," says Chris Cerf, his companion on the show and songwriting team—"with a healthy ego and sometimes wicked sense of humor."

"Sparks flew," Danny says with a smile, acknowledging the friendly rivalry between by Jeff and Joe Raposo. The two composers delighted in one-upping each other musically, to the benefit of all.

"Jeff and my father were like brothers," says Nico Raposo. "They worked side-by-side in one room for those first five years. They could fight like cats and dogs, but most of all, they respected each other." The two composers often vacationed together with their families, sharing ideas and co-writing more than seventy songs, most often uniting Joe's music and Jeff's words.

"Jeff's wonderful lyrics and music reflected the mood and the style of the show—fun, energetic, sometimes sentimental, and always entertaining," Joan Ganz Cooney said of Jeff, who was lost to *Sesame Street* when he developed colon cancer and died at the tragically young age of 56.

"A true music visionary" is how Joan describes him.

> "From the beginning, Jeff played a critical role in the educational and creative standards of *Sesame Street*, which led to the instant success of the show.
>
> —JOAN GANZ COONEY

NEWS FLASH "Rubber Duckie" sold more than one million copies as a single and reached #11 on the Billboard charts in 1971. It's been recorded in French, Spanish, Dutch, and German. "I feel like the Mick Jagger of the 5-to-11 set," Jeff told *The New York Times* in a 1993 interview.

Jeff Moss squeaks the duckie in the original recording and no other rubber duck has had that unique sound, so the same track is reused each time the song's redone

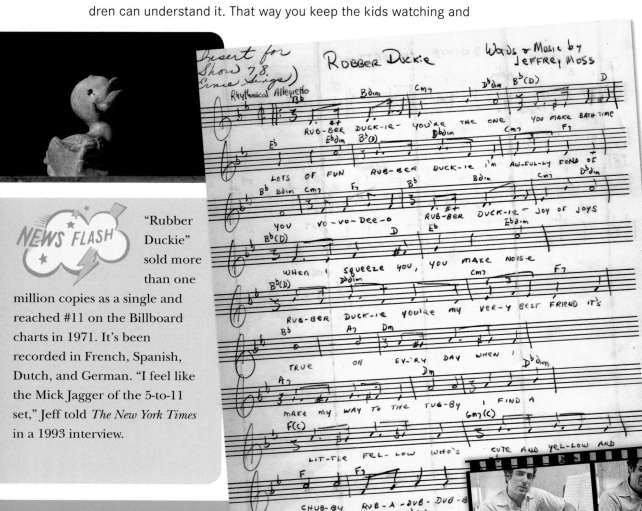

Joe Raposo and Jeff Moss took childlike pleasure in poking at each other musically, as evidenced by Joe's sly aside on the lead sheet he penned for Jeff's "I Love Trash," right. But both worked long hours side by side—the writing staff often bunked at the office, working through the night—so perhaps it was their roller-coaster relationship that inspired the rueful lyrics of Jeff's "Still We Like Each Other": "We are friends / You and me / And it doesn't matter what we look like / Or if sometimes we don't agree."

Aaron Neville sang an especially moving version of this song with Ernie on the show

They give 105 percent, which makes any song into something special.

—JEFF MOSS

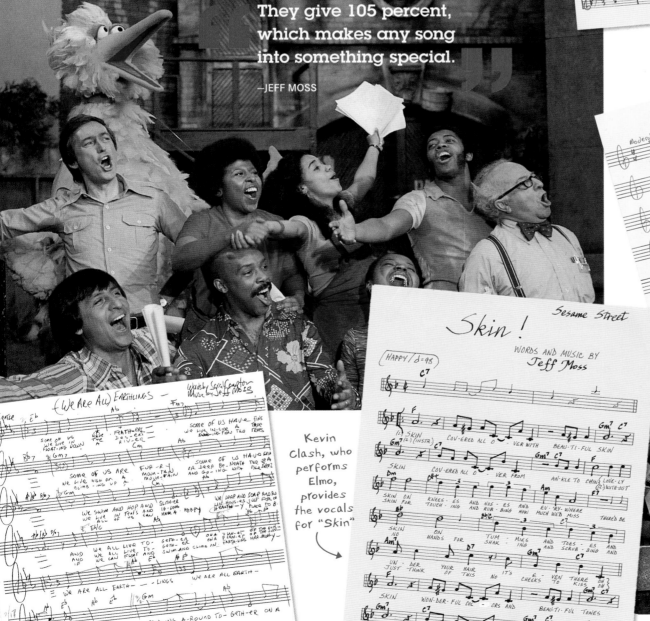

Jeff, Joe, and Chris share a laugh backstage at "Sesame Street LIVE!"

Kevin Clash, who performs Elmo, provides the vocals for "Skin"

Chris Cerf on location with the cast, shooting the cover art for 1974's "¡Sesame Mucho!"—Sesame Street's first bilingual album—which features guest turns by Malo, José Feliciano, and Vikki Carr singing in Spanish

Show Me The Silly

writers writers writers

Chris Cerf with jazz artist Joe Williams, one of the "Put Down the Duckie" singers

T here was so much composing talent on *Sesame Street* that it's not surprising it sometimes overflowed into other venues. Jeff Moss moonlighted over at what was then Henson Associates, providing the Oscar-nominated score for *The Muppets Take Manhattan*. Sam Pottle—who cowrote *The Muppet Show* theme song with Jim Henson—briefly replaced Joe Raposo as music director, writing the *Sesame Street* mainstay "What's the Name of That Song?" while he was on staff.

At times, changes came about for unhappy reasons. In another of the show's great losses, Joe tragically passed away at age 52. In 1989, Robby Merkin (musical director of *The Little Mermaid*) took over the helm, writing songs like "Elmo's Rap Alphabet" and "Write Your Name" during his seven-year tenure.

Danny Epstein, who served in a variety of musical roles on the show since its inception, left the role of director of music operations in 2009 with great reluctance. As he puts it, "This show is musically head and shoulders above the others."

These days, Mike Renzi is music director of the show. "Mike is a wonderful songwriter and arranger whose songs have a rather more contemporary feel in some respects than perhaps Joe's and Jeff's," says Bob McGrath. "The show has always been cutting edge in its musical selections and spoofs, and the aim is to keep the classics alive but add new tunes for each new generation to call its own. Mike's on top of it."

"We updated the sound a little bit, and Mike has put his own stamp on it," says Danny. "He is probably as world class as it gets."

Some of the songwriters who penned early classics are following *Sesame Street* into its next decade. One is Chris Cerf, a writer who originally came on board as a publishing executive in the fledgling products group back in the early 1970s. On staff at Random House, Chris had been writing and editing *Sesame Street* books when Joan asked if he wanted to make the jump over to the Workshop. Chris leaped at the chance.

As a student, he had been a few years behind Joe Raposo at Harvard, and Joe knew from those days that Chris could write rock and

roll. So early on, Joe let Chris try his hand at a song for the show.

Chris ended up penning "Count It Higher," which has gone on to become a *Sesame Street* classic. (The Count labeled it his favorite song during a DJ stint on the show.) What's more, Chris sang it on the show—as a Muppet (puppeteered by Jim Henson) named Chrissy, lead singer of "Chrissy and the Alphabeats." Chrissy was one of the earliest Muppets based on actual people. The band, whose name morphed to "Little Chrissy and the Alphabeats," performed a number of Chris's tunes over the years.

Another Muppet rock group was formed a little later, called "Little Jerry and the Monotones," with Jerry Nelson as its lead singer. Jeff Moss wrote a lot of the Monotones' songs.

Chris soon became the go-to guy on *Sesame Street* for classic rock and roll as well as song spoofs. He has an infallible ear, a head full of tunes, and

During season 24, guests were asked to sing this tune, just as Chris suggested

Cerf/Stiles — Lyrics for "PUT DOWN THE DUCKIE" — Version #6 — 8/4/86

3. It'd be great — for both musical and visual reasons — if we wild, swinging sax-and-horn section in this song. Such horn is very hot right now in pop music circles. Besides, the Sesam band already has two musicians — Mel Davis and Wally Kane can play this stuff wonderfully. Can we have a special arrang done? (The choreographed horn players in "Face the Face," fr Townshend's recent record-and-video "White City," might se good source of inspiration here.)

4. As Ernie plays his saxophone (both with and without the he should bob and weave around the stage in the great tradi wailing sax players (e.g., Clarence Clemons, Junior Walker an All-Stars, and Sam "The Man" Taylor). Danny DeVito does a parody of this in the video for "When the Going Gets Tough," Jim might want to take a look at before he tackles "Put Dow Duckie."

5. Following is a far-from-complete list of celebrities who m might not! — be appropriate choices to help make "Put Down Duckie" the huge video spectacular we all know it can be (h modestly). No doubt they're all standing by, waiting for our

Whitney Houston
Janet Jackson
The Rev. Jesse Jackson
Reggie Jackson
Mick Jagger
Don Johnson
Grace Jones
Senator Edward Kenned
Kermit the Frog
Jeanne Kirkpatrick
Ed Koch
David Letterman
Cyndi Lauper
John Madden
Madonna
Wynton Marsalis
Jim McMahon
Senator Daniel Pat
Eddie Murphy
Bill Murray
Martina Navratilo
Jack Nicholson
Leonard Nimoy
Richard Nixon
William "The R
Miss Piggy
Prince
Richard Pryor
Ronald Reagan
Molly Ringw
Fred Rose
Pete Lee R
David Lee R
Willard Sc
Brooke Sh
Sylvester
Sting
Meryl St
Sugeon
Mr. T
Lily To
Kathle

Christopher Cerf Associates, Inc.

TO: Dulcy Singer, Lisa Simon, Arlene Sherman
CC: Norman "Normie" Stiles, Dave Conner, Danny Epstein
FROM: Chris Cerf
SUBJECT: "PUT DOWN THE DUCKIE" — (Song for <u>Sesame Street</u>)
DATE: 4 August 1986 (Version #6.0)

Hi Everybody!

Here — at last! — are the lyrics for Norman Stiles' and my long-awaited jazz/rock epic, "PUT DOWN THE DUCKIE!":

PUT DOWN THE DUCKIE!
Music and Lyrics by Norman Stiles and Christopher Cerf
(C) 1986 Splotched Animal Music (BMI) and Sesame Street, Inc. (ASCAP)

ERNIE

[VERSE #1]
Excuse me, Mr.Hoots, I hate to bug a busy bird,
But I wanna learn the sax, and I need a helpful word,
'Cause I always get a silly squeak when I play the blues.

HOOTS THE OWL

Ernie, keep your cool, I'll teach ya how to blow the sax,
I think I dig your problem — it's rubber and it quacks,
You'll never find the skill you seek till you pay your dues!

[CHORUS #1]
YOU GOTTA PUT DOWN THE DUCKIE!
PUT DOWN THE DUCKIE,
PUT DOWN THE DUCKIE,
Ya gotta leave the duck alone!
PUT DOWN THE DUCKIE,
PUT DOWN THE DUCKIE,
PUT DOWN THE DUCKIE,

Chris Cerf's submissions for songs commonly took this form: he would provide detailed (and often wryly humorous) production suggestions along with the lyrics.

"CO-OPERATION"/Lyrics and Production Notes   Page 2

"CO-OPERATION"

Well, I'm sittin' on a seasaw seat
Thinking seasawing would be neat,
And I can't find a friend to sit on the other side;
Yes, I tried it all alone
But I crashed down like a stone,
Couldn't get no CO-OPERATION if I tried.

No, no, no, no CO-OPERATION,
No, no, no, no CO-OPERATION,
No, no, no-no-no CO-OPERATION if I tried,
If I tried....

Well, I'm dying to jump rope,
But I've just about lost all hope,
'Cause I'm so mad, I'm just fit to be tied;
'Cause I can't find a friend
To pick up the other end,
Couldn't get no CO-OPERATION if I tried.

No, no, no, no CO-OPERATION,
No, no, no-no-no CO-OPERATION,
No, no, no-no-no CO-OPERATION if I tried,
If I tried....

Well, I'm in an awful fit
'Cause I'm dying to be "It",
And I can't find anyone to go and hide.
Every time I start to play
Everyone just runs away,
Couldn't get no CO-OPERATION

Emily Kingsley's hilarious "I Go Beep" song ended with the TV screen covered in animated dots

Now, here's that moment you've all been waiting for, 'cause here comes the song at the top of the *Sesame Street* hit parade! For 327 weeks and still holding strong, the number one song on the Count's Count Parade—number one! 'The Song of the Count'! *Ah-ah-ah-ah-ah!*

—THE COUNT

a clever yet simple rhyming style that adults and kids love. Among his familiar songs are "Letter B" (cowritten with Judy Freudberg) and "Put Down the Duckie" (with Norman Stiles on lyrics).

There have been other songwriters over the years. Notable are Alan Menken, who also wrote scores for some of the great Disney animated films; Sammy Cahn, who wrote "There's Always Room for One More"; husband-and-wife composer Paul Jacobs and lyricist Sarah Durkee, who came from the world of rock and roll; and Robby Merkin, to name just a few. Currently, Mark Radice and Russell Velázquez are composing for the show, bringing to it a highly contemporary sound.

Scriptwriters on *Sesame Street* often write their own lyrics, submitting them along with their scripts. Emily Kingsley, who created the character of Polly Darton, is one. She wrote "Under the Weather Over You" for Polly, as well as the "Nine to Five" spoof "Counting One to Five." A few other scriptwriters, like Tony Geiss, write both lyrics and music. He estimates that he's written about a hundred and fifty tunes for the show.

The research department helps guide the direction for songs to ensure they support the curriculum—these tunes have to teach as well as entertain. Tony recalls how that worked in a show centered on the theme of sibling rivalry, using cast member Buffy Sainte-Marie and her son Cody's relationship with

Big Bird: "Lewis Bernstein was head of research, and he sent me this monograph. It said, 'Don't say I'll have enough love for you,' because it makes it seem like you have a finite amount of love, and maybe you get a smaller share of this love pie. You say, 'I have a special kind of love for you, a Big Bird love—and I have baby love for the baby.'

"So we wrote a Buffy Sainte-Marie song: 'I'll love you because you're yellow and tall; I'll love him because he's tiny and small. Yellow and tall love, tiny and small love, everyone loves, throughout their days, different people, different ways.' "

The song was perfect.

Puppeteer Jerry Nelson with his Count von Count

Writer Emily Kingsley; her "Song of the Count," cowritten with Jeff Moss, debuted in season 6

Danny Epstein and Sam Pottle on location on a Navajo reservation

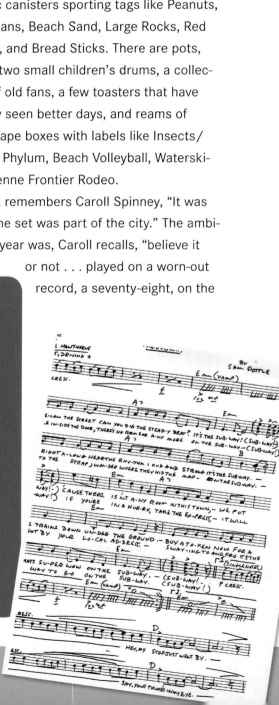

Make Noise

Over the years, many talented songwriters have labored at *Sesame Street*. But the process is generally the same. A songwriter submits a tune—in the form of a written lead sheet or some sort of audio file—to the music department, where, after it's approved, Mike Renzi almost always arranges it, writing the various instrumental parts and ensuring that the song embodies the show's signature sound. (Mike also writes underscoring for the show.) A copyist then creates final copies, and the song goes to the band for performance.

Forty years of music composition have resulted in thousands of pages of music, currently being scanned into a computer by

Dick, below, and the rubber duckies for the Pops event

audio archivist Eric Goldin (who's already archived 6,200 songs, with more to come). The whole operation is managed by coordinator Vicki Levy, whose knowledge of the music library is encyclopedic. (In addition to Jeff Moss's plaintive anthem "I Don't Want to Live on the Moon" and Joe Raposo's classic "Sing," she admits to a particular fondness for Sam Pottle's "Fur.")

But music isn't the only thing heard on *Sesame Street*. Sound engineer Dick Maitland's job is to create the endless

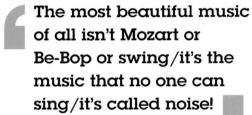

> **The most beautiful music of all isn't Mozart or Be-Bop or swing/it's the music that no one can sing/it's called noise!**
>
> —OSCAR,
> IN THE SONG BY POTTLE, "NOISE"

variety of sound effects on the show, from the Honkers' honks to the Muppets' footsteps.

"Jim hated the fact that the Muppets were just floating in air; he wanted to give them footsteps and weight," Dick explains.

Dick's office is down a crowded hallway filled with shelves haphazardly stacked with large plastic canisters sporting tags like Peanuts, Big Beans, Beach Sand, Large Rocks, Red Bricks, and Bread Sticks. There are pots, pans, two small children's drums, a collection of old fans, a few toasters that have clearly seen better days, and reams of audiotape boxes with labels like Insects/Lower Phylum, Beach Volleyball, Waterskiing Championships, and Cheyenne Frontier Rodeo.

Before Dick came on board, remembers Caroll Spinney, "It was so quiet, you'd never believe the set was part of the city." The ambient street noise provided that year was, Caroll recalls, "believe it or not . . . played on a worn-out record, a seventy-eight, on the

Want the sound of someone walking in snow? Dick Maitland crunches fistfuls of kosher salt. Cookie Monster eating? Croutons crushed right next to the mic. (These days, Dick confides, croutons tend to have garlic on them. "It takes days to get it off your hands.") Squishy footsteps? Wet paper towels in a tub of water, squished with his hands while Dick makes the footsteps with his feet. "Jim was just in tears laughing over that one," Dick recalls. "It sounded so stupid, he just couldn't see straight."

On My Pond

WORDS AND MUSIC BY
Christopher Cerf & Sarah Durkee

© 1986 SPLOTCHED ANIMAL / JIVE DURKEE / SESAME STREET INC.

Sarah Durkee teamed with Chris Cerf to pen this classic

NEWS FLASH One of the pieces of equipment Dick has in his studio at *Sesame Street* is one of Pink Floyd's Putney synthesizers. It's now thirty-five years old, and he still uses it every day. Among other things, it provides great wind or whooshing sounds for when Super Grover flies.

cheapest little thing, and they'd put a mic to this phonograph."

Dick was working in sound effects at ABC Network News when there was a call about some work at a kids' show on 67th Street.

"The first job I had was for a song called 'Windy,' " Dick recalls. "They wanted a big crash at the end.

"In those days we didn't have electronic equipment buttons we could push. So I went and I got all the stagehands, and we made this big pile of crap in the middle of the stage. And at the right point, I threw myself at the pile and smashed it all over the floor.

"Everybody was in the control room," Dick goes on, "including Jon and Joan. And Jon says, 'We gotta do that one more time.' We

build the pile again, and the song came around, and, bang, I threw myself at it.

"Jon said, 'We need to do this one more time,' " Dick continues, grinning. "And I realized at that point that the actors weren't even acting, the camera had been turned on me, and they're all in the control room laughing their asses off at this young kid throwing himself into this pile of garbage to make this crash."

Dick has moved from using scratchy records to three turntables to tape to synthesizers and computers. But he still creates sounds the way foley artists have always done—with odd bits of stuff and an incredible, infallible ear for what sounds like what.

Composer Sam Pottle's copy of Grace Hawthorne's humorous "Subway Song" lyrics appeal to both kids and parents—its gritty on-screen sound effects also showcase the talents of the sound department

For thirty-eight years, vocal coach David (Dave) Conner coaxed outstanding vocal performances from the cast members of *Sesame Street*, most of whom are actors, not professional singers. (Judith Clurman replaced Dave in season 39, and currently, Paul Rudolph has taken on the job.)

"[Dave] made me sound like I can actually sing," Caroll Spinney says.

Dave, who also arranges music, confides that his most amusing memories are of his sessions with the professionals who appear as guests.

"Itzhak Perlman came in to play 'The Minuet in G,'" he recalls. "I asked him, 'What key do you want to play this in?'

" 'Let's try G," Perlman answered."

And then there was the time that Seiji Ozawa was conducting the immortal All Animal Orchestra.

"He's conducting," Dave says. "It's all prerecorded. And suddenly, he yells, 'Stop! The pigs are not watching!' "

"Dave once had to tell tenor Andrea Bocelli that he was off pitch," Caroll recalls, shaking his head.

Sing After Me

Whatever the song, the human and Muppet cast of *Sesame Street*, along with their many guest stars, perform it with integrity, heart, and humor, whether indoors, on set, or out on location. "The intent," says Danny Epstein, "is a high level of arranging and delivering of music."

And they make it sound effortless.

The gospel group Listen My Brother appeared on several episodes the first year of the show; Their musical director, Peter Long, was Loretta Long's husband at the time

The cast assembles under Jon Stone's direction on the beach at City Island, New York, for a series of segments that aired in season 8; above, Judy Collins is on the far left

> "Fuzzy and blue, that's me / I'm fuzzy and blue / It's just the way I grew / Love being fuzzy and blue / I do!"
>
> —GROVER, SINGING "FUZZY AND BLUE," MUSIC BY STEPHEN LAWRENCE AND LYRICS BY DAVID AXLEROD

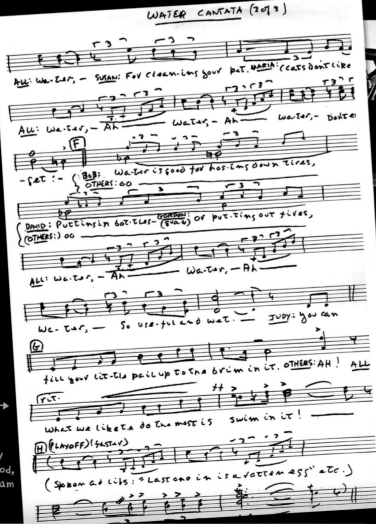

Lyrics by David Axlerod, music by Sam Pottle

Some vocals are prerecorded, so talent simply lip synchs during taping; at other times, performers such as Kevin Clash, shown here with musical guest John Legend, belt out the tune on set

Songs such as Chris Cerf's 1979 spoof of Bruce Springsteen's original are a huge hit with fans (especially parents)

The song that fans commonly call "Mah Nà Mah Nà" got its start 4,500 miles away—as the underlying music for a scene in a risque sixties documentary about Swedish sex habits, called *Heaven and Hell*. (It accompanied some giggling college girls into a sauna.) In 1968, the tune was collected onto an Italian album with other cuts from popular soundtracks. No one is sure when Jim Henson first heard the tune, but he's the one who suggested it be used in a Muppet segment. The wild-haired puppet Jim used for the piece was later modified and came to be called Bip Bippadotta; he's heard on the album "Everybody's Song."

Bert's bath gets interrupted by the whole cast, even though he refuses to sing along

"One of my favorite lesser-known Muppets of *Sesame Street* is Hoots the Owl . . . the saxophone-playing jazz owl," show writer Mark Saltzman reveals. "I was happy to create a venue for him on the Street, naturally enough called Birdland.

"I wrote for Hoots and included a role for a jazz trumpeter. *Sesame Street* being *Sesame Street*, the role was cast with Dizzy Gillespie. In person. The kids in that show were agog, watching his cheeks bulge when he blew. There was some consternation in the control room—how, exactly, does one address this jazz legend? 'Dizzy' seemed too familiar. 'Mr. Gillespie' seemed unredeemably square. A compromise was arrived at: We'd call him 'Mr. G.'

"After a take, Dizzy did what all trumpeters must do, and emptied his spit valve. One of the kids stared and pointed at the liquid flow, shouting,

> 'What's THAT?'

" 'That?' Mr. G answered softly. 'That's jazz.' "

> " Aaaahhh. . . . I love taking my bath, peace and quiet, all alone . . . Ernie! Wh-what are you doing with a piano in the bathroom?!? "
>
> —BERT

Released worldwide by Putumayo, "Sesame Street Playground" is the first album to feature songs from the show's coproductions around the globe

THIS CHAPTER IS BROUGHT TO YOU BY THE KEY OF F AND THE NUMBER $\frac{4}{4}$.

The key of F is what the "Sesame Street Theme Song" (often called "Sunny Day" by fans) is sung in, based on the original lead sheet, says Danny Epstein, music coordinator at the time it was written. **The number 4/4** is the time, which measures the beats—one, two, three, four, one, two, three, four—in a song. The *Sesame* theme is four-four time. In a song sung in cut time, you would accentuate every *other* beat: one, three, one, three.

11

"What I'm not looking for is something that would be typically thought of as something that would appeal to children."

—ARLENE SHERMAN,
FORMER COEXECUTIVE PRODUCER

I BELIEVE IN LITTLE THINGS

From Ladybugs to Fairies

Many animations and live-action films, as well as some longer-form segments like "Elmo's World," are specially themed to coordinate with specific episodes of *Sesame Street*. After their debuts, they become part of a library of shorts, which are available for use in any number of episodes. But sometimes, a film or animation is created to be a recurring, regular segment on the show. One of these stand-alone animations breaks new creative ground for *Sesame Street* and is scheduled to begin airing as part of every episode in season 40.

It's being produced in the small, five-room second-floor office of SpeakeasyFX, a computer animation studio where, at the moment, about twenty people sit silently at their computer screens. All are focused on the work they're doing for the new series. It's called "Abby's Flying Fairy School."

All you can hear are the clicks and ticks of computer keys. Some people are wearing headphones, listening to their own private soundtracks. An Abby Cadabby doll perches next to a white board. Another hangs from a lamp as inspiration. But the Abby you can see on screens around the office has never been glimpsed before. She's a computer-generated (CG) character, carefully matched in 3-D animation to her original Muppet incarnation.

The appeal of any given Muppet is unique. It's a combination of color and texture, mouth and eye shape, and the skill of the puppeteer, who can with a tilt of the head or a quirk of voice summon up a host of emotions. Understandably, many of the Workshop staff were leery of attempting to animate the puppets in 3-D. In fact, only a few fleeting attempts had ever been made (Big Bird and Cookie cameos in two vintage shorts; the opening for an international co-production). Should they go any further?

It was a legitimate question. But given that *Sesame Street* is all about experimentation and finding new ways to reach and teach its audience, the answer had to be yes.

To win the job of animating Abby, SpeakeasyFX was one of a number of studios that did a test. "The idea was to have her feel like a puppet," recalls owner and executive director Scott Stewart, "but then have all this beautiful secondary movement."

Animation director Jan Carlée nods. "It really is a 50/50 mix between an animated character and a puppet performance," he explains.

In the test footage, Abby looks down at her

Blog A revised 2

In each episode, Abby and her friends are given a challenge by their teacher, Mrs. Sparklenose. Here, they help Blahg, a stand-in for Cinderella, prepare for the ball

 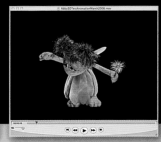   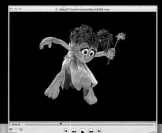 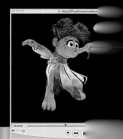

Blahg

Animator Peter Sepp—a veteran of Pixar who created the characters in the film *Ice Age*, among others—designed all of the new characters in the segment, like Gonnigan, Blahg, and gerbilcorn Niblet

Gonnigan

feet in wonder, as befits a Muppet who suddenly has a fully operational bottom half. She hops once and then flies delightedly out of frame. After all, that's what CG animation can do for a puppet: enable her to do anything at all, including fly.

SpeakeasyFX's early attempts at an animated Abby were far from perfect, insists Art Director/Designer David Michael Friend. So Andy Zazzera, head of 3-D animation, studied Muppets and puppeteering in general before coming up with what was probably the feature that gave SpeakeasyFX the edge over the competition.

When a person—or a "normal" animated character—opens his mouth, his jaw typically drops. But that's not what happens with a Muppet. The puppeteer's thumb, in the jaw of the Muppet, moves down. The rest of the hand, in the head of the Muppet, curves up, creating a movement that's unique to puppets.

"Andy set up a mechanism," explains Jan, "so that when you open Abby's mouth, it makes her head go back." It looks remarkably similar to the live puppet's movement.

"What I think the Workshop responded to," he goes on, "was the fact that it reads as a Muppet." But it was a Muppet with a difference . . . a Muppet who could go where no Muppet had gone before.

> ## Let's twinkle think!
>
> —ABBY CADABBY
> (THIS RECURRING MANTRA ENCOURAGES INTERACTION BY VIEWERS)

Storyboards are used to plot out the shots

The adventures in the Flying Fairy School are crafted to enhance a problem-solving curriculum—Abby and her original-to-the-series classmates are excellent models for figuring things out and asking questions, encouraging viewers at home to advise the characters.

The problem-solving skills of its preschool audience are encouraged even more by the segment's online version. Kids can watch episodes the same day they air, but with game-like, interactive elements added. They can thus help solve a dilemma or suggest a strategy. In some ways, the medium of CG animation lends itself more easily to interactivity than traditionally puppeteered segments.

Most of the action takes place in this floating school (to get there, Muppet Abby boards a bus on the Street and during her ride transforms into CG-Abby)

FLYING FAIRY SCHOOL

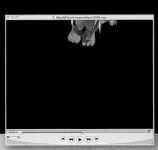

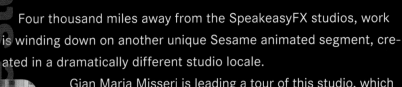

"The tools are sacred," says Monica, who crafts each figure by han

Four thousand miles away from the SpeakeasyFX studios, work is winding down on another unique Sesame animated segment, created in a dramatically different studio locale.

Gian Maria Misseri is leading a tour of this studio, which he runs alongside patriarch Francesco Misseri. It's housed in a crumbling medieval castle in a suburb of Florence, Italy, where Charlemagne paused on the way to being crowned. And the studio has been supplying the Workshop with all forms of animation since the 1970s, using media as diverse as water, sand, and paper.

Francesco, busily sweeping leaves in the backyard, is easy to mistake for a genial gardener. He has "no English at all," Gian explains. But his casual clothes and warm but silent greeting disguise a highly efficient and effective leader, long known in Italian media circles as the hard-driving partner of a 1950s advertising firm and later as a worldwide leader in animation. Francesco is still in charge of all pre-production in the studio, but he hands off English-speaking guests to Gian Maria.

Post-production work hides the many sticks used to hold characters in active poses

In rooms scattered throughout the castle and even tucked into a shed in the backyard, animators are working on "Bert and Ernie's Great Adventures," launched in 2008 and the very first series of animations ever to star the *Sesame Street* Muppet characters. First slated as an international offering, it was tapped for the U.S. show and had its domestic debut in season 39.

The work going on today is a reflection of the four decades of Misseri partnership with *Sesame Street*. In fact, this series began serendipitously, when lead creative/director of production Monica Fibbi playfully attached a brief claymation Ernie and Bert bit at the end of another submission as a little "thank-you" for the job. The Workshop production team was instantly smitten.

Today's tour makes one thing very clear: creating high-quality stop-motion animation like this is a painstaking, slow business. After three-dimensional characters are sculpted (often in a clay-like plasticine) and posed, minute sequential changes are made to the figures, and endless photographs taken. Ultimately, these photos are strung together—nowadays on computers—in a kind of complex flip book that makes the characters seem to move and speak.

"We work with a range of six to nine animators to deliver four [five-minute] episodes in forty working days," Gian Maria explains. Each animator averages just under four seconds of film a day—sometimes even less. That's partly because Misseri Studio works in "ones," Gian Maria explains. He sketches a diagram with three hands of a clock, one stopping at one o'clock, one at two o'clock, and one at three. Then he draws another, with additional arms inserted. Each represents a pose; having more poses makes the animation appear seamless. Misseri uses twice as many poses as other studios.

"This is why our movements are very smooth," Gian says. "This is the standard of our studio. We are really proud of it. Most studios, in order to save time, they do not do this."

Gian Maria Misseri (far left) explains how his animators are now using digital photography and computers in the venerable claymation process: "There is a lot of work in the post-production that you don't see, you think it's not there. There is a lot of work doing wire removal and chroma keys to replace backgrounds. To fix a light, it might take half a day. I cannot afford to stop an animator for half a day. Since I have these raw digital files, I can do this in post-production."

in the studio
in the studio
in the studio

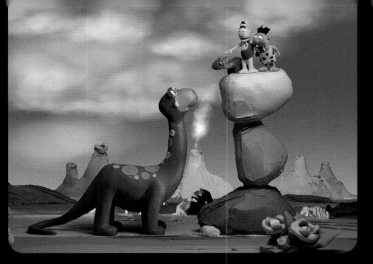

A pasta machine is used to create wide, flat slabs of clay that are used to form the characters and much of the furniture and landscapes

Nearby, Monica sits at her desk, taking bits of clay from a huge pile of scraps. She's creating some possible designs for Roman sandals that the characters will wear in an upcoming scene. Monica creates the basic models and "look" for every episode: the costumes, props, and backdrops that will establish a sense of place and time (the characters frequently travel back in time on their imaginary adventures). Her final designs will be applied by the additional modelers, who will be making all the actual pieces used in the episodes.

She rolls a pinch of brown clay into a snake-like strip to make a sandal strap. Then she frowns comically at her efforts. It's difficult, she reports ruefully, to make proper sandals for the characters'

stubby and tiny feet. Making the characters can be challenging as well, though some are harder to make than others.

"Bert is easiest—his eyebrow," Monica reports, through a translator, making an exaggerated scowl. "I use it a lot. Ernie's got such a big mouth, it is hard to animate. He's got a dimple that is very hard to make, very risky. Sometimes you get an awful Ernie."

Gian laughs, "I can hear Monica sometimes on the set: 'How did you make Ernie? He's a monster!' "

Monica says of the process: "Being handmade, it is not precise, not mechanical. If you just take orders from someone it's a sort of prison. The animators must put something of their own into a scene."

SESAME STREET
Bert and Ernie's Great Adventures

" **If only the water wasn't so wet and watery.** "
—BERT

Animated Faces

The show's first contributor, Fred Calvert, and his wife work in studio with a team of animators, supplying many films in collaboration with Ken Snyder Industries

When Joan Ganz Cooney created her proposal for an educational television show, she envisioned a series of "commercials" for letters and numbers that would carry much of the show's core curricular messages. This innovative (and initially controversial) idea would come to define the look of *Sesame Street*, resulting in innumerable counting and literacy-based shorts—both live-action and animated—that have resonated with the show's viewers over the last forty years. Each generation has its favorites, but many have become so iconic, they've been seen and memorized by every successive crop of preschool fans.

The commissioning and directing of all those filmmakers has been the responsibility of surprisingly few people over the years. First was Lu Horne, working as a supervising producer for the show's first season, when everyone on the team was wearing many hats.

"The Workshop wanted a mixture of styles and techniques," recalls Lewis Bernstein, who was on the production team early on. "What was decided was to go outside to the world of film and anima-

tors and bring them in for curriculum seminars and give them assignments."

Lewis remembers when these films got their second overseer—and first dedicated champion. "Edith Zornow was Film and Animation Coordinator," he says. "Her vision was to ask, 'Who are young artists that are hungry and would like to try out on *Sesame*?'" And because of her interest in emerging talent, the show would end up working with animators and filmmakers on the cusp of fame.

At first, Edith gave assignments to animators and film producers she knew or had sourced through a variety of film and animation festivals. But soon, as *Sesame Street* made a name for itself, she was overloaded with requests to make pieces for the show. In some cases, animators or filmmakers were able to deliver the entire piece, including writing and music. At other times, the Workshop was able to offer collaborators from its own talented staff of

Arlene Sherman with Bert. Animator Sally Cruikshank and others call Arlene "wonderful to work for." Arlene's choices hugely influenced the show into the new millennium.

By the second year of the show, queries from artists, animators, and filmmakers started flooding in. Pitches were colorful and creative and reflected the passion the show was already generating. Some, like Andrew Loring's, below left, led to an assignment. More often, the educational needs of the show made it tricky to find the perfect partners.

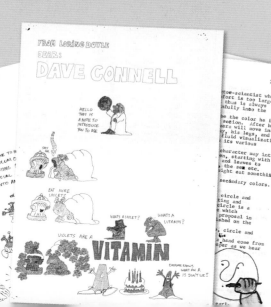

The show's pitch reel featured a series of variations on the basic "10 to 1 Countdown" animation, ending in one where the announcer himself blasts off, which delighted kids (and cofounder Joan Ganz Cooney) in early testing

musicians, composers, and writers. Songs could be provided before a film was made, with underscoring added later. Edith coordinated all this back-and-forth for hundreds of films each season, a role she continued to fill for many years.

One contributor, Paul Fierlinger, remembers her straightforward methods.

"Edith was wonderful because she would stick to her word—and she didn't say much," he recalls laughingly. "She'd throw out numbers: 'What if you did number 2 or number 5?' We'd talk very briefly and then I would bring it in. She'd look at it and say, 'Yes, we'll be doing this.' That was all. She was wonderful that way."

Edith's eventual successor, Arlene Sherman, began working at *Sesame Street* in 1977, after attending NYU film school and spending a number of years in Europe making experimental films and working as an extra for legendary French movie director François Truffaut. A number of years later, she began working with Edith. When Edith left to work on other projects, Arlene became the principal person involved in sourcing film and animations for *Sesame Street*.

Original art for a letter C animation from season 3

Arlene was interested in talent, not in an artist's history. In fact, many of the people she hired had never done work for kids before. What she did—and what the other producers on *Sesame Street* still do—is look for, as Arlene described it, "incredible colors, wonderful music, and innovative styles that are captivating" to both children and adults.

"The . . . films that appeared on the show during Arlene's years speak for themselves," says Carol-Lynn Parente, executive producer of *Sesame Street*, in tribute to her friend. Sadly, Arlene passed away in 2008. "They're just groundbreaking. In the film and animation world, it is a badge of honor to have any of your work appear on the show. And that's largely due to the quality of work that Arlene Sherman produced."

Coming from the world of real commercials, Tee Collins would say of the assignments: "Everything you do doesn't have to come out at precisely 58 seconds. You have more latitude, much more freedom"

NEWS FLASH

Animator Tee Collins created some of the first shorts—his "Wanda the Witch" appeared in the first episode, in 1969. Tee was one of very few African-American animators who was forging a career at the time. Here, testing with children, who laugh along, proves his success.

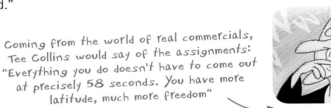

All That Jazz

Some names and images that even casual fans will likely recognize: Bud Luckey's 1975 "Country#5" (center of the page) and (top, left to right) Mo Willems' "Suzie Kabloozie," Karen Aqua's "Pass-Along Alphabet," Sally Cruikshank's "Beginning, Middle and End," Gahan Wilson's "Bridge-keeper," and Pixar's "Luxo Jr.," and (left) Ken Snyder's "Alice"

Over the years, *Sesame Street* has featured some of the most groundbreaking animation in the business. Respect-ed animation talent like Wil Vinton (who raised the profile of California raisins with his claymation ads in 1986), Jeffrey Hale, Derek Lamb, Ron Campbell, Faith and John Hubley, Mo Willems, and the folks at Pixar all contributed. So did noted artists such as Ted Shearer, Harvey Kurtztman, Keith Haring, and Gahan Wilson.

An instinctive talent who got his start as a child drawing on sidewalks with the edge of a brick, Bud Luckey is among these *Sesame Street* veterans. Currently designing for Pixar, where he's helped create films like *Toy Story* and his own Academy Award-nominated short, *Boundin'*, Bud worked as a 2-D animator before moving into the digital Pixar world. It was during those earlier years, when he was affiliated with Jeffrey Hale's studio, Imagination, Inc., that he made a number of classic films for *Sesame Street*. His "Ladybug's Picnic" and "The Alligator King" remain on most fans' top-10 lists even decades later. Don Hadley and Walt Kraemer created the infectious tunes for both.

Imagination, Inc. also produced the psychedelic "Pinball Number Count" series, which first appeared in 1976. It was Walt who hired The Pointer Sisters to sing the vocals.

"Four of them showed up, even though we only budgeted for three," he recalls of the voice-over session for the Pinball series. "No one ever turned down an opportunity to work for *Sesame Street*." The animation for "Pinball Number Count" was directed by Jeffrey Hale, who came up with the idea and its Yellow Sub-marine-influenced designs. Imagination, Inc., also created the similarly iconic "Jazz Number Count" series, with songs recorded by Jef-ferson Airplane's Grace Slick. Over the years, in fact, Hale's group generated an astonishing number of *Sesame Street*'s greatest hits.

Dozens of artists have since contributed the animations that pepper the show, building on Joan Ganz Cooney's promise to create informative "commercials" that would support the *Sesame Street* curriculum. As former head writer Norman Stiles would later say, these pieces "taught like crazy"—and people who saw them never forgot them.

The race cars and hands appear in each of the nine jazz entries

This detail of one of the "Pinball" cels shows the vibrant colored-pencil work

The "Jazz Number Count" se-ries was given pop-culture status with songs recorded by Jefferson Airplane's Grace Slick. Oddly, neither Pinball nor Jazz featured the number 1.

Ernie Fosselius (whose *Star Wars* parody, *Hard-ware Wars*, would later gain fame) was one of the animators responsible for the classic "Pinball Number Count." Walt Kraemer composed the catchy music, sung by The Pointer Sisters.

Examples of work by Dan Haskett, an animator who later designed the characters of Belle and Ariel for the Walt Disney Company

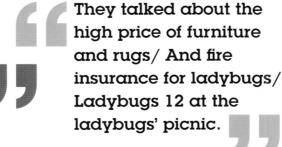

> **She's a real Martian beauty/ My number 9 cutie.**
>
> —"MARTIAN BEAUTY #9," FROM DIRECTOR JEFFREY HALE AND DESIGNER BUD LUCKEY

> **They talked about the high price of furniture and rugs/ And fire insurance for ladybugs/ Ladybugs 12 at the ladybugs' picnic.**
>
> —"LADYBUG'S PICNIC" FROM DIRECTOR BUD LUCKEY

"A loaf of bread, a container of milk, and a stick of butter" were on the grocery list in Jim Simon's season 8 animation

> **Why should I be someone else? I'm happy being me.**
>
> —CECILLE

"She can bounce, she can roll, she can spin like a wheel/ She's got a rubber soul and her name is Cecille" went the lyrics to Chris Cerf's theme song for animator Will Vinton's superstar

Clockwise, Ted Shearer and Ray Favata give life to ace detective Billy Joe Jive and Smart Suzie Sunset; the Hubleys' "V is for Violin"; Ken Snyder's Swami sprouts four arms in order to count to 20; and Global Thingy, from Jim Jinkins and David Campbell, which promotes conflict resolution

Robby Merkin, *Sesame Street*'s music director for six years, contributed the score to Ken Snyder Industries' "Fishing Boy Alphabet Soup" animtion in season one.

Darby Slick (who wrote "Somebody to Love" for Grace Slick) scripted the dreamlike narration for John and Faith Hubley's "E" animation: "Eating a peach, sitting on my eagle/Chasing a beagle to the queen on her knee under a tree by the sea"

Animations like this one are submitted with only a few backgrounds, which are reused in the sequence

> **Whichever of you can cheer me up, gets to wear my crown.**
>
> —"THE ALLIGATOR KING #7," BY BUD LUCKEY

"It was too good to last," the snake says regretfully when his newly acquired legs walk off to rejoin the sheep to whom they belong in "Simple Simon," jointly credited to Derek Lamb and Jeffrey Hale

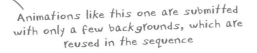

Control Room

It's really all about getting the style and point of view of the artist and interpreting that to teach curriculum.

—CAROL-LYNN PARENTE,
EXECUTIVE PRODUCER

Color television was still so new in 1970 that technician Walt Rauffer had to issue a set of guidelines for the companies submitting *Sesame Street*'s independent films, with tips on colors to avoid, make-up application, and establishing color balance. But for the most part, the experimental TV show encouraged its contributors to break the rules. And as a result, artists pushed themselves to try new forms and tell stories in ways they never had before. Over the years, those efforts never abated, and even longtime contributors continued to work outside their comfort zones with the help of the Workshop team.

Producers Shyrlee Dallard and Lu Horne review early film

"I made my first film for *Sesame Street* in 1971," says filmmaker Paul Fierlinger, who enjoyed a special relationship with Workshop writer Jim Thurman. "I could pick anybody I wanted to or write it myself. [Jim and I] just automatically did everything together; he was a great help. An insider, he knew exactly how to write these things."

Most of Paul's early work was in classic 2-D, but one day, he came up with a new character that was a departure from his other animations. It was an invention born of necessity.

"It was always a struggle to stay alive as a freelance animator," Paul explains. "I asked [EVP] Dave Connell if I could get a series. He said it could never happen: 'You're a one-man operation, you'd have to make a show every two weeks,' he told me. I started wracking my brains to come up with a way to do it."

Jeffrey Hale's "Lost Boy" animation cracks up a film editor at Teletape

That way turned out to be his stop-motion animations of "Teeny Little Super Guy," an improbable character painted on a clear plastic cup.

"The thing was prefab. Every one of those was done in two weeks . . . it was a cottage industry," Paul says of the process, which included collaborators Larry Gold (music), Patrick McMahon (editing), and Jim Thurman (voices). "Funny thing . . . a lot of it *was* shot in a cottage next door."

The classic that resulted is cemented in the minds of a generation of watchers. For Paul, it was a practical success as well. "It meant we'd be able to pay my bills for the next eight months."

Technician Walt Rauffer worked at Teletape Studios that first year on the Street. He remembers that Street scenes were initially shot piecemeal, constantly interrupted as editors spliced interstitial films into the sequence right on the spot. He was one of the early advocates for building a separate library of films that could be edited into street scenes later, creating a kind of film factory.

NEWS FLASH

William Wegman was already well recognized as a fine artist before contributing more than sixty short films to *Sesame Street* in seasons 20 to 34. These films star some of his famous Weimaraners: Fay Ray, Battina, Crooky, Chundo, Chip, Bobbin, and Penny. Sometimes costumed, the dogs help kids learn concepts as diverse as rhyming ("Jack Sprat") and science ("Fay Family Makes a Cake").

"Teeny Little Super Guy" isn't rendered on the typical animation cel's acetate overlay; instead, he's painted on a drinking cup, which made animating him more economical for creator Paul Fierlinger. The population of his imaginary world was shifted by hand and by stick in miniscule increments to create the stop-motion action. In today's digital world, this seems almost shockingly low-tech, but it produced an emotionally satisfying result: a character who is still a favorite among generations of *Sesame Street* fans.

Household objects were roped into use: a child's balloon, coffee mugs, the kitchen sink

" Teeny Little Super Guy/
Pops right up before your eyes/
He's no bigger than your thumb/
'So snap your fingers, here I come!'"

—"TEENY LITTLE SUPER GUY"

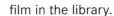

Mini Movies

Jon Stone used "pixelation" (stop-motion) in a series of live-action films with the human cast

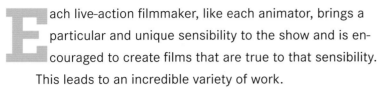

Each live-action filmmaker, like each animator, brings a particular and unique sensibility to the show and is encouraged to create films that are true to that sensibility. This leads to an incredible variety of work.

There are films like Rachel Harms' *Poetry Project*, featuring the poetry of both hearing and deaf children as voice-overs for outdoor shots saturated with light and shadow.

There are films of visits to factories, with detailed exposés on how to make steel, ice cream, dolls, shoes, peanut butter, or crayons—many fondly recalled by grown-up graduates of the show.

Then there were the hundreds of animal films, many with tunes sung by Joe Raposo.

The Workshop commissioned photographers to prowl New York's streets, shooting street signs for the frequent montages showcasing "sight words" that even pre-literate preschoolers should recognize: stop, exit, danger. Once, a savvy filmmaker spotted a sign being lowered into place at the hotel across the street from the Workshop's offices. By the end of the day, the event had been immortalized as a

film in the library.

And there is Marc Brugnoni, who has tackled all those subjects and more in the several hundred films he has made for *Sesame Street*. Marc created a number of them during the first season, doing everything himself: script, music, and shooting. His very first assignment was about cleaning.

"It was my idea," he reports. " 'You Can Clean Almost Anything' was the title of it. I ended up using my little daughter in it." He chose to use some Swingle Singers music for the film.

Marc also worked with Joe Raposo on a variety of films throughout the years, including the classics "Everybody Eats," which featured a hilarious shot of a hippo scarfing down his veggies; "Everybody Sleeps," which began with a man thrashing around in bed and cut to a peacefully snoozing camel; and the beautiful "I Believe in Little Things," a gentle and virtually perfect synthesis of film and song.

Making films for *Sesame Street* has become a family affair for Marc. He recently filmed his granddaughter for an "Elmo's World" episode about noses.

Some of Marc's films

The show's short live-action films had an important purpose: to drive the curriculum home in focused ways that the Street stories could not. This YouTube comment from a fan, "afriendofbean," shows their impact:

"This Mad Painter #5 skit helped me to learn how to write the number 5 when I was very young...I always used to try to write a 5 but, every time I would try, I would always make a capital letter S. Then I said to myself, 'Wait, I remember the painter and the gorilla making a 5 together, let me do what they both did.' First I did what the painter did, then what the gorilla did, after that, I made a 5 well."

The Number Painter, also known as the Mad Painter, appeared in ten skits beginning in 1972 and was played by Paul Benedict (aka the eccentric British neighbor in the 1970s CBS comedy "The Jeffersons"). And yes, that's Stockard Channing eating the number 3s he paints in mayonnaise, mustard, and ketchup

Local kids are recruited and a school playground is commandeered

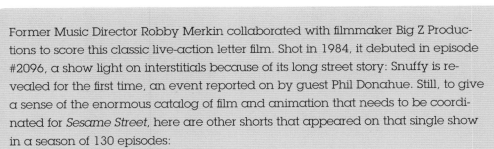

Former Music Director Robby Merkin collaborated with filmmaker Big Z Productions to score this classic live-action letter film. Shot in 1984, it debuted in episode #2096, a show light on interstitials because of its long street story: Snuffy is revealed for the first time, an event reported on by guest Phil Donahue. Still, to give a sense of the enormous catalog of film and animation that needs to be coordinated for *Sesame Street*, here are other shorts that appeared on that single show in a season of 130 episodes:

Animations: "Pinball Number Count #6"; "Obstacle Mix"; "Farm Animal #6"; "S-Snake"; "Balloon S"; "Ball-Down"

Live Action Films: "Dressed Up"; "Peanut Butter"; "Me and My Chair"; "Sno-Cone"; "Kittens"; "Elephant–Zoo"

The second time the segment aired, 21 other interstitials were in the same show.

Film makers

Jim created an iconic claymation short with twelve Munchkin-voiced clay boulders that gleefully transform into numbers

Virtually all animators and filmmakers supplying the show cite the enormous freedom given by producers, calling it a liberating force that let creativity explode on screen. Fred Calvert, who worked on dozens of animations, says, "Of all the films I've made, the *Sesame Street* animation segments are still at the top of the list of my most enjoyable and worthwhile accomplishments."

Another case in point: Jim Henson and Frank Oz both stepped away from their familiar Muppet characters to experiment with films for the show. Frank's venture was a single live-action piece, featuring a red ball that travels along a roller-coaster-like structure until it is finally ground into powder (which kids found so tragic an ending that it was changed for later airings).

Jim supplied more than a dozen shorts, in all kinds of media, from stop-motion with clay, tabletop puppetry (with help from Dan Sahlin and Kermit Love), to live action and hand-drawn animations. The creativity the show unleashed was boundless.

> **" Once upon a time in the land of 8, there stood a castle very great. "**
> —"KING OF EIGHT"

Jim Henson was experimenting in computer animation years before most artists were even thinking about the new medium. This puppet-like face was rendered digitally in 1970 on a system called Scanimate, at Computer Image in Denver, Colorado. Numbers morphed and colorful graphics pinwheeled on the screen, while a mellow voice directed kids to, among other things: "Watch the screen and we will try to count how many dots go by."

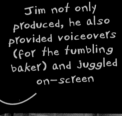

Opera-singing Carmen the Orange is assembled on-screen from found objects

Jim not only produced, he also provided voiceovers (for the tumbling baker) and juggled on-screen

Jim's original drawings for the sequence in his counting series

Jim Henson's daughter Cheryl distinctly recalls her father's work on the films, like the animated "Song of..." number series: "He painted all the numbers himself. He would obsess, doing these all night long. He'd paint a little, film a couple of frames. Paint some more, another layer of paint, then film some more. And he loved matching animation to music. I have this image of him sitting up all night, painting under the camera. He and Frank Oz considered themselves as much filmmakers as puppeteers. They really enjoyed doing short films."

Internationally, animation is a treasured form (see its use in an animal-themed short by Dhaneesh Jameson and Rohit Iyer, at left, from India's "Galli Galli SimSim") and the Workshop's "Sesame Street English" language learning program reflects this interest by offering adorable anime-influenced shorts

Workshop producers are always experimenting with new ideas for recurring segments along the lines of breakout hit "Elmo's World." One upcoming project involves animating the characters, while others take advantage of the huge domestic and international library of live-action films. These new recurring segments are targeted for international audiences but might someday appear on the show in the U.S., too.

Soon you may be watching episodes based on one of several "proof of concept" ideas—a term for show pitches as they are shopped around to distributors—that are being floated right now: a science-of-discovery series, "Elmo's Backyard"; "Super Sesame Heroes," which tackles conflict resolution; or "Munchin: Impossible," a healthy-eating, seed-to-table-themed spoof of an action series with Cookie Monster.

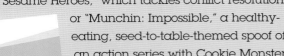

In 1972's surreal "Lost Boy Remembers Way Home" (aka "Yo-yo Master and the Lost Boy"), a little traveller passes a psychedelic street clock, plastic house, and animal fountain. He's REALLY lost...

Sesame Street Number Film #3
December 1970

Frank Oz has said of his direction of a live-action film for the number 3, which aired in episode 1707, "I built [a] kind of bizarre wire sculpture and shot it over many months. Looking back on it, I'm thinking, " 'My God, why?' "

SEGMENT #0003-0620

Lost Boy: Can you help me get unlost?

Yo-yo Master: Well, you should figure it out for yourself, little guy. But I'll give you a hint.

Lost Boy: Oh, thank you.

Yo-yo Master: Try to remember everything you passed, but when you go back make the first thing the last. Ha-ha! Yeah!

This 3-D sculptural source material used for three animations from the nineties might surprise viewers who see only the 2-D on-screen versions

"
Behind your face there is a place that's called your brains and your mind.
"

—"THE YO-YO MASTER,"
LYRICS BY JOHN MAGNUSON

THIS CHAPTER HAS BEEN BROUGHT TO YOU BY THE LETTER Y AND THE NUMBER 10.

The letter Y is for the jovial Yo-yo Master, who guides a lost boy back home in an animation directed by Jeffrey Hale, of Imagination, Inc. **The Number 10** is for the familiar "ten-nine-eight-seven-six-five-four-three-two-one" refrain heard in the "Jazz Number Count" series of animation/live-action films by Jim Henson.

making magic

12

"The rest of the world needs what we were able to do here. We gave a country a safe street, a place where it found its soul."

—MELVIN MING, COO, SESAME WORKSHOP

WE ARE
ALL
EARTHLINGS

06°09'SOUTH
106°49'East

In a small, semirural suburb of Jakarta, Indonesia, a modern glass-and-concrete television studio sits across from a school on a narrow, quiet street. All around are small houses with red clay–tiled roofs, characteristic of houses in the region. Some are in disrepair. Many have no indoor plumbing.

Debris and construction materials ring the studio. Out in front, barefoot workers laying a pattern of bricks on a walkway wrap T-shirts around their heads to stave off the heat and humidity. Inside, where the hubbub of construction is muted, visitors find themselves in a different world.

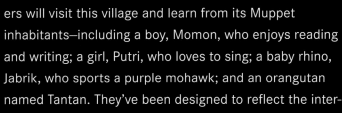

Here, an idyllic village flourishes in a lushly green setting typical of the Indonesian countryside. On the road that runs down its center is an oddly familiar street sign. It reads *Jalan Sesama*.

A generation of preschoolers will visit this village and learn from its Muppet inhabitants—including a boy, Momon, who enjoys reading and writing; a girl, Putri, who loves to sing; a baby rhino, Jabrik, who sports a purple mohawk; and an orangutan named Tantan. They've been designed to reflect the interests and traditions of Indonesia in ways American Muppets cannot.

Charlotte Cole, VP of international outreach and education, explains the process by which they were developed, which is strikingly similar to the one that shaped domestic production in the U.S. "Because our coproductions are produced by local teams that include educational experts for a given country or region who determine a given project's educational priorities, we are able to create material that is tailored to the specific needs of the children we reach," Charlotte says.

But before that can happen, there is a ceremony to perform.

In the center of the studio, a number of blue plaid prayer rugs form a carpeted surface on which a ring of people sit, praying. Others stand behind them. In the center of the rug are four or five bowls of brightly colored sweets and a plate of what looks like hard-boiled eggs, the necessary ingredients for a traditional ritual to celebrate new ventures.

The *Jalan Sesama* street stretches out against a painted backdrop of sky and mountains. The house farthest down the street has been built small, with a forced perspective that makes the street feel longer than it is. This only becomes noticeable when humans enter the street from the rear; the crew and cast has accepted the convention that the small house is home to a Muppet character.

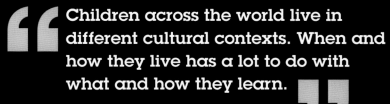

Script ID :
Episode # : INDO-01-STU-032-Ver1- APPROVED BY NY 4 April 2007
Segment :
Title :
Goal : Hari Hujan (script in a box #1-010-Rainy Day)
Writer : Cognitive (B) -> Cognitive Development (I) -> Creativity (i)
Draft : Pahala Sigiro
Date : 2
Character : 15 Maret 2007
Location : Tantan, Pak Bagus
Costume : Ext.Bale-bale
Props : Pakaian sehari-hari
SFX : 2 payung dan air
Song : efek hujan
Synopsis : None
payung karena kehujanan, melihat Tantan menggunakan payung secara terbalik. Pak Bagus pun berusaha
menjelaskan pada Tantan bahwa cara memegang payungnya itu salah. Tapi Tantan merasa bahwa dengan
memegangnya begitu payungnya dapat bekerja lebih baik.

PAK BAGUS BERJALAN DI DEPAN BALE-BALE MEMAKAI PAYUNG

1.Pak Bagus

(KE KAMERA) Oh, halo. Hari ini di jalan Sesama hujan sepanjang hari.

Karena itu saya memakai payung.

Tapi kelihatannya hujannya hampir berhenti

Mari kita lihat

MENENGADAHKAN TANGANNYA UNTUK MERASAKAN HUJAN

Ya, hujannya sudah berhenti.

PAK BEGUS MENUTUP PAYUNGNYA, MENEPI KE BALE-BALE DAN MERAPIHKAN
PAYUNGNYA.

TANTAN DARI ARAH BERLAWANAN MENGHAMPIRI PAK BAGUS

MEMEGANG PAYUNGNYA DI ATAS KEPALA SECARA TERBALIK

3.Tantan

Halo Pak Bagus.... Hari ini hujannya indah sekali, ya?

Saya suka hujan, karena hujan membuat bunga-bunga saya tumbuh subur.

Dan akhirnya saya bisa pakai payung

Bahasa Indonesia is one of the most widely spoken languages in the world

1

Nearby, a large yellow cone of rice, called a *tumpeng*, sits on a table. The tip of the cone will be cut, and then the rice served to cast and crew. The servers must be careful not to drop a single grain of rice. If they do, the production will have bad luck.

Watching closely is Ginger Brown, AVP, senior producer, global television; Marty Robinson, puppeteer, who has trained the Indonesian Muppet performers; Jim Martin, director, who's there to help the local director, Key Mangunsong; Muppet builder Jason Weber; and Dini Parsudi, production coordinator for *Jalan Sesama*, who was born in Indonesia but currently works at Sesame Workshop.

It is after 10 o'clock now, and the Americans are eager to get started on the first day's shooting. The cone of rice is carefully served. Luckily, not one grain is spilled.

Everyone applauds. The production is destined for success.

> " **Children across the world live in different cultural contexts. When and how they live has a lot to do with what and how they learn.** "
>
> —DR. CHARLOTTE COLE,
> VP INTERNATIONAL OUTREACH
> AND EDUCATION

NEWS FLASH

When Sesame Workshop personnel got to Indonesia after the set had been built they discovered that all the walls had been constructed of Styrofoam. If you rubbed against it, it made a lot of noise—not a good thing on a sound stage. And it was very fragile—in fact, holes began appearing in it from the start of production. Ultimately, the Indonesian crew rebuilt the entire set with wood and plaster.

Street to Strasse

Finchen is seen on Sesamstrasse today

Puppet designer Kermit Love, seen below right with Bert as Santa, travels to Germany with a team in the seventies to help train local puppeteers—right, Kermit's original sketch of puppet Samson

The producers of *Sesame Street* are fond of saying that it's the world's longest street. But in the early days, no one believed that the show's impact would be felt outside the United States. Joan Ganz Cooney's original pitch for the show included no plans for international production. In fact, Joan and the original team thought the riffs on pop culture she envisioned would be too "quintessentially American" to resonate anywhere else.

Dr. Lewis Bernstein, who was hired to work on research and review scripts but who quickly became involved in the Workshop's international efforts, explains how wrong they were. "From the very first days, there were countries who said, 'We want your show,' " Lewis relates. "And we'd say, 'you know our show wasn't made for you. It was made for the social, cultural, and educational needs of American children. If you want to do your own show, we'll *help* you by telling you what worked for us, but then you have to bring in your own educators, and sit down with your own producers and creative people, and come up with what makes sense for your own children.' "

The ideal that Lewis describes is a coproduction. Less perfect, from the Workshop's perspective, is a dubbed version of the U.S.'s

Sesame Street, but in some cases that is all that countries are able to produce. So the Workshop and its global partners must weigh both need and capability to determine which route to take.

"The important thing," says Sesame Workshop CEO Gary Knell, "is to figure out how to make each international show self-sustaining. That means you can't necessarily use the American model for production from the 1970s, where early government and foundation funding was key, in places with

The pink puppet is the alligator, Abelardo, created for the original Mexican coproduction, seen here at the grand opening of a local park—in 1995 Parque Plaza Sésamo, an actual Sesame theme park, opens

different economic and political structures. You need models that also work for countries like Bangladesh."

During the first years of *Sesame Street*, some countries were able to commit to locally produced versions. With a cast of all-new puppets and an open plaza-like location, a pilot Portuguese-language *Sesame Street* was created for Brazil: *Vila Sésamo*. It ran for five years and was recently brought back on TV Cultura. In fact, Brazilian performer Fernando Gomes, who's taken on the role of Garibaldo, became a puppeteer because of his love of the original show, which debuted in 1972. Series in Germany, Mexico, and Canada followed.

These days, it's estimated that *Sesame Street* is seen by 75 million viewers, all around the globe. The latest full coproductions are in Bangladesh, India, Indonesia, and Northern Ireland. There's also a version of *Sesame Street*, called *Open Sesame*, with culturally specific content removed, ready for dubbing into local languages.

"We definitely have a social agenda," says Shari Rosenfeld, vice president, developing and emerging markets. "In a country like Egypt, we focus on girls' education. In Israel, we focus on mutual respect and understanding and child empowerment. In Palestine, on boys' education and positive role models. In South Africa, we focus on HIV/AIDS. But we don't dictate that agenda. We try to engender the local point of view. It's about giving people the Sesame tools."

In Latin America, where neighbors typically gather in a town's open plazas, that locale stands in for the American street. Here in Mexico, a grocery, center, does similar duty to the U.S.'s Hooper's Store. And a nurse character reflects the role of Susan and the evolving roles of women.

The New World

SESAME PARK

Sesame Street began airing its U.S. shows in Canada in 1972; it was reformatted in 1996 as *Sesame Park* and features a full-body polar bear character named Basil. A version of the show was adapted for French-speaking Canada in 1975.

A more nature-centric locale was preferred by Canadian broadcasters

Because the Workshop strives to make its international productions specific to their regions, the familar street may be a park, a *rue*, or a plaza.

"This is not an American show that's being imposed on countries around the world," Sesame Workshop CEO Gary Knell says of Workshop efforts to find global partners to localize the series wherever it's seen. "These are indigenous programs that are locally developed, produced by local people, local writers, local actors, local musicians, and local puppeteers. What we do is help train them on the techniques of television and how to apply education to an entertainment medium. It's really their show to produce."

"Plaza Sésamo" also airs in some U.S. states where there are many Spanish speakers

The effervescent, pink Lola and, below right, the parrot Abelardo (formerly an alligator)

PLAZA SÉSAMO

Plaza Sésamo was first broadcast in Mexico in 1972. "Yo crecí con *Plaza Sésamo*," Vice President of Columbia Francisco Calderón told producer Ginger Brown when they met unexpectedly on a flight. In English that means "I grew up with *Plaza Sésamo*."

Just as in the U.S., international shows test content with kids

Garibaldo was originally pale blue, seen below, which looked good on the black-and-white TV sets of the time but not so great for today's color sets, so Garibaldo is now a canary-yellow Big Bird clone

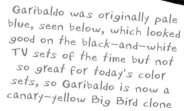

VILA SÉSAMO

The character of Garibaldo was the centerpiece of the original series in Brazil in 1972, and he appears in the current production, relaunched in 2007. "People just went crazy for Garibaldo when they saw him again," says fellow cast member Magda Crudelli. "It was like he had never left."

Across the Pond

Sesame Street moved to Europe in the early seventies, when the German series *Sesamstrasse* began airing. The show bounced to the Netherlands (*Sesamstraat,* 1976) and then took root in France.

In 1979, the Workshop celebrated the Street's tenth American birthday with the premiere of *Barrio Sésamo* in Spain. Turkey, Portugal, Sweden, and Norway followed.

Fast-forward to 2002, when the United Kingdom began broadcasting *Play With Me Sesame*. The American show had actually aired there years earlier, to some debate—British press initially decried the decision to bring over the "vulgar" import. Overt Americanisms were removed and Zs changed to Zeds to address some concerns, but cultural worries turned out to be groundless, and decades later, a generation of adult fans of the U.K. series fondly recalled the show, lobbying for its comeback in the new form.

More expansion (and revisits to regions formerly served by the show) are always in the works. The latest European *Sesame?* A full coproduction in Northern Ireland, which began airing in 2008. There, the show is set in and around a fantastical tree. Set-based characters include Irish hare Hilda and inventor monster Potto, both of whom live in the tree's hollow trunk.

These Muppets are unique to Northern Ireland. But other international faces would look eerily familiar, says Shari Rosenfeld. "Japan and France, for example, have their own localized Elmos."

123 SESAME TREE

After returning from training the *Sesame Tree* team of puppeteers in Northern Ireland, Marty Robinson raved: "These guys are better their first day of taping than I was on my tenth."

123 RUA SÉSAMO

There have been three productions in Portugal, including a full-fledged coproduction with a Portuguese Big Bird and Grouch. *Play With Me Sesame* is the version currently on air.

123 BARRIO SÉSAMO

The original production in Spain, which hit the airwaves in 1979, featured a snail character who could hide a thousand and one things in her shell. Today's characters include owl Bubo, monster Vera, and humanoid Gaspar.

This teletype press notice announces the debut of "1, Rue Sesame"

In Sweden, Cookie Monster is called Kakmonstret

5, RUE SÉSAME

After first airing a version of *Open Sesame* in the early seventies, by 1978 France had a full coproduction. Then, its address was *1, Rue Sesame*; today, the set can be found at 5. Here, life revolves around the courtyard of a building in a small French town.

A very early version of a French Sesame Street first aired in 1974: "Bonjour Sesame," which had no street stories—episodes were just 15 minutes long. Current episodes feature Muppet Griotte, left

SVENSKA SESAM

Sweden's *Svenska Sesam* began production in 1981, airing on Sveriges Radio Channel 1. It's currently a dubbed version of *Sesame Street*.

SESAMSTRASSE

Sesamstrasse has been in continuous production since 1972—the very first German Muppets debuted on that show in 1978.

Hundreds of international books and toys are developed each year—all vetted by Workshop staff

NEWS FLASH

Sesame English was a series introduced in 2001 as a multimedia educational initiative aimed at familiarizing kids and their families with the basics of the English language and elements of American culture. Coproduced with Berlitz, it starred Tingo, a Muppet performed by John Tartaglia. It aired on TV in a number of countries, including Japan, Korea, and Italy.

"Sesamstrasse"'s Samson sports enormous tennis shoes

Small World

Working in international project management, Shari Rosenfeld has seen a shift away from coproductions as countries find more creative ways to build on the existing *Sesame Street* library. Sometimes the Workshop will help build a region's production capabilities literally from the ground up, but often, it's about making small changes and creating just one or two local Muppet hosts to make *Sesame Street* unique to each nation. With more than 4,000 episodes and countless short films and animations in its catalog—many produced in the U.S. and others coming from abroad—the show offers options even in countries where coproductions aren't economically feasible.

"In ten years," says CEO Gary Knell, "our digital library will be available for producers to use around the world. That way, someone in India can find a piece produced in South Africa and use it on their show. . . . What we need to do is move toward being a truly global company, so that we actually have people who can keep our work going in Europe, Japan, India, South Africa, Egypt, etc. . . . We've put flags down in lots of places around the world."

SESAM STASJON

In Norway, the show began airing in 1991. Soon after, when broadcaster NHK issued viewers an open invitation to tour the set, a crowd of 30,000 showed up, effectively blocking all of downtown Oslo.

SESAM KLUBBEN

In March 2009, TV2/Denmark signed a contract with Sesame Workshop for a Sesame programming block containing elements such as *Play With Me Sesame* and locally produced Elmo segments.

SESAMSTRAAT

The Netherlands opened its own Street in 1976; the show has sometimes aired in both Dutch and Flemish.

"I like the American method, consisting in very precise consultations with children about how they imagine someone or something," said Andrzej Kostenko, the Polish series' director

SEZAMKOWY ZAKĄTEK

Poland's show is called *Ulica Sezamkowa;* the logo above references its version of the branded block, loosely translated as "Sesame Nook." For some time beginning in 1996, an original series aired. Actor Andrzej Buszewicz was cast by children, who chose his face as the most grandfatherly; the show also featured a dragon named Bazyli.

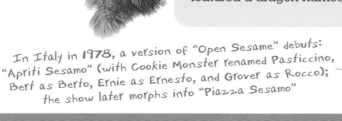

In Italy in 1978, a version of "Open Sesame" debuts: "Apriti Sesamo" (with Cookie Monster renamed Pasticcino, Bert as Berto, Ernie as Ernesto, and Grover as Rocco); the show later morphs into "Piazza Sesamo"

RRUGA SESAM. 123   ULICA SEZAM. 123

Kosovo pioneered a new *Sesame Street* format that's being called the "visual dictionary," which allows a balance between languages of the region and introduces children to the sounds of Albanian, Roma, Serbian, and Turkish—instead of showing words on screen, children label objects verbally, learning that there are different ways to say the same thing.

Children in Kosovo receiving sets of the Workshop's outreach kits

Bert and Ernie are huge stars internationally, outshining even Elmo, inspiring the new claymation series, "Bert & Ernie's Great Adventures"

SZEZÁM UTCA. 123

This show in Hungary is the hub of a Sesame-branded block of programming that includes *Elmo's World*, *Global Grover*, *Play With Me Sesame*, and *Bert and Ernie's Great Adventure* segments. It's broadcast to Romania, Moldova, Slovakia, portions of the former Yugoslavia, and the Czech Republic.

Louis Mitchell, of the U.S. office, art-directs a shoot with Turkey's Simi

> "We try to produce the best show we can, working with the local resources, and many times we actually end up improving the overall quality of a country's television as a result. . . . We give a country a model of how television can be used effectively to address people's needs."

—LUTRELLE "LU" HORNE, IN 1987, THEN VP/EXECUTIVE PRODUCER OF INTERNATIONAL TELEVISION

SUSAM SOKAGI. 123

Turkey, which straddles the divide between Europe and Asia, has featured various Big Birds (blue and orange). Nowadays, it airs a branded block with an exuberant little-girl Muppet host, Simi.

Minik Kus means "little bird" in spite of his Big Bird size

УЛИЦА СЕЗАМ. 123

Though no longer on the air, Russia launched its own version of *Sesame Street* in 1996. Life in a newly opened society was its curriculum focus.

Global Reach

Country-hopping monster Khokha laughs with one of her friends in Cairo and, far right, helpful Filfil takes kids the long way 'round by camel

The commitment of *Sesame Street* to its audience of young children worldwide is perhaps best captured in words from the Workshop's own "mission" reel, narrated by Alicia Keys and first shown at a 2009 fundraising event:

Can you imagine what the world could look like as a better place? A place where all kids have access to education, where boys and girls have equal opportunities, where every child counts? So when you think of those who have the power to open our eyes, to bridge the divides, to inspire change . . . what about a Muppet?

This is a story about one child and one Muppet, playing out all the world over. Just imagine: 12.7 million girls live in Egypt, and many don't dream the same dreams as their brothers of becoming teachers, doctors, or world leaders. Because they are girls. Then there is Fatma, one of nine million Egyptian children who watch Alam Simsim. *Fatma dreams of being a lawyer. Fatma is a girl.*

Fatma got the idea from [Muppet] Khokha, who inspires Egyptian children, both boys and girls, to be anything they want to be. So if Fatma and those nine million Egyptian children grow up to become lawyers or doctors, if they inspire their daughters to become teachers or astronauts, and if those daughters inspire their daughters to become world leaders, can the future course of women change forever?

AIDS is a difficult subject to talk about, but especially necessary to talk about in South Africa, where 5.5 million people are infected. Where one in ten children has lost a parent, and even more suffer from silence. Tamryn's mother has AIDS but didn't know how to tell her. Then they met Kami, a Muppet who is HIV positive. Tamryn is just one of over two million children who watch Takalani Sesame, *a show that helps parents and children talk about AIDS. If Tamryn and her mother start a conversation, and millions of other families join in, can their voices be loud enough to break the culture of silence?*

There are 32 million children in India with no access to preschool education. Children who can't count to ten or spell their name, children who work instead of play. Aman is one of 17 million who watch Galli Galli Sim Sim. *Each day, the Muppet Chamki teaches*

Nimnim from South Africa

NIGERIA

A Nigerian version of the show that features characters created in South Africa is being developed with the goal of teaching tolerance and compassion. It's called *The Adventures of Kami and Big Bird.*

TAKALANI SESAME

AIDS became a focus on *Takalani Sesame* with the creation of HIV-positive Muppet Kami in 2003. UNICEF next appointed Kami its global "Champion for Children." Now the South African show is being adapted for similar needs elsewhere in Africa—in Tanzania, Kilimani will reach approximately five million children at risk for malaria, teaching basic health and hygiene.

Aman lessons. For Aman, it's all fun and games. What he doesn't know is that he's learning how to count. How to spell his name. How to unlock possibilities. Now, if Aman and his 17 million classmates grow up educated, could they open the doors for their children to have better lives and a brighter future? Can you imagine? Nine million Egyptian children increasing the potential for women everywhere? Two million South African children breaking the culture of silence around AIDS? Seventeen million Indian children today unlocking the promise of a nation tomorrow?

Can you imagine?

عالم سمسم
١٢٣

Egypt's show began encouraging education right from the start, in 2000. Funded by the U.S. Agency for International Development (USAID) through the Egyptian Ministry of Education, it's adapted throughout the Arab world.

Egypt's Khokha, seen here with her friend Fatma, is now making appearances in adapted shows throughout the Middle East

كوچهٔ سسمی
١٢٣

In 2004, Afghan children first saw *Koche Sesame*, created from material developed in Egypt and dubbed in Dari.

حكايات سمسم
١٢٣

The Jordanian series *Hikayat Simsim* is part of a larger effort, says Charlotte Cole. "With great hope, we continue working with our partners in the region to promote respect in the face of conflict." The show fosters a deliberately comic and lighthearted feeling with monsters Tonton and Juljul.

IFTAH YA SIMSIM
123

The first *Sesame Street* in the Middle East arrived in Kuwait in 1979. After testing, it was decided to use modern standard Arabic, and the show was broadcast simultaneously in 22 Arab nations. Decades afterward, the show's name recognition is still strong, and a new version is currently in discussion.

Behind the scenes in Kuwait

شارع سمسم
123

In Palestine, where the show is called *Shara'a Simsim*, the goal is to serve as a catalyst for positive change by promoting children's senses of their own Palestinian identity. Workshop CEO Gary Knell says of the series: "Anyone who knows about conflict resolution will tell you that the first element of conflict resolution is about self-esteem. If you don't feel good about yourself, you're not going to feel good about anyone else."

רחוב סומסום
123

Israel began producing *Rechov Sumsum* in 1983. "In a region where children of different cultures seldom get to spend time together in everyday life, the series gives them an opportunity to 'meet,'" says project director Danny Labin.

NEWS FLASH

In 1978, when the first Israeli *Sesame Street* production was being discussed, Lewis Bernstein (seen below) recalls a discussion about what kind of characters would live on the Street. A version of Big Bird was suggested by Moshe Dayan's nephew, Yehonatan Geffen. But then an artist attending the session held up a drawing of a hedgehog.

"Hey," he said. "What about this? Because we're prickly on the outside, like a hedgehog, and we're sweet on the inside." The hedgehog, Kippi, would become Israel's Big Bird.

The Rim & Beyond

What's the first thing a producer should do when a country expresses interest in a series? Sesame Workshop's Ginger Brown has a short answer: "You go there," she says, smiling.

It's impossible to get a feel for the needs of a nation long-distance, so Ginger begins on the ground, by starting the search for a local producer for the show. This process almost invariably involves incredibly complex and delicate negotiations—political, financial, and creative. In the meantime, Dr. Charlotte Cole, who leads research and outreach efforts from the Workshop's offices, finds local educators to work on the new show's curriculum.

Then there are meetings . . . meetings to establish the local educational messages, meetings about the setting and characters.

If it's a full-fledged production, new puppets are constructed in the U.S., originally by Kermit Love and currently by Jim Henson's Creature Workshop, overseen by Connie Peterson. Most counties are delighted to have puppets built by these expert craftspeople, with their 40 years of experience designing Muppets for TV.

But not always. In Bangladesh, the craft of puppet-making is even older—thousands of years older. As Chief Creative Advisor Mustafa Manwar explains: "This a poor country, a developing country. But one thing we are very, very proud of is our literature, culture, and song. So we want to keep those things. And in this world, the modern world, the internationalism doesn't mean that you must copy each country. Internationalism means your best thing, your own country's best thing; when you can give it to the world, they will appreciate it."

The solution? Manwar worked closely with the Henson team, and there is a recurring segment on the show using traditional Bangladeshi puppets.

SABAI SABAI SESAME

Beginning in 2005, a version of the English show is dubbed into Khmer: "When Cambodian children see Muppets speaking their language, their mouths drop open in utter amazement," says Peter Wilson of Educational Television Cambodia.

JALAN SESAMA

Indonesia, an archipelago made up of 17,508 islands, presented a challenge. The show strives to reflect the country's motto: "*Bhinneka tunggal ika*," meaning "Although in pieces, yet one."

NEWS FLASH

For the many countries with limited production facilities or budgets for educational television, the Workshop created the best possible option to original coproductions: an alternative series named *Open Sesame*. Lu Horne, who headed international production when *Open Sesame* was created, described it this way: "The series contains universally acceptable material . . . and is as nearly 'culture-free' as TV material can be."

Shari Rosenfeld explains that the collection of Muppet skits, short films, and animations was offered as source material. Partners could pick and choose from the library of segments. "It was sold into many countries around the world, and then dubbed into a local language, or just broadcast in English," she explains. Some countries found it so successful that it became the gateway to production of all-new material.

In addition to airing in different nations, the show is also broadcast to the military's overseas locations.

गली गली सिम सिम

India's *Galli Galli Sim Sim* aims to increase girls' literacy rates, so producers developed the character of Chamki, who is dressed in a school uniform, chosen to neutralize cultural stereotyping, making her representative of all girls. Outreach initiatives in the country bring the show to outlying villages, delivered via repurposed vegetable carts toting battery-charged TVs.

Five-year-old Tuktuki shows children watching "Sisimpur" that girls can have the same opportunities as boys

সিসিমপুর™

১২৩

Halum, a tiger, is a starring Muppet on *Sisimpur* (the Bangla spelling is shown above), the Bangladeshi version of *Sesame Street*, which launched in 2005. Its aim is to help remedy low achievement and high drop-out rates in grades K–3.

"Most children don't really have a childhood. By the time you're five, you end up working and supporting your family."

—SHAILA RAHMAN, RESEARCHER, NAYANTARA PRODUCTIONS, BANGLADESH

芝麻街®

123

When a Chinese version of *Sesame Street* opened in 1998, there were so few people in the country with experience writing for children that an auto mechanic became the head writer of the show.

The Chinese cast includes a grocer, like Mr. Hooper, and other friendly neighbors, like Little Plum, below

SESAME STREET®

123

For decades, *Sesame Street* aired in Japan in its original form; it was a popular way for adults—especially teens—to learn English, and products were geared to this older audience. In 2004, a children's version launched, with green-and-purple monster Mojabo as host.

Theme park Universal Studios Japan created a 4–D movie that drew record crowds

SESAME!®

123

The Philippines aired the first fully bilingual version of the show in 1983, broadcasting in Tagalog and English. *Play With Me Sesame* now airs there.

OPEN SESAME®

123

The Australian *Open Sesame* was augmented in 2004 by the addition of Ollie, a monster emcee of short segments that were created expressly for the region and that air between other shows all day.

"I have worked in television for a number of years and feel confident that I can overcome the ordinary challenges that face a project, but when the problems you face are power outages, floods, political turmoil, and the like, you need to develop a new set of coping skills . . . the one that seemed to help the most was a good sense of humor!"

—NADINE ZYLSTRA, PRODUCER

Pass It On

Recent workshops in Palestine, above, help orient performers to the unique challenges of television puppetry. The French puppeteers, below right, are being trained by Kevin Clash

O nce the curriculum of a new international show is established and the setting and the characters are determined, it's time to cast the puppeteers—typically, the responsibility of American performers Marty Robinson and Kevin Clash.

At first, aspiring performers work with bare hands, with a Ping-Pong ball rig for the eyes. They work on lip-synch, and then Marty and Kevin put them on monitors. "Where your brain is destroyed," Marty says with a grin. "Because of the right-left thing. You learn how to find your focus—where your character is supposed to be looking. You learn how to operate monofilament, how to stand up, sit down, do a double take, a triple take, how to faint, how to get up from a faint, how to lie down, how to fall asleep . . . even how to breathe."

Cheryl Henson and Kevin Clash traveled to South Africa for the puppeteer workshops that trained the *Takalani Sesame* performers there. In 2001, when the events of September 11th temporarily curtailed travel just when the Egyptian puppeteer workshop was scheduled, the South African team stepped in and led the workshop instead, paying it forward.

Working in front of both mirrors and cameras, sixty or so puppeteers dwindle to forty, twenty, ten, then a final few. By the time it's clear who will make it, the performers have received more advance training than their American counterparts ever did.

Then come the writers' seminars, often run by *Sesame Street* scriptwriters Molly Boylan or Annie Evans and usually held in the States—though the team will travel if needed to assist a new staff.

"We sometimes have to impart to them how to *write*, not just how to write for kids," Shari Rosenfeld says, "because so often we have unskilled writers. I think our head writer for the Palestinian show is an architect. . . . You get people from such different walks of life, because there's no TV industry in some of these places."

Finally, when the show is ready to go in front of the cameras, Workshop personnel travel abroad to help out for a week or two, answering questions and smoothing out the rough spots.

During production, Ginger Brown heads a New York staff that has always included a producer who's a native of the country and speaks the language, although the goal is someday to shift all oversight to the regions themselves. Ginger's team reviews rough edits of the show, providing feedback and support. But ultimately, each country runs its own production, ensuring it's accessible to and appropriate for its own children.

And that makes all the difference.

Around the world, the street becomes a rue, a train station, and a plaza

" At a time when so much of the world news is troubling, progress on 'the longest street in the world' gives us cause for hope—one step, one child at a time. "

—DR. CHARLOTTE COLE,
VP INTERNATIONAL RESEARCH

"I'm looking for people who can take a bit of technique and start having fun with it," says Marty Robinson, describing the task of finding a crew of puppeteers to perform variations of *Sesame Street* around the globe. "Good actors, who can make you feel. I'm looking for the guy or girl who can convey without talking . . . you know, in the long take before you speak. A sense of comic timing."

THIS CHAPTER HAS BEEN BROUGHT TO YOU BY
THE LETTER G AND THE NUMBER 140.

The letter G is for Global Grover. Producer Melissa Dino helped usher in a series of Grover segments that debuted in season 34, with the stated goal of teaching children to respect the diversity of people from all over.
The Number 140 is for the number of nations and territories where *Sesame Street* is currently seen in its varied iterations.

13

"Foundation support is impermanent. Governmental funding is uncertain. Every organization needs a stable financial base in order to attract talented people."

—DR. LLOYD MORRISETT, COFOUNDER,
ANTICIPATING THE NEED FOR LICENSING
(THE RANDOM HOUSE BOOK DEAL IS SIGNED BELOW)

BECAUSE WE'RE FRIENDS

EPISODE 4141

Every taping of *Sesame Street* requires some degree of problem solving, but an extra level of wizardry is needed this morning on set. Today Elmo will be riding his tricycle.

For Elmo/trike close-ups, Kevin lies on his back on a rollie while performing the small red Muppet. Elmo's hands are attached to a pair of handlebars that have been removed from a trike. By scuttling forward with his feet, Kevin makes Elmo—who is tightly framed in the camera—look like he's steering and pedaling along.

For wide shots, though, in which the whole tricycle needs to be seen wheeling around the set, the trike is operated via joystick, much like a giant remote-controlled toy car. Elmo's feet and hands are wired to the trike's pedals and handlebars, so it will look like he's in control instead of what's really happening—the trike is doing the pedaling and steering, and Elmo's along for the ride.

That means the set has to be cleared of cables that usually snake everywhere, getting under camera wheels and tripping up unsuspecting visitors. "When are we going to wireless cameras?" camera operator Jimmy O'Donnell asks plaintively.

To add to the technical challenges, the shot is also going to involve what is called a dirty feed. There will be graphics fed into the shot during the take—in this case, the alphabet—so director Emily Squires and the people in the control room can see exactly how everything will look in the finished show.

The feed happens off the *Sesame Street* stage, in a truck filled with taping and recording equipment parked behind Kaufman-Astoria studio, where tape op Ernie Albritton and video engineer Jim Meek work.

A hidden engine installed in the back basket will power the trike

"Roll tape, Ernie," assistant director Frank Campagna calls through his headset. Ernie leans forward again and presses two buttons . . . one for the feed, one for the tape. "Speed," he murmurs quietly into a goose-necked microphone.

Disembodied voices fill the truck as a small girl and a boy meet up at the top of the scene.

Kevin focuses on Elmo's performance as puppeteer Matt Vogel, who's controlling the trike's joystick, steers Elmo in a smooth arc past the kids and around the street sign. On the monitor, miraculously, a Muppet rides a trike . . . solo.

A red foam mouthpiece remotely controls Active Abby's movements

More toys: In season 40, a new segment with Elmo's trike is taped. This time, Elmo is joined by the "Active" version of Leslie Carrara-Rudolph's puppet, Abby. Puppet builder Rollie Krewson and electro-mechanical ace Tom Newby show her the remote-control ropes.

Puppeteers Marty Robinson, Eric Jacobson, and Matt Vogel take the controls for this test drive, jealously watched by crew members and puppeteer Carmen Osbahr

Kevin's vocals were prerecorded and his lip-syncing was done remotely as Elmo rode

The electromechanical team makes minor adjustments to a remote-controlled car for season 40's Squirmadega Races story line. Everyone wants to get in on the act when it's time to test the worms' cars on the Street set.

Play Things

The MONSTER at the end of this Book starring LOVABLE, FURRY OLD GROVER

Hello, everybodee!

Jon Stone, the show's original head writer, authors one of the first books—it goes on to become the all-time best-selling title for Sesame Street

Jim Henson shares an introspective moment with Bert, one of the first Sesame Street toy puppets created. Jim was very supportive of licensing the characters

When Joan Ganz Cooney and Lloyd Morrisett obtained initial funding for *Sesame Street*, they foresaw that foundation and government money would not support the show for long. (In fact, it was fully funded that way only for the first two years.) The cofounders presciently began planning a financial portfolio for the Workshop—investments that, like a university's endowment, could sustain the company when the funding ended.

At the same time, Joan carefully investigated a possible licensing program—the creation of products based on the show. As a nonprofit, the Workshop would be required to use all licensing revenue for its programming and outreach efforts, which was exactly what the founding team intended.

Joan began with books, working with editor Jason Epstein at Random House to set up a *Sesame Street* publishing program. Chris Cerf—who would become one of the most successful songwriters on the show—came on board to run it. It was a very cautious first step. Even coloring books were verboten, for fear they might be too restricting to imaginations, recalls Anna Jane Hays, one of the first editors on the Workshop staff. When licensing demonstrated the ways content could be adapted to promote the show's literacy and social-emotional curriculum, though, researchers gave activity books the nod.

The next thing to be licensed was music, with the first *Sesame Street* original cast album released by Columbia Records in 1970.

THE SESAME STREET BOOK OF NUMBERS

The very first Sesame Street books were an ill-fated Time Life Book series, right, considered too costly for the audience. Later books, seen here, were more successful

"The whole world looked at what they were trying to do," explains Bill Whaley, who was brought in to run the products division a few years later when licensing began to expand. "So they really wanted to do music and publishing first, and not any of the noneducational or exotic or expensive products."

Ann Kearns, currently vice president of licensing for Global Toys, credits Bill with reorganizing the division, creating a licensing model followed by many children's shows today. The team's goal was to create a line of products that reflected the show's educational mandate but could bring in income to make production possible when funding levels dropped.

"We needed to make up the difference with our own revenue," Ann says.

Licensing grew to include every other kind of experience that proved to be in line with the show's ethics: live shows and theme parks, plus a range of educational or imaginative toys, games, music, and albums. The team actively seeks options that are more affordable for its viewers as well as partners who are willing to sponsor the show and its many outreach efforts.

Licensing's continued success became the foundation of what would become the Sesame Workshop "endowment."

> **That's the thing that I'm really proud of . . . when we got the engine roaring, and all the stuff that went away from the government was now supplanted with the income from the Workshop . . . from licensing.**
>
> —BILL WHALEY,
> LONGTIME HEAD OF *SESAME STREET* LICENSING

WESTERN PUBLISHING COMPANY, INC.

January 7, 1970

Mrs. Joan Ganz Cooney, Director
Sesame Street
Childrens Television Workshop
1865 Broadway
New York, New York 10023

Dear Mrs. Cooney:

Western's original note inquiring into the license. Bill Whaley, below, helped build the Workshop's licensing business

EVP Dave Connell and then-head of licensing Chris Cerf review panels of the Sesame Street newspaper comic with its artist, animator Cliff Roberts. Syndicated by King Features, the strip ran from 1971 to 1975

Books, music, toys, plush, clothing, home videos, feature films, Internet content, even podcasts . . . the heads of the Workshop's domestic and international licensing divisions today continue this effort, under the same mandate to reflect the show's mission in its products. This nonprofit mission comes first, which means partners even receive very careful guidelines about where and how they may advertise.

"Everything that we do in this group is to enhance and reinforce our on-air promises," explains Maura Regan, vice president and general manager for global consumer products. "I look at a day in the life of a kid, how kids are getting their content, how they interact with products. Then I look at how I can add value to that day—but along the lines of what *Sesame Street* can deliver."

That includes new ways to deliver the show itself.

"Digital distribution has become an essential complement to broadcast television for our video content," says Terry Fitzpatrick, executive vice president of distribution. "The multiple touch points of digital media allow the Workshop to expand the accessibility of

> **The licensing division is the more commercial part of this company, true. But it's because of what we can deliver that this company can do more of what it does. You know the quote, 'No man is so tall than when he stoops to help a child'? I always feel very tall when I talk about working for *Sesame Street*.**
>
> —ANN KEARNS,
> VP LICENSING, GLOBAL TOYS

Sesame Street." Digital's interactivity, portability, searchability, and personalization offer a powerful way to connect with the show's audience and increase the relevance and impact of its educational content, he explains. "Many of these new media devices also offer an opportunity to encourage parent and child interaction with our content, which dramatically increases learning outcomes."

The same goals and guidelines hold true for international licensing—the child always comes first. In areas of economic hardship, it's a balance between need and local capability.

"That's a point I make a lot when I talk to our licensing partners," says Ann Kearns. "I say, you know, we're in Bangladesh because the kids need us, not because there's a huge licensing opportunity. We're there *despite* the fact that there's no licensing opportunity. It's important that our partners recognize what we do around the world and support us in other ways."

Danny Horn, a contributor to fan sites ToughPigs.com and Muppet Wiki, and senior community development manager at Wikia, remembers: "Nineteen seventy-five: I'm four years old and I'm sitting cross-legged on the living room floor. My parents give me my Chanukah present—a Cookie Monster doll that's as big as I am. He sits on the floor in front of me, and I look into his googly eyes. That's my earliest memory, right there. Chapter one: Me and Cookie Monster.

"I don't remember watching the show, actually; I must have. My memories are all about the things, not the show. I had a six-foot-long wooden puzzle with a photo of Mr. Snuffleupagus; when you put it together, it stretched all the way across the rug. One of my records got scratched, and when I played 'M-M-M Monster Meal,' there was a skip right after Herry said 'melons.' An hour after I was put to bed, my mother found me with the lights on, reading my book about Grover and the Amazing Mumford.

"Who remembers watching TV? You watch it, and then it's over, and you turn it off. But you could carry the toys around with you. You could sleep with them, and break them, and find them under the couch six months after you thought they were lost forever. For kids growing up in the seventies, *Sesame Street* wasn't a TV show; it was part of the environment. We ate off Cookie Monster placemats and slept in Big Bird sheets. Nobody dreamed of living on *Sesame Street*. We didn't have to. *Sesame Street* lived with us."

Toy Timeline

Here's a snapshot of what was happening in the wider world during the show's history. What were your parents doing while you were watching *Sesame Street*? What was happening at the Workshop? Check it out!

1971

- The Rolling Stones' "Sticky Fingers" album cover, conceived and shot by Andy Warhol and complete with actual zipper, ignites controversy.

1973

- The Endangered Species Act is passed.
- President Nixon calls for austerity to combat the recession; initiates oil/gas price controls.
- The trial of the Watergate burglars begins.

1974

- "I shall resign the Presidency effective at noon tomorrow," President Richard Nixon announces on August 8th. "Vice President Ford will be sworn in as president at that hour."

1975

- American forces pull out of Vietnam.
- *Saturday Night Live* makes its debut.
- Paul Allen and Bill Gates work on the first computer language.

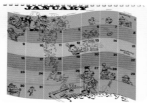

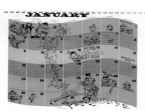

In the 1970s, these characters mark the first time Little People figures from Fisher-Price are based on actual people

1973's Questor finger puppets expand on 1971's original Topper lineup

In 1970, Sesame's first album goes Gold and wins a Grammy

Clips from the Ice Follies skate show, which debuts in 1974, later appear on the show, in episode #0796

Hugely popular Mad magazine artist Jack Davis is commissioned to do the first Sesame Street calendar

The very first Sesame Street puppets are released by Child Guidance in 1973

An array of toys displayed in the early seventies shows the range of licensing right from the start

1970

- *Sesame Street* books (published by Western Publishing and Random House) and a magazine launch.

1971

- Linda Bove arrives as a regular cast member on *Sesame Street*. Books with Random House follow in the eighties: "Sign Language ABC" and "Sign Language Fun."

1973

- Fisher-Price's first *Sesame Street* toy is the Movie Viewer.
- Colorforms releases a Neighborhood set.

1974

- The 123 Sesame Street brownstone appears as a float in the Macy's Thanksgiving Day Parade.
- *Children and Television*, by *Sesame*'s Gerry Lesser, hits book stores.

1975

- Bert and Ernie are exhibited at the Smithsonian Institute.
- Kermit sings his signature Sesame tune, "Bein' Green," with Ray Charles on the *Cher* show.

1976
- The country celebrates the bicentennial with a big party on July 4th.
- *One Flew Over the Cuckoo's Nest* wins the Academy Award for Best Picture.

1977
- Jimmy Carter is sworn in as the 39th president, succeeding Gerald Ford.
- A first-class stamp costs 13¢.
- *Saturday Night Fever* and *Star Wars* premiere.

1978
- The Middle East peace process begins at the Camp David Accords.
- Jim Davis' "Garfield" comic debuts.

1979
- Willie Mays enters Baseball's Hall of Fame.
- Sony introduces the Walkman.
- Disco's popularity peaks with diva Gloria Gaynor's "I Will Survive."

1980
- The U.S. Hockey Team wins a gold medal at the Winter Olympics.
- Ronald Reagan is elected the 40th president of the United States.

Books by Random House and Western Publishing, including pop-ups, storybooks, and paperbacks, are deliberately priced low to enable the intended audience to build a library of quality books

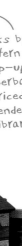

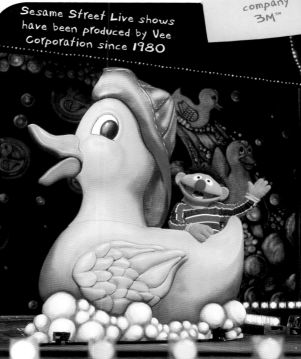

Sesame Street Live shows have been produced by Vee Corporation since 1980

Post-it notes are introduced nationally by company 3M™

The concept sketch for Sesame Place and the actual opening gate, right, plus later sketches and attractions. The park is constantly being updated

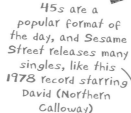

45s are a popular format of the day, and Sesame Street releases many singles, like this 1978 record starring David (Northern Calloway)

1976
- Milton Bradley's first puzzle shows that Cookie eats healthy. (He eats *everything*!)

1977
- Macy's Thanksgiving Day Parade stars Kermit—the balloon travels abroad for the International Year of the Child.
- The first Spanish *Sesame* book is printed.

1979
- Elmo's puppeteer, Kevin Clash, performs for *Sesame* for the first time (as Cookie Monster) in the Macy's Thanksgiving Day Parade, celebrating the show's tenth year.

1980
- Sesame Place, the *Sesame Street* theme park, opens in Langhorn, PA.
- *Sesame Street Live* begins to tour.

1981
1981
1981

1982

- The Falklands War begins . . . and ends.
- Sony releases the first commercial CD player.
- Michael Jackson releases the megahit album "Thriller."

The compact disc, or CD, is introduced in 1982

1984

- Ronald Reagan is reelected to a second term as president.
- Band Aid is formed to help Ethiopia, which is suffering from a massive famine.

1985

- "We Are the World" is recorded by USA for Africa.
- Nintendo releases its first games console.

Among Nintendo's first array of games in 1985: Super Mario Brothers

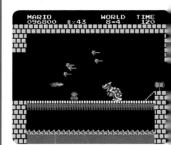

Despite the arrival of the high-tech CD, the low-tech Sesame phonograph, with wind-up action, is successfully introduced in 1984

Big Bird StoryMagic books, tapes, and animated dolls are developed by Ideal Toys in 1986—Big Bird is later joined by Cookie Monster and Oscar

SESAME STREET MUPPETS

Would you buy a sheet from these guys?

Bradley Time had the license to produce Sesame Street watches and clocks from 1974 to 1983

NEWS FLASH

Children's Computer Workshop (CCW) was created in 1982 within the company to apply the goals and research savvy of the show toward the development of technologies for preschoolers. It teamed with partners to create educational computer and video games, testing with kids to adapt existing controls to the needs of its young audience. Games ran on Apple (using AppleSoft BASIC, then Integer BASIC), the Atari 2600 VCS computer and game system, Radio Shack's TRS-80 Color Computer, the Nintendo Entertainment System, and home computers. The division was disbanded in the late 1980s, emerging as an Interactive Group with a focus on all forms of digital media.

1982's Sesame Street characters are the last original-style Weebles produced

FISHER-PRICE

I'll Miss You, Mr. Hooper

Susan and Gordon Adopt a Baby

1981

- Big Bird visits China, looking for the phoenix: "What a good thing it would be if a great big American bird went to meet that beautiful Chinese bird!"

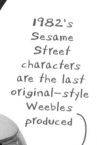

Sesame Street was added to the Viewmaster line in 1982. (The device was considered high-tech when it debuted at the 1939 New York World's Fair)

1983

- Actor Will Lee dies; the grief-stricken cast goes on to tape an episode addressing the death of his character, Mr. Hooper. The episode goes on to win an Emmy Award.

1984

- In season 16, Big Bird goes to camp, a rare excursion off the set.
- Elmo joins the cast, along with Telly.
- Computers are introduced on the show.

1985

- *Follow That Bird* is released, the show's big-screen debut.
- Rand McNally creates a Sesame globe.

1986

- *The Muppets: A Celebration of 30 Years* debuts on CBS.
- The book *Susan and Gordon Adopt a Baby* reflects an earlier story line on the show.

1987

- "Walk Like an Egyptian" tops Billboard's charts.
- Aretha Franklin becomes the first woman to be inducted into the Rock and Roll Hall of Fame.

1988

- George H. W. Bush is elected as the 41st president of the United States.

1989

- *The Simpsons* premieres.
- The Berlin Wall comes down.

1990

- Peace activist Nelson Mandela is released from a South African prison.
- NBC's *Seinfeld* debuts.
- Martina Navratilova has a record-breaking ninth Wimbledon win.

Grunge becomes mainstream with 1991's best-selling album *Nevermind*, featuring hit single "Smells Like Teen Spirit"

1992

- Jay Leno takes over from Johnny Carson as host of *The Tonight Show.*
- Bill Clinton is elected as the 42nd president.

Astro-Grover is a *Sesame Street* game for home computers developed by Hi-Tech Expressions and Children's Television Workshop, released in 1987. The game teaches counting, adding, and subtracting

Promotional postcards celebrate the show's 20th birthday

NEWS FLASH

The flagship Sesame Street General Store, dedicated solely to Street merchandise, appeared in 1990. Soon after, satellites popped up in malls nationwide. But the ultra-quick expansion to 35 stores nationwide was too ambitious, and the chain ultimately closed.

The show's tolerance curriculum is supported with storybooks and coloring books

Vee Corporation's live shows in the early nineties include "Where's the Birdie," "Let's Play School," "Sleeping Birdie," "Big Bird and the ABCs," and "Silly Dancing"

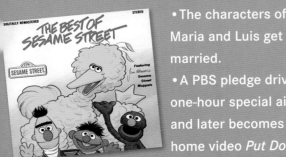

1987

- The characters of Maria and Luis get married.
- A PBS pledge drive one-hour special airs and later becomes the home video *Put Down the Duckie.*

1988

Big Bird's balloon flies in the Macy's Thanksgiving Day Parade

1990

- *Sesame Street* celebrates its 25th anniversary, then tragically loses Jim Henson when he dies suddenly.

1991

- *Sesame Street Home Video Visits the Firehouse* is released and later used in outreach programs.
- *Sesame Street*'s preschool education program (PEP) originates.

1992

- Research indicates that *Sesame Street* reaches 92 percent of Caucasian, Latino, and African-American preschoolers living below the poverty line.

1994

- 1994 is designated "Year of the Family."
- *Forrest Gump* is released.
- *Friends* premieres on NBC.

1995

- Yahoo! is founded.
- American astronaut Norman Thagard flies on a Russian spacecraft, part of the joint Mir Program.
- Pixar's *Toy Story* premieres.

1999

- Napster debuts.
- The Euro officially replaces national currencies in the Eurozone.
- Many fear a Y2K meltdown. They needn't.

In 2000, teams of scientists working on the Human Genome Project announce that they have completed mapping the genetic code

2001

- Publicly generated online encyclopedia Wikipedia launches on the Internet.
- *Sesame Street*'s hometown, New York City, is devasted by the events of 9/11.

One day, inventor Ron Dubren had an idea after seeing two kids helplessly giggling as they tickled each other. How could he re-create that feeling of utter hilarity in a toy? He and engineer Greg Hyman began to design, gutting a toy monkey to create their prototype, Tickles the Chimp, who simply laughed. Twelve companies turned it down until Tyco Preschool's Stan Clutton saw its potential. But in the preliminary testing, moms wanted more. Movement did the trick, courtesy of the kind of motor used today to make cell phones vibrate: put that together with a little red monster, and Tickle Me Elmo was born. It was a groundbreaking toy that giggled contagiously when kids touched his hand.

Although Tyco Preschool had envisioned a holiday hit, Tickle Me Elmo's astonishing popularity took even them by surprise. Supply couldn't keep pace with demand; stores ran out of the toy the day after Thanksgiving. Appearances on shows like *The Today Show, Good Morning America*, and *The Rosie O'Donnell Show* (where the talk show host tossed the doll to audience members whenever a guest mentioned the word "wall"), plus Toy of the Year awards, fueled the fire. Demand reached a point where parents fought for the toy in aisles, and auctions reportedly brought in bids as high as $1,500 for a toy that retailed for under $30.

Sesame's evolving curriculum tackles "green" subjects, reflected in partner efforts like Sesame Street Live's "Elmo's Green Thumb" and Reader's Digest's pop-up book "Let's Help the Earth"

Internationally, licensing also helps to support the Workshop's productions—toys and books reflect the various cultures

Tickle Me Elmo has fathered a dynasty: Tickle Me Ernie, Big Bird, and Cookie Monster; a "Surprise Edition" of the doll programmed to reveal prizewinners months later; Let's Pretend Elmo; Hokey Pokey Elmo; Chicken Dance Elmo; Limbo Elmo; Check-Up Time Elmo; Bird's the Word Elmo; Elmo Knows Your Name; and Elmo Live (which senses its environment); and, in 2009, Tickle Hands: furry red interactive gloves.
To be continued . . .

Fisher-Price, one of the Workshop's early licensees, has released new playsets for every generation of fans

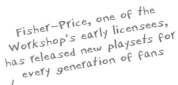

1994

- *Sesame Street's All-Star 25th Birthday: Stars and Street Forever!* airs on ABC.
- *Let's Be Friends* premieres, the fourteenth live show.

Parque Plaza Sésamo opens in Monterrey, Mexico, 1995, joining Universal Studios Japan and Vila Sesamo Kids' Land (inside the Hopi Hari amusement park) as international parks

1997

- Cookie Monster becomes a poster boy for the "Got Milk" campaign.

1996

2000

- Children's Television Workshop becomes Sesame Workshop to acknowledge that the company's mission stretches far beyond television into a wide variety of new media.

2003

• The Iraq War is launched with an air strike on military targets in Baghdad, the start of a "shock and awe" campaign by the United States and the United Kingdom.

2004

• The Boston Red Sox win the World Series—their first since 1918.
• *Avenue Q*, a Broadway musical reimagining *Sesame Street* for grown-ups, wins a Tony Award.

2005

• Hurricane Katrina catastrophically strikes the U.S. Gulf Coast just one year after a tsunami devastates Southeast Asia.

2006

• Pluto loses its status as a planet.
• President George W. Bush signs a renewal of the Patriot Act.

In 2007, the space shuttle Atlantis successfully completes mission STS-117

2009

• Barack Obama is sworn into office as the 44th president of the United States, the first African-American to serve in America's highest office.

Elmo is added to Random House's 2004 edition of the "Sesame Street Dictionary"

Spanish-language and bilingual titles from partners like Dalmatian Press expand in the new millennium

In 2007, Abby joins the classics in soft-doll lines by Gund and Fisher-Price (often called a "plush" license)

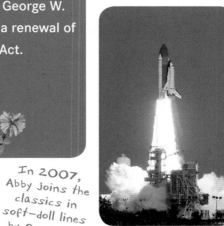

Licenses with Earth's Best, Stemilt Growers, California Giant Berry Farms, and Apple and Eve provide food products that support the show's Healthy Habits for Life initiative

In 2003, Sesame begins a sunny partnership with Beaches Resorts

Busch, the Workshop's parks partner, signs a deal in 2006 for expansion around the world—here, Elmo greets a new pal at Sea World Australia

American Greetings, Sesame's greeting card, stationery, gift wrap, and party goods partner, helps sponsor the show and outreach programs

Books enter the digital age, with downloadable options plus animated storybooks from Publications International and Hinkler Books

Grandma,

Sprout
PBS KIDS
Let's grow!

SESAME STREET
Park Day
PLAY ▶

In 2008, Sesame debuts a new, research-driven Website with customizable playlists, and on PBS Kids Sprout, the show hits 18 million downloads in one month

Fans experience the show on Hulu, YouTube, and Apple's iTunes (where "Word on the Street" segments become the number-one ranked podcast)

2005

• To comfort children affected by Katrina, the show rebroadcasts its "rebuilding" episodes.
• The "*Sesame Street* Presents the Body" exhibit begins a tour of science centers.

2006

• Sesame Workshop launches "Talk, Listen, Connect: Helping Families During Miliary Deployment"— a second program, in 2009, helps families cope with injuries suffered during service.

LIBRARY
🎵 Music
🎬 Movies
📺 TV Shows
🎙 Podcasts   15
📻 Radio
STORE
iTunes Store
🛒 Shopping Cart
Purchased

◀ ▶ 🏠 ▸ Podcasts ▸ Today's Top Podcasts

TODAY'S TOP PODCASTS

1. Sesame Street ...
Sesame Street
Category: Kids & Family
Free SUBSCRIBE

Big Screen
Little Screen

The expansion of the *Sesame Street* brand into films, videos, and television specials was a natural. The first film foray occurred in 1985, with *Follow That Bird*. Sandra Bernhard, John Candy, Chevy Chase, Joe Flaherty, Waylon Jennings, and Dave Thomas made cameos in the cross-country romp as Big Bird's friends search for him after he's convinced to leave the Street and live with a family of dodos. Show writers Tony Geiss and Judy Freudberg scripted the Warner Bros. movie, which featured new Muppet characters developed by Michael Frith, who first came to Jim Henson's attention from his work as an editor and illustrator on *Sesame Street's* Random House books and later became EVP and creative director for Jim Henson Productions.

New York City's Metropolitan Museum of Art opened its doors (and a prop sarcophagus) to the Muppet and human cast

The next movie, *The Adventures of Elmo in Grouchland,* hit the big screen in 1999. In the meantime, several television specials were produced, beginning with *Christmas Eve on Sesame Street* in 1978 and continuing with the characters' invasion of New York's Metropolitan Museum

In 1974, Sesame Street and The Electric Company characters take over the ABC studio and spoof its shows in a prime-time special aired on that network

of Art in *Don't Eat the Pictures* (1982), 1983's Emmy-winning *Big Bird in China* (the first U.S.-China co-production ever), *Big Bird in Japan* (1989), the globe-trotting *Sesame Street Stays Up Late!* (which visited the show's international sets), *Elmopalooza* (1998), and more. The puppets have also made appearances on other programs, from *Arthur Fiedler's Evening at the Pops* on PBS in 1971 to guest shots on Comedy Central's *The Colbert Report* in 2008 and ABC's *Scrubs* in 2009.

The show's library of home videos began to be produced in 1985. They allow specific goals to get even more focus (*All-Star Alphabet, Elmo Visits the Doctor, Happy Healthy Monsters*) or encourage children to celebrate their imaginations (*Abby in Wonderland*).

"I don't think I'm on Sesame Street," Abby wonders in that lushly filmed script.

But, of course, she still is . . .

The cultural exchange works both ways—Big Bird learns about Japan in this 1989 special and "Elmo Saves Chistmas," in 1998, is dubbed for Japan's audiences

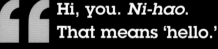

Hi, you. *Ni-hao.* That means 'hello.'

—OUYANG LIANZI, AS XIAO FOO, BIG BIRD'S NEW FRIEND IN CHINA

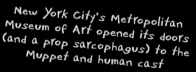

Jon Stone directs a scene in China, where Big Bird explores the Great Wall

"Abby in Wonderland" is given a full-on, movie-musical production; though it's developed for DVD, it's also screened in selected movie theaters

Guest star Paul Rudd clowns on set—here with "Being Green" director Emily Squires and writer Christine Ferraro

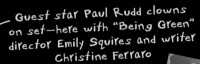

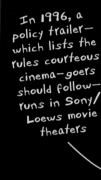

In 1996, a policy trailer—which lists the rules courteous cinema-goers should follow—runs in Sony/Loews movie theaters

One year, as a subversive Christmas present to the staff, Workshop staffers Chris Cerf, Joe Raposo, Danny Epstein, and Bill Effros (from the products group) hatched a joke inspired by the care the Workshop took with all its licensing endeavors. They created a fake product, Imperial Sesame Street Polish Kielbasa, complete with a label featuring Cookie Monster alongside an educational "Disclaimer" pledging that the product was educational. The sausages were stashed in the Workshop fridge.

That night, Chris relates, an employee discovered them and called the chief legal counsel and Joan, who were horrified. A hunt began to find out who could possibly have licensed kielbasa. The prank expanded in response: Joe made a commercial, sent to Joan and the legal team, with Cookie Monster affirming that the sausages were "better than cookie!" Joan was appalled. Legal was out for blood.

"The day before Christmas," Chris says, "Joe got the *Sesame Street* band to dress up in hats and lederhosen, and they marched into Joan's office with cooked sausages." The joke was revealed and, because Joan (of necessity) has a sense of humor, all was forgiven.

Noted movie poster artist Steven Chorney did the striking painting for "Follow That Bird"

In "Follow That Bird," Bob outlines the plan to search for Big Bird, who has left a family of dodos to return to Sesame Street. En route, the Bird is duped by the Sleaze Brothers into appearing as the "blue bird of happiness" in their traveling circus

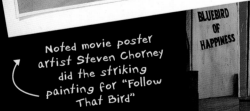

BLUEBIRD OF HAPPINESS

THIS CHAPTER HAS BEEN BROUGHT TO YOU BY THE LETTER E AND THE NUMBER 1.

The letter E is for Elmo—Tickle Me Elmo, that is. **The number 1** is for one million—the lowball estimate for units sold of the toy in 1996, the first year it appeared. The enormous popularity of Tickle Me Elmo's iterations in the decade since have helped to sustain the nonprofit Workshop during tough economic times and have made preschoolers (plus a disproportionate number of adults) giggle helplessly.

14

"*Sesame Street* has your back."

—GARY KNELL, SESAME WORKSHOP CEO,
QUOTING A RETURNING SOLDIER WHO
BENEFITED FROM OUTREACH EFFORTS

A Workshop field research team works
together to overcome a travel-related
challenge during a study conducted
in Jamaica in the 1970s

WE'LL DO IT
TOGETHER

SPECIAL
EPISODE

This morning, Staff Sergeant Ramon Padilla is being introduced by Gary Knell, Sesame Workshop's Chief Executive Officer, to a gathering of the staff in the offices of Sesame Workshop. More than two hundred people have gathered to applaud him—as Gary puts it, Ramon is "a role model for many, many soldiers"—and to honor his work in *Sesame Street*'s "Talk, Listen, Connect" outreach project, a groundbreaking multiphase series of DVDs and related material for young children and their military families. *Coming Home: Military Families Cope With Change* is about to air as a prime-time special on PBS on April 1, 2009. It's part of an initiative born from a strong and singular hope, Gary reminds everyone, to recognize the thousands of American children and families who know all too well what it's like to see a loved one go off to war—families like the Padillas.

Ramon is visibly moved but a little discomfited by the attention. He quickly shifts the focus to his "beautiful wife, Judith," and children, crediting them with being his source of strength.

"Thank you for inviting us here," he goes on. "I was born in Mexico; I came to California when I was two years old and I joined the army when I was 25, the year 2000." Ramon tells of his service on international bases until he was assigned his first tour in the Middle East. "It was pretty tough; Emily was four months and Ramon Jr., on the way. After I was deployed, I was scared there wouldn't be a chance to see him."

Outreach kits are available in both English and Spanish

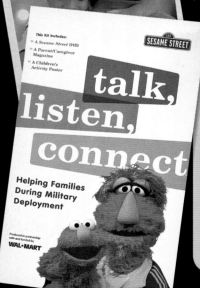

It is often said that when a parent or sibling is deployed, the entire family is deployed

A brief leave enabled the sergeant to meet his son. But soon after his return to duty, his family's worst fears were realized.

"I was there 45 days when an RPG [rocket-propelled grenade] came to our firebase," Ramon explains. "I guess they aimed it at me. I was also hit by an AK-47." His confident voice and buoyant attitude dim slightly as he relates the event that cost him an arm and changed his life. "I was hit in my head, so I have moderate TBI [traumatic brain injuries]. They flew my family out, also my brother who was in Iraq. I thank the Army for that."

Ramon first became involved with the Workshop's outreach efforts when he used them himself. "We saw a commercial for 'Talk, Listen, Connect' and I knew we had to see it," he explains. "I said, 'We need to make this a family event,' especially for Emily—she was asking 'Where's Daddy?'

"It was a blockbuster," he goes on. "The kids watched it all the time. The stuff they portrayed, it really helped—how to keep in contact with the family. Two weeks later there were posters from Emily, pictures from Ramon. It was great."

The Workshop's live-events group has teamed with the United Service Organization on a performance of "Talk, Listen, Connect," currently touring bases and installations. Kids get to meet their Muppet friends while local agencies are able to gather in one place to offer all kinds of financial and emotional support to the families that attend.

Ramon Padilla and his family

> "I agreed to do it under one condition: I had to meet Elmo."
>
> —STAFF SERGEANT RAMON PADILLA

Ramon expresses his gratitude humbly, but it's his own efforts that are currently making other recovering soldiers' lives easier. These efforts began when he was approached by show staff to be featured in the second program in the series, dealing with changes in family life when a soldier comes home injured.

"I thought about it . . . for one second," he says.

This second program is already changing lives. "We had a triple amputee come in recently who had not seen his three-year-old daughter since his injury and was afraid of how she would react," another Army staff sergeant, involved in distributing kits at Walter Reed Army Medical Center, told the Workshop. "I gave him the TLC kit and explained the materials to him. He was so happy that he started to cry with joy."

During his talk, Ramon screens segments from the DVD component of the "Talk, Listen, Connect" kit featuring other soldiers and their families. By the end of the tape, many Workshop staffers are wiping away tears, moved by the stories on-screen and by Ramon's gratitude for the program.

"Thank you all for making this DVD," he finishes. "This is a hard subject—nobody else has done anything like this for the Army. This is the first time you can involve the kids in the integration."

Outreach has been the heart and soul of the Workshop's mission since the beginning. It's a commitment articulated by Gary Knell as he rallies the team for the next installment of the series, a kit dealing with even graver need: helping military families who have lost a family member.

"When people ask, 'What are you doing to help?' " Gary says, "I hope that we as a family at Sesame Workshop can stand up and feel proud about what we've accomplished."

The Workshop knows the power of familiar and comforting faces—and laughter—so it uses the charm of Elmo and his friends to help kids open up and talk about what they are feeling about stressful subjects

"As macho as you think you are, that you're a U.S. soldier and a fighting machine, this particular fight, you can't do alone—you need [your] family," said one of the veteran soldiers interviewed during taping for "Talk, Listen, Connect." The documentary component of the outreach kit contains interviews with families and offers strategies for keeping the talk flowing. The Muppet story lines, meanwhile, reflect typical family dynamics. "If even Elmo and his family are feeling it, then there are other families feeling it, too," said the wife of a deployed Army sergeant first class. "This helps us feel like we're not alone in this."

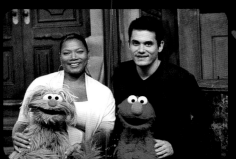

Queen Latifah and John Mayer are enlisted as the engaging hosts of Talk, Listen, Connect's "Coming Home"; Cuba Gooding Jr. hosted 2006's special: "When Parents Are Deployed"

A mobile viewing unit makes a stop at the Estrada Courts housing project in Los Angeles, CA

Early Outreach

From the beginning, Joan Ganz Cooney recognized that *Sesame Street* had the potential to benefit children. But first, children and their families had to know about the show and its educational goals. When *Sesame Street* debuted in 1969, the families of its intended low-income and minority audience were barely aware of public television. The Workshop needed to reach out to these families in original and creative ways.

It needed outreach.

"*Sesame Street* and the Community," an early document from the Workshop, described outreach's mission: "To ensure that all children, particularly children of the poor, have an opportunity to watch the program and benefit from its educational message." Joan herself called outreach "second in importance only to the actual production of *Sesame Street*," going on to assert that "it is only when we reach and teach children that we can consider the program a success."

Beyond making people aware of *Sesame Street*, outreach addressed the need to build on its curriculum in ways a television show could not. Because no matter how effective and ubiquitous television may be, that first outreach mission statement continues, "it cannot respond to a child's specific questions, and it cannot provide objects to touch, to walk around, to smell. Preschool children need this direct experience of the world. [Outreach provides] real people—adults, teenagers, and other children—with whom the children can play and learn."

CAN YOU TELL ME HOW TO GET TO **Sesame Street**

Evelyn Payne Davis, a tireless advocate for disadvantaged and marginalized families, was hired as vice president of the new outreach division, called Community Education Services. Her initial goal was to encourage family viewership among populations in need: in New York, Boston, Chicago, Detroit, New Orleans, San Francisco, Oakland, L.A., Dallas, and Biloxi. She established small satellite offices staffed with dedicated workers eager to work with families in their communities.

"We ultimately had around two or three people per field office," recalls Ann Kearns, who worked with Evelyn in the show's first decade. These grassroots workers distributed literature, badges and buttons, posters, and other material that promoted the show, meeting families on street corners, in supermarkets, anywhere mothers (the primary caregivers at the time) could be reached. Their job, Ann recalls, "was to work with parents and teachers and caregivers and really teach them what the show was all about and how they could use it to help their children."

Early outreach programs included mobile viewing units that brought the show to inner-

Below left, the show's educational curriculum was introduced to families in Appalachia via home visits and mobile units; below, bookmobiles with donated material make it possible for children in poor inner-city neighborhoods to own what was for many their first book

city neighborhoods, to Appalachia, to the Choctaw and other Native American communities, and to the children of migrant workers. Donated television sets were provided to storefronts, day care centers, housing projects, libraries, and churches—often linking with Head Start centers and the Jaycees (the United States Junior Chamber, working with teenagers). Routines at the centers were designed to use the program as a springboard for post-show "reinforcement." After viewing, facilitators led children in group activities and conducted workshops to provide caregivers with the tools to build positive parent-child relationships.

In Appalachia, for instance, a rural coal-mining region where high school drop-out rates were as high as 50 percent in the seventies, there was a desperate need for early-childhood education: children performing well in lower grades were more likely to stay and suc-

ceed in school. So a mobile classroom offered facilities for fifteen children at a time to watch the show and participate in playful learning activities directed by teachers. Field office directors Paul Elkins and Robert Bright coordinated with the local Dilenowisco Educational Cooperative to train home visitors to tutor children in weekly sessions, working with parents to establish learning routines that could continue when the field officers moved on.

Over time, as *Sesame Street* gained traction, the work of its Community Education Services group evolved and expanded. The idea was to use the show as a catalyst for larger explorations of its curriculum.

Evelyn Davis continued as the face and vice president of the Workshop's outreach into the nineties. Her advocacy for communities in need and her belief that the best way to do that was to bring whole communities together is demonstrated by the simple statement she uses to close that first outreach document:

"There's more that can be done. Will you help?"

Evelyn Davis, Sesame Street's head of outreach, joins the staff in 1969, leading such programs as the mobile inoculation units, like the one below

In the seventies, the Workshop initiated a program called *Sesame Street* Summer Camps, in cooperation with New York City's Youth Services Agency. Workshop-trained tutors supervised viewings of the show and then led follow-up lessons, sometimes involving older children to help mentor younger ones.

Road Trip

Highly expressive faces give one indication of why the show's music, rather than its Muppets, tested best in this community

I t wasn't merely lip service, a quick promise made in order to obtain government and foundation funds. The Workshop's determination to test the educational effects of *Sesame Street*—and, as Joan Ganz Cooney's initial proposal ambitiously suggested, the effects of television itself—was and remains a passionate conviction: a mission, not simply a mission statement. From the first, the team was committed to the hard work of finding out if the show could actually teach and meet its goals.

Dr. Ed Palmer, head of the research division at the time, wanted to test the show's success with children who had no daily exposure to other kids' shows—exposure that might lead to deceptively positive results—as well as with children whose options for community support of education were few. But how, he wondered, was it possible to do so in an increasingly media-saturated society?

After careful research in conjunction with Harvard University, he decided to go to Jamaica.

The team settled on a remote mountain town, where limited electrical access meant most kids had never even seen a television, let alone watched educational children's shows.

Weeks of testing revealed some surprises. Oddly, the very segments that tested so well domestically—the Muppet bits—didn't seem to capture the imaginations of Jamaican children...perhaps due to difficulties in translations. This meant interest dropped sharply when puppets appeared on screen.

Any segments with music, however, tested through the roof.

Most important—far more so than the success of any one element—was the show's overall impact: even the earliest returns indicated that kids were learning. Their recognition and, even more critically, comprehension of the underlying principles of letters and numbers—why they mattered, what they represented—increased measurably.

The show was meeting its goals . . . even in isolation.

Ed Palmer and Harry Lasker add their muscle to local drivers to reach the isolated communities

Decorated bus shelters promote the study locally

Sony and other corporate sponsors, as well as government grants, help supply the equipment for outreach—in Jamaica, television is supplied for the study by battery—powered units

Photographer Bill Pierce, who accompanied the Workshop team to Jamaica, remembers that when the televisions were first turned on, some of the villagers, who had never before seen a television, ran away screaming. During the study, they grew tolerant of the new medium, labeling the technology "Monkeys in a Box." Research showed a clear improvement in comprehension and literacy skills from routine viewing of the show.

HARVARD UNIVERSITY
GRADUATE SCHOOL OF EDUCATION

LABORATORY OF HUMAN DEVELOPMENT

Roy E. Larsen Hall, Appian Way
Cambridge, Massachusetts 02138

February 10, 1972

Dr. Lloyd Morrisett
Markle Foundation
50 Rockefeller Plaza
New York, New York 10020

Dear Lloyd:

The Children's Television Workshop's proposal to study the use of mobile videocassette television in remote areas provides a totally unprecedented opportunity to learn about the effects of televised experiences upon children.

The proposal itself anticipates this opportunity:

"... we will be bringing television to areas where it has never been seen before. As such, the experiment offers a unique opportunity to study and record the reactions of absolutely inexperienced television viewers. The methodological problems involved are complex. However, one possible means of data collection might be the use of cassette units in the video taping of the reactions of the children while viewing the programs. Such video tapes could help determine if the capacity to learn from television is itself a distinct skill which must be learned." (Harry Lasker, "A Collaborative Study of the Use of Mobile Videocassette Television in Remote Areas," Children's Television Workshop, February, 1972)

How does viewing television affect a child's basic perception of his world? There has been great speculation about this absolutely fundamental question, but research cannot be done in regions where television already has wide usage because children are simply too sophisticated in their television viewing — they have gone far beyond the point where we can examine such basic changes in their perception of the world. The question can be studied only where children are confronting television for the first time and the proposed CTW videocassette study provides a unique opportunity that probably will never occur again. It would be unforgivable to ignore this opportunity when there is so much to be learned from it for a relatively small investment of money, time, and personnel.

> I love the program. The children who watch are more alert to teachers' questions and approaches, and teachers have been stimulated to improve their methods.

—LYNDON KELLY, SCHOOL PRINCIPAL, ST. PETER'S, JAMAICA

Prison
Project

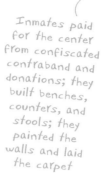

Sesame Street was born during a period of convulsive social change, with Americans reinventing their ideas about culture, gender, race, and economics. The prison environment didn't escape scrutiny. After the four-day standoff that followed the Attica Prison riots of 1971, changes were made to treatment and rehabilitation models in the nation's prison system. And for one unprecedented program, Sesame Street went to jail.

Studies of recidivism among prison populations had shown that convicts were more likely to return to jail—and be violent within it—if they lost ties with family while inside. But children were reluctant to visit their parents in prison (and parents resistant to expose them to the environment). Also, families had limited access to day care that would make visits between parents possible without children present.

In 1975, the Workshop organized a number of Sesame Street children's centers in prisons, complete with books, toys, and child-size furniture, which encouraged inmates to form better relationships with their visiting children. A more revolutionary move was the training of inmates as tutors for the children of other prisoners. Sesame Street leveraged its high profile to obtain government and local support to create these centers, and worked closely with nearby community, religious, and medical groups to prepare and train the prisoners. (These local groups would remain on-site later to supervise the program.) After intense psychological screening, a group of inmates in each prison was chosen to work with the children. It was a hugely successful program among the prisoners but eventually lost critical funding.

Inmates paid for the center from confiscated contraband and donations; they built benches, counters, and stools; they painted the walls and laid the carpet

While some were serving life sentences for crimes as violent as murder and armed robbery, all inmates selected first passed rigorous psychological testing and screening processes.

Inmate Frank E. Cook is trained to work with children using supplied materials; training enabled inmates to guide kids through educational activities based on the show's curriculum goals

> " **This is a valuable program because it helps strengthen family ties, which our experience shows us is one of the most important factors in an inmate's successful readjustment into society.** "

—NORMAN CARLSON, DIRECTOR OF THE FEDERAL BUREAU OF PRISONS, 1977

NEWS NEWS NEWS
CHILDREN'S TELEVISION WORKSHOP

FACT SHEET: SESAME STREET PRISON PROJECT

SPONSORS: The Children's Television Workshop, New York City, and the Federal Bureau of Prisons, Washington, D.C.

SITES: Federal Correctional Centers at Fort Worth and Seagoville, Texas; Lompoc, Calif.; New York City; Butner, N.C.; Oxford, Wis.; Alderson, W. Va. and Lexington, Ky.

Plans are underway to extend the project to state and federal institutions in Massachusetts, New York, Arkansas, Wisconsin and Washington state.

The settings include long, intermediate and short term prisons; urban and rural locations, maximum, medium and minimum security arrangements and male, female and co-educational programs.

GOALS: The prison project seeks to help maintain and strengthen family ties between inmates and their spouses, to help inmates learn and apply new skills and to provide useful experiences for children of inmates during prison visits.

BENEFITS: (1) Children of inmates are provided with a systematic program of educational and entertaining activities on visiting days.

(2) Inmates and visiting spouses are able to communicate in a positive emotional climate without having to worry about the behavior of their children.

(3) The family has the opportunity to interact together, as parents participate with their children in activities contributing to the child's development.

(4) Inmate care givers are trained in the fundamentals of working with children and are able to participate in a meaningful experience. Inmates have the opportunity to explore their interests in the possibility of a career in the field of child care.

(5) Inmate care givers and parents have the opportunity to expand their understanding of parental roles.

(6) Custodial officers responsible for the visiting area have improved control in a more positive environment.

> ❝ I don't intend to come back here, and this child care is an indication to me that there can be more I can do outside. ❞

—CYNTHIA, BEDFORD HILLS
CORRECTIONAL FACILITY FOR WOMEN

"Wherever there are children and adults, we will try to reach them," said Evelyn Davis, the Workshop's then vice president of community education. The prison project did just that. Inmate Harold Graham's hope was that kids he taught would "learn from the tutors' transgressions not to do the same and end up in jail." And several of the inmates trained as tutors went on to work with children as counselors even after their release from jail.

Kendrick "Snake" Davis
Kirkland Correctional Institution
4 Mun Broad River Road
Columbia, South Carolina, 29210

29,March 1979

Mr. Robert Bright
Regional Representative
The Childrens Television Work Shop.

Dear Mr. Bright;

I wish to take this oppourtunity to express my personel "Thanks", to you and everyone who made it possible for this program "Sesame Street" to be innovated at this institution.

The children enjoy the program very much, and speaking for myself I know I enjoy it twice as much just observing the interest & happiness shown in a child's face during the hours with us.

It is a rarity that an inmate in an institution receives the chance to give of himself in a worthwhile project, and I for one am proud to be able to plan,participate and perform any duty in the program to make it a success and a pilot program for others I hope will follow.

My sincere thanks to you again for your support.

Sincerly yours
Kendrick "Snake" Davis
Kendrick "Snake" Davis

Since it began, the Sesame Street Program has made a big difference in my personal life. I have always loved kids but until now, I have never taken an active role in the education of children. Since its implantation I have missed only one weekend working with the kids due to illness. I never thought I'd see the day that I acually missed working with the kids. Its rewarding to realize that you are playing such an important role in the development of these children. Their energy is endless and it does tend to rub off on you. After coming to Kirkland, I attended a two-year college program obtaining an Associate at Arts Degree. I was planning to go into Electrical Engineering however after working with Sesame Street for a length of time I am considering working with underprivileged children, and abused children. I believe that had I had not come to prison and Sesame Street, I would have missed a very important part of my life.

Thank you,
Michael E. Carriker

> ❝ To come visit her daddy . . . it used to be a terrible thing, you know. My little girl came to me two weeks ago and I got a hug just because this wasn't such a bad place to come anymore.

—TOWNES RAWLS, KIRKLAND CORRECTIONAL INSTITUTION

Audio Cassette Included

Fire Safety on Television for Preschoolers

FA-2
APRIL 1980

Fire Education for Sesame Street: Highlights of a research study on
mass media fire education for preschool children
Produced by: The Children's Television Workshop for
Federal Emergency Management Agency/U.S. Fire Administration

federal emergency
management agency
U.S. fire administration

Reach Out

Curriculum specialist
Makeda Mays says
of taping the latest
fire–safety edition:
"You could tell that the
children felt that these
people were not only
their friends, but also
people they could go to
in an emergency"

I n the nineties, Sesame Workshop created *Sesame Street* PEP (Preschool Education Program): an ongoing multimedia out-reach project that gathered show-related content, from the television show to books, to help prepare young children for school. The program provided content to day care centers nationwide. The Workshop also created programs to support children's health and well-being, including projects that taught fire safety, provided infor-mation about lead poisoning, and empowered children who have asthma. Nowadays, the Workshop's outreach group carries the title Education, Research, and Outreach to reflect its broad scope, as it creates assets for kits and advises other Workshop divisions on exhibits and special events for kids.

This division partners with the show's production, publishing, and interactive groups to develop material. Sponsors are found to fund distribution and any needed new content. Sometimes the Workshop creates original multimedia material for its outreach efforts. At other times outreach is built around *Sesame Street* episodes that have struck a chord with audiences or that seem par-ticularly appropriate. Materials include informative pamphlets—in as many as five languages—DVDs, podcasts, and Web sites with educational interac-tive games as well as parenting tips. These continue to be created by Outreach to help families and communities use *Sesame Street* programming to help their own kids.

Production

Research Content

Sesame promoted library card registration
with a campaign in the nineties, and
a new effort got under way with New
York's Brooklyn Public Library in 2009

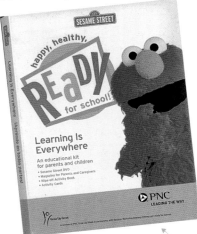

happy, healthy,
REAdY
for school!

Learning Is
Everywhere

An educational kit
for parents and children

PNC
LEADING THE WAY

Preparing children for school
is a focus of outreach
efforts like this
multimedia kit with DVD,
parenting magazine, kids'
book, and activity cards

"Learn and Grow" is filled
with messages promoting
healthy habits; like many outreach materials, it's available
in English and Spanish

Fire safety is one of the first emergency–
related outreach efforts. That kit continues
to be updated, while new preparedness kits
are developed for other emergencies

¡Preparémonos!
Planificando juntos para emergencias

An exhibit now touring museums
teaches kids about the body—but
the Strong National Museum of
Play in New York was the first
to develop a Sesame–based
exhibition, an ongoing
celebration of the show

Strong
NATIONAL
MUSEUM of PLAY

Aprender y
CRECER
con Sesame Street

> **Kami, one of the things I do is talk to people about things that are important to them, about things that will make a difference in their lives.**
>
> —FORMER PRESIDENT BILL CLINTON

Programs have been created to alert kids (and their grown-ups) to avoidable dangers, like lead, and to help them cope with and manage an existing condition, such as asthma

Outreach sometimes enlists support from influential figures. Kami, a character developed for the South African series, teamed with former President Bill Clinton to create a public service message about HIV/AIDS in 2006.

The Muppets were recruited by NAMM, an association dedicated to promoting music, to spread the word about how music can help kids' cognitive and emotional development

Sesame Street's outreach efforts don't end at the U.S. border. Internationally, culturally appropriate material is developed and distributed worldwide with the help of organizations like UNICEF, USAID, and SIDA, communicating messages about literacy, health, and tolerance.

"We aim to fill in the big educational gap at early ages," says UNICEF's head of office in Kosovo, Robert Fuderich. He explains that the kit, provided free to care centers, will "reinforce the message to children and parents . . . that there are children 'on the other side of the hill' who speak a different language and have different cultural traditions and beliefs."

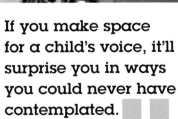

> **If you make space for a child's voice, it'll surprise you in ways you could never have contemplated.**
>
> —NADINE ZYLSTRA, *SESAME STREET* PRODUCER

In Bangladesh, outreach means that kids in rural areas can watch the show (delivered by rickshaw)—in that country, teenagers are taught to film live-action sequences for the show in a program designed to give them a voice

Just Ask

The Workshop partnered with Liberty Alliance Project, a special program set up through the New York State Office of Mental Health, to help families in the tristate area who were affected by the events of 9/11.

Photo 20: "What Makes You Proud?"

What is it that makes you proud?
The flags that people are hanging up
Why does this show "the very best of America"?
It shows the best of America because people are caring for eachother.

9) MY "SPECIAL POWERS" COLLAGE

Outreach is a two-way street at *Sesame Street*. The team at the Workshop utilizes its unique relationship of trust with children and families not only to produce materials and tools to help this audience but also to find out more about children's educational and developmental needs. They do this by going directly to the kids themselves through a variety of ongoing studies.

This research has shaped outreach projects as diverse as those about healthy eating (targeting America's obesity epidemic), serious illness, and disaster recovery.

One timely study, completed in spring 2001, showed that preschoolers were very aware of war and other violent events being reported on television and discussed at home. "The Fear Study" helped shape the Workshop's responses to subsequent tragedies, such as 9/11 and, later, Hurricane Katrina. The resulting Workshop kits built on what staffers had learned about how best to reassure children.

"We found in our research that it is rarely acknowledged how young kids really experience stressful situations, or even what a stressful situation might be," explains Jeanette Betancourt, vice president of outreach and educational practices, who's helped to develop *Sesame Street*'s emergency-preparedness programs.

After 9/11, the Workshop packaged four shows—two on fear and two on coping with intolerance—into one kit, providing them in Chinese, in Spanish, and in English to children around the area of Ground Zero.

"They were funded by New York's Department of Mental Health, and they really helped parents talk to their kids," explains outreach head Lewis

PICTURE OF MY FEARS OR WORRIES:

WAR!

Bernstein. "From doing things like that, we learned that we could create a program that was for parents as well as kids."

The Workshop tackles tough issues like emergency preparedness in a uniquely family-centric way. Messages focus not on the fears but on empowering children with knowledge, like helping kids to remember their names, addresses, and phone numbers. The Workshop also responds to disasters like Hurricane Katrina by sending its producers and performers to suffering communities.

"It really is magical," says Leslie Carrara-Rudolph, puppeteer of Abby Cadabby and other characters. "Going on the Katrina tour, it became evident that puppets can reach children in a way that is whimsical, unthreatening. That's why they're used in therapy."

"I've gone all over," adds Kevin Clash. "Every time there's a disaster where we can help with the children—in Kansas City after the tornado, with Katrina—I'm just happy that the show is around, that these characters are so popular, that we can do something.

"To be able to give back," he goes on wonderingly . . . "it is amazing to be able to do that through Sesame."

Sesame Workshop, Adler Planetarium & Astronomy Museum, and Liberty Science Center in the U.S. and Beijing Planetarium in China collaborated on a binational cooperative project, promoting science education and cross-cultural appreciation that tackles intolerance

OneWorld, OneSky
Big Bird's Adventure

"We are offering parents a trusted place to go to address emotions that children feel when they are faced with any kind of disaster."

—DR. LEWIS BERNSTEIN, EXECUTIVE VICE PRESIDENT FOR EDUCATION, RESEARCH, AND OUTREACH

DVDs, posters, magazines—all kinds of materials have been developed for outreach; this special publication was part of the kit dealing with disaster recovery

Cookie Monster became the subject of controversy when it was announced he'd become the show's poster child for healthy eating—fans had to be reassured he still ate cookies (a "sometimes food") as well as fruits and veggies

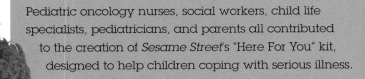

In a time of upheaval, children need familiar faces to feel comfort. After Hurricane Katrina, *Sesame Street* responded quickly and effectively with a kit that collected components from an earlier project, "You Can Ask," already designed to help families cope with stressful situations and facilitate communication between kids and caregivers. The new kit was distributed free by PBS stations in affected areas. Lynn Chwatsky, senior project director for outreach, saw the reaction firsthand:

"It was amazing the response that they had from these materials. They needed these so badly. It really helped the dialogue between parents and kids. Parents felt better. Kids felt better."

Interestingly, the kit was built around shows that first aired in 2001—long before Katrina. "It came out of a season of a lot of terrible weather around the country," recalls show writer Lou Berger. "We were sitting around a table and talking about what we could do that would show kids that bad things do happen . . . but communities continue."

NEWS FLASH

Because what happens to parents happens to kids, the Workshop's outreach extends to events like the recent economic downturn, as in "*Sesame Street* Getting Through Tough Times: Family Stories and Strategies." That's the working title for a project being developed as a prime-time television special. Outreach project directors Rocio Galarza and Cynthia Barron explain that it will feature brief documentaries focused on real-life families, including the story of a *Sesame Street* family coping with the ups and downs of these uncertain economic times. Elmo and his friends will join a guest host in a script that will offer help, hope, and concrete strategies. The goal is to encourage children to express their feelings and ideas as their families adjust to lifestyle changes.

Pediatric oncology nurses, social workers, child life specialists, pediatricians, and parents all contributed to the creation of *Sesame Street*'s "Here For You" kit, designed to help children coping with serious illness.

"Kids want to talk about it, but they're afraid to talk about it with the adults in their lives, because they're afraid to make the adults scared. They're trying to protect them," relates Jeanette Betancourt, who conducted research for the kit. The DVD stars Elmo's cousin Chester and Danny, a leukemia patient, who uses his personal experience to help others.

"When we weren't shooting, Danny was underneath the bed, puppeteering Chester," says Elmo's puppeteer, Kevin Clash.

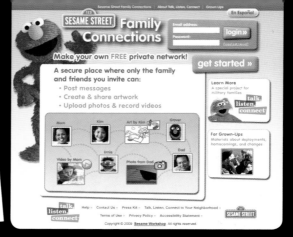

Now And Then

The first outreach projects were very local in nature—field offices worked with kids in their own neighborhoods. Today, localized efforts continue in programs like National WIC (Women, Infants, and Children) Association's health and nutrition initiative, which began as a program centered in California. Other outreach programs start as more national efforts, like the one supporting military families.

"Because whatever your political view about war, put it aside," says Lewis Bernstein. "We discovered a need: seven hundred thousand children have parents who are sometimes in their lives and sometimes not. We met with psychiatrists, we met with members of the military, we came up with a project, we created material for them. And when we did and we got it out, it was amazingly effective. All of a sudden, here was something that the military supported that allowed [military families] to talk, allowed them to communicate and share and build support systems."

It's not enough, though, just to produce the materials; it's about getting them to the kids who need them. Early outreach in the seventies was often restricted by distance. But now, the ability of *Sesame Street* to offer help is global and 24/7. Complete outreach kits for a number of the show's educational initiatives are available for download on the Web by parents, facilitators . . . *anyone* in need. And in the case of "Talk, Listen, Connect," funding grants have enabled distribution of the physical kits—containing a DVD, poster, guides, and many helpful referrals—free of charge to any military family that requests one. The hundreds of thousands of kits already distributed demonstrate that more than 90 percent of families affected by deployment have already asked for and received them, benefiting from the point of view shared by the families and children filmed.

"We were honored to be able to go into their lives and hear what they have to say because it's so important and makes such a difference for everyone, no matter what challenge they may be meeting," says Vice President of Outreach Jeanette Betancourt.

All these outreach efforts, from 1969 to today, are simply extensions of the mission of the show itself: to entertain and educate children in need, giving them a safe place to meet, to laugh, and to learn with friends . . . a place called *Sesame Street*.

As part of outreach efforts to military families, *Sesame Street* and its partners have created a room-in-a-box, a kit that contains children's furniture, wall art, toys, books, DVDs, and other materials designed to establish safe, fun environments. These boxes are being made available to family assistance, medical treatment, and child development centers to "Sesamize" otherwise grim or cold spaces, and they can be assembled to suit their locales. Here, military staff and their families volunteer to help customize one such space at an airport where families are reunited with soldiers—often injured—who are returning from duty, providing a space that quietly encourages love, care, and talk. Photographer Gil Vaknin says that through his viewfinder, he's seen that Workshop projects "share a search for truth regarding tough situations children and families face together."

Jane O'Connor, near left, helped lead the effort in the seventies to train young people to mentor even younger kids in their neighborhoods and to get the word out about the Street to families and community groups around the country

pictures of families

the different types of homes that people live in, not only ones like in this country but also an igloo, grass hut and so on.

Training materials clearly identify the show's goals and methods, helping to recruit and inform youth and community leaders

In 1971, the National Youth Corps helped the Workshop connect with teenagers and their families in urban neighborhoods, as seen in these then-described "rap sessions." Decades later, in 2008, Youth Corps teens in Palestine helped to launch the show there.

WHICH GANG
ULD YOU CHOOSE
OR YOUR CHILD?

THE 18th AND VENANGO STREET GANG

"The task of reaching and teaching preschoolers of poor families of all races can only be accomplished by the active interest and participation of all parts of the community."

—EVELYN DAVIS, VICE PRESIDENT, COMMUNITY EDUCATION SERVICES

THIS CHAPTER HAS BEEN BROUGHT TO YOU BY THE LETTERS CES AND THE NUMBERS 123.

The letters CES are for Community Education Services, the first outreach division set up at the Workshop back in 1969, headed by Evelyn Davis. **The numbers 123** are for one of the most famous addresses in the world: 123 Sesame Street, an imaginary locale that, through outreach efforts, touches children in neighborhoods all over the world and has become a safe second home to children worldwide.

15

**Keep going.
It's bigger than we are.**"

—JIM HENSON TO KEVIN CLASH (1984)

SEE YOU TOMORROW

SESAME STREET

УЛИЦА СЕЗАМ

عالم سمسم

PLAZA SESAMO

SESAMSTRASSE

RECHOV SUMSUM

芝麻街

TAKALANI SESAME

SHARA'A SIMSIM

SESAMSTRAAT

THE NEXT 40 YEARS

When Joan Ganz Cooney and Lloyd Morrisett first created *Sesame Street*, they knew they were doing something unusual. But neither of them thought that their two-year "experiment" would last so long—or that it would become the extraordinary exemplar of children's educational television excellence that it is today.

The show's longevity begins to seem almost inevitable, though, when you consider the fundamental and timeless ideals upon which it was built.

" 'Dignity' may sound like an odd word to use in describing boys and girls whose ages are only three to five years old," Joan once remarked. "The Workshop has found it a very important ingredient . . . and the only legitimate way to convey this dignity—this sense of self— is to provide as much relevant education as possible, as soon as possible, to children."

Forty years later, those ideals still govern. But what does that mean for the future of *Sesame Street*?

Lloyd has wondered the same thing. "*Sesame Street* was born in a favorable hour," he has said. "There is still reason to ask whether conclusions drawn from *Sesame Street* can provide guidance for others who wish to turn the power of mass communications to new social goals."

CEO Gary Knell believes they can. He sees a future that grows from the *Sesame Street* fundamentals and spreads to neighborhoods Joan and Lloyd could not have imagined: neighborhoods in places like Bangladesh, Kosovo, Palestine, Israel, South Africa, Jordan.

"There's nothing that's more directed to our mission than meeting the educational and social-emotional needs of kids everywhere," Gary asserts. "We need to move toward being a truly global company."

And just as *Sesame Street* at its inception utilized a relatively new technology (television), the *Sesame Street* of the future needs to look to new media platforms to deliver on its promises.

"We have to work creatively to apply the *Sesame Street* curriculum to any new technology that has the power to reach, educate, and entertain kids," says Scott Chambers, vice president and general manager of

> " It is my honor and privilege, as a parent and as president, to say on this wonderful occasion that this is brought to you by the number 40!
>
> I'm pleased to join all of you in supporting and celebrating this program, as someone who remembers fondly watching *Sesame Street* with my younger sister and as a parent of two girls who learned a great deal while spending time with Elmo and Big Bird and all of their pals.
>
> *Sesame Street* has, over the course of four decades managed to remain at once relevant in changing times, timeless in the values that it instills in our children. In fact, there are many adults who could stand to learn again the lessons that *Sesame Street* offers: lessons of compassion and kindness and respect for our differences. The world is a better place for the world you create on *Sesame Street*, a world that enriches our children's minds and hearts each and every day.
>
> Congratulations on this milestone and thank you. "
>
> —PRESIDENT BARACK OBAMA, 2009

Worldwide Media Distribution. "Yesterday, that meant almost solely television. Today it means a rich Web site, podcasts, mobile applications, e-books, and audio downloads. Our goal, our job, our responsibility is to anticipate what it means tomorrow."

So with new media presenting renewed power for change, *Sesame Street* finds itself at the frontier of a whole new universe . . . in a sense, at a whole new beginning.

Yet, in a future that is unknown, there are these certainties:

Tomorrow, Big Bird and Elmo, Chamki, and Kami will make children laugh around the world. Bob and Leela and other friendly faces will nurture self-confidence.

Tomorrow, writers, musicians, researchers, puppeteers, and producers will experiment with new ways to teach.

Tomorrow, outreach initiatives will make a difference.

Tomorrow, Sesame Workshop will look behind while forging ahead.

Tomorrow will be another sunny day on *Sesame Street*.

INDEX

head start–mitchell
head start–mitchell
head start–mitchell

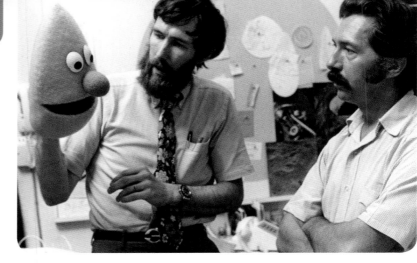

mitchell-sesame street
mitchell-sesame street
mitchell-sesame street

sesame street-zylstra
sesame street-zylstra
sesame street-zylstra

This book was
Brought to you by...

(Numbers in parentheses indicate clockwise placement on the indicated page)

Diane Adams: 72 (7), 231 (11) **U. Adaggi:** 262 (6) **Brigitte Barrett:** 303 (1) **John Barrett:** endpapers (2), 6 (1), 7 (1), 13 (1), 32 (1), 38 (7), 43 (4), 45 (1), 47 (7), 48 (1, 3), 51 (4), 55 (1), 87 (1), 88 (1), 94 (4), 99 (4), 102 (4), 107 (1), 127 (1), 128 (1), 132 (5), 133 (4), 134 (2), 142 (1, 2), 149 (1), 173 (1), 193 (1), 198 (2), 201 (6), 215 (1), 249 (1), 252 (1), 253 (6), 254 (3), 255 (2, 5, 6, 7), 256 (1), 257 (2), 258 (3), 263 (9), 265 (1), 269 (2), 279 (1), 280 (1), 291 (1, 4), 293 (3), 295 (1) **Charles Baum:** 92 (1-3), 94 (2), 104 (1-4), 188 (2) 301 (1) 303 (2) **Janet Beller:** 191 (16) **Michael Benabib:** 118 (6) **Charlotte Brooks, LOOK Magazine Collection, Library of Congress, Prints & Photographs Division:** 18 (1, 2), 20 (1, 2), 25 (7), 31(7), 152 (3), 154 (2), 155 (1), 156 (1), 202 (3), 239 (1) **Anthony Causi:** 34 (2, 3), 35 (2), 37 (1), 38 (1-6), 64 (1), 135 (2, 3), 138 (2), 177 (3), 108 (1-4), 109 (1-4), 117 (4), 121 (7) **Bonnie Carlson, used by permission of United States Agency for International Development (USAID):** 289 (1) **Victor DiNapoli:** 95 (1), 276 (6-8) **Robert Fuhring:** 20 (3), 23 (4), 24 (3, 4), 25 (2-5), 32 (1), 40 (2-4, 7), 41 (1, 2, 4, 5), 43 (2), 46 (1-6), 47 (8), 51 (1), 52 (3, 5), 53 (2-6), 55 (2), 56 (1-3, 6, 7, 10), 58 (1-3, 5-8), 61 (1), 66 (1-2), 67 (2, 3), 72 (1-6, 8, 9), 83 (10, 16, 18), 85 (4, 5, 7), 105 (4), 106 (1), 110 (1-4, 7-9), 111 (3), 116 (2), 152 (1), 155 (2, 3), 157 (2), 158 (1, 6), 159 (1), 170 (1), 171 (1-4), 179 (2), 183 (1), 186 (5), 190 (3, 8, 9), 191 (6, 11, 18), 201 (2), 220 (8-10), 222 (1), 224 (3-6), 243 (6), 282 (5), 293 (1, 4, 7, 8, 11), 294 (1), 296 (2), 298 (1) 303 (3) **Catherine Gibbons:** 99 (5), 102 (1), 105 (6, 7), 160 (1) **Jesse Grant:** 113 (7), 116 (11), 117 (1, 13, 14), 119 (4) **Ryan Heffernan:** 150 (1), 253 (5), 258 (1), 259 (1, 2, 6), 263 (5, 6, 8, 10), 280 (3, 7, 8), 281 (1-4, 6) **Jim Henson Co.:** 41 (3), 145 (2), 268 (1) **Richard Hutchings:** 69 (1), 75 (1), 83 (17) **iStock:** 253 (3), 254 (4), 256 (5), 258 (2), 260 (2), 271 (1, 2), 272 (1), 273 (1), 274 (1), 275 (1) **Eric Jacobson:** 74 (7), 79 (3), 84 (3), 86 (1), 92 (4), 130 (5), 181 (5) **Darren Kidd:** 154 (1, 2) **Emily Kingsley:** 180 (1) **Eric Leibowitz:** 207 (2) **Peter Linz:** 131 (5-7) **Betsy Loredo:** endpapers (1), 56 (8), 162 (3), 166 (3-5), 179 (1), 202 (2), 216 (1-5), 217 (1-3), 236 (1-7), 237 (1, 2, 6-8), 247 (6-8) **Mark Magner:** 136-137 (1), 207 (1), 208 (3) **Kevin Mazur:** 113 (17), 125 (11) **Paul McGinnis:** 15 (1), 35 (1, 3, 4), 36 (2, 3), 39 (1), 62 (1), 63 (1), 69 (5), 81 (1, 5), 89 (4, 5), 102 (2, 3), 103 (3), 119 (7), 121 (5, 8-10), 122 (5), 124 (2), 125 (7), 128 (2), 129 (2), 130 (2), 131 (4), 132 (6), 134 (1, 4), 135 (4), 138 (1, 4), 139 (4-6), 140 (2), 142 (3), 143 (4), 150 (2), 151 (4), 177 (1, 5, 6), 179 (3, 5), 185 (1, 4), 186 (4), 187 (3), 197 (1), 201 (2, 5), 208 (1, 2), 209 (5), 210 (3), 211 (1-3), 217 (4), 227 (3), 228 (2), 229 (3), 266 (3), 267 (1-7), 297 (1, 3), 298 (3), 299 (1), 300 (3), 302 (2,3) **Michael Melford:** 1 (1) **Gary E. Miller:** 113 (10, 13), 114 (11) **Nancy Moran:** 43 (4-8), 55 (3-6), 57 (3-5), 144 (1) **Nancy Ney:** 227 (3) **Eduardo Patino:** 118 (2, 3), 119 (11), 122 (7), 123 (2, 11, 12), 125 (1, 6, 10), 165 (1-4), 208 (7), 210 (4), 277 (5), 291 (2) **Don Perdue:** 112 (4), 115 (2), 117 (12, 15), 119 (3), 125 (12), 206 (1) **Bill Pierce:** 1, 19 (1), 40 (5), 43 (1), 45 (2-4), 48 (4-6), 59 (3-5, 8), 69 (7), 75 (9), 90 (8), 114 (15), 115 (9), 116 (1), 117 (2, 3), 118 (5, 8-12), 119 (1), 121 (2, 4), 123 (3, 4), 124 (4), 130 (4), 145 (1), 170 (5), 172 (1), 199 (1, 2), 205 (5), 214 (1), 220 (1-5), 221 (2-4), 222 (2), 223 (2), 225 (5), 227 (4), 228 (3), 242 (1, 3, 5), 244 (1-7), 278 (1), 284 (1-6), 285 (1-4), 300 (1) 303 (4) 304 (1) **Luiz Ribeiro / Wire Image:** 112 (7-9), 114 (13), 119 (2) **Judy Ross:** 55 (7), 67 (4), 69 (1-4), 70 (1, 5-7), 73 (2-5), 74 (1-4), 75 (3-6), 78 (3-6), 83 (11), 104 (8, 10, 12), 190 (7), 191 (1, 7, 13, 15, 17), 200 (1, 3), 204 (4), 205 (2-4), 208 (5), 218 (2-5), 224 (7), 225 (1-3), 226 (1-4) **Gail Russell:** 93 (3) **Anita and Steve Shevett:** 24 (1, 2), 28(1-4), 75 (8), 76 (1), 77 (1-4), 117 (9), 139 (1), 160 (5), 191 (12), 229 (4), 231 (9, 10) **Pete Souza:** 296 (1) **Geert Teuwen:** 33 (1), 112 (3) 140 (5), 141 (3), 164 (6), 229 (2), 256 (4) **Richard Termine:** 14 (1), 16 (1-5), 17 (1-5), 36 (1), 40 (1), 45 (5, 10), 54 (1), 56 (4, 5), 57 (1), 62 (2), 64 (2-4), 65 (1-3), 69 (6), 73 (7), 74 (5), 75 (2, 7), 78 (7), 79 (4), 80 (1-6), 81 (2-4), 82 (1-6), 83 (1-3, 5-9), 84 (1), 88 (2), 89 (1-3), 90 (1-3), 91 (1-4), 93 (10), 94 (7), 95 (1), 98 (1), 99 (7, 8) 100 (1, 2), 102 (5), 103 (1, 2, 4), 104 (6, 7, 13), 112 (10, 11), 113 (4, 8, 9, 11, 12, 15, 16), 114 (1-4, 7, 9, 12), 115 (6-8), 116 (6, 10), 117 (6, 16), 118 (1, 7), 119 (14), 121 (6), 122 (2, 4, 6), 123 (1, 10), 124 (3, 6-8), 125 (8,9), 129 (1, 3), 130 (1, 3), 131 (1-3), 132 (1, 3, 4), 133 (1, 2, 5), 134 (3, 5), 135 (1), 138 (5-7), 139 (2, 3), 140 (1, 3, 4), 141 (1, 2, 4-6), 142 (4, 6), 143 (1-3, 6), 146 (1-5, 7-9), 147 (1, 3, 5-9), 150 (3), 151 (1-3) 164 (4, 5), 165 (5), 166 (2), 167 (1), 168 (1), 169 (1-7), 171 (8-11), 174 (1-4), 175 (1-8), 176 (1, 2), 177 (2, 4), 179 (4), 180 (6, 7, 10), 183 (3), 185 (2, 3, 5, 6), 186 (1-3, 6), 187 (1, 2, 4-6), 188 (1, 3-5), 189 (1), 190 (2, 4, 6), 191 (5), 192 (1), 194 (1-4), 195 (1), 196 (1-3), 197 (2-4), 199 (4), 200 (4), 201 (4), 206 (3), 207 (4), 208 (4, 8, 9), 209 (2), 210 (1), 211 (4-6), 212 (1-5), 213 (1-10), 217 (5), 231 (1-4), 260 (1), 266 (1, 2), 267 (8), 280 (2, 4, 5, 6), 281 (5), 288 (2), 290 (1-4), 291 (5), 300 (2), 302 (1) **Mitzi Trumbo:** 100 (3) **Gil Vaknin:** 292 (1-6) **Theo Wargo:** 99 (6), 114 (8), 116 (4), 117 (11), 119 (12, 13), 125 (14, 15), 166 (1), **Leigh Wiener:** 238 (2, 3)

Meet a few of the photographers whose images made this book possible:

Richard Termine

As Sesame Workshop's official on-set photographer for many years, Richard's close association with the Muppets and their puppeteers is clearly shown in his ability to capture unguarded, intimate moments on set. Richard's history and unique closeness with the *Sesame Street* family was honored in the show's 40th season when he was cast as an extra in one of the show's "gems"—special shots dropped into the show as a wink to knowledgeable fans. Specializing in performing arts photography, Richard has snapped dancers in flight and players on the stage for his work as a frequent contributor to the *New York Times* and other prestigious venues. This book could not have been completed without access to his thousands of images from the show, past and present. He originally used two Nikon F3 film cameras, shooting black & white and color transparency film. He currently shoots on-set with digital Canon D5 cameras. Discover the exhilarating range of his work at **richardtermine.com**.

Paul McGinnis

The unique perspective and unequaled insider status Paul has as a *Sesame Street* puppeteer means that his shots are often of the most candid moments on set. Paul originally began bringing a camera along to the set informally but, as this book progressed, began snaring many shots that *Sesame Street* fans specifically requested. He also meticulously documented its 40th season.

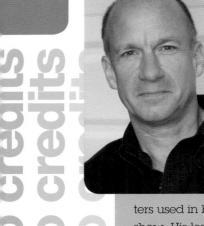

John E. Barrett

No photographer knows more about how to make a posed Muppet look alive and kicking (sometimes literally) than John. He is the preferred photographer for the countless shots of characters used in books, products, and promotion for the show. His less fuzzy but always striking work is found at **johnebarrett.com**.

Charles Baum

A chronicler of key moments in the show's pioneering days, Charles later took a hiatus from working as an editorial photographer and joined his father, legendary restaurateur Joe Baum, and became a co-owner of the celebrated Windows on the World and the iconic Rainbow Room in New York City. Now revisiting his art, Charles is currently developing a book which details the evolution of Atlantic City. Photographs from the project can be seen at **charlesbaumphotography.com**.

Robert Fuhring

Some of the show's earliest moments were captured by Robert, whose journalistic and starkly dramatic black and white photography is often the Workshop's only visual record of some of the first and most adventurous Outreach projects, as well as of behind-the-scenes tests of the show. Thought lost but recently unearthed from Workshop archives, these photos preserve rarely-seen moments that few imagined would be of such interest decades later.

Anita & Steve Shevett

Working as a team, the Shevetts are noted for portraits of actors and angels in the New York theatre world. Their artful work is also showcased in the children's book "Babies ABC," from Random House. Anita's solo photographs are best known to *Sesame Street* fans from the pages of *Sign Language ABC*. Although out-of-print, that title's appealing presentation of actress Linda Bove's demonstration of American Sign Language continues to be recommended by ASL instructors and organizations like the Anti-Defamation League and Gallaudet University.

Luiz Ribeiro

New York-based Luiz routinely covers global events and people in danger zones as well as more relaxed locales. His unerring timing has netted candid and telling moments with celebrities as well as moving, often visceral documentary photography.

Theo Wargo

Film, TV, political, and fashion icons—from Sandra Day O'Connor to Daniel Radcliffe—are among those shot by Theo for photo services like WireImage. His crisp images and pristine lighting make celebrated faces instantly recognizable yet somehow fresh and new.

Judy Ross

Vivid portraiture that creates strong emotional links between subject and viewer are Judy's forté, in work hailed by curators in numerous galleries and museums like New York's MoMA.

Charlotte Brooks

Charlotte joined the likes of Walker Evans and Dorothea Lange in documenting the life and struggles of America's rural poor for the Farm Security Administration. In 1951, she broke ground as the first woman hired by *Look Magazine* as a full-time staffer.

Bill Pierce

Bill's experience as a photojournalist covering hard-hitting news is reflected in the sometimes haunting, storytelling quality of his work behind the scenes at *Sesame Street*. His other assignments in war zones around the world, however, caused concern on the set. Various Muppets could be quite vocal in their disapproval, wanting to keep him safe. But it was fortunate that Bill didn't listen to them, as his documentary photography of conflict or abuse in regions around the world (including Staten Island's infamous Willowbrook institution here at home) has significant impact. For that work, he has been presented with the Overseas Press Club's Olivier Rebbot award for best photoreporting from abroad, The World Press Budapest Award and the Leica Medal of Excellence. Work by this highly respected photojournist has been showcased in museums and exhibit spaces such as the Corcoran Gallery of Art, the International Center of Photography, Pace MacGill Galleries and the Leica Galleries and has appeared in *Time*, *Life*, *The New York Times* and countless other publications. His involvement with *Sesame Street* led to an interest in passing on his photographic knowledge as a guest lecturer and contributor to numerous magazines and websites.

In photographing *Sesame Street* in the days of film, Bill used Leicas (small and quiet) for close work behind the scenes with wide-angle and normal lenses. Shots of action on the set during rehearsals and takes were made with longer lenses on single lens reflex cameras. Bill has currently given up film and today shoots his images digitally. Look for his shots on the web at **billpiercepictures.com**.

NEED TO Read

Want to find out even more about *Sesame Street*? Tune in to your local PBS station to see the show or Hulu to screen popular clips. A visit to sesamestreet.org and sesameworkshop.org is your next step, as well as friending the show on Facebook or subscribing to podcasts on iTunes for several Sesame-related series. Then, to dig a little deeper:

Find out what the true fans know....
There's no readier, more ever-expanding resource for learning about the show than fan-driven, Muppet-dedicated web sites. Of special note are Muppet Wiki (we found **muppet. wikia.com/wiki/Season_1** to be an excellent starting point), managed by Danny Horn, Senior Community Development Manager at Wikia; **muppetcentral.com**, a fan site created by webmaster Philip Chapman; **toughpigs.com**, a blog maintained by Joe Hennes and Ryan Roe; and **muppetnewsflash.com** and its related twitterfeed, overseen by blogger Greg James. Google Groups offers more options with searches for "Sesame Street" and "Muppet."

Learn more about the show's genesis and early years....
Local bookstores can order a current edition of the meticulously documented *Sesame Street and the Reform of Children's Television* by Robert W. Morrow (Johns Hopkins University, 2005), or hunt down an out-of-print copy of *All About Sesame Street* by Phylis Feinstein (Tower, 1971) or a 1972 publication of *Children's Television Workshop: How and Why It Works*, by consultant Herman W. Land, Nassau BOCES. *The New York Times'* Jack Gould frequently wrote about PBS and the show; try searches through the newspaper's online archives at **query.nytimes.com/search/sitesearch** for him or Joan Ganz Cooney. The National Public Broadcasting Archives at the University of Maryland contain thousands of Workshop documents.

Read the minds of the show's creative team....
A series of interviews with *Sesame Street* personnel collected by the Academy of Television Arts & Sciences Foundation for the Archive of American Television provides unparalleled access to the memories of insiders. A complete list can be found at **emmytvlegendsinterviews.blogspot.com**. Look for these names, among others: Joan Ganz Cooney, Lloyd Morrisett, Kevin Clash, Caroll Spinney, Danny Epstein, Tony Geiss, Lewis Bernstein, Sonia Manzano, and Bob McGrath. (Interviews with James Day, of NET, and *Captain Kangaroo*'s Bob Keeshan are also informative.) Or delve into a copy of *Street Gang: The Complete History of Sesame Street*, by Michael Davis (Penguin, 2008).

Become an expert on Jim Henson....
Go to the source. The Jim Henson Legacy, founded and supported by Jim's family and friends—**jimhensonlegacy.org**—is your gateway. Read *Jim Henson: The Works—The Art, the Magic, the Imagination*, by Christopher Finch (Random House, 1993); *Jim Henson's Designs and Doodles: A Muppet Sketchbook*, by Alison Inches (Abrams, 2001); and *The Art of the Muppets*, from Muppet Press (Bantam Books, 1980). YouTube searches for "Jim Henson" plus "commercial" or "films" will launch a trip through Jim's pre-*Sesame Street* productions. For a stepping stone to the craft of creating puppets yourself, try *The Muppets Make Puppets*, by Cheryl Henson (Workman, 1994).

Read up on Public Broadcasting's story....
Online, **current.org/history** offers insights straight from the archives of *Current*, the newspaper about public TV and radio. Offline, check out *PBS Companion: A History of Public Television*, by David Steward (Simon & Schuster, 1999) and *Vanishing Vision: The Inside Story of Public Television*, by James Day (University of California Press, 1995).

Hear the voices of the people in your neighborhood....
Autobiographies and other titles by show talent give them their say: *The Wisdom of Big Bird (And the Dark Genius of Oscar the Grouch): Lessons from a Life in Feathers*, by Caroll Spinney with J Milligan (Villard, 2003), *My Life as a Furry Red Monster: What Being Elmo Has Taught Me About Life, Love, and Laughing Out Loud*, by Kevin Clash with Gary Brozek (Broadway Books, 2006); and *Sesame Street Dad*, by Roscoe Orman (Inkwater Press, 2006). Numerous children's books by Sonia Manzano and Bob McGrath (plus his many recordings and songbooks) also reflect the voices of the people and characters you love.

> **I'm really part of that first generation of people who grew up on *Sesame Street*. The work of *Sesame Street*, in its own way, is similar to my work in the sense that [it's] fundamentally about universal access to preschool education and my work is about universal access to knowledge. We both play a role in what I think has become much bigger than the time when *Sesame Street* started: the world of informal learning.**
>
> —JIMMY WALES, COFOUNDER OF WIKIPEDIA

Find out who's visited the show....
The category "Sesame Street Guest Stars" on **muppet.wikia.com** provides virtual reams of data about guest stars. So does the search term "Sesame Street" on **imdb.com**.

Bone up on how curriculum shapes Sesame Street....
The complexities of teaching through TV are outlined in *Children and Television: Lessons from Sesame Street*, by Gerald S. Lesser (Random House, 1975) and *G Is for Growing: 30 Years of Research on Children and Sesame Street*, edited by Shalom M. Fisch and Rosemarie T. Truglio (Lawrence Erlbaum, July 2000). For playful ways to extend the learning at home, visit the parent pages of the *Sesame Street* Website at **sesamestreet.org/parents**.

Enjoy the wit of the show's writers, directors, and producers....
Watch the show. Watch the show. Watch the show. And score an out-of-print copy of *Sesame Street Unpaved: Scripts, Stories, Secrets, and Songs*, by David Borgenicht (Hyperion, 1998). Explore Jim Henson's own humor and production process in *Of Muppets and Men: The Making of The Muppet Show*, by Christopher Finch (Random House, 1993).

Hum to the music of Sesame Street....
Listen for the "Sesame sound" on many compilations; *Songs From the Street: 35 Years of Music* also has informative liner notes. Then make music yourself with these: *The Sesame Street Songbook: 40 Favorite Songs* (Hal Leonard, 2007) or *The Sesame Street Songbook: Words and Music by Joe Raposo and Jeffrey Moss*, arrangements by Sy Oliver (Simon & Schuster, 1971).

Watch some of our classic animations and read all about 'em....
Sesame Street's own website allows you to build playlists that include favorite animations. YouTube keyword searches for "Sesame Street animation" will yield others. Animation World Network (home to digital *Animation World Magazine*), can be found at **awn.com** and is an excellent resource for information about artists and producers; search for "Sesame Street."

Travel the world with international productions....
Visit **sesameworkshop.org**'s pages on productions around the world to get the most current info and photos. Also, screen a copy of the moving independent film, *The World According to Sesame Street,* by Linda Goldstein Knowlton and Linda Hawkins Costigan. It offers a behind-the-scenes look at versions of the show in Kosovo, South Africa and Bangladesh—more about that at **pbs.org/independentlens/worldaccordingtosesamestreet/film.html**. Best of all, travel and watch a local version yourself.

Share the show with a new generation....
Think about how rare it is for three or more generations to share the same experience in today's rapidly-changing media world, or to experience that same cultural phenomenon at a similar point in their lives—childhood—and later have that vocabulary in common. So, see the show with a child you love and talk about how you watched it as a kid, too. Share a book, video or CD, or get down on the floor together with a toy. (A search on ebay for "*Sesame Street* vintage toy" will remind you of the childhood zeitgeist of your own generation.) If you're in the neighborhood, visit the Strong National Museum of Play in New York, Atlanta's The Center for Puppetry Arts Museum, one of the Sesame Street live shows or its traveling exhibits, like "The Body" and "One World, One Sky."

Explore a catalyst for change....
Visit pages on **sesameworkshop.org** dedicated to community outreach projects that empower children's literacy and numeracy, health and wellness, emotional wellbeing, and respect and understanding. You support all those efforts when you support *Sesame Street*.